GARDEN PLANNING AND CONSTRUCTION

GARDEN PLANNING AND CONSTRUCTION

A.K. Davidson and D. Roberts

Ward Lock Limited · London

First published in Great Britain in 1984
by Ward Lock Limited,
82 Gower Street, London WC1E 6EQ,
a Pentos Company.

House editor Denis Ingram
Designed by John Wallis

Text filmset in Monophoto Plantin 110/663
by Santype International Ltd., Salisbury, Wilts.

Printed and bound in Great Britain by Hollen Street Press.

British Library Cataloguing in Publication Data

Davidson, A. K.
Garden planning and construction
1. Gardens—Design 2. Gardening
I. Title II. Roberts, D.
712′.6 SB473

ISBN 0-7063-6209-8

Contents

Preface

In writing this book we have tried to bring together the techniques for constructing the bones of a garden with some detailed discussion of the actual materials to be used. Thus, while the book is not a guide to planning layouts, we hope that it will be useful in helping to choose the right materials and suggesting how best to use them. In this way the aim of the book is to help owners of new houses to make the basic transformation from building-site to the first stages of a garden, or the owners of houses with established gardens who may wish to make some fundamental alterations to the garden layout.

In enlarging our earlier book, *Simple Garden Construction*, we have included material that takes the work in the garden right through from detailed preparation of the site to all the small additional jobs that help fill out the basic design and enable the garden to answer all the demands made upon it, both recreational and practical. This book is not, however, a guide to the selection, propagation or planting of garden flowers or shrubs.

Planning a new garden is both a challenge and an adventure. Spending time deciding on the shapes and relationships between beds and lawn, the size and position of a pond, and choosing the right materials or combinations for walls, paths or terraces is time well spent. A well-planned and balanced garden will, after planting, give increasing satisfaction as it matures and the different elements of stone, wood, earth and plant life blend together.

To help with this initial planning we have included a short chapter on some basic points to keep in mind, suggesting various alternative approaches, and provided a short introduction to each type of wall, fence, terrace, etc., to enable you as far as possible to select the right type to suit your plan. Once the layout and the materials have been decided on it is as well to visit local garden centres or gardens to see how the various types of finish look 'in the flesh' to help confirm your choice. To help also with the actual purchasing of materials we have covered some general points about where to buy, and look in detail at buying the different materials to help you avoid the inevitable pitfalls.

Throughout the book we have tried to indicate the point at which a job becomes too large or technically difficult for the amateur with non-specialized tools, and have suggested how the job can be done as cheaply as possible by contractors. In the main, however, all the work included here, especially if the garden is not above average size, can be done at weekends or in the evenings by an unskilled person with very few specialized tools. We have also tried to indicate where a person working on their own will need help.

Each section of the book contains not only the method of construction, but also a detailed breakdown of how to measure up a job and estimate the quantities of materials you will require, including the comparative costs of the different materials.

Since the book is aimed at amateurs who wish to make their own gardens, we have also included many basic tips, diagrams and household measurements to help with the work as it goes along. There is also a chapter on the tools that will be needed.

Throughout the book measurements are given in both metric and imperial and although these may not always be exact equivalents, they are sufficiently accurate for gardening purposes.

Be sure to read *all* the relevant pages before starting a job, because important points indicated thus: '*Note* ...', may, for clarity's sake, have been included after the step-by-step instructions.

A.K.D., D.R.

Acknowledgements

Throughout the writing of this book we have been indebted to a number of people for their help and advice, and would like to take this opportunity to express our thanks. In particular we would like to acknowledge the contribution of David Ellis to our knowledge of the subject over the years.

We should also like to thank Alec and Sue McDonald and Barry and Marcia Phillips for letting us use their gardens and Paul Chidlow for his advice and assistance with the carpentry.

For their help in producing the book we would like to thank our editor Denis Ingram, Bob Challinor for photographing the sites and Sue McDonald for typing the manuscript.

A.K.D., D.R.

Publishers Note

1 Tools

One of our aims in this book has been to ensure that none of the jobs covered require tools that are technically difficult to use or hard to acquire. There are a few exceptions to this, and in these cases we generally advise that you seek the help of a skilled contractor. On the whole, therefore, you will probably already have most of the tools mentioned for general work around the house and garden.

To help you get organized before you start a job we have included a list of the main tools required for each task at the beginning of the job instructions, under the heading 'What you will need'. This chapter, therefore, should be referred to if you require further description of any of the tools mentioned, or for generally useful ideas. If there are some tools that you cannot readily get hold of, use the local paper or telephone directory to locate a tool hire firm; most of these will hire you anything from a pointing trowel to a small dumper truck. We have therefore included a detailed discussion of points to note about hiring that may save you money and help avoid any problems.

Tools for work on surveying, excavation and drainage

The most important thing to notice here is that accuracy is going to be crucial for getting the right results. Thus when measuring up long lengths of boundary, fencing, etc., always try to use a long tape, i.e. 10 or 20 m (33 or 66 ft), rather than a short 3 m (10 ft) one. On a long run, a few additional centimetres here and there can soon become a few metres of surplus materials. Alternatively, **surveyor's chains** can be hired, and these may give more accurate results on rough ground. **Cowley levels**, described in detail on p. 22 are the most practical instruments for the amateur to use for surveying, but for most jobs, a **sighting board** and **staff** will give sufficiently accurate results. For draining, some long-handled **scoops** and **pipe hooks** can be hired if you are working with particularly deep trenches. Otherwise the all-purpose shovels and pickaxes, etc. outlined below will be all that is necessary.

Tools for work on walls, terraces, paths and features

Most people will be familiar with or own a **pickaxe**. It is used for loosening soil for removal by shovel, and has pointed and chisel ends to its head. **Shovels** should be used for mixing and digging, rather than the narrower-bladed **garden spade**. The **wheelbarrow** used should be a heavy-duty builder's barrow, since most garden barrows will not stand up to the weight loads required during the movement of concrete, mortar, blocks, etc. A **crowbar**, or **'jemmy'**, is a very useful general-purpose tool which will come in handy on many occasions. **Gloves** are almost essential when handling blocks or cement, and should be of the stout leather gardener's type.

Two kinds of **tape-measure** are useful. The small, steel automatic ones, 1.8, 2.4 or 3 m (6, 8 or 10 ft) for detailed work, and the longer 10 or 20 m (33 or 66 ft) wind-up ones for use when measuring up large jobs.

A bricklayer's **trowel, spirit-level** and **hammer** (Fig. 1.1) should be used. The **trowel** should be large size (much quicker and more efficient when you get used to them), and have one straight edge. **Spirit-levels** should be 60 or 90 cm (2 or 3 ft) long for maximum accuracy, particularly for laying terraces. The bricklayer's **hammer** (having one end of the head chisel-shaped) is useful for cutting and marking blocks, etc. A **lump hammer,** a stout, short-handled hammer with a head weight of 1–2 kg (about 2–4 lb) and **bolster chisel** will also do this job and the lump hammer is a useful tool anyway. About 12 m (40 ft) of **builder's line** will be required. This is nylon cord that comes in various lengths wrapped round a piece of card. Buy as many lengths as you need, tie together and wind on to a peg or **mason's block** for easy use and storage. Care should always be taken to pull the lines very tight, to take up all natural stretch. The **blocks** are useful to hold the line in position, hooking on to the ends of the wall. A **rubber mallet** may also be useful for tapping bricks or blocks down where there is a tight fit, etc. A **spot-board** of wood, about 75 cm ($2\frac{1}{2}$ ft) square, is needed to hold the mortar while you are working. It should be carefully cleaned after use. Larger spot-boards should be used for mixing on. For **earth rammers** see the section Tools for work on fences.

A **wooden square** will be required to check the accuracy of corners, but for squaring large corners, when digging out footings for example, a system of string and pegs can be used (Fig. 1.2). To square line AX with AY: place peg 1 at point A. Place peg 2, 90 cm (3 ft) from A along line AY. Pin a 1.2 m

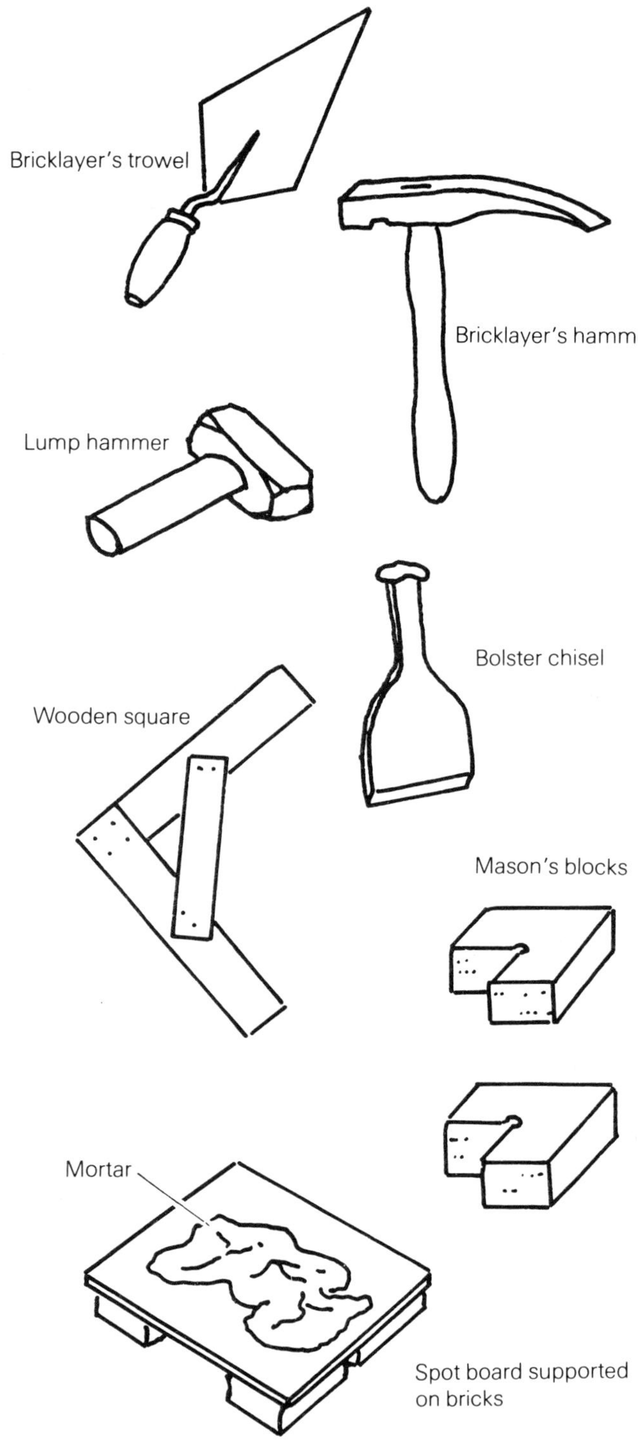

Fig. 1.1 *Some useful tools for construction work.*

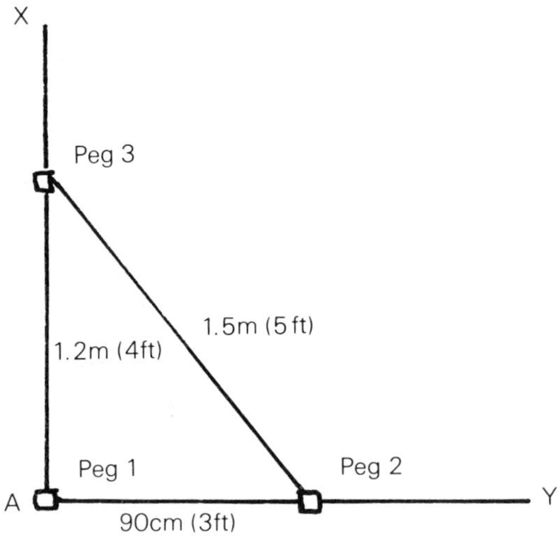

Fig. 1.2 *Making a right-angled corner.*

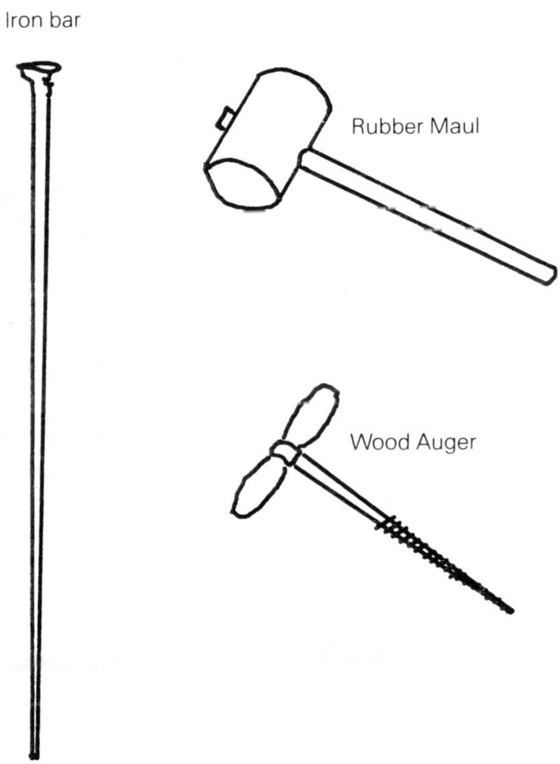

Fig. 1.3 *Some useful tools for work on fences and gates.*

(4 ft) length of string to peg 1. Then, pulling the 1.2 m (4 ft) string from peg 1, and using a tape-measure from peg 2, mark on the ground the point where the end of the 1.2 m (4 ft) string meets the 1.5 m (5 ft) mark on the tape-measure. Place peg 3 on this mark and bring line AX to lie flush with pegs 1 and 3. The corner will be square.

Finally, on large jobs, a **cement mixer** will save a lot of time and effort. Small portable ones are available on hire from many sources, and some quick phoning around should secure one. If available, try to hire an electric one since these are much more convenient and pleasant to work with. Also **masonry saws** might be worth hiring for large jobs where there will be a large number of blocks or slabs, etc. to cut. They consist of a small two-stroke engine which drives a fibre disc at high speed, and are a lot faster and more accurate than a hammer and bolster chisel; they are also extremely noisy! A dust mask and goggles should be worn at all times when using these saws.

Tools for work on fences, gates and additional jobs

Many of the tools mentioned above will be required for this work. In addition you will need a **hand saw** and carpenter's **claw hammer**. Other useful tools will be a **rubber maul** (Fig. 1.3), (sledge hammers are not suitable for knocking in stakes or prick-posts, etc.) and a large **iron bar**, 90 cm or 1.2 m (3 or 4 ft) long at least. **Bars** are available at a number of Army Surplus Stores, ironmongers and similar outlets and are useful for their weight when opening up holes and also as **rammers**, having a flat top at one end.

You may also need a **hand-winch** when straining long wire fences and these, like cement mixers etc., are available from hire companies. For fitting hinges on gates, and a number of additional carpentry jobs, a **wood auger** or **electric drill** will be required (Fig. 1.3). If you do not already own a drill, these, like **jigsaws** (useful for the carpentry work), can be hired from 'small tool' hire firms.

Tools for work on preparing ground and hedging

The most suitable kind of **rake** for preparing ground is the 90 cm (3 ft) wide, fine-toothed garden rake. Do not try to use the springy, long-toothed kind of grass rake.

Back-pack sprayers for weedkillers can be hired, but for an average-sized garden, a standard 14–18 litre (3–4 gal) **watering can** with a rose attachment will do the job just as efficiently, but be sure to wash it thoroughly after use. The most handy-sized **rollers** are the small 100–150 kg (2–3 cwt) garden ones, even for large areas. The most convenient type to hire are the hollow cylinder rollers that are filled with water for use and emptied for transportation. **Forks** should be robust garden models, and **shovels** as for above.

Rotavators are useful for breaking up clean soil, i.e. soil from which the weeds, roots and stones have been removed. They have 3 or 5 hp petrol engines driving blades which cut the soil up, while pulling the machine along, breaking up the soil to a depth of about 15 cm (6 in). We have found them most useful for preparing ground that has been forked and weeded, creating an excellent 'tilth'. Do not put too much faith in them for clearing ground; there is no substitute for fork work. Should one be required, they can be hired by the day from most tool hire firms, small contractors and agricultural engineers.

For hedging, the most useful kind of saw will be a small **bowsaw** (Fig. 1.4). The shaped frame shown in the diagram helps you cut between closely spaced stems. As well as the saw, a trimming **sickle** will be necessary to shape the hedge and clear around the foot of the plants. For laying the hedge a **billhook**, or **small axe** will be required for cutting the boughs and a **rubber maul** (as for above) for banging in the stakes. **Gloves** as for above.

Some points about hiring tools

Few people should encounter any problems when hiring or returning tools, since most companies have carefully worded invoice forms that spell out the exact terms of the hire agreement. Occasionally, however, misunderstandings do arise and so we outline below a few points to bear in mind that may help to save unnecessary bother and expense:

1 Be sure to check the exact terms for the length of hire. Does a day mean morning to night of the same day, or first thing the next day? Is it cheaper to hire at week-ends? Are there any special and cheaper rates for short-term (a couple of hours) hire periods etc?

2 Before taking the tools, check the terms of agreement. See if they specify who is responsible for cleaning the tools and, more important, who pays if the machine breaks down. If these points are not immediately clear, be sure to ask since you may be liable for extra payments. In addition you should check the machine over (for loose or damaged parts etc.) before taking it away.

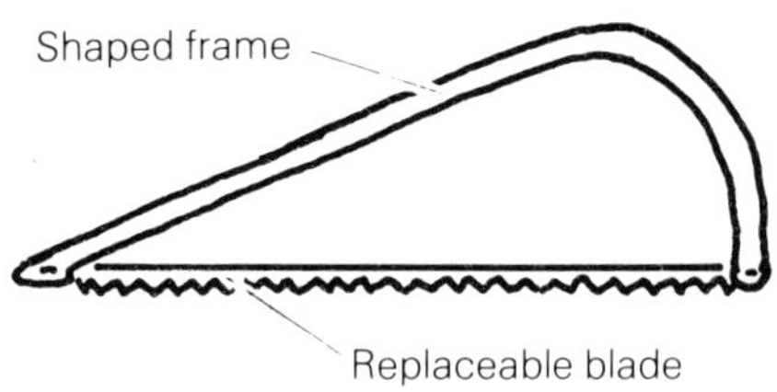

Fig. 1.4 *Bowsaw for hedging work.*

3 When using hired power tools, be sure to follow any instructions given concerning oiling and greasing. Ignoring these and having the machine seize up can be very expensive.

4 Similarly, be sure to follow any safety warnings, i.e., 'Dust mask and goggles must be worn when using this machine', etc.

5 Any power tool is potentially dangerous if used improperly or carelessly.

6 If you are using a skip and it is left on a public road during loading, check first that it can legally be left where you want it, and be sure to get an authorization ticket from the local council. Note also that a skip left on a public road overnight will, in certain situations, need to be marked by lights.

2 Mixes

A 'mix' of mortar or concrete means that given quantities of cement and sand, or in the case of concrete, sand and gravel, have been mixed together and then turned into a wet paste by the addition of water.

Throughout this book the exact elements of the different mixes are given for each job. The standard all-purpose mixture for mortar is one part cement to four parts sand, i.e. 1 : 4 (the mixes range from 1 : 3 to 1 : 6 or 1 : 8). For concrete the mixture is one part cement to six parts sand and gravel, i.e. 1 : 6 (mixes range from 1 : 4 to 1 : 9). For our purposes 'one part' indicates one shovelful. Therefore, 1 : 4 = one shovelful of cement to four shovelfuls of sand. To the dry mix (whatever the quantities) is added sufficient water to turn mortar into a wet but self-supporting paste, while concrete at the right consistency will adhere into a ball if squeezed in the hand.

One further ingredient is commonly used nowadays: plasticizer. This is a solution which is added to the water which ensures that the mortar is of a 'plastic' nature – more elastic and adhesive than if just water were added. It is not absolutely essential but will make life easier, particularly for laying bricks, blocks, etc. Plasticizer is available at all builders' merchants and has instructions for use on the container, although a general rule is one capful per mix. A substitute for plasticizer if you run out or have only a small job to do is washing-up liquid, which is used in the same quantities will cost much the same. Plasticizer is, in fact, the modern-day replacement for lime which was used for the same purpose. Should you wish to use lime, it should be added at a rate of one shovelful for each shovelful of cement used.

Note Plasticizer is mainly used for mortar and should not be used for concrete except in special circumstances. Your supplier will advise on this.

To mix

(a) Using a cement mixer Start the machine, pour in approximately 1 gallon of water, load in quantity of sand or sand and gravel, required for the strength of mix, add more water if necessary to make the sand water mix sloppy. Add cement to mixture.

When the machine has thoroughly turned the components together, that is when the sand in the mix has turned a uniform grey, add small quantities of water (with plasticizer, if required) until the desired consistency is reached. (This differs slightly from job to job, and where important is specified in the job instructions.) Test the mix regularly by removing small handfuls. If the mix becomes too wet, add more ingredients, making sure you retain the correct ratio.

When the mix is ready, tip it out into a barrow. Care should be taken not to overload the mixer, since this will result in inefficient mixing.

(b) By hand First of all make sure that you have a firm, clean area to mix on. A large spot-board (p. 10) is ideal. Using a shovel, measure out the components in the ratio required until you have a reasonable pile or enough mix for your needs. About 12 shovelfuls of sand, or sand and gravel, is plenty to mix at one go.

The most efficient way to mix is to work round and round the pile, lifting a shovelful from the outside and turning it over, dropping it into the middle of the pile. Go round once and then flatten the heap out. Repeat until everything is thoroughly mixed.

To add water: Pile the mix up, and using the shovel open up the middle to form a crater shape. Pour a small amount of water (plus plasticizer if required) into the middle. Then, using the same 'round and round' technique, gently sprinkle dry mix from the outside of the pile into the water. Repeat until all the water is absorbed.

When the water is absorbed, turn the pile thoroughly, ensuring that the mix gets an even dampness. Then pile it up again and open out the centre. Add more water and repeat the whole operation again until the required consistency is achieved.

Points to note

1 Be sure to plan your working session carefully, whether it is a couple of hours, an evening or a whole weekend. Do not, for example, mix too much mortar at once, since it may get wasted. Similarly, do not over-commit yourself by trying to lay too many bays of concrete at once. (A 'bay' of concrete is the area formed by the shutters erected to hold the concrete while it is setting. Thus on small jobs only one bay will be necessary, while on larger jobs the total area will be divided into a number of bays which can be laid one at a time or in combination, depending on the amount of time or material available.) Make sure that you have all the necessary tools, materials and assistants before starting; delays can result in wasted time and materials, particularly since cement is only capable of forming a bond for a few hours after wetting.

2 If mortar or concrete is left standing in a barrow, the water in the mix will rise to the surface; this causes a constantly sloppy consistency on top, whilst the mix at the bottom is drying out. Therefore, when working, remember to turn the mix over periodically in the barrow to maintain the correct consistency throughout.

3 Keep an eye on the weather. If there is likely to be a frost at night, do not leave fresh concrete or mortar exposed to it. Postpone the job or cover carefully. If it is likely to rain, do not start laying concrete, or pointing or rendering a wall.

4 Remember that all finishes can be altered by painting or staining. If you need the strength of a concrete fence post, for example, but do not like the cement finish, you should think about painting the surface rather than using an alternative material. Special paints are available at garden centres and builders' merchants.

Common mistakes in mixing

1 Too dry a mix. This can easily happen and will make block or brickwork extremely difficult. To avoid this, test a sample of the mix between two blocks, etc. while mixing is in progress.

To test: Trowel some mortar on to a block and place another on top. If the mortar supports the top block, but allows you to tap it down, then the consistency is correct. If the mortar runs out and the block slides about, then the mix is too wet. If the mortar is so stiff that you are unable to tap the block down, the mix is too dry.

2 Insufficient cement. This is the cause of a lot of the cracking or breaking away on new walls. Careful attention to quantities will help avoid this.

3 Weakening the mix by revitalizing it when it has 'gone off'. Adding water to a mix that is drying or dried out is a bad idea since cement is being lost all the time. (The cement rises in the mix with the water and is washed away or remains unmixed.) To revitalize a mix, add extra cement and then water, and re-mix thoroughly.

3 Planning-layouts

The work of planning a garden, both the ground plan and the planting, lies outside the scope of this book, concerned as it is with the actual construction work, but we feel that a brief discussion of some of the factors that should be considered during the planning stage will help put the material covered in this book into some kind of perspective. We suggest that it will save you time, effort and money, as well as leading to more successful results, if the construction work is taken into consideration during the early planning stages and in this chapter, therefore, we will be looking at how the planning should be approached so that the construction of the components becomes an integral part of it.

The site

It is important, first of all, that any plan should be drawn up in the light of detailed knowledge of the site. Thus, before starting work on the plans, have a really good look at the site, removing if need be any existing and unwanted plants and features so that you have a clear understanding of its character (its proportions and the relative positions of higher ground, level changes, flatter areas and so on) and its setting (whatever immediately surrounds it, or, in more open situations, any good views visible from it, etc.). This may seem an obvious point, but incorporating the natural site features into the plan where possible will not only save work during construction, in that less rearranging of soil etc. will be necessary, but it will also produce a more natural result, while appreciation of the setting will help you exploit good views or pinpoint places where screening is necessary.

Over and above these points, there is the third dimension to allow for (crucial for successful landscaping), and this cannot be done by working from two-dimensional plans alone; the most carefully worked out plan, and one which incorporates all the required components, may prove a disappointment when it is actually laid out. Perhaps a fence or wall is just too high or too low to be effective, an important feature is masked by planting or higher ground, or maybe a carefully laid out terrace appears to slope, or takes on an unattractive pattern due to optical illusions created by the surrounding levels or the angle from which it is viewed. These effects cannot be allowed for on a plan, but can be eliminated to a large extent by knowledge of the site itself. In the same way, you can save a considerable amount of work by, for example, positioning lawns on the flatter parts of the site or using level changes to create backdrops for water features, etc.

A final point to note is the orientation of the garden, which direction the sun will come from and which areas of the garden will benefit from it. Noting the areas of sun and shade and designing to allow for them will help you develop the full potential of the site and position plants in the most suitable spots.

Uses

The second point for consideration is that before finalizing a plan be sure to have a clear idea of the various uses to which the garden and its component parts will be put. Since it will usually be both expensive and disruptive to alter things once construction has been completed, make sure that your plan makes sufficient allowance for all the various activities that will be carried out in the garden. Are there enough firm surfaces? If so, are they for pedestrian or vehicular use? Do you have enough room for all the flowers, shrubs, trees or vegetables you require? If there are children in the household, is the lawn large enough for play or will a separate area for their activities be necessary? Do you have paths in the right place to provide access to sheds, incinerators, washing lines or rotary driers? Do you need room to turn or park cars, and so on? Clearly a garden, particularly in urban areas, will have many demands made on it, and if these can be allowed for in the planning stage and the exact uses of the different areas identified, then the better it will be able to fulfil its practical and recreational roles, and the easier it will be for you to get an idea of the ground preparation that will be necessary and the most suitable construction techniques.

Styles

Following on from this comes our third point. Once the allocation of space has been decided on, planning the actual layout and the individual components that go to make this up will be simplified if you have a clear idea of the kind of style you wish to use. Gardens on the whole fall into three main categories of style: the formal, geometrically laid out type; the informal, more natural looking type, where beds, lawns, paths, etc. merge and inter-relate without distinct divisions, and those gardens that combine a bit of both. Knowing which style you want to use will help not only in designing the layout, but also with the choice of materials for the paths, steps, terraces, walls, fences, etc., that you wish to include.

To illustrate this point in action we will look at the job of designing layouts for two common garden shapes; long, thin sites, and small rectangular ones. In both cases you have two basic choices. Either you can deliberately use the distinct geometrical shape of the site to create a formal style garden that mirrors and emphasizes the existing straight lines, angles and perspectives, or you can aim to disguise the real shape, breaking the space up with an informal, asymmetrical design. Alternatively, if you have sufficient room, you can use both methods, creating one part (near the house maybe) along formal lines, with paths or grass leading away to a more informal background.

When you have decided which style to use, overall or for different parts of the garden, the type of layout required and the materials suitable for it will become more apparent. For example, if the garden is to be in the formal style, the design should be bold and uncluttered with distinct shapes clearly divided by clean lines, using materials such as slabs, blocks, metal gates, etc., that will help define the different areas by their regular shapes and patterns and which will stand out from their surroundings. On the other hand, an informal garden depends for its effect on blending the different components, unifying the overall picture, and yet creating as much localized detail as possible. This style, therefore, calls for layouts that avoid symmetry by following or accentuating the natural levels and shapes of the site and using materials such as stone, stepping-stone paths, crazy-paving, etc., that create irregular shapes and patterns and will merge as far as possible with the plants and soil around them.

Some final points should also be noticed here. First, whatever type of layout you design, try to fill in the details of the plan as fully as possible. By doing this you will be able to work out with some accuracy the quantities of different materials you will need, and this in turn will enable you to place bulk orders, where applicable, which can lead to appreciable savings on the cost of the job, even if you are not doing all the work at once. (An exception here is orders of cement which should be bought as you need it.) Secondly, when the plan is complete and construction work begins, success in bringing a layout to life will depend, in part at least, on attention to detail. This applies not only to the details on the plan, such as creating the correct sight-lines and backdrops, framing views, or fully developing the potential of path surfaces, edgings and features, but also to the details of the construction work. Do not be tempted to skimp on ground preparation and the other jobs that may be out of sight once the surface is finished, since tilting slabs, loose steps, terraces that hold puddles, or bulging walls will inevitably spoil the look of the garden and may even become a serious hazard.

4 Planning–the work

In the previous chapter we looked at some ideas on how to set about planning the finished garden. Later in the book we cover in detail the actual construction of the various features. In this chapter we will be discussing the background work necessary for preparing the site and estimating correctly the time and materials needed to do certain jobs. After this we will look at some points to consider when actually buying the materials. A basic knowledge of the points covered here will be very useful to anyone undertaking small jobs in helping to prepare the site properly, and in particular to anyone starting large-scale work, either in a new garden or when radically re-designing an old one, since errors in levels or quantities, whether materials or time, can prove costly.

Basic surveying

The objective of surveying is to determine the size, shape and contours of a piece of land, or the position of things relative to their surroundings. To carry this out successfully a working knowledge of the basic principles of surveying is required. For the purposes of this book, however, a number of these surveying functions, such as mapping and positioning, are not needed and we shall only be concentrating here on determining areas and levels. These will be useful aids to building up a clearer picture of the job in hand. A knowledge of the simpler techniques used to work out areas and levels will help enormously in setting out large areas and in eliminating errors. On larger jobs it is all too easy to underestimate the amount of work required or the volume of earth to be removed, and it can also prove expensive if, on the other hand, you overestimate on materials and tool hire time.

Should your job require accurate surveying in the full sense of the word, you should call on a trained surveyor or specialist company to carry out the work. If, however, you wish to know the size of an area to be turfed or the amount of fall in one area of the garden, then a careful reading of this chapter will give you the means to do it. When you have understood the methods described and come to use them, there is one other essential factor to keep in mind and that is accuracy.

To ensure the accuracy of your calculations, over and above making each measurement as accurate as possible, the following points should be considered. The first follows the advice of the old carpenters' rule: measure twice, cut once. That is, cross-check every measurement and calculation, since an error in a chain of calculations will inevitable produce an incorrect answer. Secondly, check not only the actual readings, but also the fixed points you are using, the instruments themselves and any profile boards (see p. 22) etc., you have erected. Doing this will repay the extra time spent.

Although as mentioned before, professional surveying is a highly specialized job, the basic methods and instruments described here do not require a specialized knowledge of maths or training in how to use them; they will, however, help you in estimating accurately the size of a job and what will be needed to complete it.

1 SURVEYING AREAS

Uses of

Calculating quantities of materials for terraces, foundations, paths, etc.; lawns – either seed or turf.

What you will need

Long tapes or surveyor's chains. Pegs.

Method

Given a basic knowledge of geometry it is fairly simple to compute areas accurately. Quite simply length × width = area. If the area in question is regular in shape, then a peg should be driven in at all the corners, unless a fixed point like a fence post or corner of a building already exists. When the pegs are in position simply measure between them and calculate the area accordingly.

If, however, the area is irregularly shaped, you should divide it into smaller areas, peg the corners of these, measure and calculate their areas individually and then add these together to find your total in square metres (square yards). In the example shown in Fig. 4.1 the total area has been divided into seven more easily calculable ones. Using this method it is possible to get a pretty accurate idea of the total area. If the area has curved edges, straightening them out for calculating purposes will give a good approximation.

Note To lay out 90° corners with pegs and string see pp. 10–11.

2 SURVEYING LEVELS

Uses of

Setting levels or transferring them between buildings or fixed points in the garden. Working out volume of soil to be removed for excavations, such as ponds, etc. or levelling up for terraces, lawns, etc.

What you will need

Spirit-level. Pegs. Boards. Tape-measure. Cowley level and staff (see p. 22).

Method

To determine the relative levels of a piece of ground it is necessary to work out the elevation of the different areas that make it up; elevation in surveying is a term used to denote the height or depth of a fixed point (usually marked by a peg etc.) above or below a reference point. Therefore, before starting work it is necessary to establish a reference point on the site which can easily be seen from the parts of the garden to be surveyed. Once established the reference point is counted as 0 (zero) and the elevations of the other fixed points are then referred to as + (plus, i.e. above) or − (minus, i.e. below). If, for example, you use the back door step as a reference point and your patio is 15 cm (6 in) below it, then the elevation of the patio would be denoted as − 15 cm (− 6 in). The lawn may be 20 cm (8 in) below the reference point and thus denoted − 20 cm (− 8 in), or a fence top 1.5 m (5 ft) above the reference point and thus denoted + 1.5 m (+ 5 ft). In this way it is possible to work out the actual shape of a garden, the relative levels and the volume of soil, etc. in a given area, no matter how many slopes and level changes are present.

Once you have established a reference point you will need to choose a method for measuring the elevations of the garden and there are several ways of doing this. Depending on the size of the garden and the extent of the level changes in it, one of three methods can be used, singly or in combination. On relatively small, flat areas the simplest and quickest method for detailed levelling is to use a spirit-level, a straight board, pegs and a small tape-measure (a).

On larger jobs where the levels alter more dramatically or where the points to be

(a) Metric

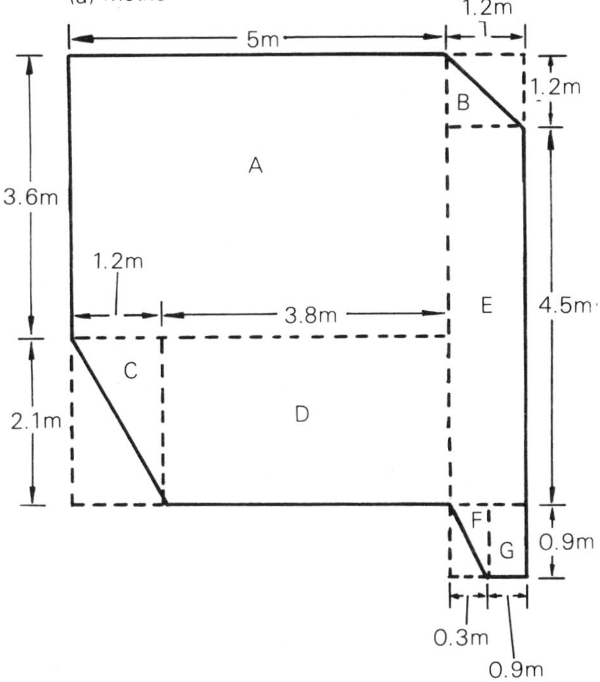

			sq m
A	5 × 3.6	18	18
B	1.2 × 1.2	1.44 ÷ 2	0.72
C	2.1 × 1.2	2.52 ÷ 2	1.26
D	3.8 × 2.1	7.98	7.98
E	4.5 × 1.2	5.4	5.4
F	0.9 × 0.3	0.27 ÷ 2	0.14
G	0.9 × 0.9	0.81	0.81
		TOTAL	34.31

(b) Imperial

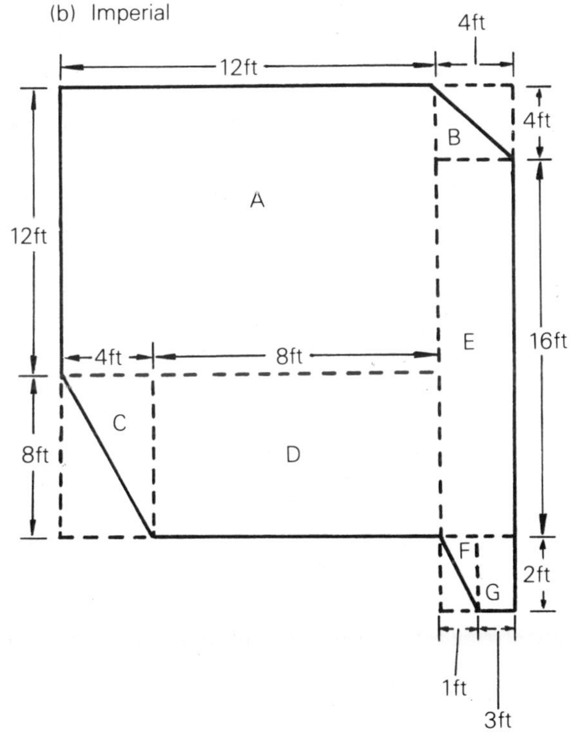

			sq ft
A	12 × 12	144	144
B	4 × 4	16 ÷ 2	8
C	4 × 8	32 ÷ 2	16
D	8 × 8	64	64
E	16 × 4	64	64
F	2 × 1	2 ÷ 2	1
G	3 × 2	6	6
		TOTAL	303

= approx. 34 sq yd

Fig. 4.1 *Calculating the area of an irregular shaped piece of land.*
(a) Using metric measurements.
(b) Using imperial measurements.

measured are at some distance from the reference point, to ascertain the relative elevations or compute volumes either sighting and profile boards (b) or the simplest of surveying instruments, the Cowley level (c), should be used.

Note Cowley levels can be hired from tool hire companies and are about the only surveyor's instrument that can be used accurately by the amateur. Other, more sophisticated instruments, such as theodolites, may also be available but if the job demands the accuracy, range and flexibility of such an instrument, you should call in a professional surveyor to do the work.

To use

(a) Board, pegs and spirit-level The board should be at least 1.8 m long × 8 × 5 cm (6 ft long × 3 × 2 in). Check that it is straight and not warped or bent at any point along its length by sighting down it. Pegs should be stout enough to be hammered into the ground without splitting or going out of shape at the top and about 23–30 cm (9 in–1 ft) long. Drive in first peg to the fixed height of required finished level above or below the reference point. Placing one end of the board on this peg, drive in another peg 1.8 m (6 ft) from it until the board, when placed on it, sits level. (Dig out earth from around the peg if necessary.) Repeat around edges of area to be levelled or along length of path etc. When the pegs are in position check between them using the board and tape that you have a uniform clearance under the board and sufficient depth to accommodate the materials to be used for surfacing the terrace or path etc. (Fig. 4.2). (For excavation depths below finished level for the various types of materials, slabs, bricks etc. see Table 5.1.) Do this along the edges and across the middle inserting more pegs if necessary, digging out excess soil or filling in hollows where required (Fig. 4.3).

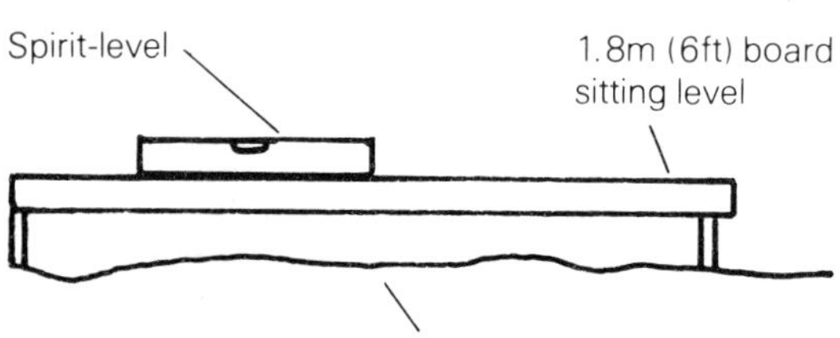

Fig. 4.2 *Levelling with board and pegs.*

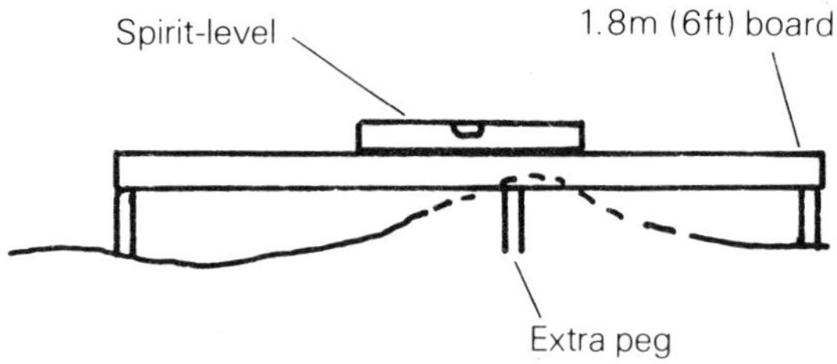

Fig. 4.3 *Using an extra peg to help level particularly bumpy ground.*

(b) Sighting board and profiles For measuring the elevations of points at some distance from the reference point or over a large area the simplest method is to use a sighting board and profiles. This involves sighting by eye over a pair or series of profile boards, set dead level at least 60 cm (2 ft) apart and at a fixed height above the reference point (Fig. 4.4). Using an assistant to hold and mark the sighting board (any straight rod or pole will do), sight across the top of the profiles and, as the assistant moves a stick or finger down the pole, indicate the point sighted and mark it. Now measure the distance between the mark and ground level. The following example indicates how these readings should be used:

Height of profile above reference point i.e. + 90 cm (+ 3 ft)	= 90 cm (3 ft)
Distance between point sighted and ground level	= 1.5 m (5 ft)
Therefore the elevation of the ground at the point	= 1.5 m (5 ft)
	− 90 cm (− 3 ft)
	60 cm (2 ft)

Therefore the elevation = − 60 cm (− 2 ft)

(c) Cowley level These instruments, which are about the size of a small camera,

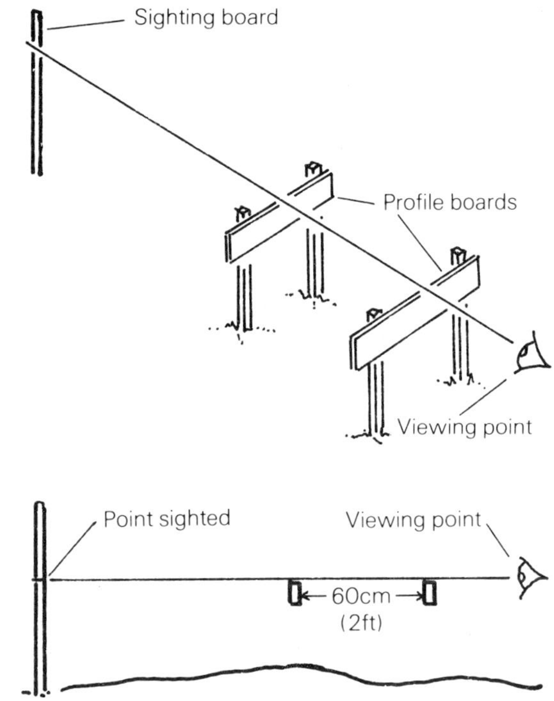

Fig. 4.4 *Sighting board and profile.*

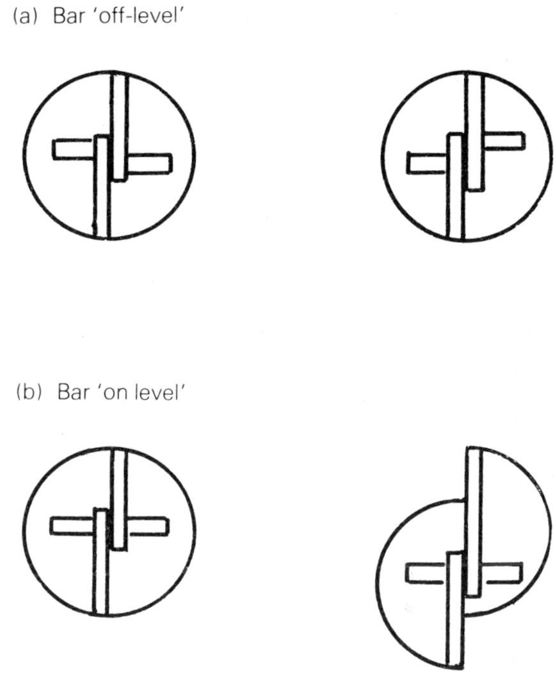

Fig. 4.5 *View of staff through a Cowley level showing various examples of on and off-level positions.*

use a system of mirrors that lock in position to read levels off a graduated staff. They need no adjusting and the tripod need only be approximately positioned. There are five mirrors inside the Cowley, one of which is attached to a pendulum which forms the automatic levelling device. When the instrument is placed on the tripod pin an internal clamp is moved locking the pendulum, and the level is ready for use. With the level comes a graduated 2 m ($6\frac{1}{2}$ ft) extendable staff with a horizontal target bar that slides vertically up and down. When the bar is 'off-level' it appears through the instrument as shown in Fig. 4.5a, and when 'on-level' as shown in Fig. 4.5b. The bar is levelled by moving it up or down and the figure indicated by the bar is then read off the staff.

Note Cowley levels are accurate to within 6 mm in 30 m ($\frac{1}{4}$ in per 100 ft). Therefore by placing it midway and reading in either direction they can be used on runs up to about 60 m (200 ft).

SETTING OR TRANSFERRING LEVELS

These jobs can be done with either sighting boards or a Cowley. If you are using sighting boards you will need a staff, and this should be a straight 1.5 or 1.8 m (5 or 6 ft) piece of wood that can be clearly marked. This equipment can be used in the same way as a Cowley (see below) using an assistant to hold and mark the staff and drive in the pegs when setting up the site. When using either method it is essential to remember that the higher the reading or mark on the staff, the lower the point sighted is.

To set levels

Fig. 4.6 shows how to set levels with a Cowley. In this example a terrace is being laid against a building. The terrace will run level along the house and, for drainage purposes, fall by 8 cm (3 in) in its width (A–B),

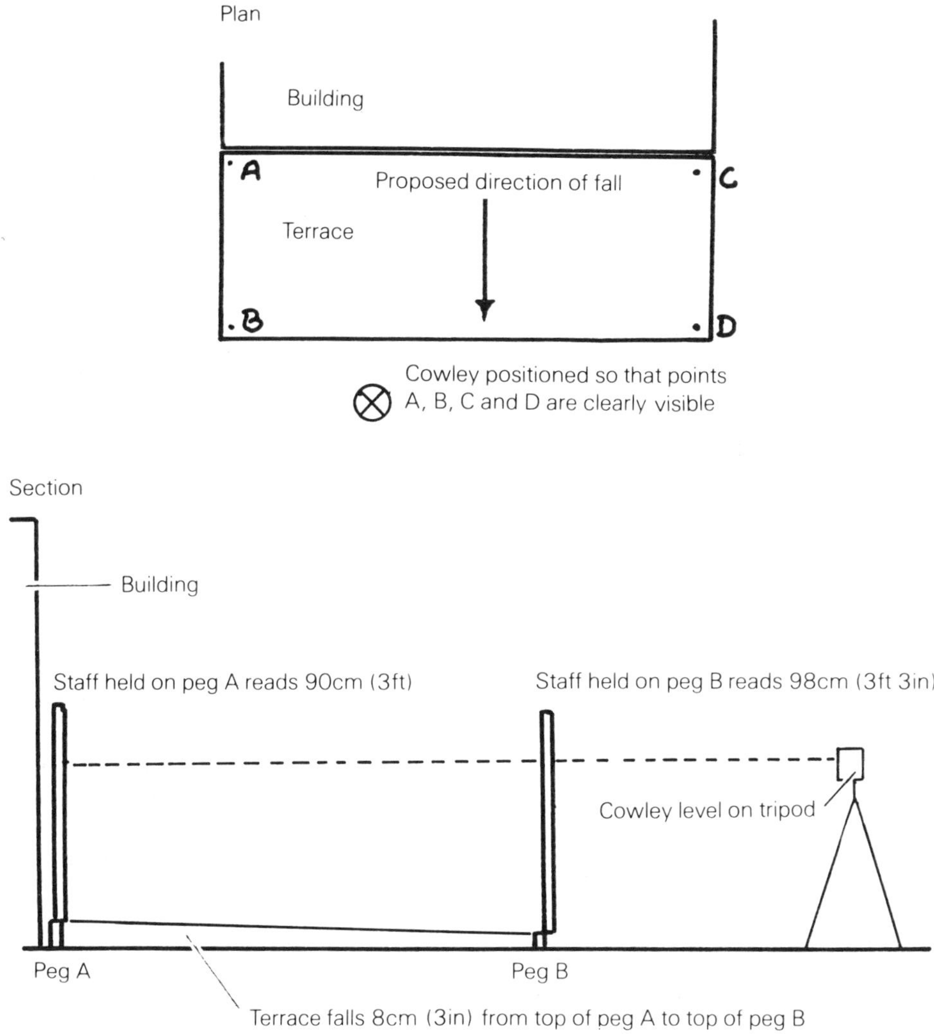

Fig. 4.6 *Setting levels with a Cowley level.*

First, drive in a peg at point A down to the required level of the terrace. Set up the Cowley somewhere outside the working area at a convenient point from which points A, B, C and D can be clearly sighted. Next, ask an assistant to hold the staff on the peg and alter the bar until it appears 'on-level' through the instrument. Read off the figure on the staff (in this example the figure reads 90 cm (3 ft)).

Remove staff and alter the bar to read 98 cm (3 ft 3 in). Position a peg at point B and checking regularly, drive it in until the bar appears 'on-level' when the staff is held on the peg. Repeat at points C and D. Do not move the Cowley tripod during this operation. The pegs are now used as guides during the laying of the terrace. When using sighting boards, mark the staff at point sighted when held at A.

Add 8 cm (3 in) and re-mark the staff. Position at B and drive peg in until the new mark is sighted.

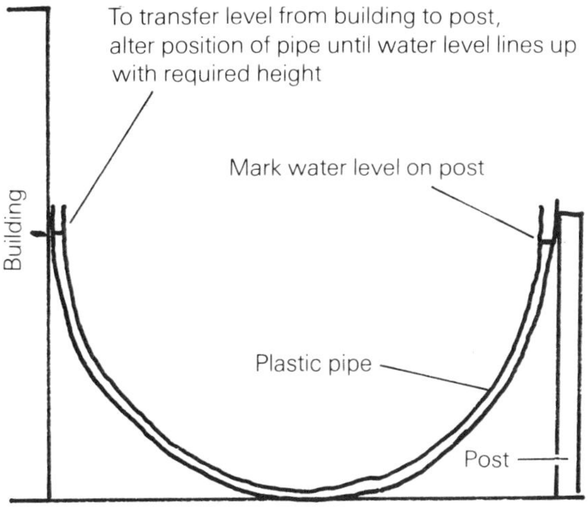

Fig. 4.7 *Using a water filled plastic tube to transfer levels.*

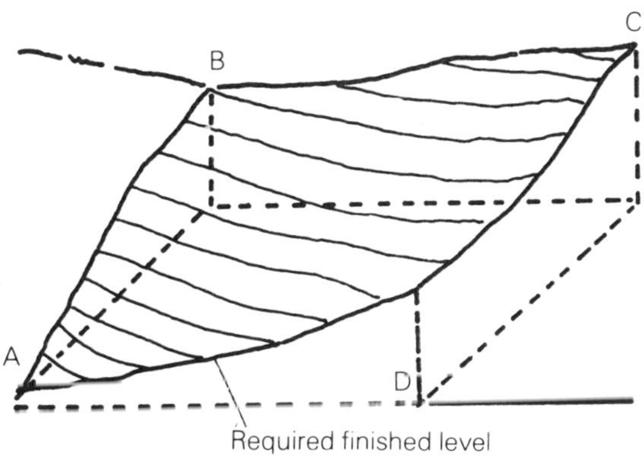

Fig. 4.8 *A piece of ground with slopes in two directions.*

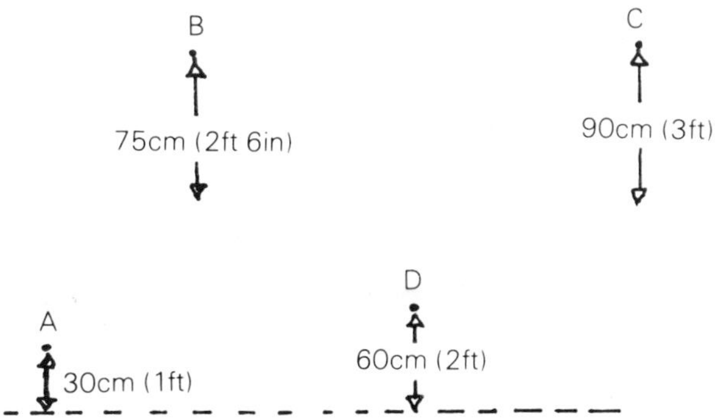

Fig. 4.9 *Calculating the elevations at points* A, B, C *and* D.

To transfer levels

Position staff on required level and mark the point sighted, or with Cowley, alter bar until it appears 'on-level'. Move staff to the point you wish to transfer the level to and drive in a peg until the mark is sighted or the bar appears 'on-level'. (Alternatively, if you are transferring levels to a building or fence post for example, mark the wall or post at the point where the foot of the staff comes when the mark or bar comes 'on-level'.) Over short distances an easy way to transfer levels is to use a length of clear plastic tubing filled with water (Fig. 4.7).

ESTIMATING VOLUMES

Earlier we established the fact that area is calculated by length × width. By extension of this the volume of a regular shape is calculated by length × width × height. The problem is of course, that few gardens are regularly shaped and land may slope in two ways at once. Thus we need a method of calculating the volume of soil contained in a piece of ground like that shown in Fig. 4.8 and the easiest way of doing this is to use the average height method.

To calculate

Establish a reference point and record the elevations of points A, B, C and D. In our example (Fig. 4.9) these read A: 30 cm (1 ft); B: 75 cm (2 ft 6 in); C: 90 cm (3 ft) and D: 60 cm (2 ft). To calculate the average height add these figures together and divide by four:

Metric: 30 + 75 + 90 + 60 cm
= 255 cm ÷ 4 = 63 cm
Imperial: 1 + 2.5 + 3 + 2 ft
= 8.5 ft ÷ 4 = 2 ft 1 in

Thus the average height = 63 cm (2 ft 1 in).

The volume of the area is now worked out by length × width × average height, and is accurate to within about 3%.

This method can help estimate the amount of soil to be removed in excavations and therefore, how many skips will be required for removal, whether it is worth getting an assistant or how much hardcore will be needed to fill in a hollow or low patch to bring it level.

Estimating: quantities and time

The most efficient method of measuring and estimating quantities for particular jobs accompanies each set of step-by-step instructions. In this section we will take an overall look at the problems of estimating and buying with the aim of getting the estimate right, saving extra expense and planning the jobs more efficiently.

As a general rule it is a good idea to allow for the unexpected in your calculations, particularly where ground conditions and the weather are concerned. When you first come to look at a job the ground may look relatively soft, but you may discover harder, more compacted or stonier ground (or even rock) just below the surface. This will clearly lengthen the time a job will take considerably, and it is worth testing the ground in several places to see what it is like. This is particularly valuable if there are indications (such as problems your neighbours may have encountered doing similar work) that the nature of the subsoil alters at any points.

The weather is always an uncertain factor and may well hold up work for days. Nothing much can be done about this, except to bear in mind the forecasts for the days on which you plan to do the work. The delay may only be a matter of hours. The problem is not so much the actual weather itself, but the effect it may have on ground conditions, turning soft, easily moved soil into sticky mud, for example. A useful rule of thumb is to add 10% to estimates of the time it will take to do a job and 5% to estimates of materials. The 10% allowance is for extra time needed if, for example, you meet hard ground or the earth turns muddy after rain, and the 5% allows for errors in calculation (it is far less annoying to be a few blocks over than a few blocks under the requirement when building a wall, for example, particularly if you are doing the work over a weekend or in the evening when you cannot go straight out and buy some more), breakages during transportation and breakages due to mistakes during construction. These figures relate to small or medium garden projects.

Having worked out the overall job it is a good idea to plan the actual working sessions carefully, whether these take up a couple of hours, an evening or a whole weekend. Do not, for example, mix too much mortar at once, since it may get wasted. Similarly, do not over-commit yourself and make sure that you have all the necessary tools, materials and assistants before starting. To help you with this initial planning it is a good idea to itemize the jobs, breaking them down into the actual stages of construction. This can be done as follows:

Let us assume you are constructing crazy-paved steps with brick risers and sidewalls (Plates 11–15). Carefully itemized the job would look like this:

Job	*Material*	*Tools*
Dig out earth profiles	—	shovel, pickaxe, wheelbarrow, tape, spirit-level
Prepare foundations for risers and sides	sand and gravel, cement or scalpings for small jobs	shovel, wheelbarrow, bucket etc.
Build riser and side walls	bricks, sand, cement, plasticizer	builder's trowel, spirit-level, builder's line, shovel, wheelbarrow, lump hammer, bolster chisel
Prepare foundation for tread	scalpings or hardcore for deep steps	shovel, wheelbarrow, spirit-level, rammer
Lay tread	crazy-paving material, mortar for screed bed and pointing	trowel, spirit-level, spot-board or wheelbarrow

Repeat for number of steps required.

Looked at this way planning the job will be much easier and you are less likely to find yourself without some crucial material or tool. If you itemize the job like this a short while before the projected working session you will have plenty of time to assemble everything you require.

The other advantage of this approach is that, as you consider each stage of the job, you can decide whether or not power tools would help to save time and effort. Is there enough mixing to do to justify hiring a cement mixer, would it help to hire a rotavator to loosen the soil, will there be a lot of blocks, bricks or slabs to cut and if so would a disc saw help? On large jobs you may even consider hiring some form of earth-moving machinery to do the initial re-shaping. This gives you a really good start but will be relatively expensive. Power tools can sometimes be an enormous help, justifying the expense in every way and often the noise. Some of the guidelines mentioned below will help you to decide whether they are worth using (for hiring tools see p. 12).

To help you estimate the time needed to do a job and to give some rough guidance on what jobs entail and the materials they require, we have included some general guidelines here. These are not scientifically or elaborately worked out, but are derived from experience and depend, inevitably, on such factors as the weather, relatively good access to the site and the fitness of the people doing the job.

Post holes (in hard or medium hard dry soil): three per hour

Setting posts in concrete (two people): 20 per hour

Laying slabs (on prepared site using mortar spots): 10 per hour

Laying blocks: 100 blocks per day is a good rate

Laying bricks: 300 bricks per day is a good rate

Ready-mix concrete: Before ordering the concrete (ready-mix suppliers can be found in the Yellow Pages or local telephone directory) work out the dimensions of the area to be concreted. Give these to the supplier who will then work out the quantity required. Specify also what the concrete is for to ensure you get the right kind of mix. Ready-mix is usually available in two sizes: 6 and $3\frac{1}{2}$ cu m; anything under these quantities counts as a part load and will be more expensive.

Two skilled people can lay one 6 cu m-load or two $3\frac{1}{2}$ cu m-loads in a day (this includes erecting the shuttering and laying and working the concrete). You should, however, be cautious of being over-optimistic in estimating your work rate because inadequate or insecure shuttering can cause a lot of problems.

Useful measurements

Approximate measurements for sand, sand and gravel. Relative quantities of sand, sand and gravel and cement: use the mix strength as a guide, i.e. 1 : 4 (see p. 14) = 4 times as much sand as cement.

7 shovelfuls of sand = 50 kg (1 cwt)
1 builder's barrowful = 100 kg (2 cwt)
Length of circumference of a circle = diameter × 3.1416
Area of a circle = diameter^2 × .7854
Area of a ring = area of outer circle − area of inner circle

$$\text{Triangle} = \frac{L \times W}{2} = \text{area}$$

One person digging and carrying soft soil without power tools should move about 7.6 cu m (10 cu yd) in a day.

If an assistant is available get two wheelbarrows. It will be considerably more efficient, allowing one person to wheel and the other to dig and fill.

For volumes of soil (unloosened) of over 15 cu m (20 cu yd) we would definitely recommend getting help either from assistants or mechanical diggers.

If there is going to be a lot of excess earth to be removed from the site, it is a good idea to hire a builder's skip which can be left on site as long as you require it and then removed when full. If you have a good workforce you may fill two or three skips in a day, in which case an empty one will be delivered when each full one is collected. Consult with your local dealer to make sure that a good supply of skips will be available and check at the same time whether or not there is an additional charge for the length of time the skip is on site. Skips are usually 10.2 tonnes (10 tons) capacity and will hold approximately 4.6–6.1 cu m (6–8 cu yd) of soil. 0.76 cu m = 1.28 tonnes (1 cu yd = $1\frac{1}{4}$ tons) approx.

Two people digging and carrying earth (less than 30 m (100 ft) at a steady rate will fill a skip in a day.

Three people with two wheelbarrows moving loosened earth – less than 30 m (100 ft) – will fill three skips in a hard day.

Most soil increases in volume by approximately 15–25% when loosened.

Buying

The most important thing to remember when buying materials is to shop around; first, to discover the full range of what is available and second, to find the cheapest sources for what you want. If you know exactly what you require we would still advise trying at least three dealers to find out the cost of the materials, whether or not you can get any discount for a bulk order, and whether or not they will deliver, and if so, the cost of this service.

The main sources of materials on which the landscape gardener depends fall into three groups, each with their own advantages and disadvantages: (1) Sawmills, quarries and factories; (2) Builders' merchants and woodyards and (3) D.I.Y. shops and garden centres.

(1) **Sawmills, quarries and factories** The sources included in this group represent the base of the consumer ladder, being the point of origin of the raw materials and sometimes of finished products. As such they have two main advantages. One is that the materials can be bought at a cheaper price than anywhere else, since they have not been handled by middlemen and will rarely have been the subject of extensive advertising, and the other is that you will be able to get the most detailed advice on the properties and uses of individual materials which can often be very useful. There are, however, some drawbacks, the main one being that many places do not sell direct to the public and if they do, they will often only sell in bulk. It is surprising though how many places will sell direct and it is well worth ringing up, or better still going in person, to find out what is available. If you have suitable transport and can load it yourself, you will often be able to get a load of stone or a quantity of fence posts for a fraction of the cost anywhere else. It is also worth remembering that cash-in-hand often makes things even cheaper. You will be able to find out the location of quarries, sawmills and factories in your local business directory.

(2) **Builders' merchants and woodyards** These form the next step up the ladder. Getting their stock direct from the sources in Group 1 they carry all the materials needed for building and carpentry. For most people these places will be the main source of supply, since anyone can go and buy from them, they will be cheaper for most things than Group 3, they will usually give discount for bulk, will deliver for a small fee, and be able to advise widely on the uses and limitations of materials since they deal directly with the building and construction trades. On the other hand, they are not good places to go and browse in or get ideas, in fact many people find the large yards and crowded warehouses very confusing indeed, and the staff are usually too busy or specialized to give general advice.

The best way to use these places is to visit those in Group 3 first, decide exactly what you want and how much, and then go and buy it from one or other of the above. It is also worth noting that if you have a lot of work to do and will be needing bits and pieces over a period of time, you can usually open an account, which can often be time saving and convenient. It also means that you may get a better discount.

(3) **D.I.Y. shops and garden centres** These are at the top of the ladder and on the whole they are good places to visit and get ideas from, but not the best places to buy your construction materials. Apart from their horticultural side, they are essentially shop windows for expensively pre-packaged products that are marketed under brand names and ready for instant assembly. This means, of course, that you are paying considerably more for pieces of wood etc. that come ready cut with the necessary screws etc., than you would for the same pieces of wood in a woodyard. Similarly, the cost per kilogram of sand and cement in pre-mixed bags is out of all proportion to the cost of the individual ingredients per kilogram at a builder's merchants. On the other hand, these centres provide a good opportunity to see the products in use, since garden centres in particular, often feature garden scenes where plants, masonry and furniture are displayed together.

The point then, is clear: if you want detailed advice, a good price for individual materials and the chance of a discount, buy from groups 1 and 2. If, however, you want to see products clearly displayed, a wide range of ideas, or convenience materials, visit a D.I.Y. shop or garden centre.

Timber

On entering a timber yard or the timber sheds at a builders' merchants you are faced with a bewildering array of shapes, sizes, lengths and types of wood, many of which go under specialized trade names. Don't be put off, tell the assistant what you want, what you want it for and how much you want. He will then advise you on the most suitable types and assemble the order for you. When the wood comes check it carefully for straightness, general condition, firm knots, splits and rot. In many cases, such as rustic fencing, the rougher the wood the better, but for structural work or where accuracy is needed, make sure you get sound, well-produced timber. Again, except for rustic work, ascertain whether the timber is dry and well seasoned, because wood often warps, shrinks or cracks as it dries out. This can lead to disastrous results when 'wet', unseasoned wood is used for structures of neat, regular designs, particularly when the weather warms up and the fence, pergola etc. is dried out by the sun.

The life of all wooden structures can be considerably lengthened by treatment with preservatives. Treated wood is readily available and slightly more expensive, but providing the wood you buy is not too 'wet' (fresh green wood will not absorb chemical treatments), you can always give it several good coats of preservative once it has been erected. Note, however, that creosote is poisonous to plants and should not be used near flowerbeds etc.

Concrete, mortar and masonry

We have already discussed the advantages of buying the ingredients for concrete and mortar individually and it is really just a matter of specifying what you want. For mortar mixes you require the clean building sand, which produces smooth 'pastes' with the most plastic consistency. (Cement when mixed with water forms a smooth, dense paste which bonds rigidly with the surfaces of blocks, bricks, etc. and sets hard. When sand or sand and gravel is mixed with it to make it workable and provide bulk, the paste surrounds the larger particles and forms chemical adhesive. The more plastic this mix is the easier it is to work with.) For concrete the cheaper, coarser grades of sand are mixed with small gravels and for the more rustic types of walling and paths, etc., these types of sand can be used for the mortar mix. Cement must be relatively fresh to work effectively so buy only as much as you will need for the various work sessions; there is no point buying it all at once if it means you will be keeping it for a long period of time.

Most masonry materials, such as blocks and reconstituted stone etc. are standard units that come in a range of sizes, but bricks are something of an exception. In this case a very wide range of types are available from the cheapest grey building bricks to the highly specialized engineering ones which can be red, brown, blue or grey. Apart from the obvious differences in price and size, each has a number of properties and therefore potential uses, and it is a good idea to have a good look round at what is available. A brick wall or terrace can be greatly enhanced by a few decoratively used bricks that stand out from the rest by virtue of their colour or size. It is worth remembering, however, that any coloured products, as with plastics and ceramics, will be more expensive, often noticeably so, than the natural ones.

This section is intended to give some general guidelines on where and what to buy. It is by no means definitive and you may well find local exceptions to our general rules. It is hoped, however, that having read it you will be able to set about getting the cheapest and most suitable materials for your job.

5 Site preparation

Preparation

As a first step when beginning work on a site, particularly if an old garden is being re-designed, the area should be cleared of all unwanted plants, shrubs, undergrowth and general vegetation. Doing this helps in two ways: it provides a better picture of the contours of the land and it helps avoid later disruption that can be caused when large shrubs or trees are taken out. You should also remove at this point any unwanted features, such as old walls or terraces, and only when you can see the whole area to be worked on clearly, the levels and spaces, should you finalize the new plan.

Once you have the new plan ready transfer it in outline to the garden by marking out the major features, terraces, paths, lawns or flowerbeds using pegs and string or sand-lines. This will give you a much better impression of what the design will look like, so that you have a chance to re-consider and alter it if the relationships between the various components or the overall balance is not as you imagined it. We advise that at this stage you try out a few variations, particularly in relation to the position of the sun at various times of the day and the direction of prevailing winds. The point to bear in mind here is that, while you might want to get on with the construction work, it is easier to move a few pegs and string than it is to move a concrete path. Over and above these considerations there is a further aspect of planning and preparation that we feel should be mentioned.

For most people who have only limited time to work on the garden – many indeed are limited to either evenings or weekends – plans will necessarily be worked on in stages and it is important while working on one stage to keep later projects and, most particularly, access to them, in mind. It would be a shame, for example, to lay a lawn or gravel a drive if at some later stage you are going to have to transport soil or stone over them. Damage or disturbance would be inevitable.

Furthermore, where the overall plan involves a number of integrated components, flowerbeds, lawns, stonework, etc., which will be built separately, it is worthwhile waiting until everything is nearly complete before sowing or turfing grass areas or planting flowerbeds so that they will not be adversely affected. In Plate 24 we have an example of this. The area of bare earth above the terrace and beside the steps is waiting to be turfed but this should be done as the final stage of the work after the terrace, steps and new contours have been completed, even if this means missing, for example, the spring growing season. Had this piece been turfed before, it would have made the job of digging out the steps and adjusting the contours of the bank to suit them much more difficult.

When the overall garden plan has been finalized you should concentrate on preparing specific areas for whatever will be constructed on them. This basic work usually consists of levelling, excavating, preparing firm bases for paths, terraces, drives, etc. and organizing any drainage that may be necessary and we discuss these aspects of preparation below.

Excavation and hardcore

Whatever kind of prepared surface (patio, path, parking area, drive, etc.) is being constructed, all will need the right kind of foundation on which they can be laid. Once you have decided on the type of surface you want, i.e. whether it is just for pedestrians or whether it will be required to carry a car or even larger vehicles, look up the relevant excavation and hardcore requirements given in Table 5.1 (p. 33).

Digging levels

To calculate the relative levels on a site and to estimate volumes of soil to be removed, see p. 25.

Before looking at the actual digging-out process it should be noted that all types of soils increase noticeably in volume when loosened for removal, and in some cases, where large areas of soil are to be removed, it will be useful to know by what percentage a given soil type will increase, since this may affect the number of skips required for removal from the site. To help you work out this increase Table 5.2 (p. 33) indicates the percentage increase in volume for five basic types of soil and these should be used as a guide. Decide which soil type is nearest to the kind you are dealing with and add the percentage shown to the estimated volume of soil present to get the total. For example if you are digging out 7.6 cu m (10 cu yd) of topsoil, add 25% to get the final total:

7.6 + 25% = 9.5 cu m
(10 + 25% = 12.5 cu yd)

of loose soil.

To dig

Always start to dig out levels at a fixed point where the finished level is correct. In Fig. 5.1 work starts at point X, where an existing path gives the required finished level. Excavation starts here, digging out a small area to the required depth (Table 5.1) below finished level.

A trench should now be dug to point A, at the same depth as the digging at X, or along any other fixed feature, such as the path, in which case the trench would run to point B. If such features border the excavation it is helpful to use them first since the damp course of the house, brick courses or the existing path level will help you keep the trench bottom at the correct depth.

Following this, trenches should be dug to the other extremities of the area to be excavated, i.e. to points C and D from trench A. Check the depths of these trenches every 1.8 m (6 ft) or so, using a board and spirit-level or a Cowley level and staff. When complete these trenches will give you the correct

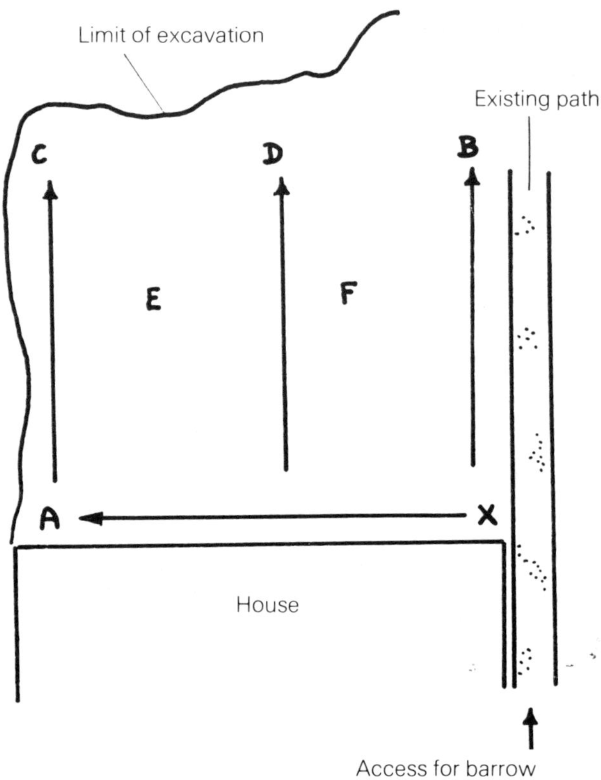

Fig. 5.1 *Terracing; preparatory excavations for a large area.*

Table 5.1 Laying techniques and excavation depths (assuming finished level equals ground level)

A. For loads up to 0.5 tonne ($\frac{1}{2}$ ton)
(pedestrians and small cars)

Surface Materials	*Method of laying*	*Base materials required*	*Depth or thickness*	*Excavation depth*
Slabs	mortar spots		2.5 cm (1 in)	12.5 cm (5 in)
5 cm (2 in)		scalping dust	5 cm (2 in)	15 cm (6 in)
thick	solid bed		5 cm (2 in)	15 cm (6 in)
		scalping bed	5 cm (2 in)	
	sand bed		2.5 cm (1 in)	
		scalping dust	5 cm (2 in)	
Bricks	solid bed		5 cm (2 in)	17 cm ($6\frac{3}{4}$ in)
7 cm ($2\frac{3}{4}$ in)		scalping dust	5 cm (2 in)	
thick	sand bed		5 cm (2 in)	
Crazy-paving	solid bed		5 cm (2 in)	15 cm (6 in)
5 cm (2 in)		scalping dust	5 cm (2 in)	
thick				
Gravel	spread and roll	scalping dust	5 cm (2 in)	10 cm (4 in)
5 cm (2 in)				
thick				

B. For loads over 0.5 tonne ($\frac{1}{2}$ ton)
(medium and large vehicles)

Slabs	solid bed		8 cm (3 in)	21 cm (8 in)
5 cm (2 in)		hardcore	8 cm (3 in)	
thick				
Bricks	screed bed		1.25 cm ($\frac{1}{2}$ in)	24.25 cm
7 cm ($2\frac{3}{4}$ in)		hardcore	8 cm (3 in)	($9\frac{1}{4}$ in)
thick		concrete	8 cm (3 in)	
Crazy-paving	screed bed		1.25 cm ($\frac{1}{2}$ in)	22.25 cm
5 cm (2 in)		hardcore	8 cm (3 in)	($8\frac{1}{2}$ in)
thick		concrete	8 cm (3 in)	
Gravel	spread and roll			13 cm (5 in)
5 cm (2 in)		hardcore	8 cm (3 in)	
thick				

Table 5.2 Percentage increase in volume when various types of soil are loosened

Soil type	*Percentage increase in volume when loosened*
Clay	40%
Earth, dry loam	25%
Gravel with sand	12%
Topsoil	25%
Wet sand	5%

depth at the extremities and across the middle of the area and the earth can now be removed from areas E and F and put at the side or barrowed out to a skip. Use the trench bottoms to check the depth as you go along with board and level. The whole area should then be checked when the digging is finished.

Note 1. Remember that topsoil is fertile and can be used elsewhere in the garden for lawns or flowerbeds, etc. Most subsoil, however, is infertile and should either be removed from the site or used in an area where it will be buried and can then be covered with topsoil.

Note 2. When choosing a starting point, keep in mind the access and exit point for the barrow. When doing the first dig across the area aim to be about 1.25 cm ($\frac{1}{2}$ in) above finished depth to avoid going too deep.

Hardcore

Hardcore, as can be seen from Table 5.1, should be used to provide a firm base for all types of load-bearing surfaces, for making up levels beneath these, or for any type of job in the absence of good firm subsoil. It does not pay to skimp on quantities and if in doubt always use it. For most purposes 2.5 cm (1 in) size stone, together with quarry dust (often called 'scalpings') is sufficient (Fig. 5.2a). It

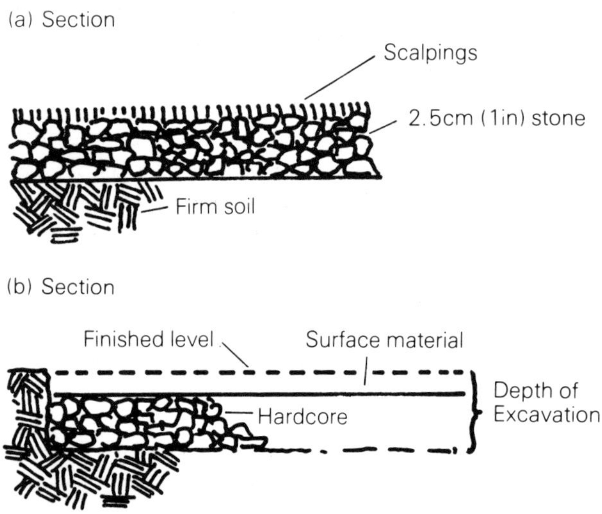

Fig. 5.2 *Hardcore. (a) Sectional view. (b) Depth of excavation.*

is cheap and available at most quarries and builders' merchants. If the hardcore is for use under load-bearing surfaces, and particularly if it is used in depth to correct levels, it should be compacted, either with a hired vibrating roller or, for smaller areas, with a hand rammer.

Note If no hardcore is required (see Table 5.1, but 'solid-bed' or 'mortar-spot' laying techniques are being used, then the earth should be covered in a thin layer of scalpings or sand.

How to use Table 5.1 (p. 33): If, for example, you wish to lay slabs to carry weights of over 0.5 tonne ($\frac{1}{2}$ ton), then you will use the solid-bed technique, and your total excavation will be 21 cm (8 in) to allow for: 8 cm (3 in) of hardcore, 8 cm (3 in) of mortar mix for the solid bed, and 5 cm (2 in) for the thickness of the slabs.

Drainage

There are three important types of drainage that concern us here: site draining, draining flat surfaces and enclosed flat surfaces, and draining behind retaining walls. Clearly the aim in each case is to control and remove as efficiently as possible any water, surface or underground, that could potentially pose a problem after construction work is complete. The destructive properties of water are often either overlooked completely or at least not given sufficient attention and this can lead to erosion, the collapse of walls, the disturbance of flat surfaces, puddles and problems of damp around buildings.

The area in which the most serious and costly damage can be done is that immediately around the house. If the line where garden surfaces meet the house or building is not 15 cm (6 in) below the damp-proof course (D.P.C.), or if the levels allow water to collect or soak-away against the walls, the effects will soon be noticed inside in the form of damp patches and peeling plaster. Thus, the cardinal rule for site preparation must be to make sure that water drains away from buildings, and on a wider scale, that surface levels should be contoured to lead water away from building foundations.

SITE DRAINAGE

Now that we have established some of the basic aims of drainage, we will look at the garden as a whole and focus on the organization of drains over large areas. For people with naturally well-drained or long-established gardens it may be hard to imagine the problems gardeners can have with wet spots, continuous surface water, or the slow drainage of puddles etc. on lawns or flower-beds after heavy rain. But for many people, particularly those who live on modern estates, or in new houses which have been fitted between existing ones, site drainage can cause a number of difficulties, and these must be sorted out before the garden can be successfully developed.

These problems often result from the widespread disturbance of levels during the construction of large estates. When this happens the natural site drainage is disrupted and, particularly where slopes have been dug away, the existing underground drainage routes through the subsoil are opened up. In addition the soil in the garden area may have become compacted by the builder's machines and will therefore not let the water drain away properly. Thus gardeners may find that water from a fairly large area around their gardens may be draining through or collecting on their land. Quite apart from the inconvenience and surface damage this can cause, it may also lead to erosion which, in turn, will make it difficult to maintain the garden. Few people will find themselves in this extreme situation but to one degree or another these are the kind of problems that may need dealing with.

In general terms there are two methods of approach to site draining: either you can interrupt the flow of water before it has a chance to accumulate, or you can remove it from an area of accumulation. In the first case surface water is channelled off where it enters the garden or at convenient points along its route and is then led away off the property. On steep slopes the water should be intercepted as near the top of the slope as possible to minimize erosion. In the second case the water in the garden is allowed or helped to accumulate, either in a natural wet spot or in a purpose-built sump, and is subsequently drained away or removed from this point. This method is suitable for gardens that are not actively eroded by surface or underground water but which are generally 'wet', and it minimizes disturbance to the garden during construction.

Whichever method of drainage is used, there are a number of ways in which it can be done, and these all basically work by channelling the water away while permitting it to collect or disperse along the length of the system.

(1) **Open ditches** These are the cheapest and easiest way of draining but have obvious drawbacks, particularly if you need to drain across the body of the garden. The idea is that a ditch is opened up across the flow of surface water and deep enough to catch water moving just below the surface. This collects the water and leads it away, either into an existing drain or into a soakaway or sump (see below). Since water will always take the easiest route, a ditch will carry it away by virtue of its open, flattened bottom and thus the bottom need not be dug with a noticeable outfall. Providing the bottom is regularly cleaned out and maintained, the outfall need only be about 10 cm (4 in) every 6–7 m (20 ft). As was mentioned above, open ditches may not be suitable for most gardens, but if there is room around the perimeter, they can be used to intercept water running down from adjacent properties. For depths and widths of ditches see p. 39.

(2) **Stone drains** The next step up from open ditches are stone drains. These are constructed by filling in the ditches with stone to permit drainage, and then either covering them with soil or, where there is a constant

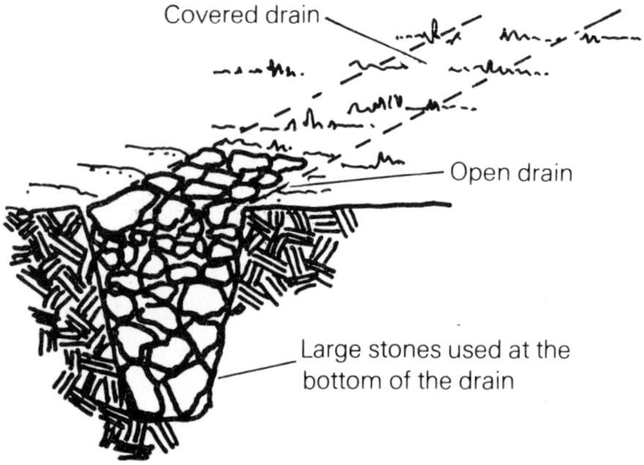

Fig. 5.3 *Sectional view of a stone drain.*

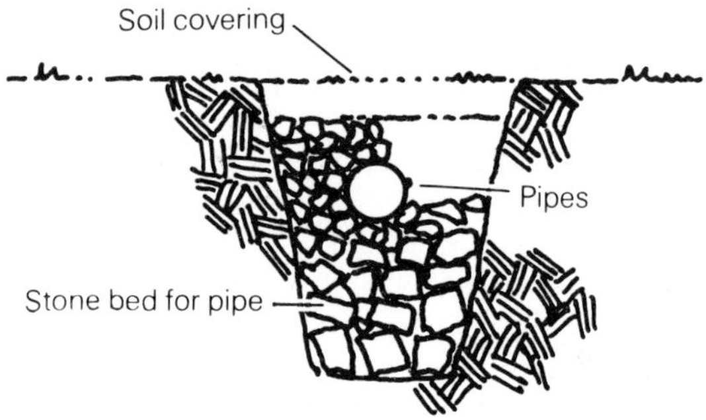

Fig. 5.4 *Sectional view of a dispersal drain.*

flow of water, leaving them uncovered for maximum efficiency. These provide one of the oldest methods of draining areas where the land is used and open ditches are therefore impractical, and Fig. 5.3 illustrates how one is constructed. The basic point to remember about this type of drain is that the larger the stones are at the bottom, the more efficiently it will work, and that the stone size should get rapidly smaller above the interception level to help seal the top if it is to be covered with soil.

For most purposes in smallish garden drains hardcore stone around 5 cm (2 in) average size is probably the most practical material to use. It is available from most quarries and some builders' merchants. If some larger stones are available these should be used on the bottom at particularly wet spots and then covered with clean hardcore stone. (For depths, widths and grid patterns see pp. 38 & 39.)

(3) **Piped drains** Perhaps the most efficient drains of all are those that have pipes, either clay or plastic, laid along the trench bottom and covered with stone. Clay is the traditional material for this kind of drain, and the pipes are usually 30 cm long × 8 × 10 or 15 cm wide (12 in long × 3 × 4 × 6 in wide) and can be bought at most builders' merchants. Concrete pipes are available but they will be unnecessarily large for most garden purposes. The pipes are laid end to end along the flattened bottom of the trench providing a clear route for the water through the soil. To facilitate maximum access, not just at the top end of the drain but along the length of the drain as well, the pipes are not mortared to seal them together so that water can enter at all the joins. Plastic piping comes in long rolls with a similar range of widths as clay pipes. The ribbed piping is perforated with hundreds of little slits which allow water to seep in along the length of the pipe. Again, for this system to work efficiently the pipe itself should be covered with a layer of clean stone and not covered directly with earth. Plastic piping is quicker and easier to lay, and will have an almost infinite lifetime. As a rule well laid pipe drains will be pretty much self-cleaning and will need only minimum attention.

Note It may seem obvious but we advise you to check the rolls of plastic piping before installing to make sure that they have been perforated. Very occasionally rolls appear on the market unperforated due to some manufacturing error. Check the pipe and change if necessary.

(4) **Soakaways** Soakaways and sumps are used as dispersal or removal points for water that has been collected in drains or that has accumulated naturally in a wet spot. Soakaways, as their name implies, concentrate on the dispersal of collected water. The stone

filling allows the water to seep down to the bottom of the pit, where it is dispersed over a wide area. Alternatively, the water can be channelled into a dispersal drain, from which it can soak-away along the length of the pipes. For this kind of drain the pipes are laid on top of a bed of stones giving the water maximum opportunity to disperse as may be seen in Fig. 5.4.

Sumps are used if the local soil type or space available makes dispersal impossible or if an accessible collecting point is required. In these cases the pit can be lined with bricks or concrete and the collected water removed with either buckets or a pump. For easy maintenance and efficient pumping the bottom of the sump, whether soil, brick, concrete, etc., should be given a fall to one side. Thus, as the water level drops while the sump is being emptied, the remaining water and any debris will collect along one side for easier removal (Fig. 5.5).

Note If your garden contains a particularly wet or boggy spot, or you have surface water running almost continuously down a bank, you might consider turning it into a feature, if this is practical, rather than trying to drain it.

TO DIG AND LAY: DITCHES, PIPES, SOAKAWAYS AND SUMPS

Type to use

The main decision here concerns which type of drain, or dispersal or removal point is most suited to your needs. This will depend on how much water is involved, whether or not there are existing drains that can be linked up to and which part of the garden is being drained. Clearly it is not possible to specify exactly what sort of drain should be installed in individual circumstances in a generalized discussion of the problem such as this, since important factors such as the exact nature of the problem, top- and subsoil types, individual preferences and the availability of the various materials all vary so much. As a guide, however, we will look at two of the common problems mentioned before and see how they can be dealt with.

(1) Parts of the lawn hold puddles for long periods after rain This problem affects a lot of gardens and is usually caused by subsoil near the surface preventing water from draining away. This is particularly true in new gardens where the ground has been levelled and the subsoil exposed in preparation for building. Although in most cases exposed subsoil is re-covered with a layer of topsoil after building is finished, it may not always be of uniform depth and the puddles will tend to collect where the topsoil is shallowest. Whether this is the reason or whether, as sometimes happens, alterations to drainage systems in the immediate vicinity cause the problem to arise in long-established gardens, a drain should be installed to remove the excess water. If the problem is not too acute, the easiest method would be to dig a small soakaway in the middle of the affected area, fill it with stone, cover with earth and replace the turf. This will remove the water from the surface and allow it to disperse over a period of time underground. Remember though, that for a soakaway to be effective it must reach a porous layer of soil.

If, however, there is too much water for

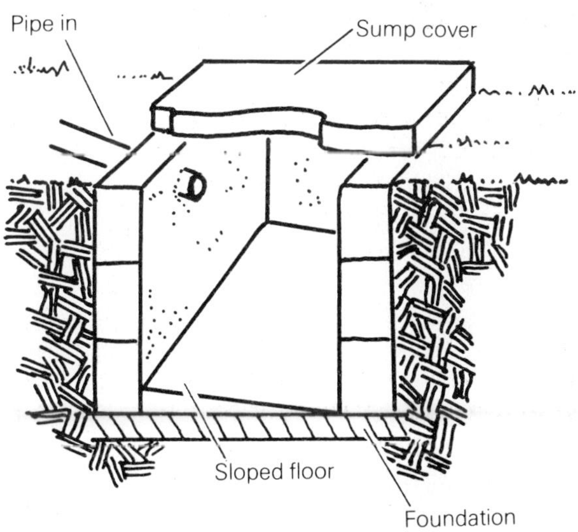

Fig. 5.5 *Collection sump : notice sloped floor. Rendering the inside will help prevent leakage.*

this to work, the soakaway, acting as a collecting point, should be connected to a piped dispersal drain. Finally, if there is too much water for this to work or if large, or widely spaced areas are affected, piped drains should be laid leading away to a soakaway, sump or exterior drainage system.

(2) **Water running in from higher adjacent property** If the water comes in at one particular point there should be no problem in intercepting it and leading it away down a piped drain. On the other hand, it may seep into the garden from a number of unspecified places. Should this be the case, the best idea is to catch it in a small, uncovered stone drain laid across the line of the slope as near the boundary as possible and to let it run along this drain to a collecting point from which it can be dispersed or removed. The stone drain need not be very big or wide and can be disguised by plants or a fence erected along the top of it.

The above examples are not definitive answers but are meant as a guide as to how to approach the problem, define it and select the most suitable remedy.

Drainage grids

Where large areas of garden or lawn are to be drained using a system of connected trenches, whether they utilize just stone or pipes and stone, it will save time and effort and will probably produce a more efficient drain if you work out the grid pattern for the system before starting. How the trenches are laid out and interconnected is a matter of choice, providing they flow into each other and towards an exit point, but the grid patterns shown in Figs. 5.6a and b, the traditional designs, are those most commonly used and they will minimize the amount of digging required. (These examples show drains using clay pipes.) Both work on the basis of subsidiary pipes feeding one main pipe which carries the water away to the dispersal point. The herring-bone grid shown in Fig. 5.6a is most useful for draining large, flat areas. The spacing of the subsidiary pipes will depend to some extent on just how wet the ground in question is, and in extreme cases more closely spaced subsidiaries may be required. For most purposes though, the spacing shown will provide efficient outlets for the water, and, particularly if you are draining an existing lawn, will minimize the disturbance on the surface. Stone fill should be to within 30 cm (1 ft) of the surface.

The half-herringbone grid shown in Fig. 5.6b should be used in situations where an existing slope in the ground, however slight, already leads the water naturally to one side. Thus the main pipe is laid along this side to collect not only the water caught by the subsidiary pipes, but also that which has percolated down of its own accord. Again, the

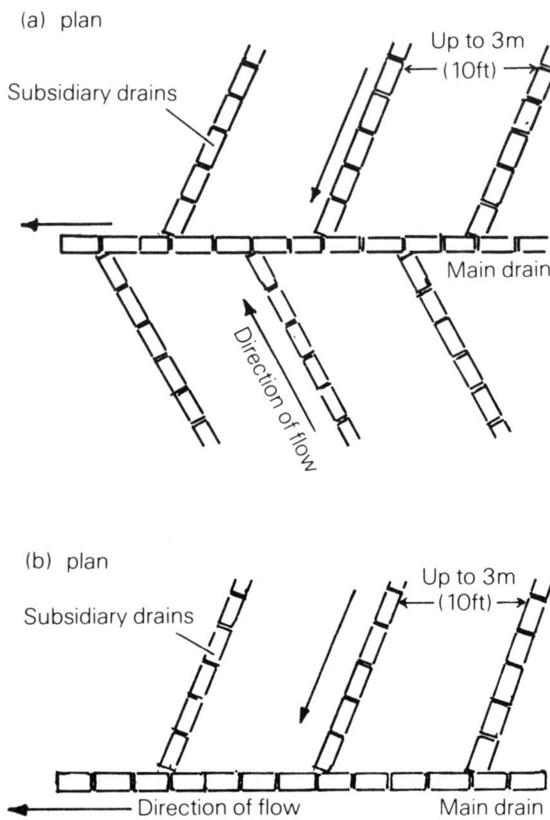

Fig. 5.6 *Drainage grids.*
(a) The herringbone style.
(b) Half-herringbone.

spacing of the subsidiary pipes should be altered if necessary to suit localized ground conditions.

There are no hard and fast rules governing the layout of drainage systems and if your garden presents particular problems in either wetness or soil characteristics you should adapt the grids illustrated here, either in the pattern used or by combining them with dispersal drains or sumps, to create a system that meets your particular needs. Whatever type of grid you use, however, for maximum efficiency try to lay the subsidiary drains across any existing slope.

Depths and widths

Before settling on a final design for your drains, it is a good idea to dig a series of test holes in the area to be drained to get some idea of the depth below ground level at which the water accumulates. Dig out the holes and leave them for a couple of days. After this period check them to see what the situation is, for by this time if any water is present below ground in appreciable quantities it will have found its level in the bottom of the hole. You should now use this as a guide to how deep the trenches need to be if the water is to be carried away. On areas such as lawns, however, where you are only concerned with surface water, the pipes need only be 30–45 cm (1 ft–1 ft 6 in) below the ground.

Trench widths, unless an extra wide stone drain is being used, need only be wide enough to facilitate easy digging and provide sufficient elbow room to lay the pipes along the bottom, i.e. the width of your shovel. This should be wide enough to take 10 or 15 cm (4 or 6 in) pipes, and allow a good quantity of stone to sit either side.

LAYING PROCEDURE: CLAY AND PLASTIC PIPES

What you will need

Pipes. Stone. Shovel. Pickaxe. Spirit-level. Stout 1.8 m (6 ft) board. Hacksaw for plastic pipes.

Measuring up

Clay pipes and rolls of plastic pipe come in standard lengths. Find out what is available and calculate your requirements accordingly. For pipe widths be sure to allow generously for the amount of water that could possibly be travelling down the various pipes. Where your system is draining areas that are only wet periodically, such as lawns after heavy rain, 8 cm (3 in) pipes will be adequate, but if you want a large number of subsidiary runs, or if the system is connected to any other interception points, it may be a good idea to use 10 cm (4 in) pipes for the main drain. This is particularly true if your main drain is to be connected to pipes draining large flat surfaces. If your drain is to channel or remove continually flowing water, larger pipes again should be used, i.e. 15 cm (6 in), depending on the amount of water. When choosing pipe sizes it is worth noting that doubling the diameter of the pipe increases the capacity four times. i.e. a 15 cm (6 in) pipe will carry four times as much water as an 8 cm (3 in) pipe.

To lay

Dig out trench, keeping the bottom as clean and smooth as possible. Start digging from the lowest point, i.e. soakaway or access to exterior drains, and work back up the system, checking every 1.8 m (6 ft) with the board and spirit-level that you are not digging too deep and causing a backfall. As mentioned before, the trench bottoms can be practically level, but if a slight fall – 10 cm (4 in) – in every 6–7 m (20–24 ft) can be included, then this will make the drain more efficient overall. If you are digging across a lawn, cut the turf off carefully in 60–90 cm (2–3 ft) long strips, roll these up and store in a safe place, to be replaced when installation is complete. (For re-laying the turf see p. 163.)

(a) Laying clay pipes Run out pipes along the side of the trench. Clear bottom of trench and lay first pipe down the middle and against the top end of trench. Tap pipe firmly into position with your heel, making sure that it sits properly along its length, and pack a small amount of loose stone or soil down the sides to hold it in position. (This helps avoid any disturbance when stone or soil filling is placed on top.) Do not, however, at this point cover the pipe entirely. Taking the next pipe, heel it into position tight up to the one before and in line down the middle of the trench. Secure it with small stones or soil (Fig. 5.7a). Continue for length of pipe run.

At junctions (between subsidiary and main pipes, etc.) it is not necessary to insert a subsidiary into the main drain. Simply ensure that the end of a subsidiary line butts up tight to a join in the main piping (Fig. 5.7b). The water will not take long to find its way through and silt up any gaps in the sides.

When the pipes are laid, go back along the runs and pack loose stones or pieces of broken pipe around all the junction points and across the top ends of the runs (Fig. 5.7c) to 'seal' them. This helps to stop soil blocking them and provides better access for the water. When you are satisfied that all the pipes are sitting properly and that the ends and junctions are well sealed, the trench can be filled. Whether you are using stone or soil or a combination, be careful when actually covering the pipes not to disturb or move them, since you may disrupt the flow or actually break a pipe.

Note The best method to 'cut' pipes for awkward lengths or to get a tight join on angled junctions (Fig. 5.8a) is to use a large adjustable spanner. Place this over the end of the pipe (Fig. 5.8b) and push down, nipping off a small piece of the pipe. Repeat this round the top until the pipe is cut to required length or angle. Use broken-off pieces to seal the pipe runs after laying is complete.

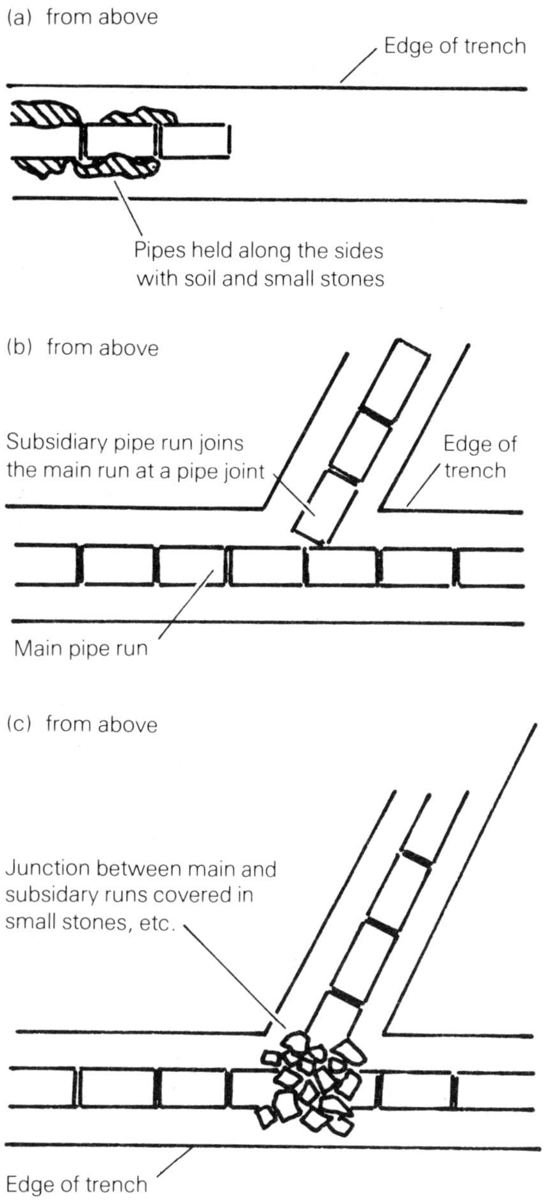

Fig. 5.7 *Laying clay pipes.*
(a) Securing the pipes;
(b) and (c) Joining pipe runs.

(b) Laying plastic pipes Clean out trench bottom and lay out the piping down the middle of the trench. If the pipe lifts up or sits out of line at any point pack loose stone around it to hold it in position. Cut any excess pipe off with a hacksaw. Seal ends and junctions with loose stone (Fig. 5.7c) and fill trench.

Note Both clay and, to a lesser extent, plastic pipes, where installed in shallow trenches are susceptible to blocking by root growth, particularly that of nettle beds. Once the roots penetrate the pipes they soon spread and collect the soils and small stones travelling down with the water, thus blocking the pipe completely. When this

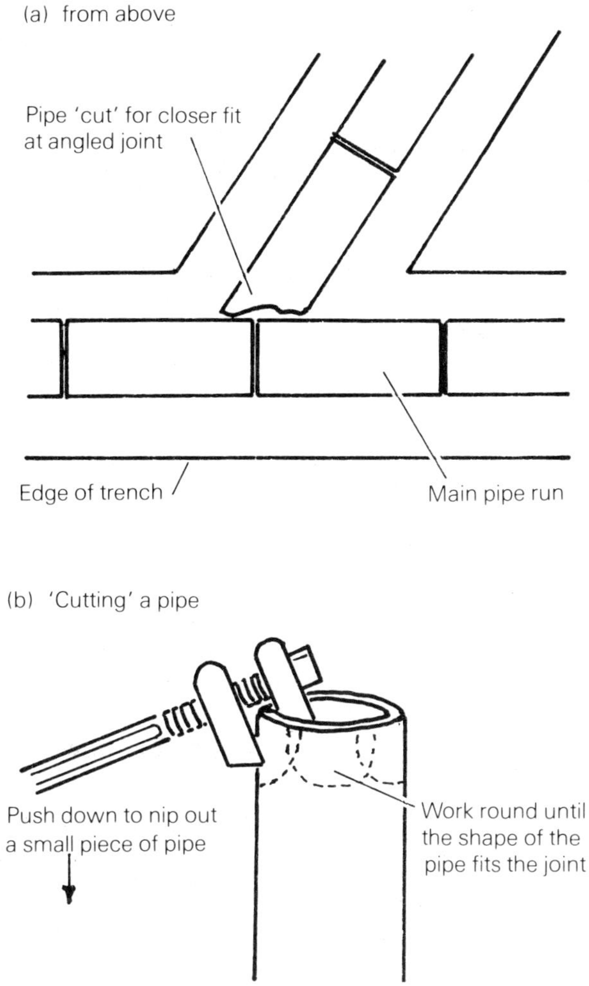

Fig. 5.8 *Cutting the end of a pipe off at an angle.*

happens, short of actually digging up the pipes, it is almost impossible to clear them. So if your pipes run under or near such vegetation, be sure either to remove the nettles etc. or rod the pipes regularly. Alternatively, where the pipes run close to bushes etc. they can be partly protected by laying plastic sacking etc., above the drain.

Flat-surface draining

To ensure efficient drainage on flat areas such as terraces, drives and parking areas, two points must be considered. First, the slight incline that must be built into the surface and second, the dispersal or removal point for the water that subsequently runs off. For the first point a detailed description of what is required is included in the step-by-step instructions for laying the various terracing materials, but you should be clear about the requirements for the second point before going ahead with constructing the terrace, etc. since the dispersal or removal drains may have to be installed first.

Dispersal and removal

Your choice of technique for dealing with run-off water from terraces etc., will depend to a large extent on the situation of the construction. If, for example, you are laying a flat surface beside a lawn or flowerbed, providing these are well drained it is sufficient to angle the run-off towards them and the water will disperse into the soil (Fig. 5.9a).

In many situations, however, you may not have direct access to soil that can act as a dispersal area, or there may be too much water for this to work fast enough, or the surrounding soil may be too heavy for the water to seep away into. Should this be the case you will need to install a drain to collect the run-off water and take it away for dispersal. Fig. 5.9b gives an example of this kind of situation, where a terrace, laid in the angle of an L-shaped house, is surrounded by higher ground held by retaining walls and is approached from the garden down a set of steps. To collect the water effectively the terrace has been laid with a fall in two directions (Fig. 5.9c), away from the long side of the house and down towards the rain-water gully pot which gives access to the rain-water drains. (If the rain-water drains were not there, this would be the best place to install a removal drain.) There are clearly a number of alternatives and variables to this layout (the downspout gully may be at the other end etc.) but this is the general principle that should be followed.

To make it easier for the water to reach the drain access it is an idea to create a shallow open gutter down one side of the terrace (Fig. 5.9d). This will help collect and channel the water after a particularly heavy fall of rain or if you wish to wash the terrace down. If you are going to include a gutter leave a 15 cm (6 in) gap along the side of the terrace between the surface material and the retaining wall or incorporate the gap in the pattern of the surface material. When the terrace has been laid and is set firm, fill the gap with mortar, following the levels of the terrace, and form the gutter in its surface. This can either be done using a piece of 10 × 5 cm (4 × 2 in) piece of wood or, to get a rounded profile, a length of 10 cm (4 in) guttering pressed into the mortar (Fig. 5.9d). When you are satisfied with the shape of the gutter, remove the wood or guttering and smooth off the surface of the mortar before it sets. Pay particular attention to the point where the gutter meets the drain access and make sure that the water can run smoothly away down the drain.

Gully pots

In situations where you are linking terrace drainage up with existing rain-water systems there will usually be a gully pot 'sealing' the access end of the drain. These pots serve two purposes. First, they catch and collect any debris, such as leaves, soil or small stones, that may be washed down the drain with the water and prevent it from entering the pipes, and second, they provide a seal that stops any smells escaping from the pipe system. If, however, there is no gully pot present, or you are laying a new system of pipes, it is a good idea to fit one at the point where the surface

(a) Hard surface sloped to one side to ensure that rainwater runs off into adjacent soil

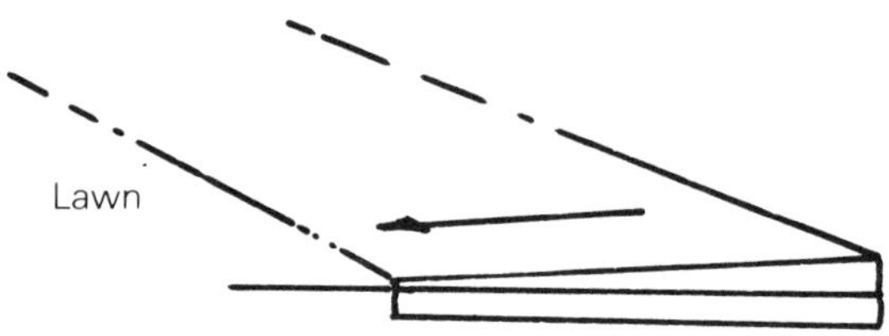

(b) Terrace surrounded by walls (from above)

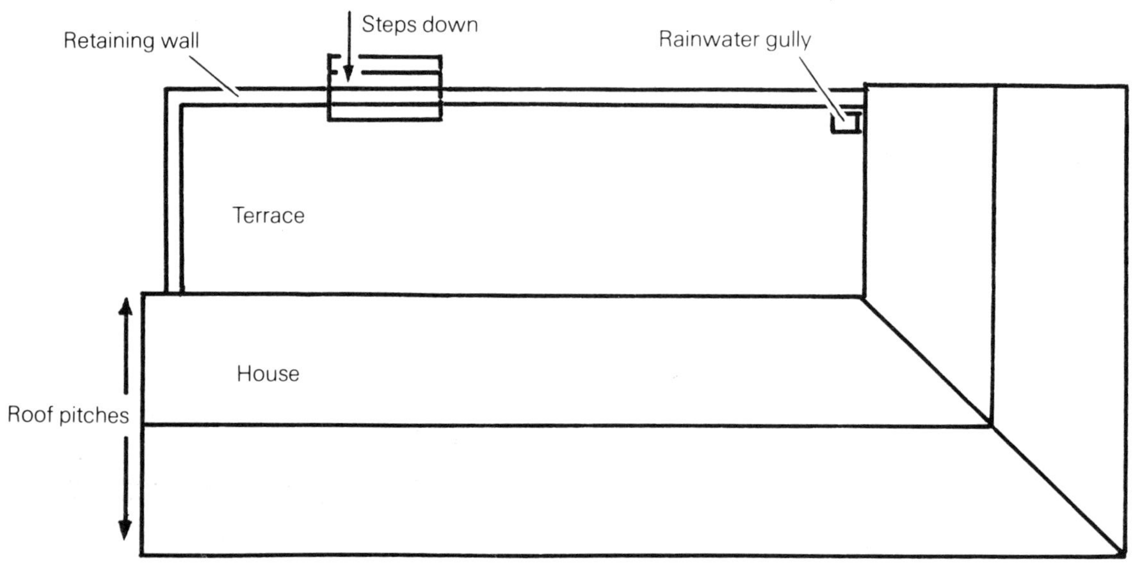

Fig. 5.9 *Draining enclosed terraces.*
(a) Draining hard surfaces into adjacent soil.
(b) Terrace surrounded by house and retaining wa
(c) Falls required to drain the terrace.
(d) Installing a gutter.

(c) Controlling rainwater with falls in two directions

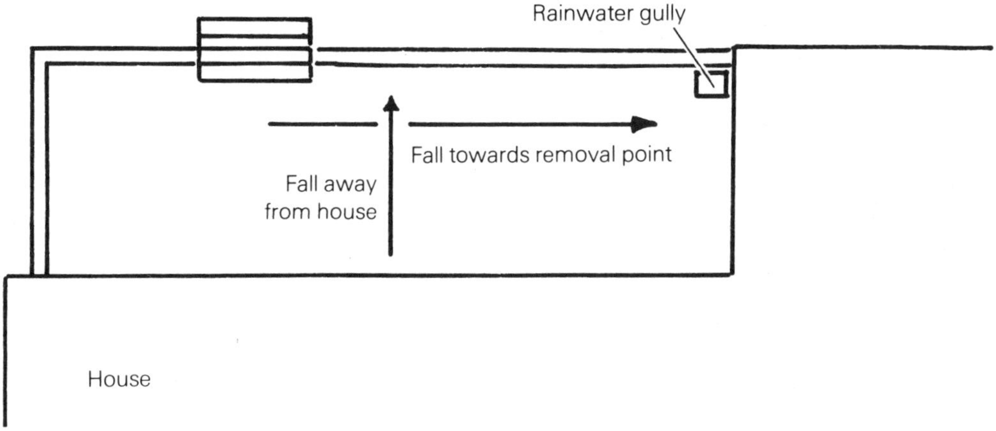

(d) Improving water collection and removal with a gutter

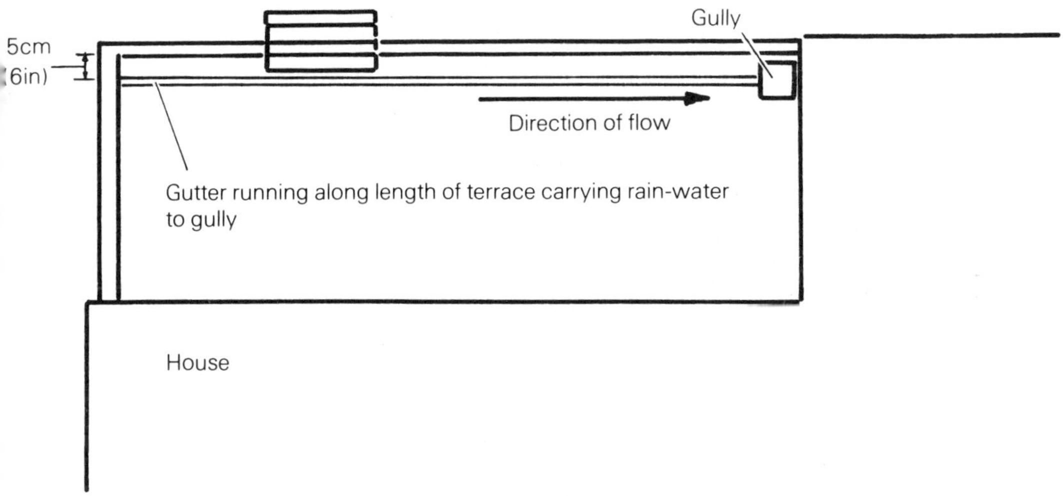

Construction of a gutter (section)

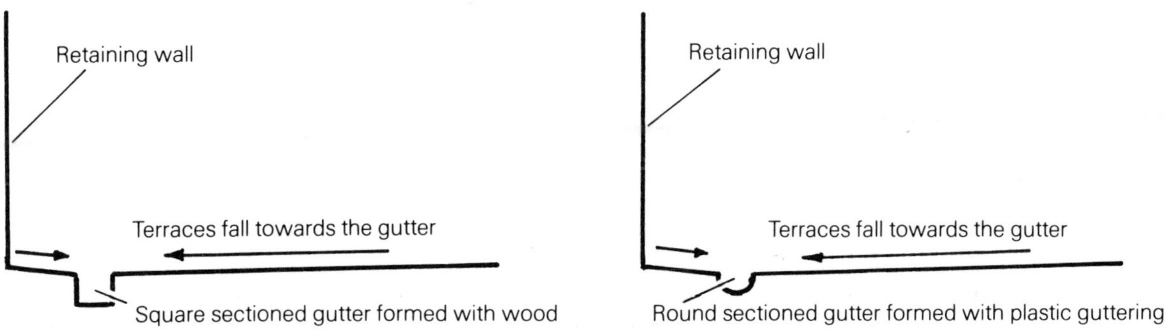

water will enter the drain. Gully pots are inexpensive and available from all builders' merchants. They should also come complete with a leaf-catching grill. To fix the pot, dig a hole deep enough to accommodate the U-bend. Place a small amount of concrete in the hole, set the pot on this and alter its position until its top lies at the correct level in relation to the terrace surface. Join pipes up to pot and fix in position with a good covering of concrete.

Pipe sizes

Whatever type of drain you use, before you buy the materials and start work, give some thought to the amount of water the drains will have to cope with. In the example shown in Fig. 5.9b, the drain must carry away water from three main sources: the roof of the house, the terrace, and the higher ground behind the retaining walls (for draining behind retaining walls, see below), including any that might find its way down the steps.

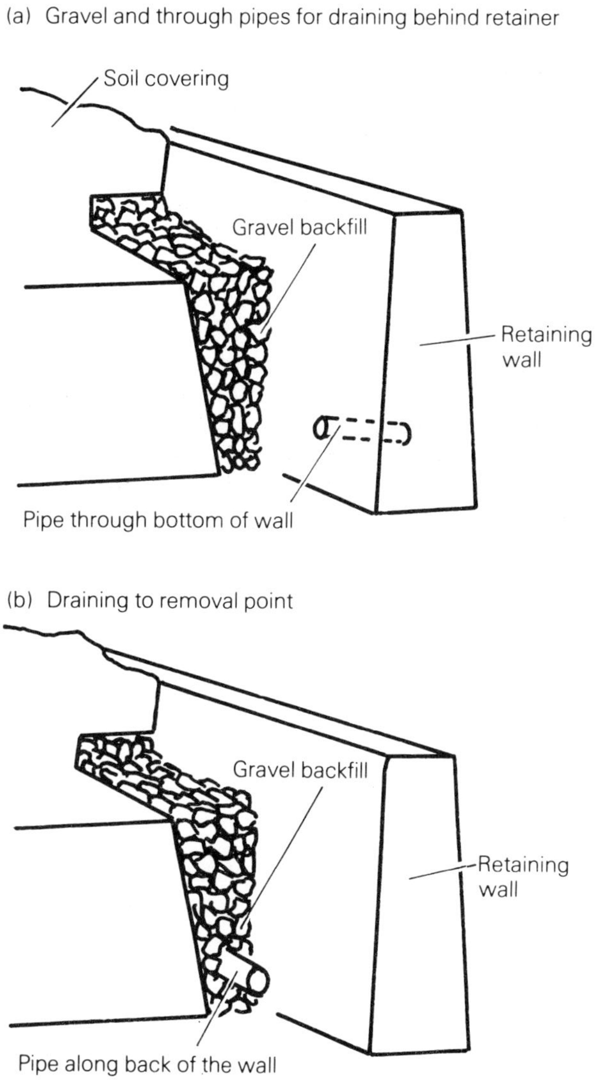

Fig. 5.10 *Arrangements for draining behind retaining walls.*

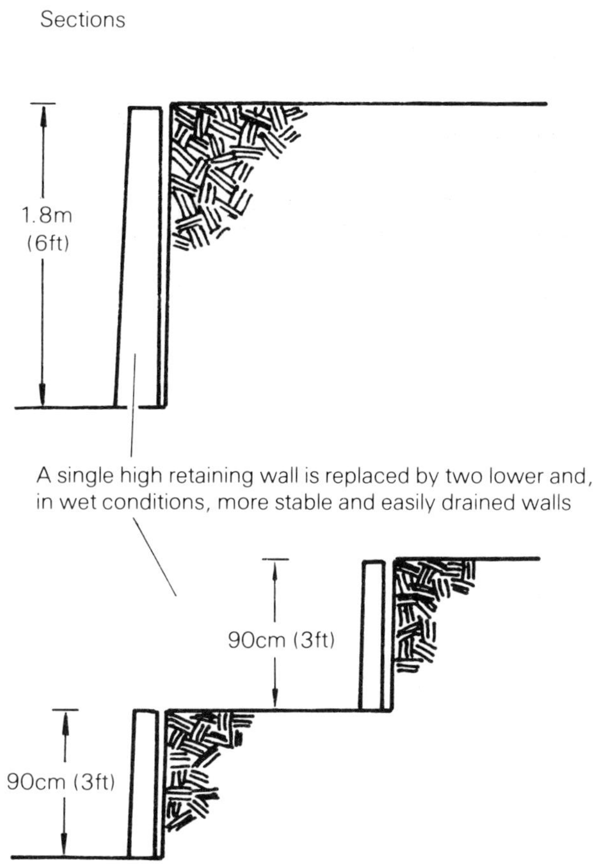

Fig. 5.11 *Terracing as an alternative to large single retaining walls.*

Thus one drain must serve a considerable catchment area, far larger than just the terrace itself. Should there be a heavy or prolonged period of rain, the pipes must be large enough (i.e. at least 15 cm (6 in) wide) to handle the water, otherwise the terrace area may well flood. It is difficult to compute the exact quantities of water, but when deciding on pipe sizes consider the potential catchment area the drain must serve, and use pipes of sufficient capacity to accept water from all areas at once. (If you are connecting up to existing drains, make sure in the same way that the pipes are large enough to handle the extended catchment area.) Similarly, the main drain in a site drainage system should be large enough to handle water from all the subsidiaries at once. If in doubt, ask your dealer for advice.

Drainage for retaining walls

A system of drainage must be considered as integral to the design and building of a retaining wall, since the wall will hold back not only soil but also any water that seeps through the ground behind. If this surface or underground water cannot escape from behind the wall, it may well undermine it and eventually cause it to collapse. Alternatively, the presence of water can create pressure behind the wall and this in turn could push sections of the wall over. For these reasons when you have worked out the kind of retaining wall you want you should then decide on how the water will be channelled away from behind it. There are two basic methods by which this can be done and these are illustrated in Figs. 5.10a and b.

In Fig. 5.10a the water is allowed to filter down through the gravel or stone backfill and is then able to run out through the wall via small pipes set along the footing. The second method (Fig. 5.10b) is to lay piping at the bottom of the stone backfill to collect water along the length of the wall and channel it away to a dispersal point. Both methods can be made more efficient by sealing the top of the backfill with plastic sheeting to prevent soil working down and eventually silting it up. For stone sizes, see Hardcore p. 34.

Note If your retaining wall is going to be particularly high (i.e. over 1.2–1.5 m (4–5 ft)) you should consider the possibility of terracing and thus using several smaller, more stable walls rather than one large one (Fig. 5.11). This will help overcome the problems of water build-up behind one wall, making the whole construction stronger.

6 Fences

Fences in gardens fall into two main categories; either they are used along boundaries or they are incorporated into the design of the garden interior. In the first category the fences are used to establish the limits of the garden and divide it from whatever surrounds it, while creating a degree of privacy within it. They therefore need to be fairly substantial and permanent structures. Within the garden, however, fences play a slightly different role and, whether they are used to separate one part from another or as screens or backdrops for features or flowerbeds, they can generally be more lightweight than those used on the boundaries. Occasionally a fence may be required to retain earth, either behind it or built up against it, and in these instances gravel boards should always be used, with the fence built along the top of them.

In this chapter we cover the main types of fence design suitable for the roles mentioned above, and these can be used as described, in a number of variations or in combination, depending on what best suits your ideas and garden. Whatever type is used, however, good results will depend upon two factors. First, the materials you buy, and second, a full understanding of the techniques to be used. In the first instance, it is clear that the finished fence can only look as good as the materials used. This is particularly true of wooden fences and so in Chapter 4 we have included a section on the pitfalls of buying timber to eliminate as far as possible any mistakes at this stage of construction. Once you have decided on the kind of fence you wish to construct, reference should be made to this section before you set off to buy the materials required. In the second instance, during the actual construction of the fence details are all important for good results, and for these to be right we advise that you first get a complete, overall view of the construction technique to be used. Before you start work, study all the steps in construction described so that you have a general impression of each stage, and then as the work goes along, study the details of each successive step. This helps eliminate mistakes.

Erecting fences on sloping ground: to avoid repetition we have covered this in some detail in the first section of this chapter (Lapped panel fences). Should you need guidance on this while erecting a different type of fence, reference can be made to this section (p. 50), where the main modifications and problems, applicable to any type of fence, are covered.

1 Lapped panel fencing

The main advantage of this kind of fencing is that it provides instant privacy. Once erected it shuts out any unwanted views and eliminates the inconvenience of waiting for hedging plants or shrubs to grow. It is therefore often used in new gardens close to the house to screen ground-floor windows from

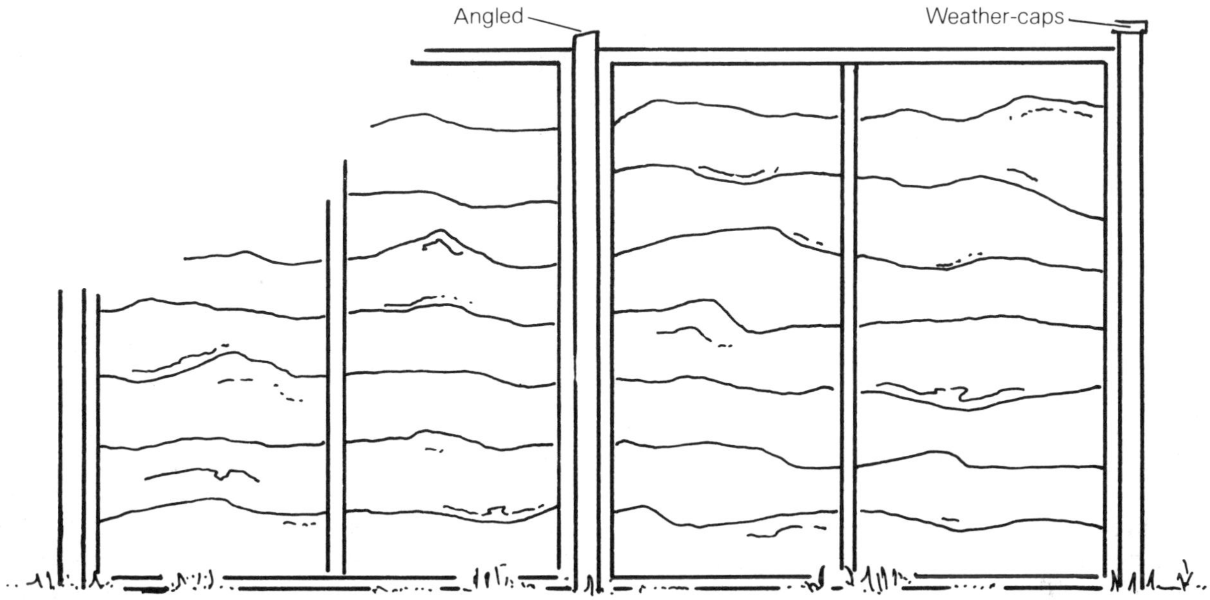

Fig. 6.1 *Standard lapped panels with 8 × 8 cm (3 × 3 in) posts. Showing alternative post top finishes. A yearly coat of wood preservative will considerably lengthen the life of the fence.*

the street or neighbouring gardens. It is also one of the easiest types of fence to erect, relatively cheap and very versatile, being useful as a boundary fence or as a screen in the garden to hide such things as the compost heap or the incinerator, while at the same time blending with the general garden colours. An additional bonus for town gardens is that, carefully erected, it is more or less pet-proof. They are stocked at most garden centres and many builders' merchants (Fig. 6.1).

It is not, however, suitable either as a retaining wall (see Lapped panel fences using slotted posts and concrete gravel boards, p. 51), or as a support for large climbing plants. In the first place it will soon rot if buried in any-way, and is not made of strong enough materials to hold the weight of earth built against it. In the second place, fully grown, heavily leafed climbing plants will tend to buckle and pull it down if allowed to climb over it unsupported by anything else, such as a free-standing trelliswork. Finally, careful thought must be given to its position and height. Panel fences which are badly erected, poorly situated or the wrong size (see Measuring up) are an eyesore and may spoil the outlook of the garden or block out important light from plants.

What you will need

Panels. Posts (allow 50 kg (1 cwt) of 1 : 6 concrete mix per post). 8 cm (3 in) nails (six per panel). Builder's line. Spirit-level. Handsaw. Hammer. Shovel. Small lengths of wood suitable for props (i.e. laths 90 cm (3 ft) long, two per post). Lengths of wood suitable for temporary struts (at least 10 × 5 × 2.5 cm (4 × 2 × 1 in). Rammer for the concrete. Wheelbarrow or bucket.

Measuring up

The panels come in standard sizes: 90 cm–1.8 m (3–6 ft) high × 1.8 m (6 ft) long. (Choose according to the job you require the fence to do.) The posts should be 8 cm (3 in) square and long enough to suit the size of panels chosen, plus 60 cm (2 ft) minimum of post in the ground, plus any extra length required for a step (see Fig. 6.2). When measuring the length of the fence and calculating

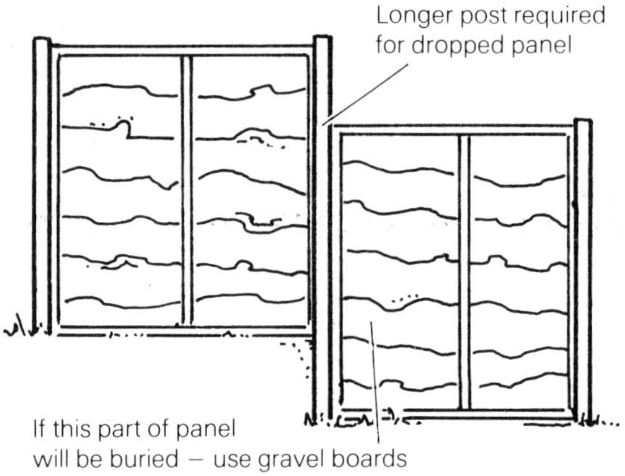

Fig. 6.2 *Dropped panel post.*

the number of panels and posts required, allow for: the length of panels, plus the width of the posts, plus one post width on each end.

Note if you are erecting the panels on sloping ground, do not skimp on post lengths when buying, as you may have to drop some panels 15–30 cm (6 in–1 ft), see Fig. 6.2. (If this means that the bottom of a panel will be buried at one end use a gravel board, see p. 51.)

Posts should be dug in to a minimum depth of 60 cm (2 ft) below ground level and should be bedded in at least 45 cm (18 in) of concrete (i.e. 50 kg (1 cwt) in an ideal hole; see To erect, Step 3). Decide now whether you want post tops flush with the panels or proud by a couple of centimetres (inches), and allow for this in the length of post you buy. Always cut post tops off at an angle (e.g. 45°) to allow rain-water to run off, or fit weather-caps (often supplied with the posts).

To erect

Step 1 Clear the ground that lies in the path of the fence, to a distance of 30 cm (1 ft) either side of the line, i.e. roughly level off any lumps of earth or clumps of rough grass, and cut back or remove any shrubs that will interfere with the fence. Any detailed levelling required can be done as each panel is erected and checked for levelness. Always start erecting from the highest point since this will eliminate any excessive digging-out.

Step 2 Mix sufficient concrete for the first two or three post holes, making the mix fairly dry to grip the posts firmly once it has been rammed.

Step 3 Dig your first post hole. The ideal hole for 8 cm (3 in) square posts is 38 × 38 cm (1 ft 3 in × 1 ft 3 in) at the top, tapering to 23 × 23 cm (9 × 9 in) at a depth of 65 cm (26 in). Position the post in the hole at the required height, standing it on a small stone if necessary, and fill the hole to 45 cm (18 in) with concrete (Fig. 6.3). Ram the concrete tightly round the post and check the post with the spirit-level. At ground level the concrete should be sloped down to shed rain-water and prevent rot.

Step 4 Attach the builder's line to the side of the post at a fixed height (e.g. 90 cm (3 ft) above ground level). Run out the line to the other end of the fence and attach it at the same height to a temporary stake, or, if it is a fixed point (a building or the garden boundary), erect the last post (as above) and attach the line. Be sure to pull the line as tight as possible. Use a temporary strut to secure the posts since the wet concrete may not hold them when the line is pulled tight (Fig. 6.4).

Step 5 Measure from centre of post to centre of post i.e. 1.88 m (6 ft 3 in) from first to next post, and dig next post hole to a depth of 1.53 m (5 ft 1 in) below the line. Using this method you can check as you go along how the overall levels are, and whether you are going to need a step.

Step 6 Re-check the first post with the spirit-level and tack the first panel to it. Support the other end of the panel with a small temporary block to prevent it dragging the post out of position. Any soil that needs removing to allow the panel to lie level should be removed before tacking. Position the second post in its hole and swing it tight against the panel edge, at the required height in relation to the panel and upright against

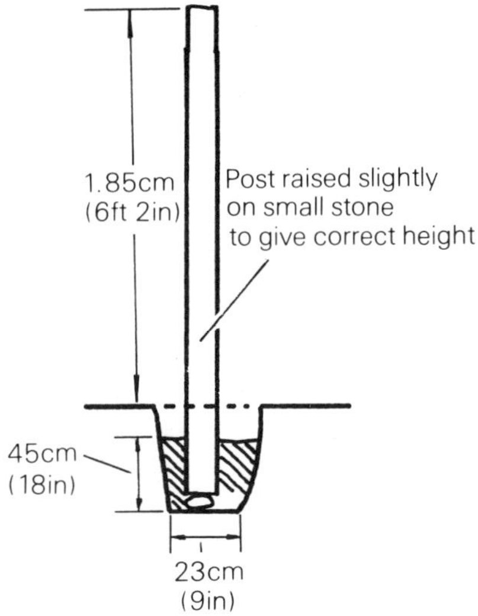

Fig. 6.3 *Post hole : panel fence.*

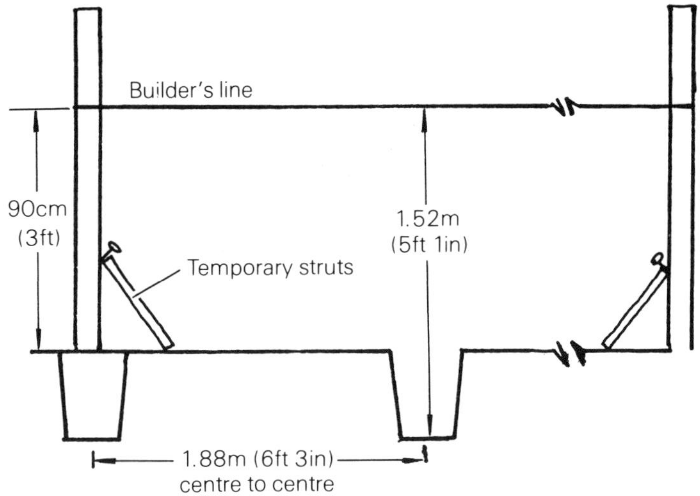

Fig. 6.4 *Determining position of second and subsequent post holes in fence erection.*

the line. Fill around the post with concrete and ram it down firmly. Check with the spirit-level on both faces. Tack the panel to the second post (Fig. 6.5a).

Step 7 Repeat the process for the rest of the fence, panel by panel, mixing concrete for the posts as required. Keep a constant check that no posts are leaning and pushing the line out and that the panel tops are lying level.

Step 8 On completion of the fence go back along the line nailing the panels firmly to the posts, ramming the concrete and checking the posts with a spirit-level. Adjust any that have moved. Finally, prop the posts with the short pieces of wood, one on either side of each post (Fig. 6.5b). Leave the props in position until the concrete has set hard, which will take about two days. A final visual check along the length of the fence is a good

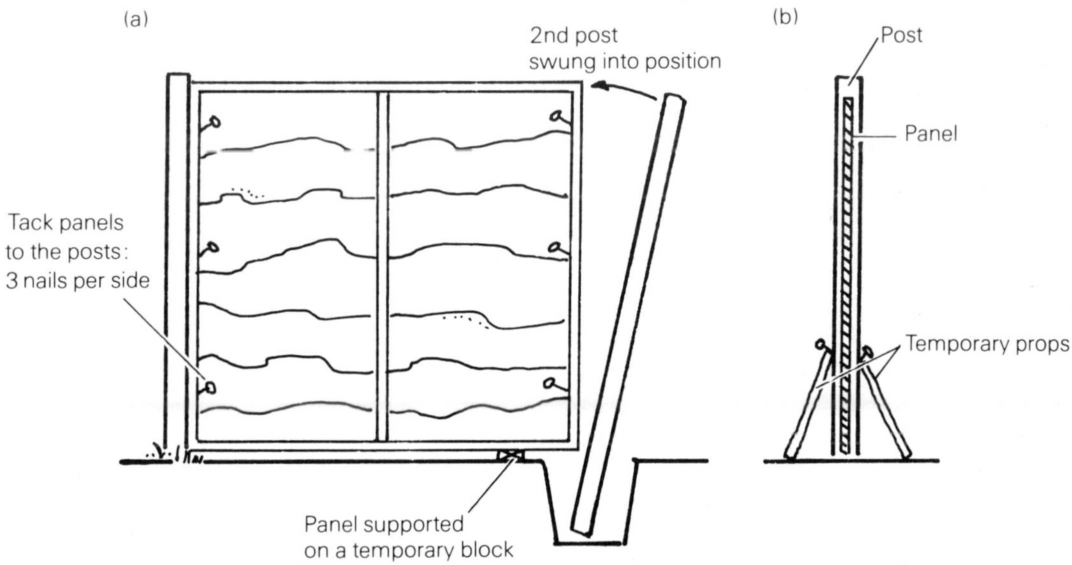

Fig. 6.5 *Erecting a panel.*

precaution. Make any necessary adjustments now. Panel fences erected in this manner should last a considerable length of time. If they either fall or blow down it is usually because the posts are too short or insufficient concrete has been used.

Note 1. If, when the fence is erected, soil is to be placed against the panels, always use gravel boards (see p. 51.)

Note 2. If the ground is sloping, erection should start at the highest point and work down. When positioning the first post, estimate the rate of fall in the ground over the first 1.8 m (6 ft) of the fence line, i.e. where the first panel will sit. Dig out excess earth to the new level and drop the depth of the first hole accordingly. Repeat as long as the slope affects the panels (Fig. 6.6a).

Note 3. If the slope is very steep at any point, it

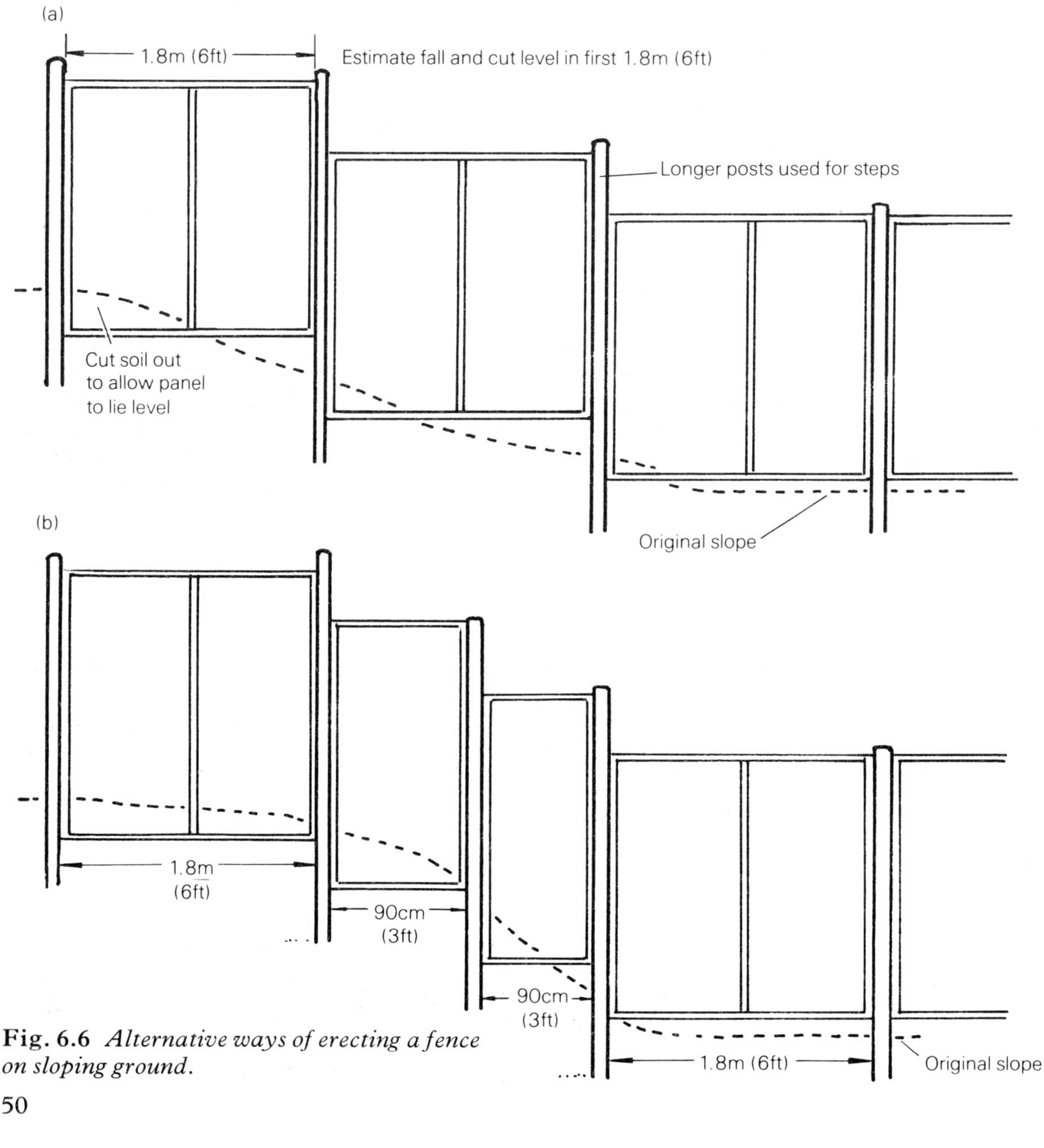

Fig. 6.6 *Alternative ways of erecting a fence on sloping ground.*

may help to cut one panel into 90 cm (3 ft) lengths (i.e. in half). Use an extra post and erect as shown in Fig. 6.6b.

Note 4. Cutting panels: should you need to cut a panel, either for an awkward length of fence or for a steep slope, remember that the new edge must have a backing spar. Therefore knock off the upright nearest to the cut (Fig. 6.7a) and re-nail it inside and flush with, the line of the cut. Saw off the excess (Fig. 6.7b). If both halves are required an extra spar will be needed (Fig. 6.7c).

2 Lapped panel fences using slotted posts and concrete gravel boards

The concrete posts are usually 13 × 10 cm (5 × 4 in) and slotted down the sides to receive the gravel boards and panels; they are also very strong once erected. The gravel boards come in standard sizes, 1.8 m long × 60 × 2.5 cm (6 × 2 ft × 1 in), and match the panels as required. The boards are slotted into the posts and dug several centimetres into the ground. The panels then slide down on top of them (Fig. 6.8). You can, of course, use as many boards on top of each other as required, the panel sizes are then selected to suit the gravel boards.

The main advantage of the boards is their extended life, and the fact that they can act as a retaining wall with flowerbeds or rockeries built against them. Also, being dug in, whether or not they are retaining soil, they will prevent weeds and grass creeping under the fence. This is particularly useful where gardens adjoin rough or unattended land. The concrete posts add considerable strength to the fence and allow the panels to support climbing plants. In addition they are available in smooth, rock-faced or pebble-dash finishes, and of course, can be painted.

On the other hand, they are about twice the price of standard wooden posts and panels. The concrete posts and panels are also very heavy and therefore more difficult to erect; at least two people are required. They are also easily cracked in handling and, if damaged after erection, are difficult to replace.

To erect

Erect as for standard panels (see p. 48), but take extra care to get the correct post height above ground level. It is as well to mark the posts with chalk beforehand showing the positions of the panels and boards, to ensure that you leave enough post height above ground level when erecting the posts (Fig. 6.9a).

Put posts and gravel boards in, using the

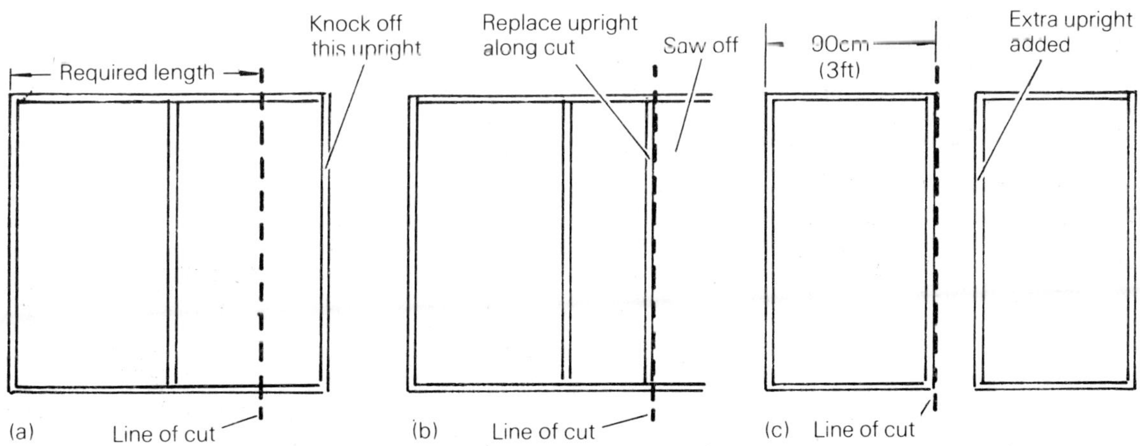

Fig. 6.7 *Altering the width of a standard panel to accommodate a non-standard measurement.*

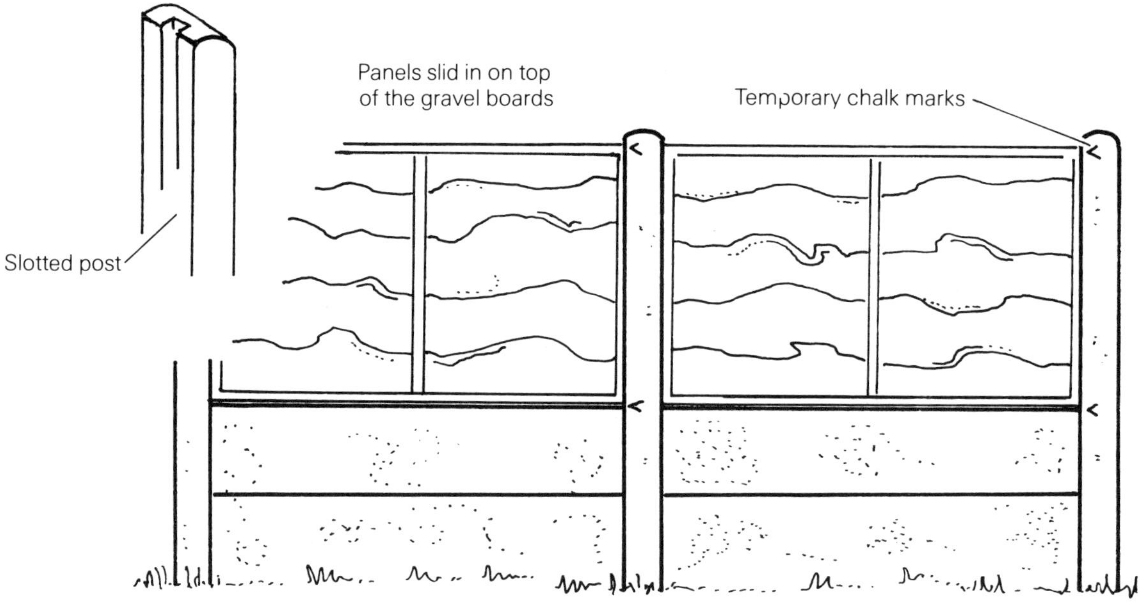

Fig. 6.8 *Standard panels with 13 × 10 cm (5 × 4 in) slotted concrete posts and concrete gravel boards.*

builder's-line method as for standard panels, and check each post carefully to see that it is standing square with the previous post (Fig. 6.9b).

Slide the panels down the slots until they rest on the gravel boards (Fig. 6.9c). Do not install the panels until the concrete around the posts has set (at least two days).

Note 1. It is a good idea to fit the middle panels first and work out to the ends of the fence; this will help eliminate the possible problems that will arise if any of the posts are out of square.

Note 2. Before sliding the panels in, check that they are square in themselves. With mass-produced panels it is possible for one or two of them to be slightly out of shape. If this is the case, alter them as required with the same method as used for cutting panels (see p. 51). At the most you will have to shave a few centimetres (an inch or so) off one side.

MAKING YOUR OWN PANELS

If, for one reason or another, the standard, mass-produced panels are not suitable for your purposes but you want to use this kind of fencing, it may be worthwhile making your own. The advantages of this are clear, in that you can make them any size you want to your own design, and in this way blend them more readily with your garden layout. The main requirements for making panels are a large flat space to work on, either a large work bench or perhaps the garage floor, and the necessary carpentry tools.

If you are going to need a number of panels, it will save a lot of time if you first construct a simple jig to make them in. Using a jig not only makes the job quicker but also helps ensure that the panels will be of a uniform size and shape.

TO CONSTRUCT A JIG

What you will need

2 cm ($\frac{3}{4}$ in) chipboard. Two 1.2 × 2.4 m (4 × 8 ft) sheets for panels over 1.8 × 1.8 m (6 × 6 ft). Some lengths of 5 × 2.5 cm (2 × 1 in) laths.

To construct

In this example the jig is designed to produce

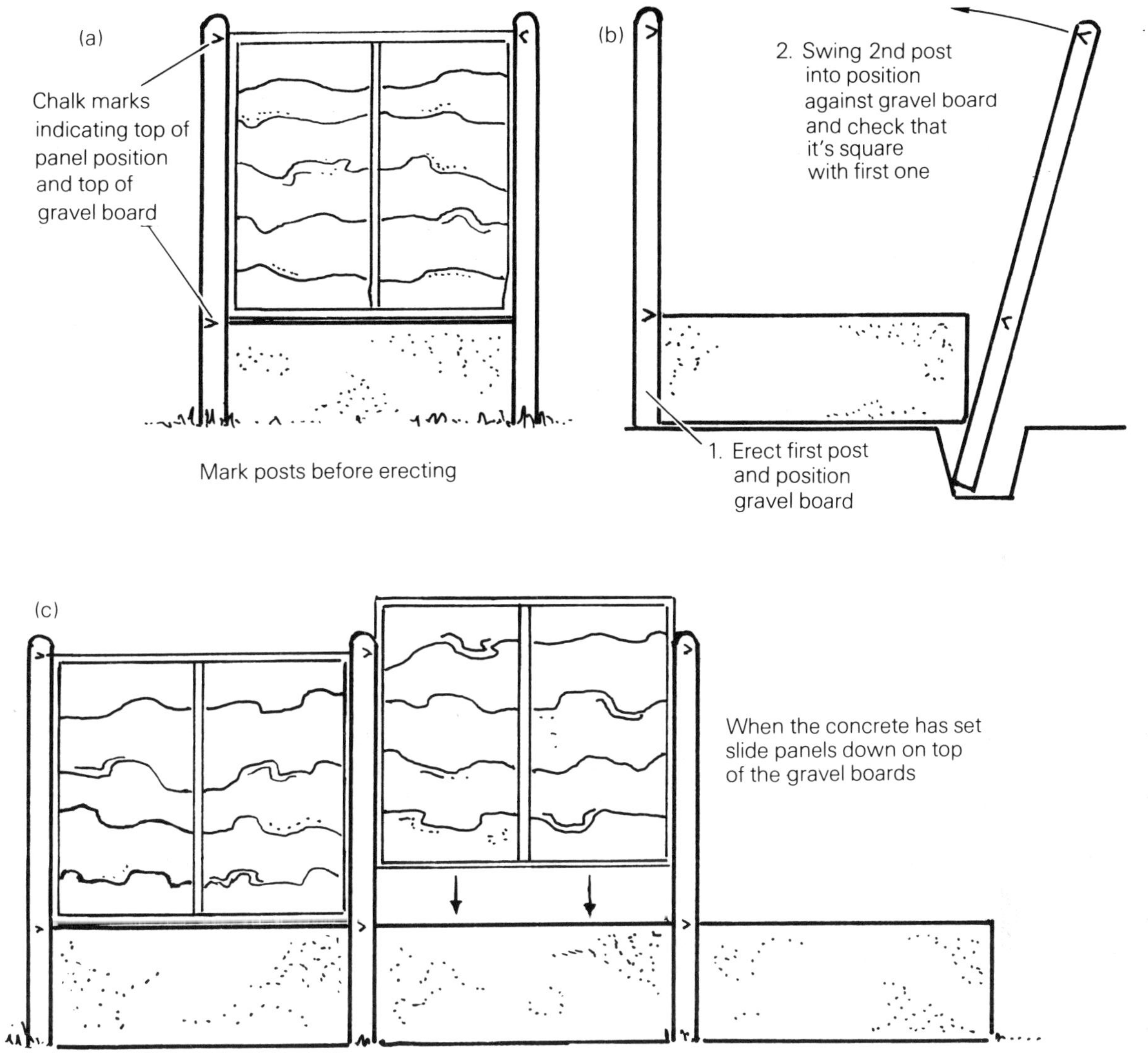

Fig. 6.9 *Erecting slotted posts and panels.*

1.8 × 1.8 m (6 × 6 ft) panels. Alter the sizes as required for the panel size you want. Lay out chipboards and nail two 1.8 m (6 ft) lengths of lath 1.8 m (6 ft) apart on to them (Fig. 6.10a), as sides for the frame. Next, nail two lengths of lath across the top and bottom of them, checking with the set square that the corner angles are all 90° (Fig. 6.10b). Finally, check that the jig is firm and secure, using extra nails if necessary.

TO CONSTRUCT THE PANELS

What you will need

5 × 2.5 cm (2 × 1 in) laths. Sawn boards for the panelling. 1.25 cm ($\frac{1}{2}$ in) nails. Saw. Carpenter's hammer. Set square. Tape-measure. Pencil.

Measuring up

Decide on the size of panel you want and

(a)

(b)

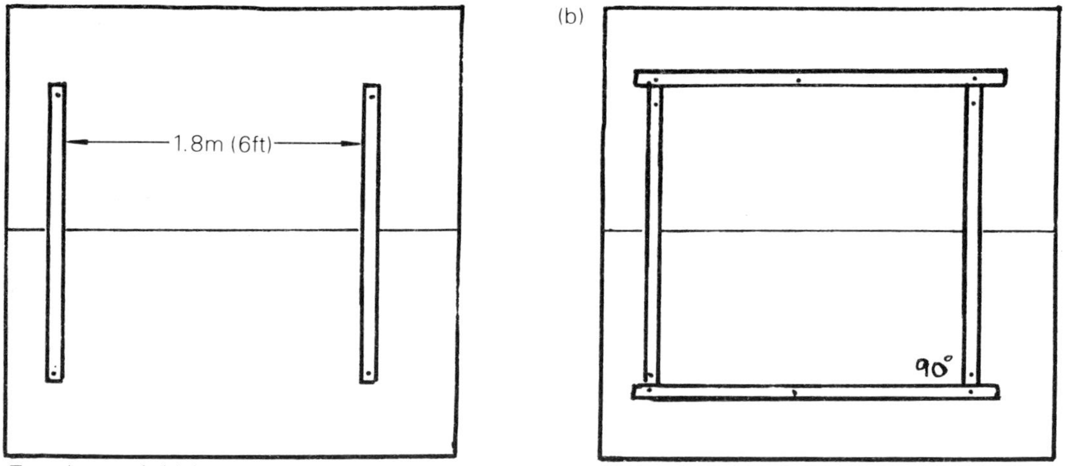

(a) Two sheets of chipboard fixed together, 1.8m (6ft) laths nailed 1.8m (6ft) apart

(b) Nail on top and bottom of frame, checking the corners are square

Fig. 6.10 *Making jig for constructing lapped panels.*

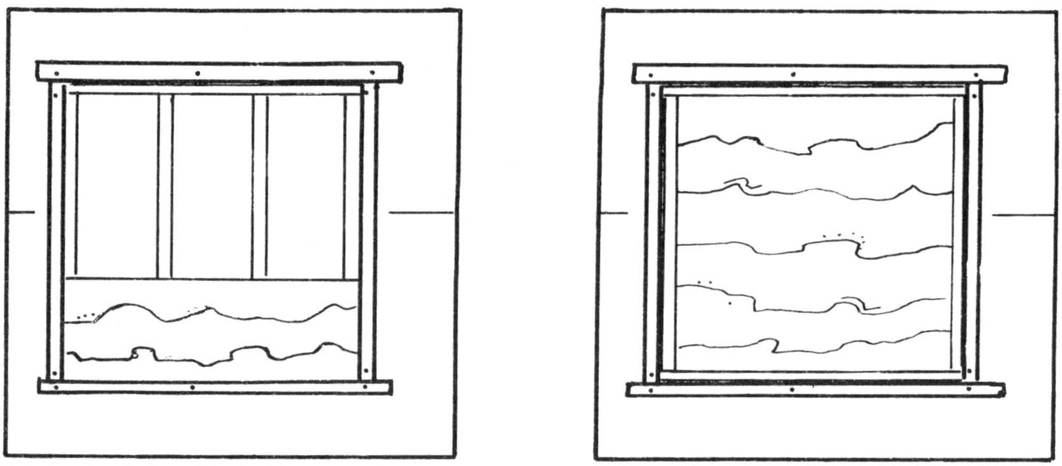

(a) Position laths in jig. Nail boards onto this framework

(b) Nail top frame in position

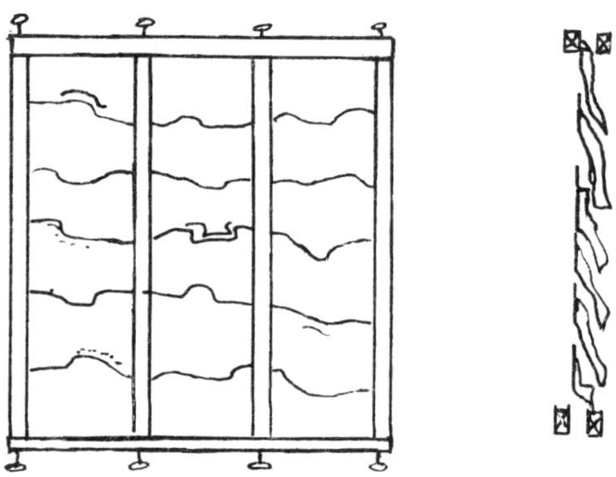

(c) Remove panel and nail frame together

(d) Section through double-frame panel

Fig. 6.11 *Constructing the panel.*

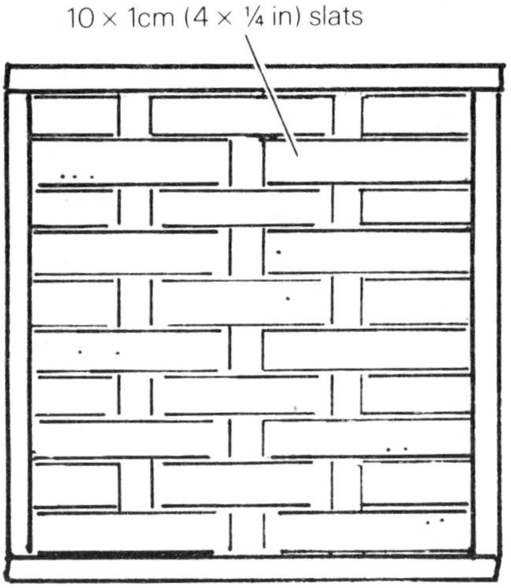

Fig. 6.12 *Interwoven style.*

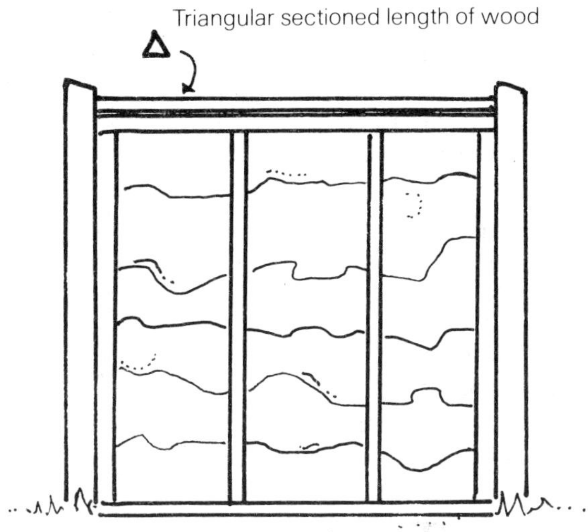

Fig. 6.13 *Additional protection.*

then work out the total length of laths required, allowing for a length along each edge on both sides of the panel (Fig. 6.11c and d), and two down the middle of one side for panels over 1 m (3 ft 6 in) long. For smaller panels under 1 m (3 ft 6 in) one centre support is sufficient. Panelling boards: these boards are usually cut from softwood poles, using the shape of the pole to give the wavy edge effect (Fig. 6.1), and therefore vary in depth (those near the centre being slightly larger than those taken from the edges). To allow for this when buying the boards, first decide on the amount of overlap you want, and then select the boards to suit the size of panel you require. For the interwoven style (Fig. 6.12 and Plate 1), three centre uprights will be needed and the boards should be straight-edged 10 × 1 cm(4 × $\frac{1}{4}$in) softwood.

To construct

Position laths in jig as shown in Fig. 6.11a. Then, starting from the bottom, place boards on this framework, nailing each one firmly to the laths as you work up. Check carefully as you go along that you are maintaining a uniform overlap. When the boards are all in position nail the last four laths in position round the edge of the panel (Fig. 6.11b). Finally, remove panel from jig and secure the centre supports by nailing them through the top and bottom of the framework (Fig. 6.11c). If you are not using a jig, construct the panel in the same way, checking carefully when you lay out the first framework of laths that all the corners are square. It may also help to tack them together to prevent any movement when the boards are being positioned. For the interwoven style, construct as above, but insert the centre supports as the final step once the framework and boards have been nailed together.

Note Once the panels have been erected they will last considerably longer if a strip of wood (triangular section) is fixed along the top to provide extra protection against the weather (Fig. 6.13), and if the whole fence (posts and panels) is carefully painted with preservative. If you are using new wood make sure it has dried out completely before treating.

3 Ranch-type fencing

This kind of fencing can be made with either rails or boards. The rails can be either 'round' or sawn in half lengthways ('half-round'), and the boards rough-sawn or planed. It is purely a matter of taste which type is used, since they all do much the same job. (Boards, of course, give slightly more privacy.)

All are available at most timber yards or builders' merchants. The method of erection is the same for all the types, although the erection of round rails is used as an example (Fig. 6.14).

Round rails have a number of things in their favour, not least of which is that they are visually pleasing. They (and the others) are also cheaper than panels, very versatile, ideal for use with hedges and will support the growth of climbing plants. Half-round rails are popular for stock fences where materials such as barbed wire may prove a danger to animals but, while they are cheaper, they are not as strong as morticed ranch fencing (see p. 59).

What you will need

Posts: 10 × 10 cm (4 × 4 in) sawn oak or treated softwood. Prick-posts: 8 × 8 cm (3 × 3 in) oak or larch. Rails: length variable depending on strength required. Boards: 3 or 3.6 m (etc.) × 10 cm × 2.5 cm (10 or 12 ft × 4 in × 1 in) sawn softwood. (Your dealer will be able to advise you on the lengths of rails and boards.) 10 cm (4 in) nails. Hammer. Bar. Maul. Shovel. Hand saw. Spirit-level. Builder's line.

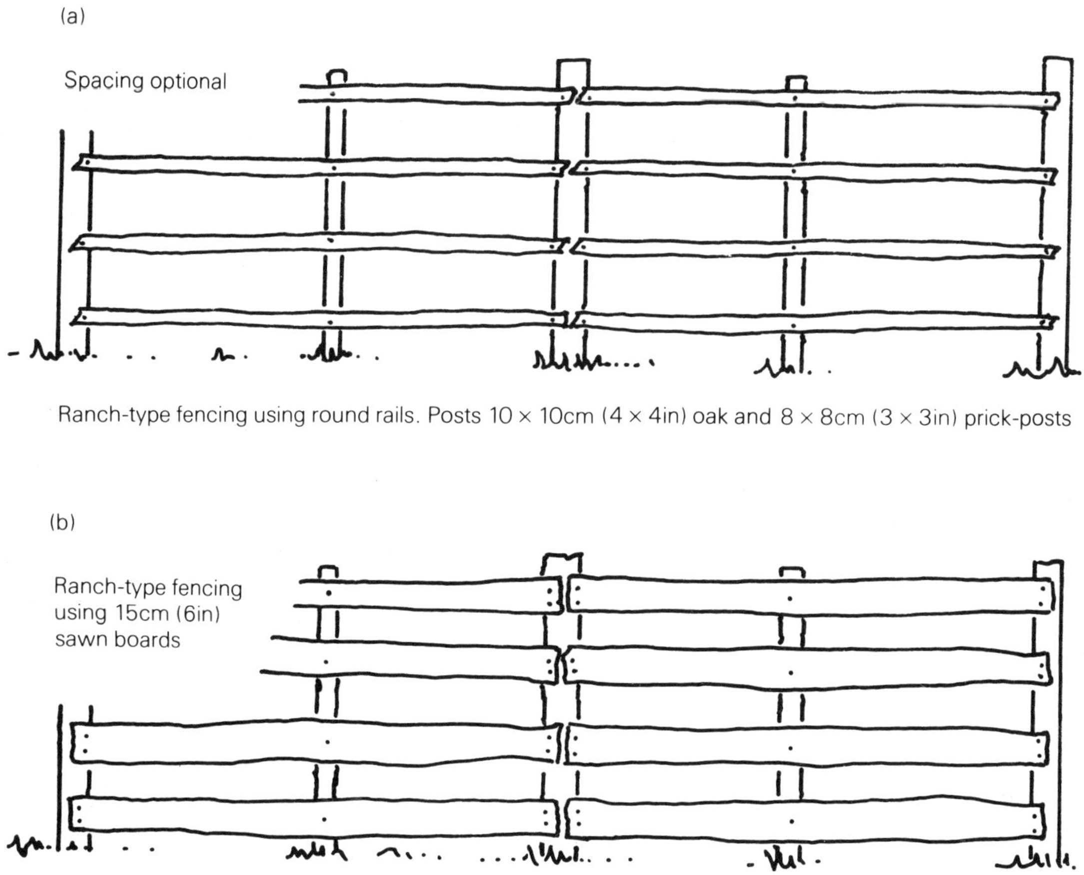

Fig. 6.14 *Two types of ranch fencing; round rails and sawn boards.*

Measuring up

Measure the length of the fence, decide on the length of rails to be used and calculate the number of rails required accordingly. Decide also at this point how high you want the fence to be, and therefore how many layers of rail will be needed and how long the posts need to be (see below). The spacing of the rails should be allowed for as shown in Fig. 6.15. One post should be allowed at either end and at the joints of rails. Allow one prick-post per rail length. For post lengths: on prick-posts add 5.3 cm (21 in) to height of top rail above ground, and for the 10 × 10 cm (4 × 4 in) posts add 60 cm (2 ft) to the same. (Measurements here are given for a typical four-rail fence; alter these as required.)

To erect

Before starting check that all the rails are the same length. If they are not, match lengths and sort them into batches of four (or however many layers are to be used). If you are working on even ground, all the ends should be cut off at an angle of 45°, so that the ends will splice together on erection. If there are any dips and hollows along the length of the fence, cut the ends at a suitable angle when these points are reached.

Erect both end posts at a height of 1.2 m (4 ft) above the ground. These are normally held firm by rammed earth, but if extra strength is required, concrete can be used (see p. 48). Attach the builder's line between the two posts. Tighten the line. Walk along the line and check that you have equal ground clearance all along. If the ground rises or falls anywhere along the length, put in temporary posts at these points to lift or lower the line as required to maintain uniform clearance.

Choose four rails for the first span. Lay one beside one end post and mark the position of the next 10 × 10 cm (4 × 4 in) post hole. This hole should be positioned so that the end of the rail will be located halfway across the post when the post is erected, and so that the post will stand against the builder's line (Fig. 6.16). Dig the hole and

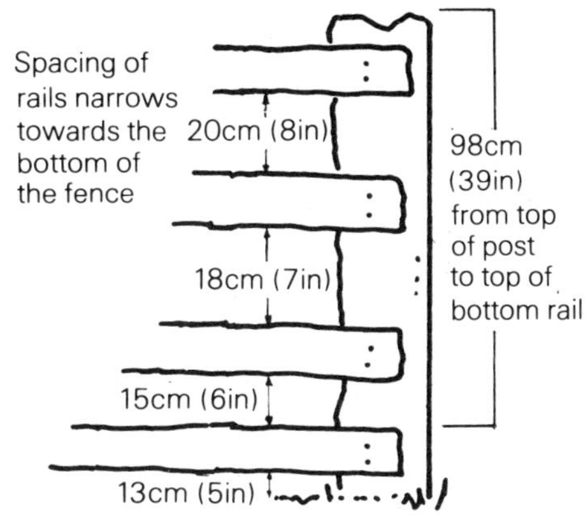

Fig. 6.15 *Spacing of rails.*

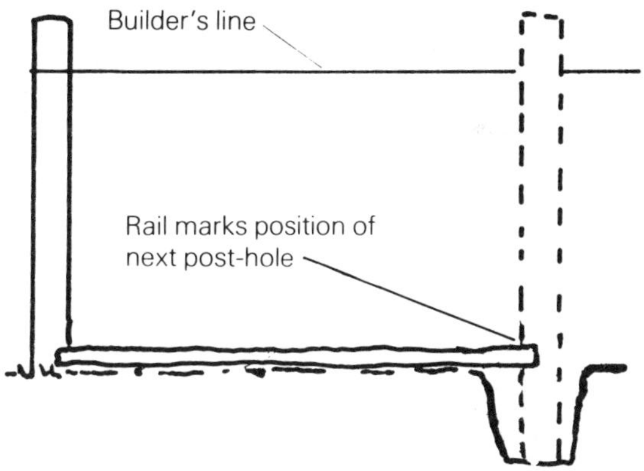

Fig. 6.16 *Positioning post holes.*

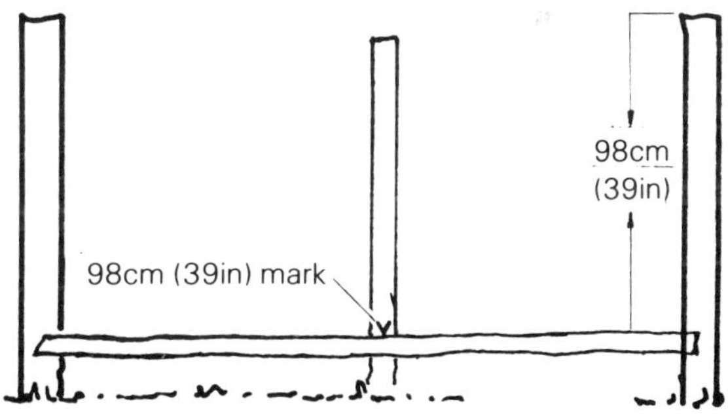

Fig. 6.17 *Erection procedure for ranch fencing.*

erect post. Check the post with the spirit-level. Ram earth firmly down.

Nail the bottom rail in position: the top edge of this rail should be 98 cm (39 in) from the top of the posts (Fig. 6.17). Take a prick-post and mark it off 98 cm (39 in) from its top. Using the bar and maul technique (see p. 70), drive the post into the ground up to the mark, tight against the bottom rail and the builder's line. Prick-posts should be driven halfway between the 10 × 10 cm (4 × 4 in) posts.

Step 1 Erect 10 × 10 cm (4 × 4 in) posts, using builder's line and tape as a guide to positioning.

Step 2 Nail on bottom rail.

Step 3 Drive in prick-post.

Note For ease of erection we advise at this point that you cut six lengths of wood, 15, 18 and 20 cm (6, 7 and 8 in) wide, two blocks of each size. These will make the job of spacing the other rails a lot easier (Fig. 6.18).

Step 4 Using the blocks to rest the rails on, nail the remaining rails in position, working upwards.

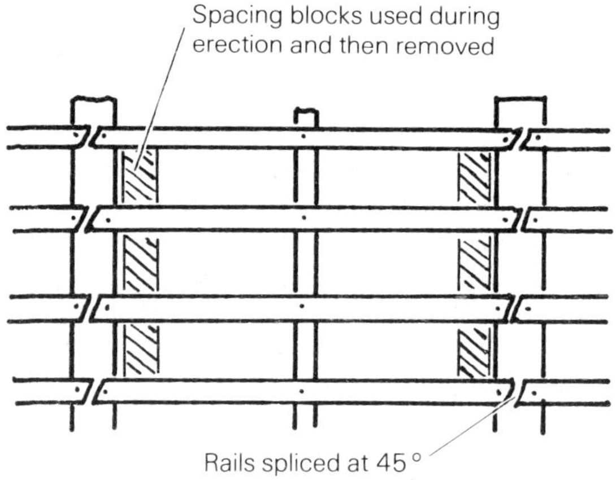

Fig. 6.18 *Use of spacers.*

Step 5 Repeat the process for the rest of the fence, splicing the ends of the rails together. When complete go back along the length of the fence, nailing the rails to the prick-posts.

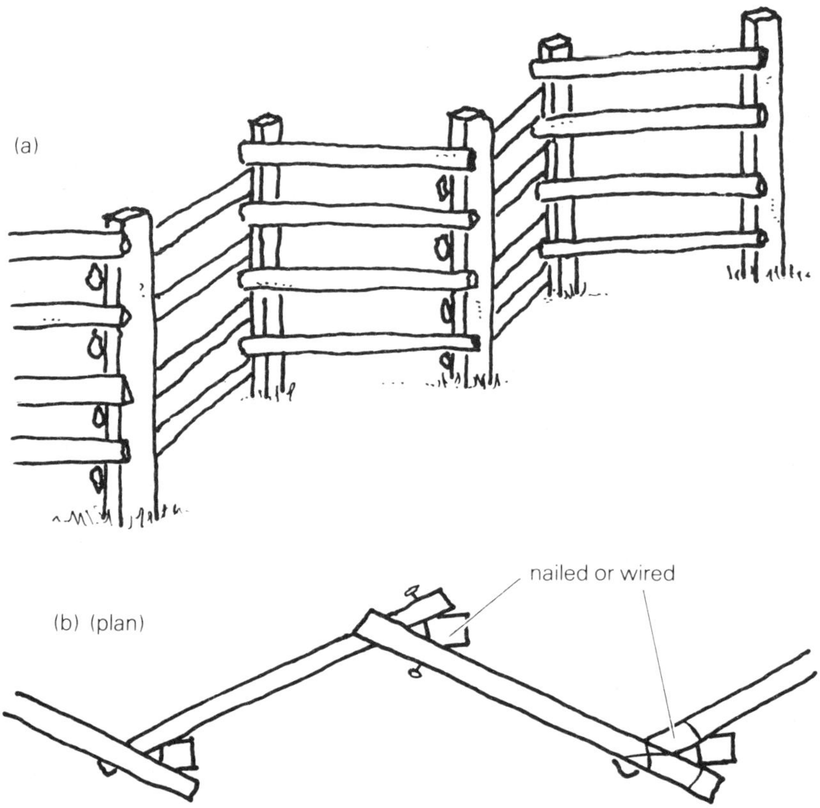

Fig. 6.19 *Staggered rail fences.*

Note The rails can, of course, be spaced equally, but narrowing the gap towards the bottom gives the fence a more balanced look.

If you require a really strong stock fence, a variation of this ranch-type fencing can be used. It involves staggering the position of the post holes, so that the fence forms a zig-zag (Fig. 6.19). This makes the fence very strong but is also more expensive since more materials will be required. This fence should be erected in the same manner as above with every other 10 × 10 cm (4 × 4 in) post moved off the line. Individual requirements will govern how much the posts are staggered.

4 Morticed post and rail fencing

The use of mortice and tenon joints in this kind of fencing has two main advantages. First, they produce a much stronger, more permanent type of fence since they do not rely to the same extent on nails, which can rust and weaken, and second, they look the same from either side. They have become increasingly popular as stock or garden fences, particularly since packages of mortice posts and rails to fit them have been available. They also look very good when combined with wooden farm-style gates.

They are, however, harder to erect than ordinary post and rails since everything has to be more accurately positioned and the procedure is therefore slightly more elaborate; they are also considerably more expensive.

The materials can be bought either, as mentioned above, in packages from specialist firms, or they can be cut to order at timber yards or fencing companies, or standard posts can be bought and cut as required at home. It is worth getting estimates from as many sources as possible to see which will work out the cheapest.

What you will need

Posts: 10 × 10 cm (4 × 4 in) oak or treated softwood. Rails: 1.8 m × 10 cm × 3 cm (6 ft × 4 in × $1\frac{1}{4}$ in) sawn softwood or oak. (Using this size will make a very strong fence. Thinner rails i.e. 10 × 2.5 cm (4 × 1 in) can be used. Ask your dealer which size would best suit your needs.) Prick-posts: 8 × 8 cm (3 × 3 in) oak or treated softwood, for rail lengths of 1.8 cm (6 ft) or over, or for additional strength. 8 cm (3 in) nails. Hammer. Bar. Maul. Shovel. Spirit-level. Builder's line.

Measuring up

Decide how high you want the fence to be and the length of rails to be used. (Measurements given here are for a four-rail fence using 1.8 m (6 ft) rails; alter these as required.) Measure length of fence and calculate the number of rails required. (For spacing of rails see Fig. 6.15.) One post should be allowed at either end of the fence and at the joints of rails. Allow one prick-post per rail length. Post lengths: for prick-posts add 5.3 cm (21 in) to height of top rail above ground, and for the 10 × 10 cm (4 × 4 in) posts add 60 cm (2 ft) to the same. Rail lengths: the actual spans are a matter of choice, but we recommend that whether you cut your own mortices or have them done by a timber yard, the rails should be set at least 4.5 cm ($1\frac{3}{4}$ in) into the posts. This will allow for any subsequent shrinking or sagging of the rails, and means that if you are using 1.8 m (6 ft) rails, the actual post-to-post span will be approximately 1.7 m (5 ft $8\frac{1}{2}$ in).

To erect

Clear the line of the fence of any plants, shrubs or tussocks of grass and level any small bumps. Erect first post so that its top is 1.2 m (4 ft) above the ground. For the fence described in this example, the posts can be held firm with rammed earth, but if the fence is to be any higher, using more rails, concrete would be a good idea (see p. 48).

When the first post is firm, erect a post at the other end of the fence in a similar manner, and attach a builder's line between them at the same height as the top rail (Fig. 6.20). Be sure to pull the line as tight as pos-

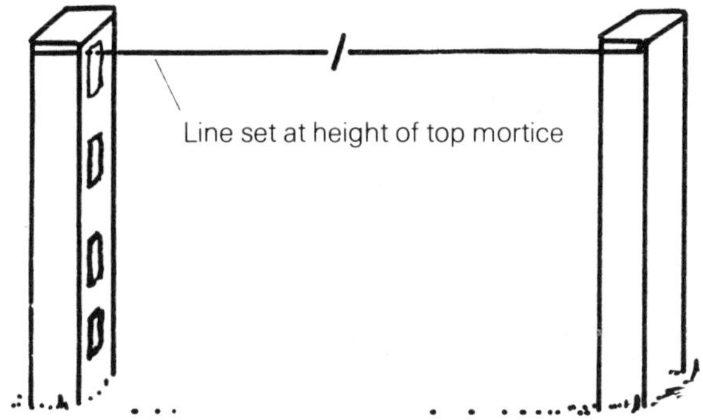

Fig. 6.20 *Setting up morticed posts.*

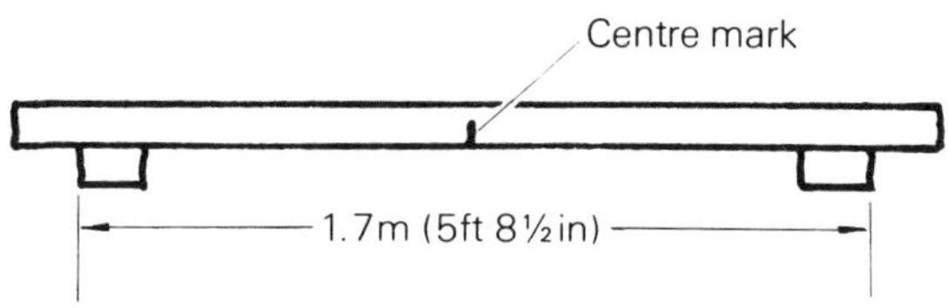

Fig. 6.21 *Spacer for morticed fences.*

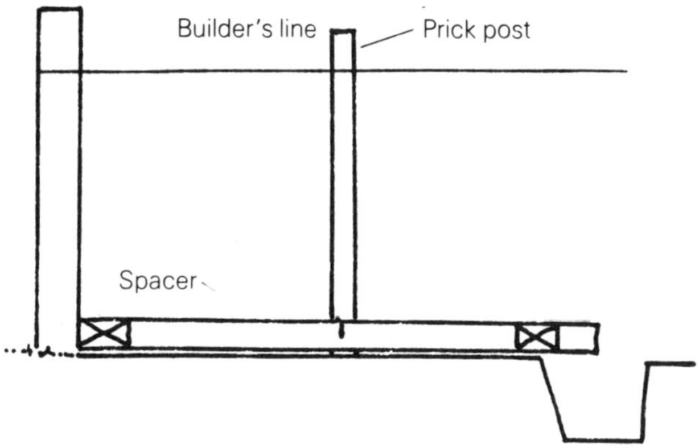

Fig. 6.22 *Positioning post holes and prick-posts.*

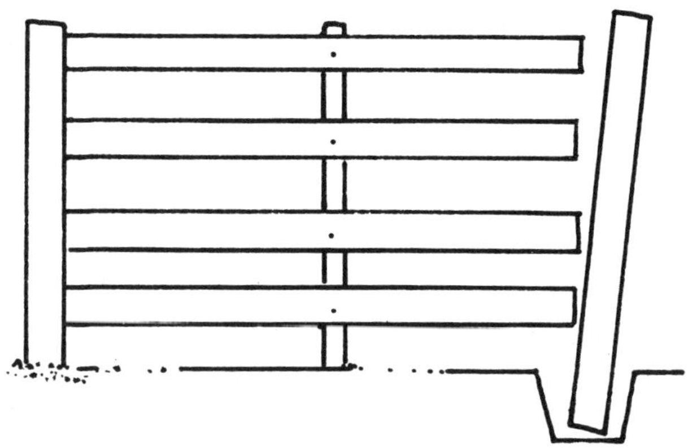

Fig. 6.23 *Erecting second and subsequent posts.*

sible. Check along the line that you have equal clearance for the whole length of the fence, and if the ground rises or falls significantly at any point, put in temporary stakes where this occurs to raise or lower the line to maintain uniform clearance.

Return to the first post and using a spacer locate and dig a hole for the second post. The spacer should be a rail (which can later be used in the final section of fence) or similar length of wood with two blocks nailed to it 1.7 m (5 ft 8½ in) apart, and marked off clearly in the centre (Fig. 6.21). Place the spacer on the ground against the first post and along the line of the fence, dig the hole for the second post and drive in the prick-post in line with the centre mark and against the builder's line (Fig. 6.22). The prick-post can either be driven down until flush with the line or left a few centimetres proud.

Leaving the spacer in position, set rails into the first post and tack them temporarily to the prick-post, at the correct heights (Fig. 6.15), starting with the top rail, the top edge of which should lie along the builder's line.

Lower second post into its hole and fit rails into the mortices working from the bottom up (Fig. 6.23), and then knock the post tight against the spacer. Check post with spirit-level and fill in the hole with rammed earth.

Remove spacer and repeat the process along the length of the fence. When the fence is complete, return along it nailing the rails firmly to the prick-posts.

5 Paling

An attractive and once very popular type of fencing suitable for a number of uses around the garden. Generally forming a low fence, it has the advantages of being more pet-proof than rails, while not shading flowerbeds as panels or close boarding might. The palings can be cut to order from timber yards and can have a variety of shapes on top. Pointed ones are probably the cheapest, but rounded or 'feather-edged' types look softer and more attractive. On the other hand, palings will be relatively expensive, time-consuming to erect and no good as a barrier to prevent grass- or weed-creep. We would also recommend that concrete be used to set the posts.

There are two methods that can be used for making these fences: 'exposed post' and 'on-the-face paling', the latter being faster to erect. For the first method, morticed posts are used and the palings set on the rails between the posts (Fig. 6.24a), and for the second, the palings run unbroken along the face of the fence (Fig. 6.24b). In this method the top rails sit on the posts, flush with the front edge, and the bottom rails are either set into the post or toenailed. Before measuring up and buying materials for 'on-the-face' paling, decide which method of construction you will use to erect the bottom rails. If they are to be set into the posts they will need to be as long as the top rails (Fig. 6.25), and the posts will have to be rebated to accommodate them. If, however, you are going to toenail them, the bottom rails need only be as long as the actual span between posts, and the posts will not need rebating. For these reasons, toenailed 'on-the-face' paling is probably the fastest and cheapest method of the three.

What you will need

Posts: 10 × 10 cm (4 × 4 in) treated softwood or oak (either morticed, rebated or plain depending on construction method used). Rails: for 'exposed post': 8 × 5 cm (3 × 2 in) sawn softwood. For 'on-the-face': 10 × 5 cm (4 × 2 in) for top rails and 8 × 5 cm (3 × 2 in) for bottom rails. Palings are usually

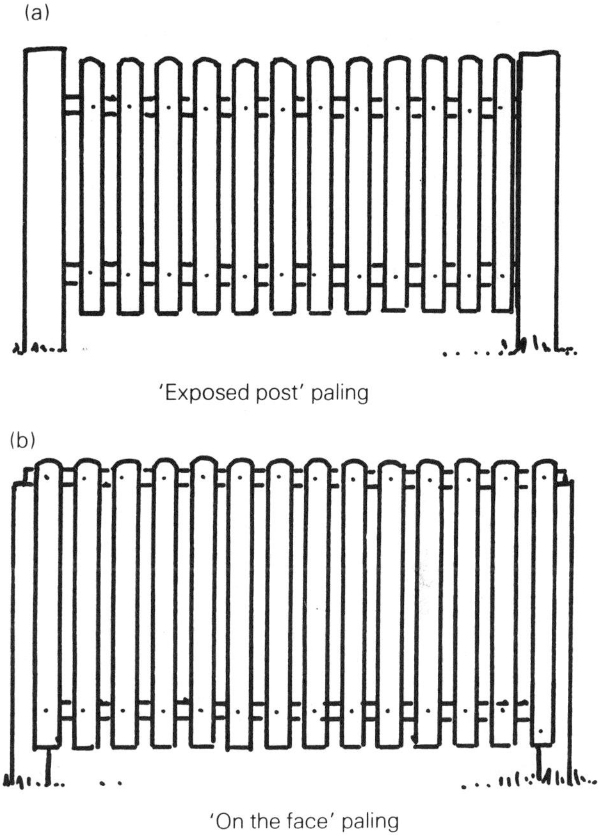

Fig. 6.24 *'Exposed' and 'on the face' paling.*

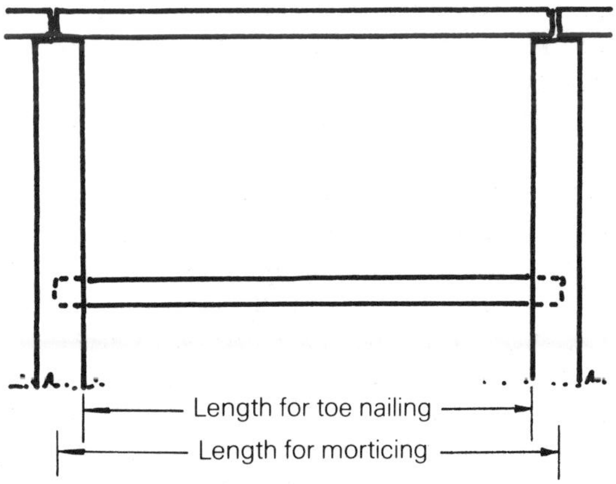

Fig. 6.25 *Arrangement for 'on the face' paling.*

8 × 2.5 cm (3 × 1 in) and come in a variety of lengths between 90 cm (3 ft) and 1.2 m (4 ft). We would not recommend ordering hardwood palings since they are likely to split or crack. 8 cm (3 in) nails for rails and 4 cm ($1\frac{1}{2}$ in) for palings. Concrete. Hammer. Shovel. Spirit-level. Builder's line.

Measuring up

Decide on height of paling required or find out what sizes are available. The length of span between posts can be according to taste from 1.2 m (4 ft) up, but should not exceed 1.8 m (6 ft) and to make erection easier for the 'exposed post' method, the length of span should allow for the width of paling to be used and the gaps between them, i.e. for 8 cm (3 in) wide palings with 8 cm (3 in) gaps, the span should be worked out in multiples of 32 cm (1 ft). Thus, to allow for the mortices and to give an actual span of 1.8 m (6 ft), the top and bottom rails should be 1.9 m (6 ft $3\frac{1}{2}$ in) long. For 'on-the-face' paling using rebated bottom rails with, for example, an actual span of 1.8 m (6 ft), the rails will need to be 1.8 m (6 ft) plus 5 cm (2 in) on either end. Toenailed bottom rails, however, need only be 1.8 m (6 ft), (Fig. 6.25). To calculate the number of palings for 'exposed post' paling work out quantity needed per span, and then the number of spans in the length of fence. For 'on-the-face' paling divide the total length of face by the width of paling and gap to be used. Post lengths: add 60 cm (2 ft) to height of fence above ground. Concrete: allow 50 kg (1 cwt) per post hole.

To erect

Before starting work it is worth measuring the actual width of the palings you have bought since rough-sawn timber may be slightly over size and planed timber slightly under. This could lead to spacing problems unless allowed for now.

The posts and rails

'Exposed post' the posts and rails should now be erected as for morticed post and rail fences (see p. 59), using a spacer that gives the required span and builder's line, setting the posts in concrete as each one is positioned.

'On-the-face'erect the posts along the length of the fence using a spacer and builder's line, filling in the holes with concrete and checking the posts with the spirit-level. Be sure their positioning is correct, because once the concrete has set it will be very hard to alter them. When the posts are ready, nail the top rails flat across the tops of the posts and the bottom ones into the rebates. For toenailing: fix temporary blocks to the posts at the height required for the bottom rail. Set the rail on the blocks and nail it to the post at either end (Fig. 6.26). (For added accuracy and to eliminate the possibility of the rail splitting while being nailed, it is a good idea to drill guide holes through the rails, if the tools are available.)

The palings

Whichever method of erection is being used, the job of fixing the palings can be made quicker and easier by using a spacer as shown in Fig. 6.27a. In this example the palings are to be set 8 cm (3 in) above the top rail and at 8 cm (3 in) intervals. To fix palings, sit spacer on top rail against the first post, set paling tight against it and at the same height and nail it to the rails. Move spacer and repeat.

6 Close-boarding

Close-boarding can be very useful as either a high or low fence. Used as a low fence it will protect plants and stop the encroachment of grass or weeds under it. As a high fence (Plate 2) it provides maximum privacy, good screening and a stronger, more permanent fence than, for example, panels which are made of much lighter materials. It will, however, work out expensive unless some second-hand boarding is available. Boards can often be found in job lots, having previously been floorboards or shed cladding; it is always worth looking around. Be sure to treat second-hand timber with a suitable preservative. Erecting a close-board fence is no more difficult than paling, since either the 'exposed post' or 'on-the-face' methods should also be used (see p. 62). A close-board fence being erected with the 'exposed post' method is shown in Fig. 6.28.

What you will need

Posts: 10 × 10 cm (4 × 4 in), morticed, rebated or plain. Rails: 10 × 5 cm (4 × 2 in) sawn softwood. Boards: 15 or 10 × 2.5 or 1.3 cm (6 or 4 × 1 or $\frac{1}{2}$ in). Concrete: 50 kg (1 cwt) per hole. 8 cm (3 in) and 4 cm ($1\frac{1}{2}$ in) nails. Shovel. Hammer. Spirit-level. Builder's line.

Measuring up

As for paling (see p. 62), allowing for the fact that the boards are nailed tight together without gaps between them.

To erect

Decide on method to be used, either 'exposed post' or 'on-the-face' and then follow the same procedure as for paling fences (p. 62). An alternative method of setting the boards for either method is to overlap them slightly to give the 'feathered-edge' effect. The size of the overlap is a matter of personal taste but an approximate guide would be to set the boards at 16 per linear m (15 per linear yd). Be sure to paint or apply timber preservative to the bottom of the boards if they touch the ground.

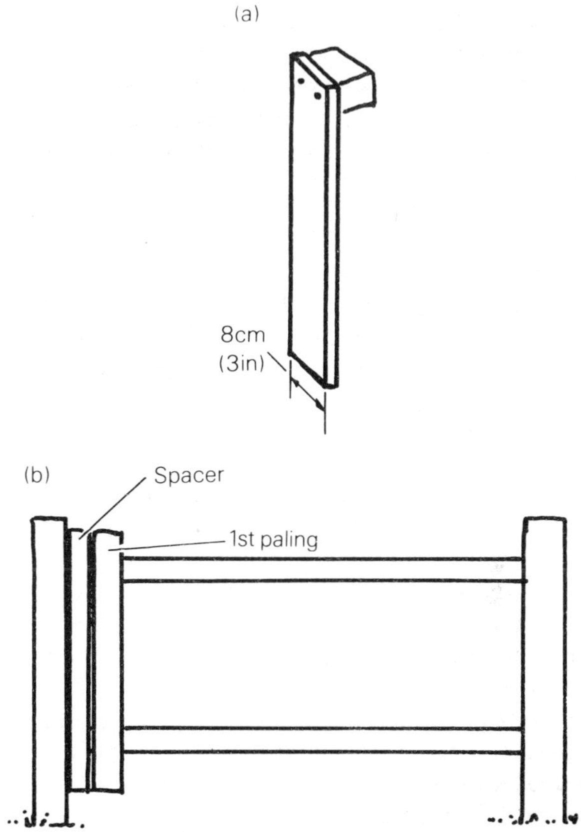

Fig. 6.27 *Use of spacer for erecting paling.*

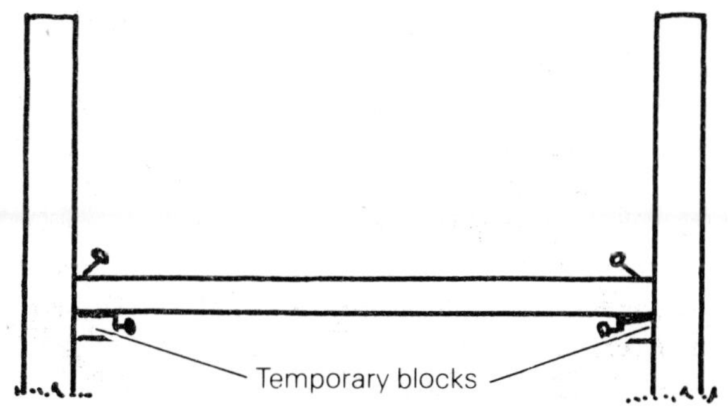

Fig. 6.26 *Toe nailing.*

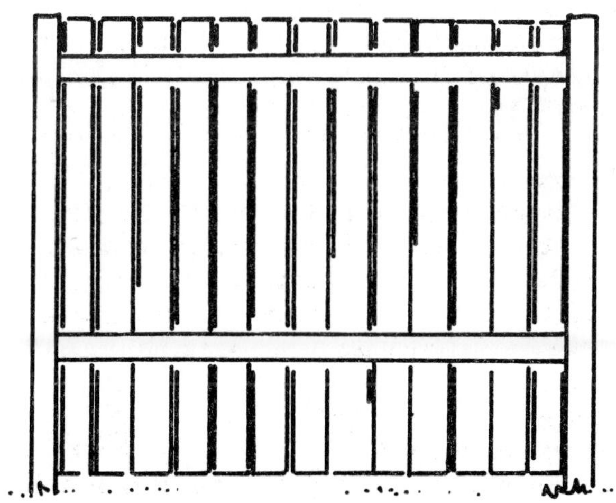

Fig. 6.28 *Close boarding.*

7 'Hit and miss' fencing

This is a very popular form of board and post fencing, both in and around the garden. It has the major advantage of offering privacy while still letting light through to the beds below. It is also a useful windbreak and will support climber growth. On the other hand, of course, it allows weed- and grass-creep underneath, is very easily climbed and is slow to erect. A coat of paint or preservative added after erection will enhance its looks and considerably lengthen its life (Fig. 6.29).

What you will need

Posts: 8 × 8 cm (3 × 3 in), for lengths add 60 cm (2 ft) to required fence height. Boards: 1.8 m × 15 × 2 cm (6 ft × 6 × $\frac{3}{4}$ in) planed softwood. 8 cm (3 in) nails. Hammer. Hand saw. Shovel. Concrete.

Measuring up

Measure the length of the fence. Decide how many boards high the fence is to be and calculate the number of boards accordingly (the boards will be spaced at 15 cm (6 in) intervals). Calculate the number of posts required, one every 1.8 m (6 ft), and then calculate the amount of concrete mix needed: 50 kg (1 cwt) per hole, or 27 post holes per cubic yard of ready-mix.

To erect

Follow the same procedure as for post and rail fencing (see p. 59) nailing on the boards from the bottom, working up on alternate sides of the posts at 15 cm (6 in) spaces. For erecting posts with concrete, see p. 48. For this job, as for post and rail, a spacing block 15 cm (6 in) wide will be useful.

For increased screening effect you can lessen the gap between the boards and add additional ones to make up the height.

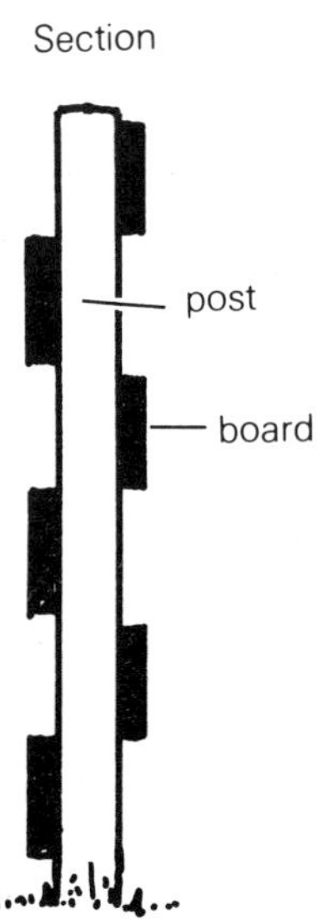

Fig. 6.29 *Hit-and-miss fencing.*

8 Larch pole trelliswork

While not strictly a fence, we have included larch pole trelliswork (Fig. 6.30) here, since it can be very attractive when combined with low fences and it should be erected in a similar way. Whether free-standing in the garden or used round the perimeter, this trelliswork provides a degree of screening and strong support for any climbing plant. It is not complicated to erect and the use of larch poles brings a pleasant naturalness to the garden, blending with any trees and large shrubs around it. Care should be taken, however, to keep it 'in scale' with the garden, because if it is too large and dominating it will seem to close the garden in, cutting out views or dividing the garden up.

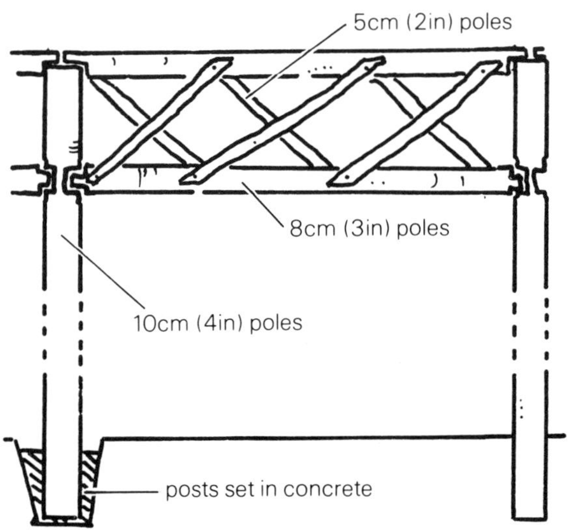

Fig. 6.30 *Larch pole trelliswork.*

Plates 1 – 3: Fences

Plate 1 Panel fence: interwoven style. Note use of central backing spar to provide additional strength (p. 55).

Plate 2 Privacy and shelter created by a robust close-boarded fence. Weathercaps are used to protect the post tops (p. 62).

Plate 3 In this arrangement terraced beds are topped by a close-boarded fence built in a 'good-neighbour' style which presents the same appearance when viewed from either side (p. 74).

Plate 4 Concrete block retaining wall, constructed of 20×20×40 cm (8×8×16 in) split-face blocks, set on a 45×15 cm (18×6 in) deep concrete footing. Note the use of the occasional light-coloured block to relieve the uniform appearance of the wall (p. 81).

Plate 5 Small, flattish stones are used to blend this low retaining wall in with the path and beds that run beside it (p. 94).

Plate 6 For this larger retaining wall bigger stones combine to create interesting patterns at the back of a small terrace (p. 94).

Designs for such trelliswork are clearly a matter of personal taste, but we would recommend using at least three sizes of pole (i.e. 10 cm (4 in) for the posts, 8 or 5 cm (3 or 2 in) for the crosspieces and 5 cm (2 in) down for the patterns) to give the finished trellis a sense of balance. This does not necessarily mean buying all these different sizes, but rather, using the various parts of the naturally tapering poles for these different purposes. Also, the span of the trellis should be kept under 1.8 m (6 ft) to ensure that the poles have a relatively uniform thickness.

What you will need

Larch poles. 8 cm (3 in) nails. Concrete (50 kg (1 cwt) per post). Shovel. Hammer. Saw. Spirit-level.

Measuring up

Decide on the length of trelliswork, the length of the spans and the finished height. Work out from these the number of uprights and crosspieces, and then work out the total length of poles required. For post lengths add 60 cm (2 ft) to height of trelliswork. At your dealers find out the average length of poles available and work out how many poles you need. (If, when the main framework of the trellis is complete, you do not have enough thin end offcuts to finish the pattern, you can always buy a couple more small poles.) Use the number of posts required to estimate how much concrete you need.

To erect

Free-standing trellis Dig post holes (65 cm (26 in) minimum depth) and erect the posts, checking their height above ground before concreting. Concrete posts firmly in position, check with spirit-level and allow them to set. The trelliswork itself can now either be assembled as one piece on the ground, or constructed in position. The latter method is best suited to single-handed work. Cut required rebates in the posts and tenons on the crosspieces. Nail these in position and fix on the pattern.

Combined with a fence In this method the sawn fence posts (e.g. 10 × 10 cm (4 × 4 in) treated softwood) extend above the fence itself and the larch pole trelliswork is fixed between them. In this way the trelliswork can combine with, for example, 90 cm (3 ft) high lapped panels to produce a very attractive fence that overcomes the limitations of both.

The fence should be erected first, using posts long enough to give the trellis the required height. Fix the trellis between these.

9 Wire fences using prick-posts and strainer posts

Wire fences are perhaps most useful for people who either have animals (ponies, etc), and therefore require a good stock fence, or those who have gardens adjoining fields where animals are kept, and therefore need a fence of a more robust nature. Certainly it will work out cheaper and be faster to erect than, for example, a ranch-style wooden fence. Another common use for wire fences is where a garden commands a fine view and a fence that does not obscure it is required.

It is, however, always useful for a gardener to know the basic techniques of wire and strainer erection for use in many small jobs about the garden, such as the erection of fruit cordons or fruit bush supports, and all large-scale trelliswork. These all require wire strands and posts to take the strain. Using the techniques described below, it is possible to erect any kind of load-bearing post without the use of concrete, e.g. gateposts, flagpoles or washing-line posts. Fig. 6.31 shows a typical length of strained wire fence.

Note On a well-erected cordon it is possible to have up to 3 m (10 ft) spans between posts, since the bushes are, to a certain extent, self-supporting. Bear this in mind when estimating the number of posts required for a cordon.

What you will need

Strainer posts: 10 × 10 cm × 1.5 or 1.8 m (4 × 4 in × 5 or 6 ft) treated softwood or oak. Estimate for one at either end and one every 23 m (25 yd) in between. Props for the strainers: 10 × 10 cm × 1.2 or 1.5 m (4 × 4 in × 4 or 5 ft) treated softwood or oak. Estimate one prop for each of the end posts and two for each of the middle and corner posts. Prick-posts: 1.2 or 1.5 m (4 or 5 ft) treated softwood. Estimate at a rate of one per metre (yard). Wire: the thickness of the wire you use will depend on what job the fence is required to do. Tell your supplier what your requirements are and he will then advise you on the most suitable thickness. Avoid, if possible, using high-tensile wire which is very difficult to handle. If available use 10 or 12 swg as both these sizes will make the job easier. Staples: use standard galvanized fencing staples. 10 cm (4 in) nails. Shovel. Hammer. Wire-cutters. Maul. Bar. Straining tool (Fig. 6.36). Hand saw. Builder's line.

Note Oak posts are considerably more expensive than softwood, and are sometimes more difficult to obtain, but their longer life and more solid qualities, once erected, may make them a more economic buy in the long run.

Measuring up

Measure the length to be fenced and calculate the number of strainers required. Allow one for either end and one every 23 m (25 yd) or at any change in direction. Calculate the number of props required (one for each end post and two for each middle post). Calculate the number of prick-posts required for supporting the wire between the strainers (one per metre (yard), except for fruit cordons where longer spans are possible). Finally, decide on the number of wire strands you want and calculate wire requirements accordingly. This will depend, of course, on how high you want the fence to be.

Remember, always allow for a strainer on any corners or changes in direction.

To erect

To erect the strainer posts Since there is no concrete involved here, to get maximum firmness on the strainer posts two things are most important: the post depth below ground in relation to the height of the fence, and the post hole itself. For post depths, see Table 6.1. For post heights over 2 m (7 ft) we recommend the use of concrete. (For erecting posts with concrete, see p. 48, Step 3.) This will be stronger and save you digging extremely deep holes. The post hole: the real

Table 6.1 Post heights in relation to post depths

Height of post above ground		*Depth of post below ground*	
m	ft	m	ft
1.2	4	0.75	$2\frac{1}{2}$
1.5	5	0.90	3
1.8	6	1.05	$3\frac{1}{2}$

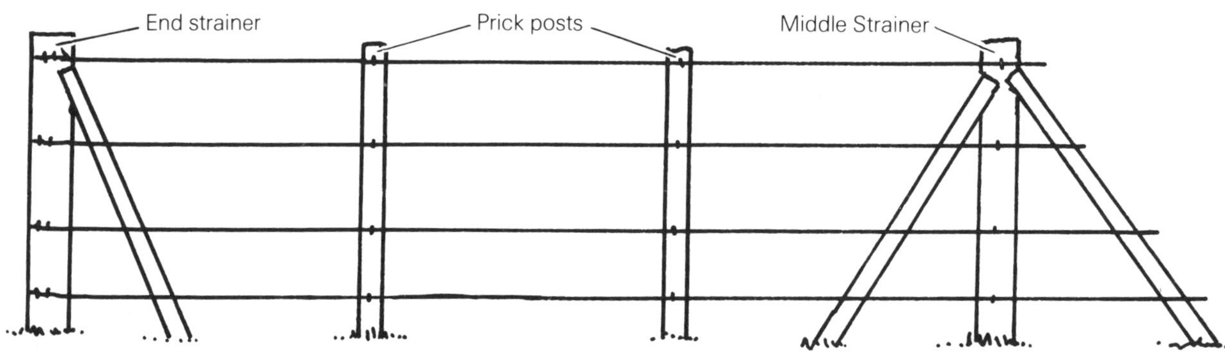

Fig. 6.31 *Length of strained wire showing end and middle strainers.*

secret of a firm post is to have a tight fit at the bottom, and the first 23 cm (9 in) of earth filling *very* firmly rammed. In addition to this the side of the hole that is taking the strain should be as vertical and as firm as possible (Fig. 6.32). A large, shapeless, crumbling hole is not as good. When digging post holes clear away as much topsoil as possible and expose the firm subsoil before starting the hole itself. For a strainer in the middle of a fence try to get both sides as vertical as possible. Do not use mud or topsoil for filling in; try to use firm subsoil or a mixture of subsoil and gravel or chippings.

Procedure: Dig a hole to the required depth. Drop the post in and hold it against the vertical side. Fill the first 23 cm (9 in) with filler and ram. When this is completely firm, fill up the rest of the hole, ramming the earth down every 15 cm (6 in). Check with spirit-level, and test post for firmness, ramming more if necessary.

To prop the strainer For efficient propping the post should be propped as near the top as possible.

Procedure: (see Fig. 6.33) (a) Ram the prop firmly into the ground along the line of the fence. Position the free end of the prop against the strainer, and mark on the strainer the point where the two meet. This mark indicates where the notch is to be cut out of the post to receive the prop. The position of the prop should be altered until this mark is within 20 cm (8 in) of the top of the post. (b)

Fig. 6.32 *Post hole for strainer.*

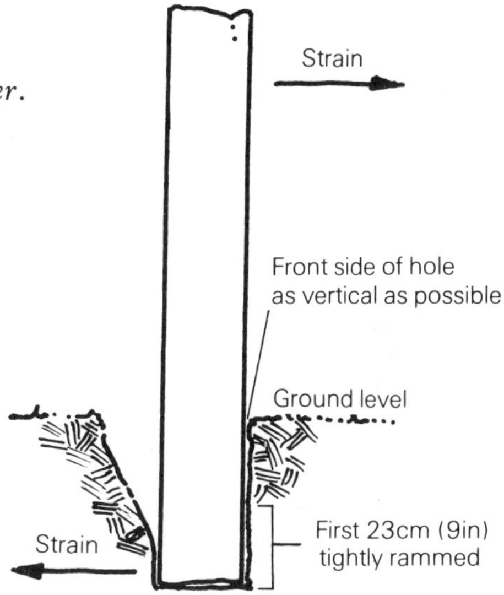

Ram earth firmly around the base of the prop and nail the top end to the post (two 10 cm (4 in) nails).

Note Try to position the prop so that when it is knocked into the notch it pushes the strainer post, giving it a slight backlean, i.e. 2.5 cm (1 in). This will help offset the inevitable inward movement of the post during the life of the fence.

For strainers in the middle of the fence repeat the procedure on both sides of the post. When erecting the middle strainers use the builder's-line method to ensure that the strainers and props are in line (Fig. 6.34) with the fence (see p. 48, Step 4). For strainers at corners or changes in direction, use the builder's line to determine the position of the props.

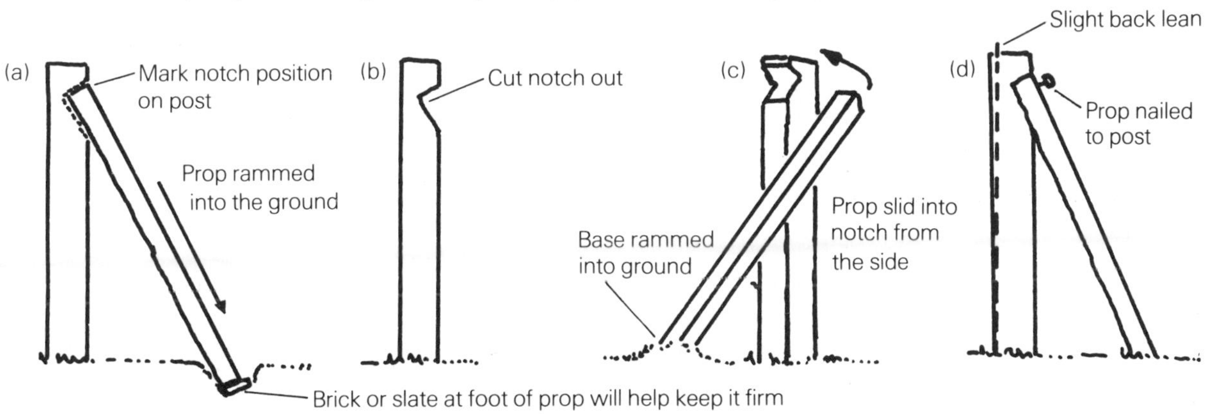

Fig. 6.33 *Procedure for propping the strainer post.*

To erect the fence Erect and prop a strainer at either end of the fence. Tie builder's line between them to give yourself a straight line to work from. Pace out and mark the position of any middle strainers or points where the fence will change direction. Dig holes, erect and prop the strainers.

Pace out the positions for the prick-posts, and using a bar and maul (Fig. 6.35) drive in the prick-posts between the strainers, and upright against the builder's line. Use the bar to open up holes for the posts and drive the posts in with the maul.

To attach the wire: staple one strand firmly (use three or four staples) to one of the end strainers. Run out the wire for the length of the fence and cut. Go back along the length tacking the wire with staples (one per post) to all the strainers and prick-posts. The wire must be able to run through the staples, so that it can be tightened later. Repeat the operation for the required number of strands. (For spacing of strands on a typical four-strand fence see rail spacing for ranch-type fencing, p. 58.)

To strain the wire: always strain the top wire first. Using a straining tool (Fig. 6.36) pull the loose end of the top wire round the end post. When sufficient tension is on the wire, staple it firmly to the post using three or four staples. Loop the excess wire round the post, staple, and cut off any excess. Go back along the length of wire and hammer all the staples firmly in. Repeat the operation for the other strands.

Straining tool: a simple device for straining fence or fruit wires is a stout piece of wood at least 90 cm (3 ft) long and about 5 × 5 cm (2 × 2 in). Staple the loose end of wire near one end of the wood, and resting that end behind the post at the correct height, push the other end round keeping the wire tight against the post. Staple the wire to the post when sufficient tension is achieved.

10 Chestnut fencing

Chestnut fencing is not a very tidy-looking form of permanent fencing and it is not popular for use in gardens since it allows a lot of intertwined weed- and grass-growth under and up it. It does, however, have some specific purposes which make it useful. It is primarily a good, cheap, re-usable temporary fence, which can be erected and re-rolled as required. Alternatively it can be used to reinforce a hedge, which is allowed to grow up and through the fence, making an attractive and animal-proof barrier. The fence is left in the hedge. It is also a good stock fence used on its own. It should be pointed out that although the technique for erection is very simple, the actual straining of the fence on a

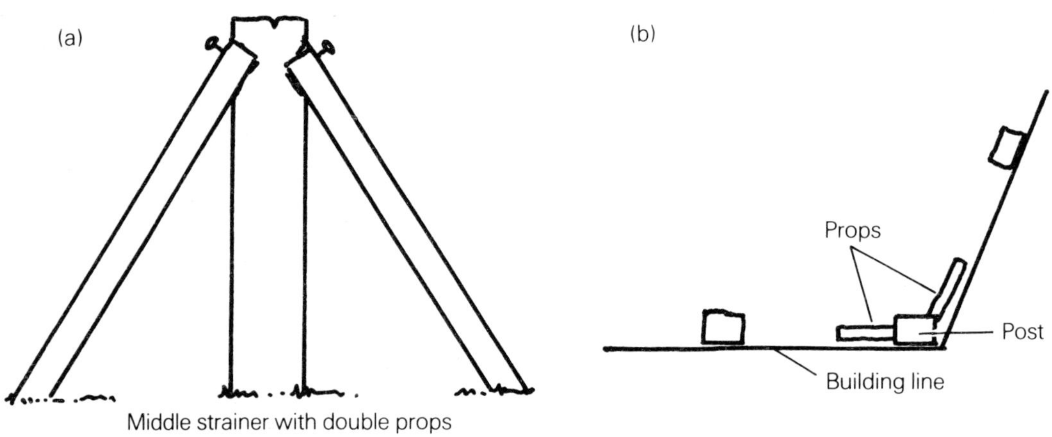

Fig. 6.34 *Middle strainer and change of direction.*

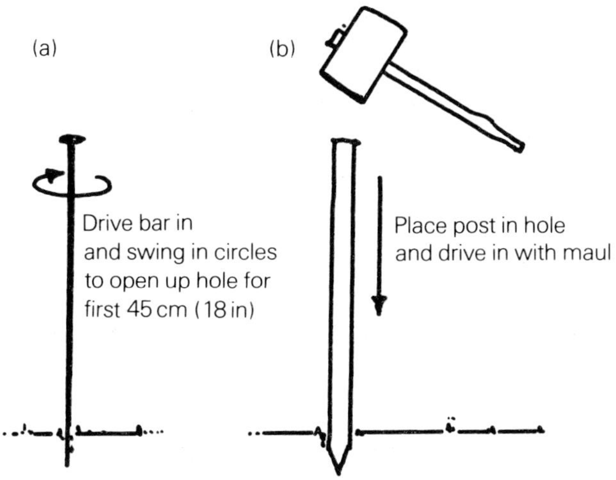

Fig. 6.35 *Making a hole for prick post.*

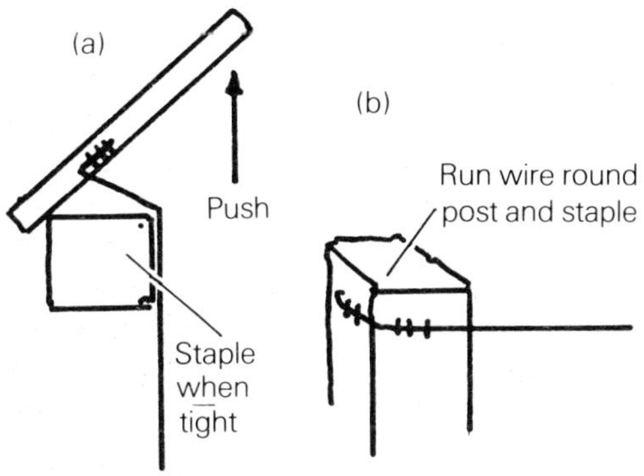

Fig. 6.36 *Straining a wire fence. (a) From above. (b) From side.*

long length is difficult. If erecting on your own, a hand-winch is advisable. If an assistant is available to help you strain the fence, then hand-tight tension is usually sufficient.

What you will need

Rolls of fencing. Strainer posts at either end (see p. 68). Prick-posts (standard larch stakes). Galvanized fencing staples. Shovel. Bar. Maul. Hammer. Wire-cutters. A hand-winch if working alone.

Measuring up

Measure the length of fencing required. Calculate the number of strainers required, one on either end and at any corners or changes of direction. If the fence is permanent allow for a middle strainer every 23 m (25 yd) or the end of each roll. Calculate prick-posts: one every 3 m (9 ft approx.).

To erect

Position and erect the strainers and drive in the prick-posts. Roll out the fence, resting it against the posts. Staple to first strainer. Strain on to next strainer and staple. Strain and staple in sections, strainer to strainer. Go back along the length of fence and staple to prick-posts. If the fence is temporary it is sufficient to strain by hand from first strainer to prick-post and so on, stapling at each post. It is advisable not to drive the staples in too far if the fence is only to be a temporary one.

11 Chainlink

This is a very useful, if somewhat institutional type of fencing. It does not look particularly attractive but is perhaps the most suitable material for such things as dog runs, pens or fencing for vegetable gardens. It is also difficult to climb. It should be remembered that once erected the rather formal and unsympathetic aspect of chainlink can be softened by allowing climbing plants, such as honeysuckle, to grow over it, or by using the newer, slightly more expensive, p.v.c.-covered fabric which can be obtained in a variety of good landscaping colours. This combines very well with wooden posts. A very attractive fence can also be made using wooden posts and rails. This is both stronger and more secure, the rails making it harder for pets or other animals to get under the wire (Fig. 6.37). Chainlink, particularly the p.v.c.-covered types, has the added advantage of durability and will last a very long time if carefully erected with concrete posts. These posts are, of course, heavier and therefore harder to erect, but they are more or less permanent once in and can be painted a variety of colours to help blend them with the garden background. For erecting chainlink an assistant will be very useful to hold and strain the fabric and for erecting the concrete

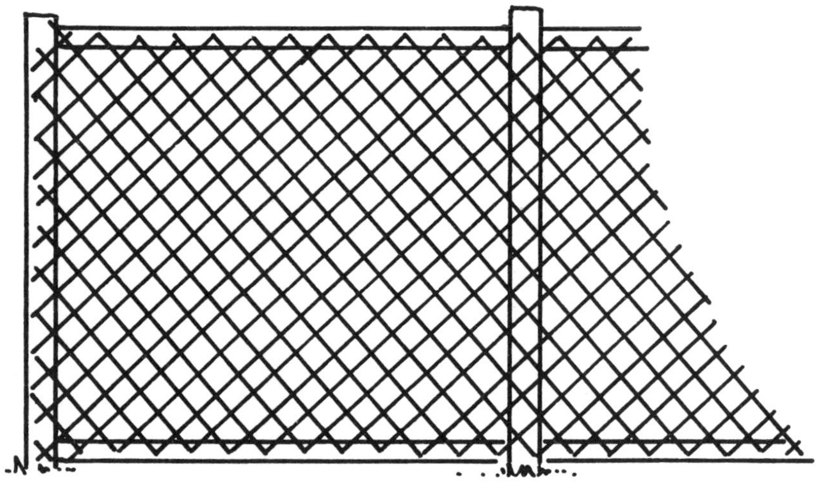

Fig. 6.37 *Chainlink fence with board frame.*

posts. The posts, with end and middle strainers, should be erected as for wire fences (see p. 68).

What you will need

Using concrete posts Chainlink fabric. Concrete posts and necessary props. Straining bars. Support wire. Wire clips. Concrete: (minimum of 50 kg (1 cwt) per post). Wire-cutters. Spanner. Pliers. Shovel. Builder's line. Spirit-level.

Using wooden posts Chainlink fabric. Wooden posts: 10 or 12.5 × 10 cm (4 or 5 × 4 in) treated softwood. Props: 10 × 10 cm (4 × 4 in). Rails (if required): 10 × 5 cm (4 × 2 in) sawn softwood. Support wire. Wire clips. Concrete (50 kg (1 cwt) per post). Galvanized fencing staples. Wire-cutters. Pliers. Shovel. Hammer. Builder's line. Spirit-level.

Measuring up

When you order the materials for chainlink fencing the supplier should provide: concrete posts with holes to take the support wires and notches on the strainer posts for the props, props, chainlink fabric, straining bars to be fixed to the end posts, small nuts and bolts to attach bars to fabric, bolts to attach bars to post, support wires, enough for two strands along the length of fence, adjustable bolts to attach wires to end posts, and wire clips to attach fabric to support wires. Chainlink comes in standard heights from 90 cm (3 ft) up. 1.8 m (6 ft) or 2.1 m (7 ft) are the most practical maximum heights for the amateur, since over this height the posts become very large and heavy and the rolls of fabric very unwieldy.

You should need only to measure the length of fence, decide on height required and order accordingly. (Middle strainers should be estimated at one every 23 m (25 yd).) Check that you have all the necessary accessories.

For wooden posts, estimate strainers as for above, and allow one post every 1.8 m (6 ft). Post lengths: add 60 cm (2 ft) to fence height. Estimate for at least two strands of support wire. (More can be used for a stronger fence.) For rails: decide on post widths and order rails long enough to give a 1.8 m (6 ft) span (i.e. using 10 × 10 cm (4 × 4 in) posts, order 1.9 m (6 ft 4 in) rails). If using rails only one strand of support wire will be required. If using rails top and bottom on fences over 1.2 m (4 ft) high use one strand of support wire along middle of fence.

To cut or join chainlink fabric

Chainlink is made up of single strands of wire

woven together running from top to bottom. Thus, to cut a roll of fabric to the required length, the fastest method is simply to unravel one strand, turning it round and round until it works itself out. This neatly separates the fabric and saves a lot of cutting. The spare strand will also be useful for joining rolls. To join two rolls together (if, for example, one roll runs out in mid-span) simply lay the two ends close together on the ground and join them by inserting a single strand, catching each end alternately (Fig. 6.38).

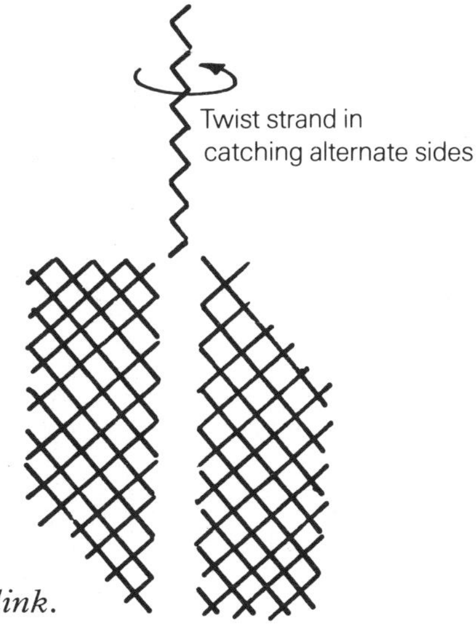

Fig. 6.38
Joining chainlink.

To erect

Using concrete posts

1 Erect strainers and posts using concrete and builder's line (see p. 48).

2 Attach strands of support wire with bolts to first post, feed it through the posts along the length of this fence and through the fixing bolt on the end post. The strands should then be pulled tight and secured. Tension can now be given to the wire by screwing up the adjustable bolts.

3 Using nuts and bolts, attach straining bars to end of first roll of fabric and fix it to the first post. Run out the fabric, leaning it against the posts and support wires. Join or cut rolls where necessary and attach to end post with straining bars. An assistant is almost essential at this point to strain the fabric while the bars are being attached to the post.

4 When all is secure, go back along the fence clipping the fabric at intervals, every 60 cm (2 ft) to the strands of support wires.

Using wooden posts

1 Erect posts as for above..

2 Staple straining wire to first post and run out along the length of the fence *tacking* it to the posts. Strain the strands and staple to end post. Return along the fence knocking the staples firmly into the posts.

3 Stand roll of fabric against first post and staple the end firmly in place, placing the staples approx 22.5 cm (9 in) apart.

4 Roll out the fabric to next post, strain it and staple.

5 Repeat for the rest of fence.

6 Clip fabric to support wires (every 60 cm (2 ft).

Using wooden posts and rails (Fig. 6.37)
Before erecting cut rebates in the posts (see p. 59) to carry the rails. (In this example we are using one rail across the top and support wire below, thus one rebate at the top is sufficient. You can, of course, use rails top and bottom, in which case two rebates will be needed.) If you are using rails props will not be necessary. Erect posts and fix rails in position. Run out support wire, strain it and staple to posts. Strain and staple fabric to posts (see above, 3 and 4) and finally, staple it to the rail and clip it to the support wire.

Note Chainlink fabric may be unneccessarily heavy-duty for some jobs, such as runs for small pets or chickens. In these cases it will be easier and cheaper to use chicken wire. This comes in various sizes and should be erected using wooden posts in the same way as chainlink. Chicken wire will, however, not need so much tension.

12 Good neighbour fences

If your garden or property adjoins someone else's and a fence between them is necessary, it is often possible to get the fence erected as a joint venture; sharing the cost and, maybe, the work. Alternatively, it sometimes happens that erecting a particular type of fence that suits your garden plan may actually spoil, or alter in some way, that of your neighbour. In these cases it is desirable to erect a type of fence that has a pleasant, finished face on both sides (Plate 3), so that it complements both gardens.

If the fence is designed as a joint venture then the needs of both gardens can be considered and ideas pooled to create a mutually satisfactory result. Any of the fence types covered in this chapter can, of course, be used but a number of them will require a few modifications to improve the backface. A major consideration in joint ventures is the height of the fence, but this does not affect the design, whereas the other big consideration, the finished face that is presented to the neighbour, does. So it is on this that we will concentrate. What we are trying to avoid here is a backface of concrete posts or props, crosspieces or strands of wire, nail points and so on – all of which may be invisible from the front. These are the areas that need modification.

'Hit and miss' fencing (see p. 64) is a good example of a good-neighbour style fence, since positioning the boards on alternate sides of the posts means that the finished faces will look the same. Using this principle we can modify some of the designs covered so far; thus, for example, we can create an 'exposed post' paling fence that presents two identical faces (Fig. 6.39). Erection procedure would be as for 'exposed post' paling (see p. 62) except that the palings would be fixed on alternate sides of the crosspieces or on alternating panels. Other styles can also be modified using this principle.

Another way of altering designs is to borrow the technique used for making lapped panels (see p. 55) where the fence material is 'sandwiched' between two frameworks. Fig. 6.40 shows a close-board fence adapted to the 'picture-frame' style. Here, instead of the boards being fixed on to one face of crosspieces, they are caught between the four-sided frameworks (one on either face) which are then nailed between the posts. For small fences 5 × 2.5 cm (2 × 1 in) timber can be used for the framework, while for larger work 8 × 5 cm (3 × 2 in) timber would be more suitable.

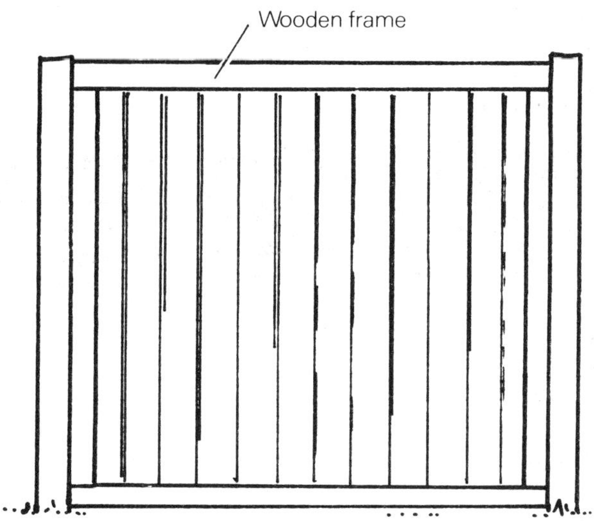

Fig. 6.40 *Picture-window style close boarding.*

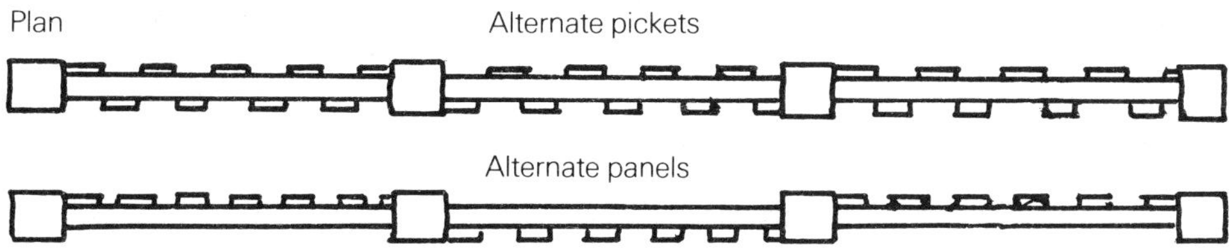

Fig. 6.39 *Good-neighbour style paling fences.*

7 Walls

The design and construction of walls, whether they are used on the boundaries or inside the garden, requires careful planning. This is not only because they involve more work than, for example, fences, but also because it is difficult and often expensive to modify them after completion. A badly planned wall may need altering for a number of reasons, the commonest of which are the line of the wall and the strength of a retainer. In the first instance, parts of the wall may be in the wrong place, and in the second, not enough thought has been given to the amount of soil the wall will be retaining and the excessive weight starts to push the retainer over. Clearly in both these cases rectifying the error will require more work and expense. To avoid this situation four points should be kept in mind.

The first is simply stated: before starting work on a wall be sure that the planned position is correct and that it fits in with any other plans you may have for the area around it. Second, consider the wall itself. The kind of walls needed in gardens are of two basic types: they either divide neighbouring gardens or one area of a garden from another (i.e. paths from flowerbeds etc.) or they retain earth (for terracing, raised beds, level changes, etc.). The main difference in construction between them is that the former need two completed faces and the later only one (Fig. 7.1). If, of course, the walls are of brick or blocks the faces will be complete and only careful pointing is needed to tidy up both faces. When thinking about building it is important to keep in mind which kind of wall it is to be, as it will affect building techniques and quantities, especially with stone walls. The building techniques shown below describe how to make the basic dividing walls and thus allowances should be made if you want a retainer.

The third consideration is the base on which the wall will stand. Known as the 'footings', these play a key role in the stability and strength of the wall. This can be most clearly illustrated in the case of retaining walls where, no matter how well built the wall itself is, if it isn't firmly anchored and supported by footings, the weight of earth behind it may eventually push it over.

Finally, when designing the wall, to ensure that it is as strong as possible allowances must be made for the type of materials to be used. Clearly, the thinner the wall the more carefully it must be designed and constructed since it cannot rely on sheer bulk and internal strength to keep it up.

For stone walls, whether dividing or retaining, strength is added to the wall by giving the faces a backlean, or 'batter'. This technique is illustrated in Figs. 7.1a and b; the dividing wall (Fig. 7.1a) tapers towards the top as the faces 'lean' gradually inwards, and the retaining wall (Fig. 7.1b) leans back into the earth. Both are stronger as a result. For masonry walls this additional strength can be added in different ways. One way is to build pilasters into the wall at regular inter-

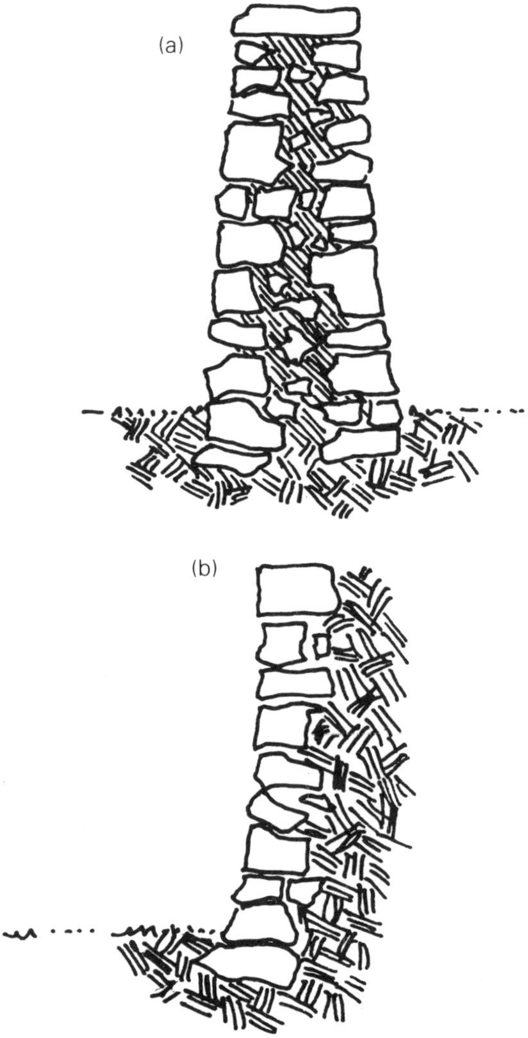

Fig. 7.1 *Dividing and retaining walls.*
(a) Section through dividing wall, two complete faces.
(b) Section through retainer, one complete face.

vals (Figs. 7.18 and 7.26). These columns act as buttresses and should be incorporated into any dividing or retaining walls over 1.2 m (4 ft) high, particularly those built of brick or concrete blocks under 23 cm (9 in) wide. The second method is to build double course walls (Fig. 7.23), which are effectively two walls built up together and strengthened by header courses (Fig. 7.25) or ties (Fig. 7.23). These make very strong walls and, if necessary, pilasters can be built in as well to provide extra stability.

The final option, and this applies to both stone and masonry walls, is to use reinforcing bars. This involves setting steel rods into the footing and then building the wall around them. This can be done in a number of ways and so in our step-by-step instructions we have included the most suitable method of reinforcing the various types of wall.

Note When building retaining walls, bear in mind that you may have problems with water collecting behind the base of the wall. If the ground behind the walls seems particularly wet or you are building a high wall, refer to the section on draining for retaining walls (see p. 45).

1 Footings

The footing of a wall is most important even though it is generally out of sight and underground once the wall is finished. Basically the footing is a shallow trench, the bottom of which is levelled for the wall to stand on. Unfirm or badly prepared footings will almost inevitably lead to cracks or collapse. Depending on the height of wall, weight of materials, firmness of the ground or the amount of 'push' on a retaining wall, the footings can be either the firm subsoil of the trench bottom (i.e. an earth footing) or concrete laid on this.

For concrete footings, two types can be used, the standard concrete footing or the 'solid pour' method. For the first type standard-sized footings are used with various wall heights and materials (see Table 7.1, p. 77) and the footings are set underground. In certain instances, however, the 'solid pour' method may save work and be stronger. If, for example, the soil along the line of the wall is particularly soft and you need to dig a deep trench before firm subsoil is reached, it may save materials and time to fill the trench with concrete up to ground level and build the wall on this much firmer footing. This will avoid burying wall materials below ground and will make the job of building easier.

Table 7.1 Recommended footing sizes

Type of material	*Wall height above ground level*	*Finished level of footing below ground level*	*Concrete Depth*	*Width*
Light blocks, bricks or reconstituted stone	up to 60 cm (2 ft)	15 cm (6 in)	8 cm (3 in)	30 cm (1 ft)
	up to 90 cm (3 ft)	30 cm (1 ft)	8 cm (3 in)	30 cm (1 ft)
	over 90 cm (3 ft)	45 cm (18 in)	8 cm (3 in)	30 cm (1 ft)
Heavier blocks or load-bearing retainers	of any height	60 cm (2 ft)	15 cm (6 in)	60 cm (2 ft)
Mortar-built stone walls	up to 60 cm (2 ft)	30 cm (1 ft)	–	–
	up to 90 cm (3 ft)	45 cm (18 in)	10 cm (4 in)	45 cm (18 in)
	over 90 cm (3 ft)	60 cm (2 ft)	15 cm (6 in)	60 cm (2 ft)
			Earth footings	
Dry stone	low dividing			
	low retaining	under 90 cm (3 ft)	30 cm (1 ft)	–
	larger work	over 90 cm (3 ft)	60 cm (2 ft)	–

Alternatively, you may wish to build the wall on exposed footings (Fig. 7.2) and for these to be stable they must be firmly anchored below ground.

The trench for 'solid pour' footings should be dug at least 45 cm (18 in) wide and 60 cm (2 ft) deep, and if carefully cut, the sides of the trench can act as shuttering. For exposed footings, shuttering should be laid along the top of the trench to give the required height above ground. On long runs the 'solid pour' method will require a lot of concrete and it will probably work out cheaper and certainly faster to order ready-mixed concrete (see p. 27). Since these different types of footing each need different preparation decide carefully before starting work whether you need earth or concrete footings and then, if you're using concrete, which method is most suitable.

Where retaining walls are concerned 'push' worth worrying about starts after the wall is 90 cm (3 ft) high (Fig. 7.3). Walls lower than this will be less affected, unless they are load-bearing retainers. It should be noted, however, that all masonry walls (i.e. brick, blocks, etc.) will require concrete footings of a depth in relation to wall height. Dry-stone walls, on the other hand, will tol-

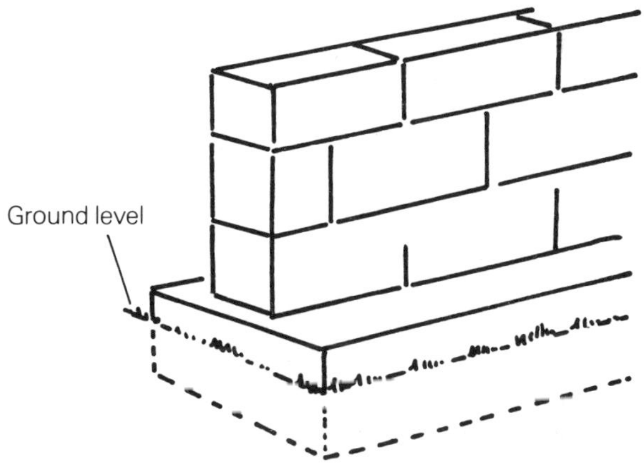

Fig. 7.2 *Exposed footings.*

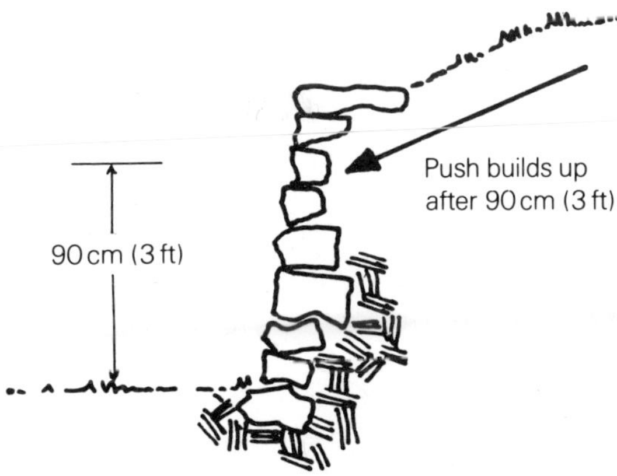

Fig. 7.3 *Sectional diagram of retainer showing 'push'.*

erate a degree of movement and can be built on firm earth. Table 7.1 (p. 77) shows the depth and type of footing required for the various types of wall.

Note 1. To calculate the footing-trench depth for standard concrete footings when digging out: add the finished level of footing below ground to the depth of concrete to be used.

Note 2. When cutting back the earth behind a retainer make sure that your cut is as vertical as possible. A sloping earth 'face' can cause problems of 'push' (Fig. 7.4).

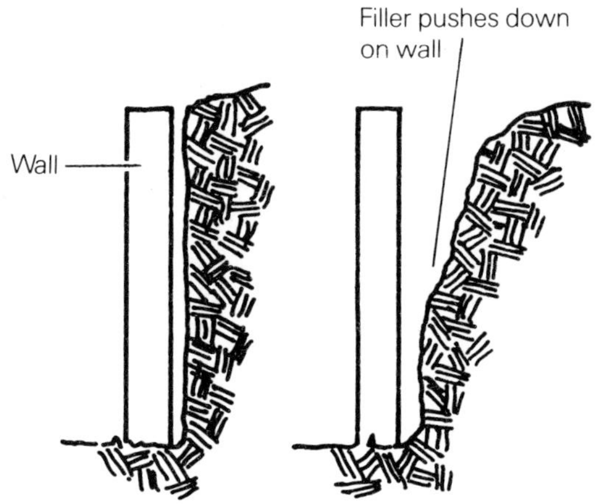

Fig. 7.4 *Cutting back behind a retaining wall.*

What you will need

For earth footings Shovel. Pick. Spirit-level. Builder's line. Stout board of 1.8 m (6 ft) minimum length.

For concrete footings Calculated quantity of concrete. Shovel. Pick. Builder's line. Spirit-level. Tape (see p. 10). Pointed pegs 23 × 4 × 4 cm (9 × $1\frac{1}{2}$ × $1\frac{1}{2}$ in). Stout board of 1.8 m (6 ft) minimum length. Lump hammer. (On particularly long runs a surveying level will be useful to set the pegs (see p. 22)).

For exposed 'solid pour' footings As above plus some shuttering boards. Stakes: 75 cm (2 ft 6 in) long, one every 1.8 m (6 ft).

Measuring up

Standard footings Measure the length of the footing in metres (yards); this should be the total length of the wall *plus* 30 cm (1 ft) extra at either end. Select the type of footing required from Table 7.1. Use Table 7.2 to calculate the quantity of concrete needed per linear metre (yard), for the recommended footing sizes. (Concrete mixes should be 1 : 6, see p. 14.)

'Solid pour' footings For these the trench

Table 7.2 Concrete quantities

*Footing sizes**	*Quantity of concrete per linear metre*	*Quantity of concrete per linear foot*
8 cm (3 in) deep × 30 cm (1 ft) wide	60 kg	40 lb
10 cm (4 in) deep × 45 cm (18 in) wide	121 kg	80 lb
15 cm (6 in) deep × 60 cm (2 ft) wide	242 kg	160 lb

* See Table 7.1

Table 7.3 Concrete quantities for solid pour footings

Footing size	*Quantity per linear metre*	*Quantity per linear yard*
60 cm (2 ft) deep × 45 cm (18 in) wide	650 kg	12 cwt

(For exposed footings; raise the base of the footing and use shuttering to give the required height above ground.)

Fig. 7.5 (Right) Marking the boundary of the footings with sandlines. The distance between sandlines will depend on footings. See Table 7.1.

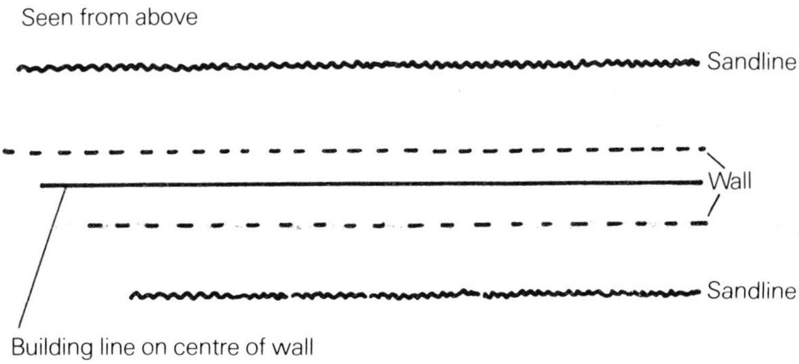

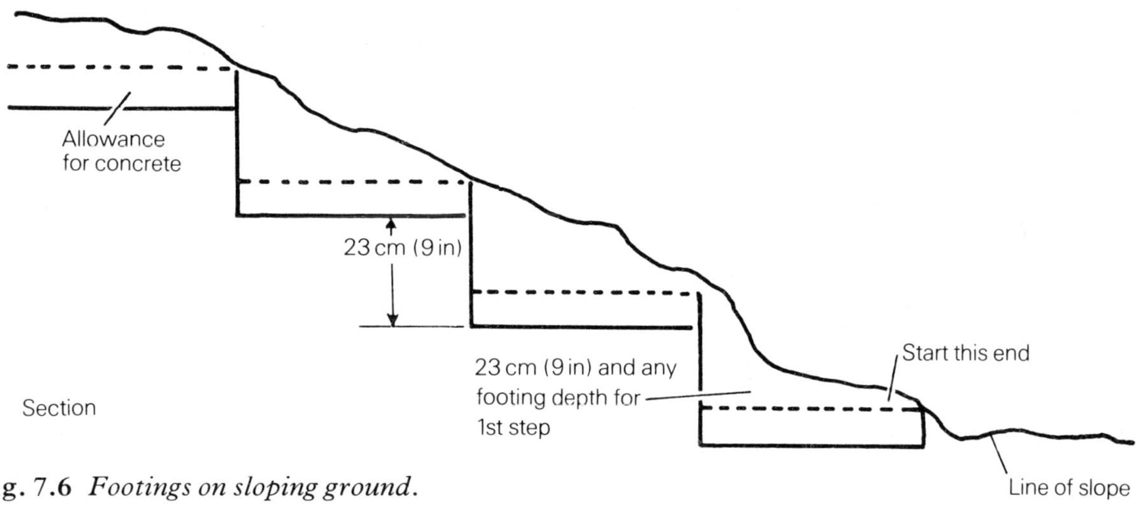

Fig. 7.6 *Footings on sloping ground.*

should be 60 cm (2 ft) deep × 45 cm (18 in) wide. Table 7.3 indicates how much concrete will be needed.

Note These concrete quantities are generous to allow for the inevitable small wastage incurred during most excavation work.

Now measure the total amount of sand, gravel and cement required for the total length of footing. One peg will be required every 1.5 m (5 ft) of footing.

To lay a standard concrete footing

(a) Digging out Run out the builder's line along the line of the centre of the wall to be. Secure both ends and tighten the line. Mark out the edges of the footing on either side of the line with sand (Fig. 7.5). Dig out the footing to the recommended depth (Table 7.1) between the sand lines, trying to maintain a roughly level bottom; use a board and spirit-level to check every 1.8 m (6 ft). Be sure to dig out to firm subsoil, even for concrete, and if the trench becomes too deep, re-fill to the depth required with hardcore (see Excavations and hardcore, p. 32).

Note If the ground is sloping, start at the bottom end and step the footing as required (Fig. 7.6). If the wall is to be built of standard-sized materials, e.g. 23 cm (9 in) blocks, then dig out the level from the bottom end until you have sufficient depth for your materials plus whatever thickness of concrete is being used, cut into the slope. Step the footing and carry on along the next stretch. Fig. 7.6 shows steps for 23 cm (9 in) blocks and these are cut to multiples of 23 cm (9 in). Alter these measurements to suit the size of material being used. If you are using random sizes, step footing wherever it is most convenient.

(b) Pegging Drive the first peg into the bottom of the trench tight to one end and to the required height above the trench bottom. For example: if the concrete is to be 10 cm (4 in) deep, drive the peg in to 10 cm (4 in) above the trench bottom. Drive in the next peg 1.5 m (5 ft) along the trench to the required height, and check for levelness from the first peg using the board and spirit-level. Check clearance along the length of the board with a tape-measure, bottom of board to trench bottom (Fig. 7.7). If it is not level or you do not have the required clearance at any point, dig out the excess now. Repeat the operation, peg to peg, along the length of the trench.

(c) Laying the concrete The concrete should be mixed fairly wet. Put it into the trench and roughly level it off between the pegs with your shovel. When the footing is full up to the peg tops, level the concrete between them with the board. Tamp the concrete surface: bang the board down on the concrete until the water starts rising to the top, making sure that there are no hollows or bumps. Avoid overworking it since this weakens the mix. This is most important since a bumpy footing will cause all sorts of problems when it comes to laying the blocks or bricks, etc. The pegs can either be left in the concrete or removed, and the holes filled once the concrete has started to set.

Note On stepped footings work up, concreting the lowest stretches first. When you come to a step, block off the end of the next one above with a brick or a piece of wood and continue (Fig. 7.8).

To lay 'solid pour' footings

Dig trench (45 cm (18 in) wide and 60 cm (2 ft) minimum depth), checking the bottom for levelness using a board and spirit-level. Drive in stakes (at 1.8 m (6 ft) intervals) as for standard footings. (The stakes are useful as guides for levelling off if the edges of the trench are crumbly or indistinct.) The stake-tops should be 60 cm (2 ft) from the trench bottom. Fill with concrete to stake-tops and smooth off with shovel.

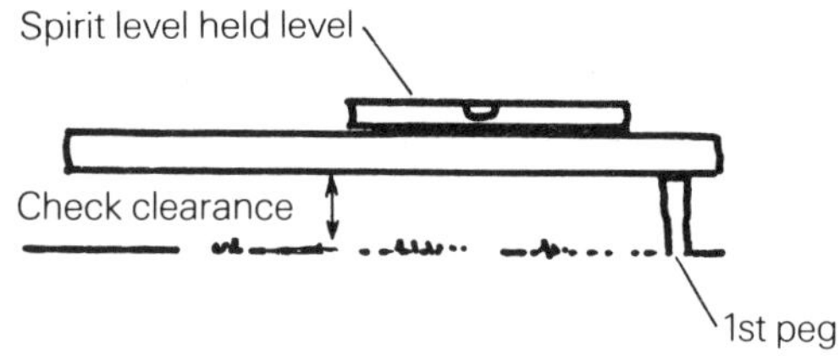

Fig. 7.7 *Checking levels of pegs and clearance.*

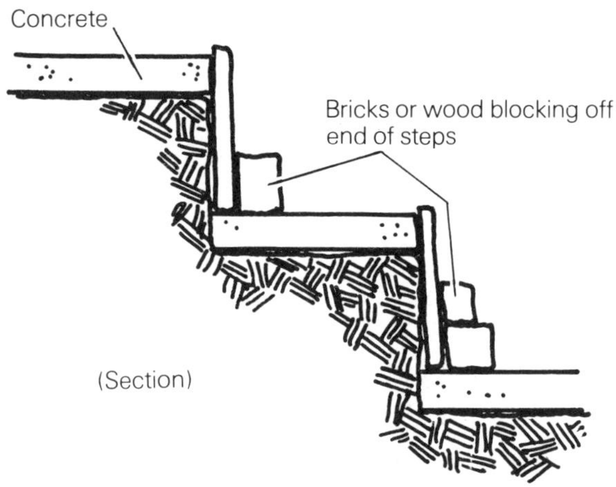

Fig. 7.8 *Stepped footing : blocking off.*

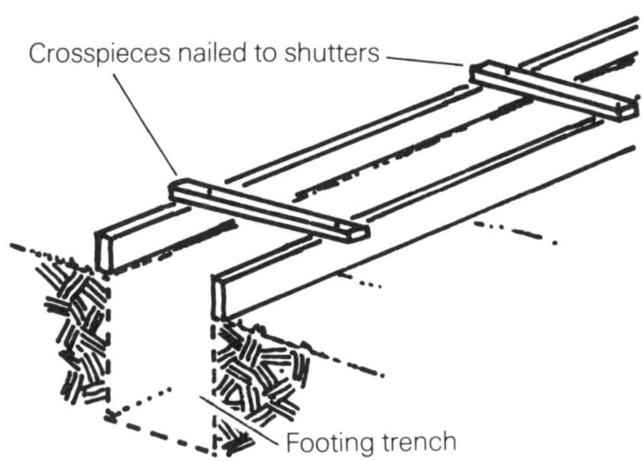

Fig. 7.9 *Crosspieces for exposed footing shutters.*

To lay exposed footings

Prepare trench as for above (omitting the stakes which are not necessary). Set up shutting along edges of trench, securing them with crosspieces (Fig. 7.9) and, having checked the shutters with a spirit-level, firm up the earth around them. Fill with concrete to top of shutters, tamp and screen off with a stout board (see p. 114).

To give the exposed sides of the footings a smooth finish, gently tap the sides of the shutters before you finish tamping. This consolidates the concrete and gives it a tidy, smooth finish when set. The top of the footing should be smoothed off with a builder's trowel when the concrete has been levelled off.

Note 1. Leave concrete footings to dry for at least 48 hours before starting to build on them.

Note 2. Reinforcing bars: reinforcing walls with steel can be done in two ways – either by laying strips of expanded metal along the courses as the wall is built up, or by setting bars into the concrete footings and building the wall up around them.

Use the expanded metal method for single walls built of brick or blocks of 10 cm (4 in) width. To lay, see p. 89. For cavity (double) walls or single walls of blocks over 10 cm (4 in) wide use bars set in the concrete.

Cavity walls: set the bars into the concrete at intervals along the line of the cavity. (Their height will depend on finished wall height.) Then, once the walls have been built and have set, the cavity should be filled with concrete, locking the walls and bars together (Fig. 7.10a). Be sure to work the concrete well down into the cavity.

Block walls over 10 cm (4 in) wide: blocks over this width have holes in them (Fig. 7.12) and the bars should be spaced along the footing to coincide with these holes when the blocks are laid (Fig. 7.10b). Thus, when the wall is complete the bars run up the middle of it. When the wall is complete go back along it filling up the holes with concrete, working the concrete well down, bonding the blocks and bars together.

To dig earth footings

Mark out footing edges with a builder's line and sand (see above). Dig to the required depth and ensure that the bottom of the trench is firm subsoil. If it is not, keep going until all the loose soil is removed. It does not matter if a footing is slightly deep, but an unfirm footing will inevitably lead to the collapse of the wall.

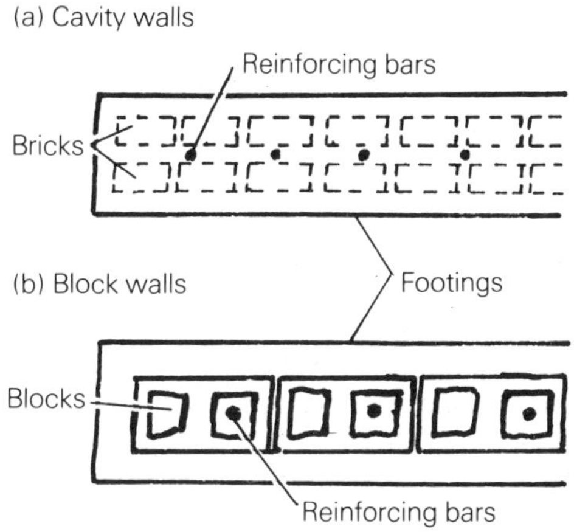

Fig. 7.10 *Reinforcing for cavity and block walls.*

2 Concrete blocks

The main advantage of walls built of standard concrete blocks is their strength and solidity over a long period of time. Concrete blocks will support considerable weight and are quicker, cheaper and easier to lay than other materials that do the same job (bricks, stone, etc.).

While many people consider blocks to be 'unsympathetic' to a garden, it should be remembered that they can be finished off with various render finishes which can then be painted. Alternatively, the face of the wall can be broken up by using a few blocks of a different colour or design here and there in random or regular patterns (Plate 4). If the blocks from your regular supplier are all the same colour, buy a few extra from another source, since few manufacturers make identical blocks. Again, variations on the standard block design are available (i.e. 'rock-faced' (see p. 89) or 'split-faced' blocks) and these can be used to add interest to the finished wall. In addition to this, moss, algae and rock plants will eventually take readily to the concrete surface, which in time softens the concrete effect. Blocks are, however, heavy and unpleasant to handle; gloves are advised.

For an unusual effect the hollow type of

block can be left without coping stones and subsequently filled with earth, making it possible to grow varieties of rock plants or bulbs along the top of the wall.

Screen blocks make very handsome patterned screens without blocking light from flowerbeds or giving a 'shut-in' effect. They can be very attractive if climbing plants, roses and so on, are allowed to grow over them. Screen blocks are not, however, suitable for retaining or load-bearing walls.

What you will need

Blocks. Mortar (mixes 1 : 4 with plasticizer, see p. 14). Builder's line. Spirit-level. Builder's trowel. Lump hammer. Bolster chisel or bricklayer's hammer (see p. 10). Shovel. Tape-measure. Spot-board. Gloves. Wheelbarrow. Mason's block.

Measuring up

Decide on the size of block you require; most blocks are approximately 45 cm (18 in) long, 23 cm (9 in) high and vary only in width. The wider blocks, e.g. 23 cm (9 in), are used for load-bearing or retaining walls. Consult your dealer as to the most suitable width for your job. The blocks are, in fact, just under 45 cm (18 in) long to allow for the mortar filling; when calculating the number of blocks required in a length of wall do not allow extra for the mortar between them. Simply calculate in units of 45 cm (18 in).

Basic figures for calculating:

Two 45 cm (18 in) blocks cover approximately 1 linear yard.
Eight 45 cm (18 in) blocks cover approximately 1 square yard.
Ten 45 cm (18 in) blocks cover approximately 1 square metre.

Using these figures calculate the number of blocks required as follows:

(a) For a level wall Measure length L, multiply this by the required height H, and multiply this figure by 8.72 when working with metric measurements and by 8 when working with imperial (L × H × 8.72 or 8). Add an extra 5% to allow for breakages and blocks to be cut.

(b) For a stepped wall on a slope Take each step individually. Measure the length of the step and estimate the number of courses required to bring it level with the next step (Fig. 7.11). Add areas X, Y and Z together to get total quantity required and add 5% for wastage.

Cutting blocks

In the standard 'stretcher-bond' block laying, every other row working upwards must start with a half-block (Fig. 7.12a). For this reason and to make up any awkward lengths (if, for example, the wall is being built between two buildings), it will be

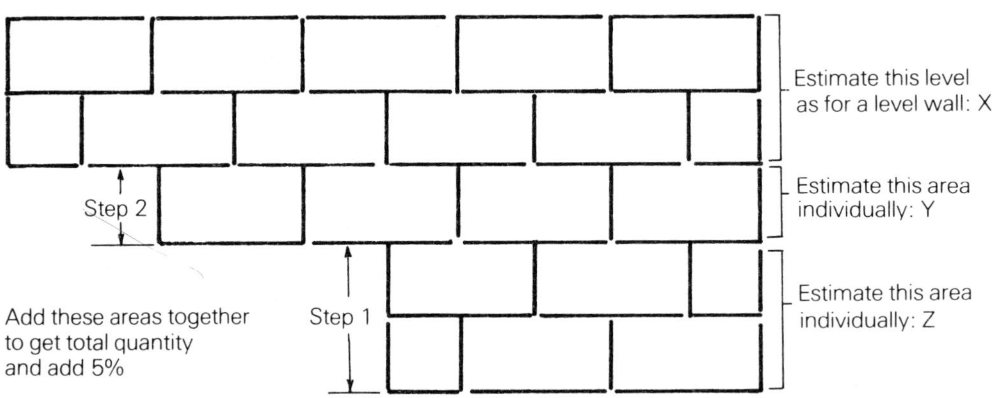

Fig. 7.11 *Estimating number of blocks required for a stepped concrete wall. In this example Step 1 requires two courses and Step 2 one course to bring them level.*

Plates 7 – 10: Construction of slab and pebble path (p. 127)

Plate 7 With the slab in position on its mortar spots fill in the gap with mortar.

Plate 8 Press small pebbles into the mortar and smooth off to required finish.

Plate 9 Lay next slab in position on mortar spots.

Plate 10 Tap the slab firmly down and check its height in relation to the edgings with spirit-level.

Plates 11 – 15: Construction of brick and crazy-paving path (pp. 129-130)

Plate 11 Checking the depth available for the second tread before building the riser.

Plate 12 Filling the tread base with mortar.

Plate 13 Lay the crazy paving material on the mortar, press it firmly in and check that it is lying flush with the brick edges.

Plate 14 The completed crazy paving pattern.

Plate 15 Fill the joints with mortar and smooth off to required finish.

necessary to cut some of the blocks. In every batch of blocks you will receive a certain number of blocks which have a slit down the middle to help you cut them in half (Fig. 7.12b). Using the bolster chisel and lump hammer, or a bricklayer's hammer, knock the block repeatedly on the sides and across the top and bottom, working round the slit, until the block falls in half (Fig. 7.12c). To cut a block into a quarter or three-quarters, mark the block with a pencil along the line of the desired cut, and knock repeatedly along the line, round and round, as above (Fig. 7.12d). To cut 'rock-faced' blocks or coping stones, use a similar method. First mark the stone or block all round where the cut is to be made. Then, going round and round the mark, knock until the cut is made.

Note 1. Hitting the block too hard or when it is lying on an uneven surface will almost certainly shatter it. Bed it firmly in sand for example, and keep going round until the cumulative effect of the knocking causes the block to fall in half.

Note 2. It is almost impossible to get an entirely accurate and straight-edged cut with a chisel and hammer, but disc saws can be hired which will do this. Should you need particular accuracy or have a lot of blocks to cut, it may well be worth your while to hire one, see p. 11.

To build

1. The mortar mix. 2. Applying the mortar to the blocks. 3. Laying the blocks. 4. Building the wall. 5. Pointing the wall.

(1) The mortar mix (For mixing technique, see p. 14.) Take care to allow for the amount of moisture already present in the sand and bear this in mind when adding water during mixing. The mix should be as workable as possible while still being self-supporting; this depends on the amount of water used. For blocks, the mix should be of such a consistency that the following will happen: (a) put mortar approximately 2.5 cm (1 in) thick on a block; (b) place a second block on top; (c) you should now be able to push the top block gently down and compress the mortar down to 1 cm ($\frac{3}{8}$ in) Fig. 7.13). This is the standard gap for all block laying. If the mortar is too solid it won't allow this pressing down, and if it is too wet it will not support the block on top of all. To be ready for laying, the mortar should now be shovelled out on to the clean spot-board.

(2) Applying mortar to blocks Apart from mixing mortar to a constant consistency, the only other knack involved in block

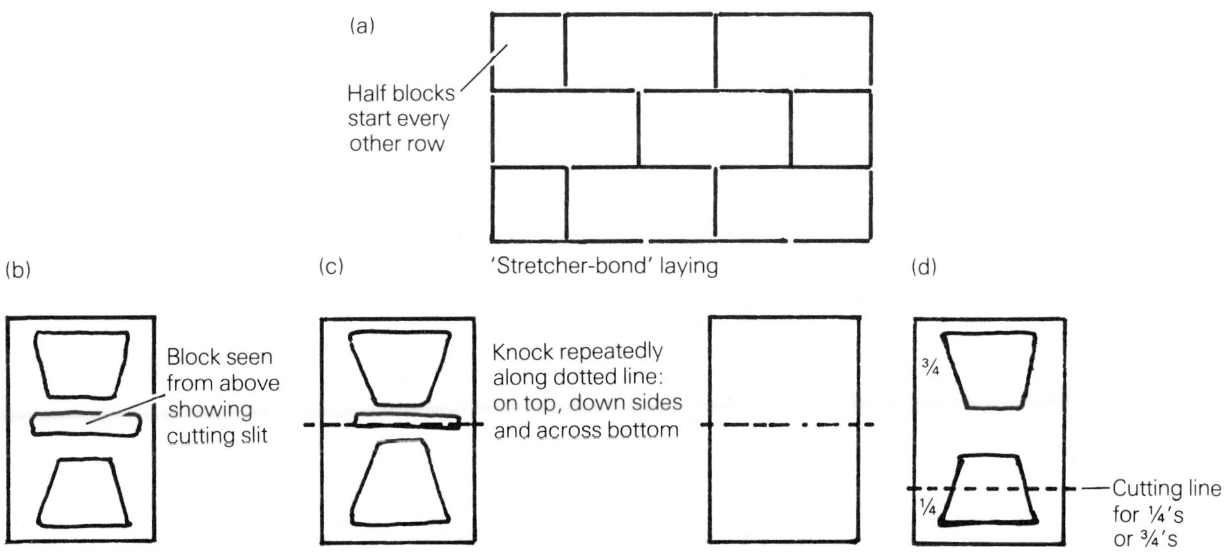

Fig. 7.12 *(a) 'Stretcher bond' laying. (b)–(d) Method of cutting blocks.*

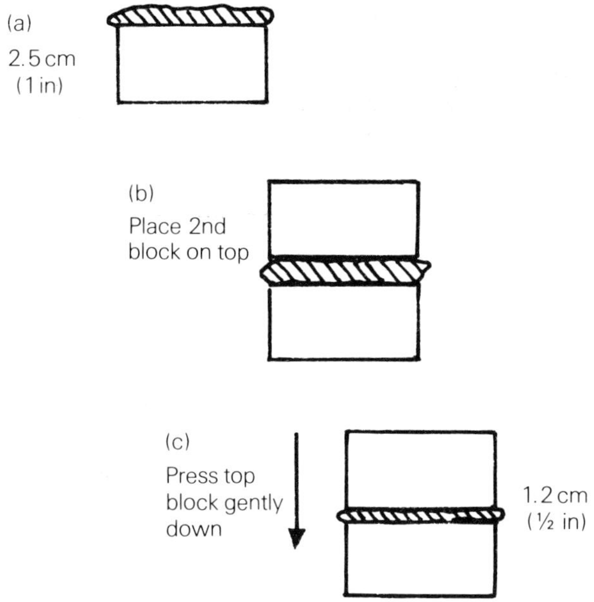

Fig. 7.13 *Mortar compression.*

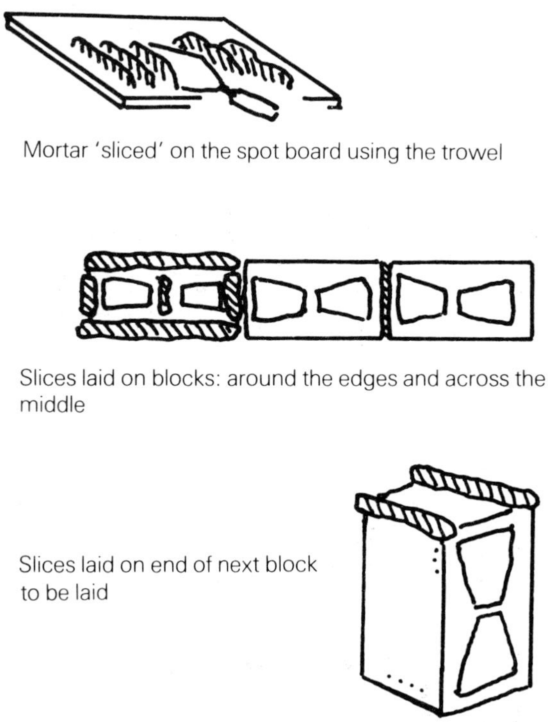

Fig. 7.14 *Applying mortar to blocks.*

laying is 'slicing' the mortar on to the blocks. Before a block can be laid, two lots of mortar must be applied: (a) mortar placed on the block or footing below on which the block to be laid will sit, and (b) the mortar placed on the end of the block to be laid as filling between it and its neighbour in the course. For both lots the mortar should be 'sliced' on the spot-board with a trowel and applied to the block in strips (Fig. 7.14).

(3) **Laying the blocks** (Fig. 7.15) Apply the mortar to the blocks in slices with the trowel. Then:

(a) Lift the block to be laid, holding it by two diagonally opposite corners, on the underside.

(b) Present the block to the wall and lay it gently in position on the mortar slices.

(c) Release the block and tap it down until it is level with the course. Butt the block with trowel against the next one to ensure a good bond. (Vertical mortar gap should be 1 cm ($\frac{3}{8}$ in) except in certain circumstances, see Note 1 below.)

(d) The mortar will now have bulged out between the blocks. Using the trowel cut this excess off clean, taking care not to smear it over the face of the block. Place the excess on the next block to be laid.

(e) Check the block with a spirit-level: first for levelness with the course, and second for flushness with the face of the wall. Any adjustments necessary should be made with small taps of the trowel.

Note 1. On a straight run half-blocks will be required at the beginning of every other course, but if there is a corner, then the interlocking ends of the blocks will do the same job (Fig. 7.16). For 23 cm (9 in) wide blocks (where the width equals half the length) the vertical mortar gap should still be 1 cm ($\frac{3}{8}$ in), but for thinner blocks (i.e. 15 cm (6 in) or 10 cm (4 in) wide) the disparity in width should be made up by making the mortar gap slightly wider along the length of the wall.

Note 2. If you are building a wall with corners, be sure to build the corners up first and then build the straight run between them. You will, of course, have to lay the first course for the whole

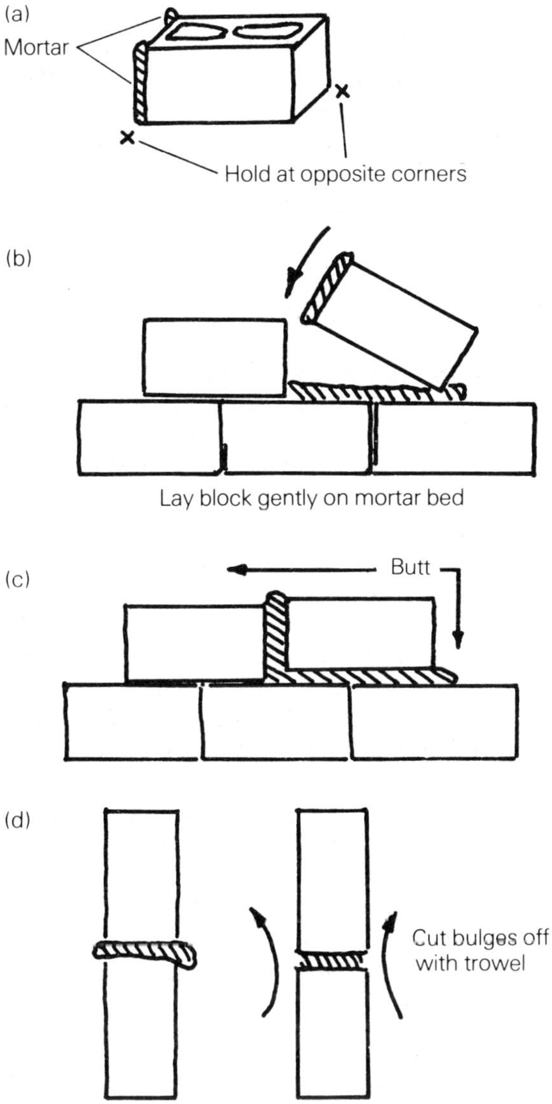

Fig. 7.15 *Laying concrete blocks.*

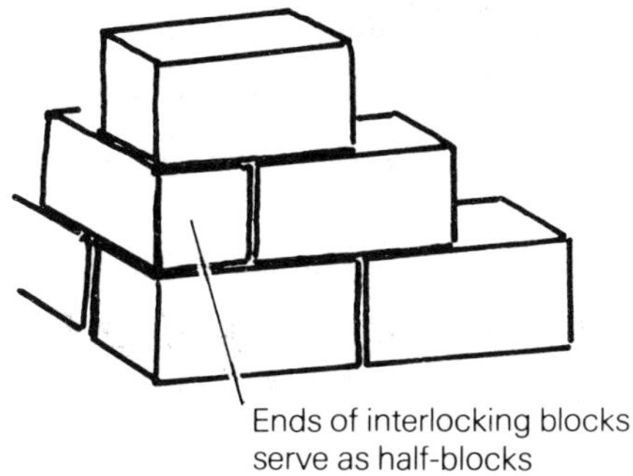

Fig. 7.16 *Interlocking blocks at corners.*

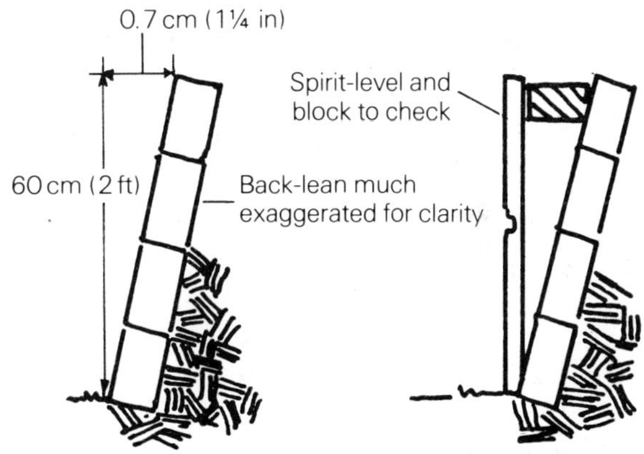

Fig. 7.17 *Back-lean or rake in a retaining wall.*

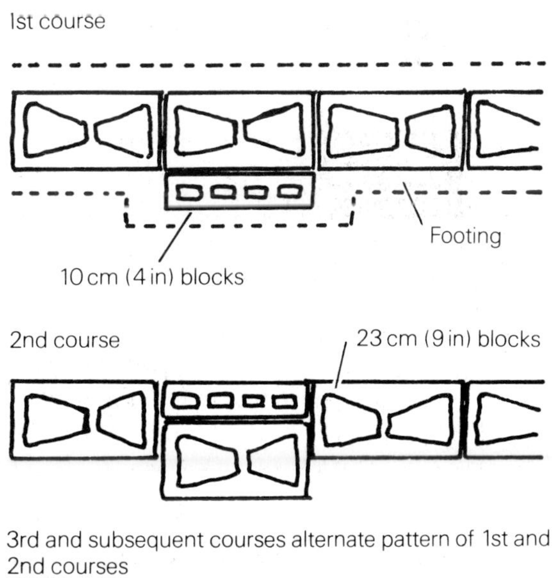

Fig. 7.18 *10 cm (4 in) blocks forming a pilaster in a 23 cm (9 in) block wall.*

length of the wall to get the correct positioning for the corners, or calculate if using multiples of 45 cm (18 in).

Note 3. If the wall is a retainer over 1.2 m (4 ft) high, added strength can be gained by giving the wall a slight backlean or batter: 2.5 cm per 60 cm (1 in per 2 ft) of height is adequate. To maintain a uniform lean check each course as you lay it with a batter-gauge (Fig. 7.17).

Note 4. Strength can also be added by building pilasters into the wall at regular intervals. For

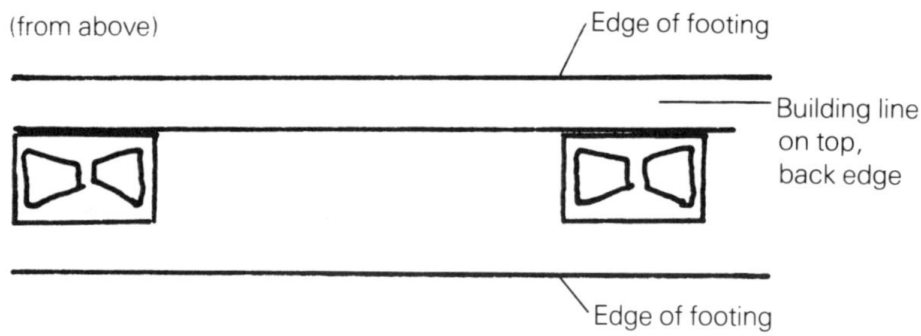

Fig. 7.19 *Building the wall: first line of blocks.*

block-work these should be incorporated into the wall as shown in Fig. 7.18. Be sure to allow for these extra blocks when measuring up.

(4) **Building the wall** To start, brush off the concrete footing to ensure that there are no bits of earth or stone on it. Run out enough blocks for the first two courses, standing them on their ends along the edge of the footing. Mix the mortar and lay a block at either end, about 30 cm (1 ft) from end and in the middle (width) of the footing. If there is to be a batter allow for it now. Stretch the builder's line from the top back edge of the blocks (Fig. 7.19) using mason's blocks or bricks to secure it. Be sure to pull it tight.

Slicing mortar on to the blocks, lay the first course straight through, checking that each block is level with and tight up to the line. This will ensure a straight, level course. If the first two courses are carefully laid the others should follow without any problem, needing only to be checked every 60 cm (2 ft) of height for batter and levelness.

As each block is laid make sure that it is correctly tapped down and tapped up to the line. Butt each block firmly up to its neighbour and finally, check every so often with a spirit-level.

Sequence: (1) Lay block on mortar; (2) Tap down to line; (3) Tap against line; (4) Butt to neighbour, check with level; (5) Cut off excess mortar.

Note Trowels usually have one straight edge. Use this for a rough check along the front of the blocks to ensure they are flush after cutting off the excess mortar.

Continue up for the required number of courses, starting each new course with a block (or half-block) at either end and the builder's line stretched between them. If you are laying on stepped footings start at the lowest point. Build up until level with the next step and continue.

(5) **Pointing the wall** Pointing is the uniform finish given to the mortar as the wall is being built. An unpointed wall will always look untidy because as the blocks are laid the mortar will not have a regular finish. Filling in any gaps and pointing finishes off the job. Depending on the weather conditions the mortar will set at varying rates. There is, therefore, no specific time at which to point but you should aim to catch the mortar while it is still soft enough to shape. There are a number of ways to point, of which the most common are:

1 'Rough' pointing: this is done with a sponge or a rag. Simply brush the sponge along all the mortar joints (not too hard) leaving a uniform textured finish.

2 'Weathered' pointing: this is done with a trowel. To do this push the trowel along the mortar lines pressing the top edge in (Fig. 7.20a). Press down the vertical joints, smoothing the surface. (Do not pull the trowel since the point is likely to leave a mark).

3 'Raking' (for use with rock-faced blocks): rake out the joints (leaving a semi-circular impression) with a 1.25 cm ($\frac{1}{2}$ in) diameter steel bar or an old bucket handle etc. by pulling it along the joints (Fig. 7.20b).

Variations

Rock-faced blocks These are standard blocks with the difference that one face has been left rough-textured rather than pressed flat as on all other blocks. This type of face has extra visual appeal and is a useful alternative to the standard finish. Lay as for standard blocks with 'raked' pointing. Estimate the quantities as for standard blocks.

Reconstituted stone This is an attractive and popular walling material. To produce this stone the manufacturers mix cement with very fine quarry dust (rather than cement and sand), and with the later addition of dyes, they can reproduce, at a fraction of the cost, the textures and colours of various types of natural stone: sandstone, slate, Cotswold stone, etc. For types and descriptions there are detailed manufacturers' pamphlets available at most garden centres and builders' merchants. The basic size of the stones is 45 × 15 × 15 cm (18 × 6 × 6 in), i.e. approximately 14 per sq m (12 per sq yd). Lay as for block work and use 'weathered' pointing.

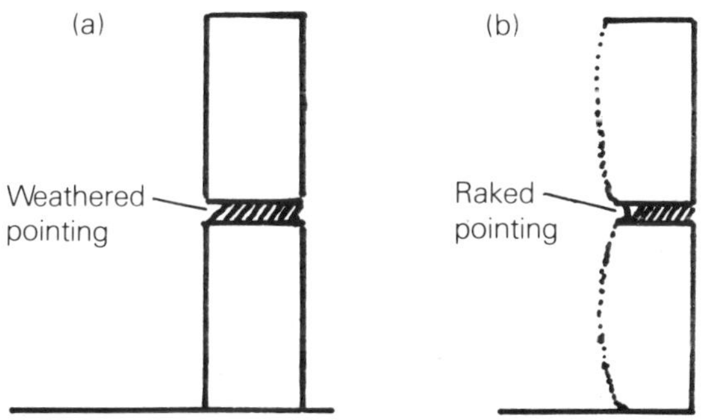

Fig. 7.20 *Pointing the wall.*

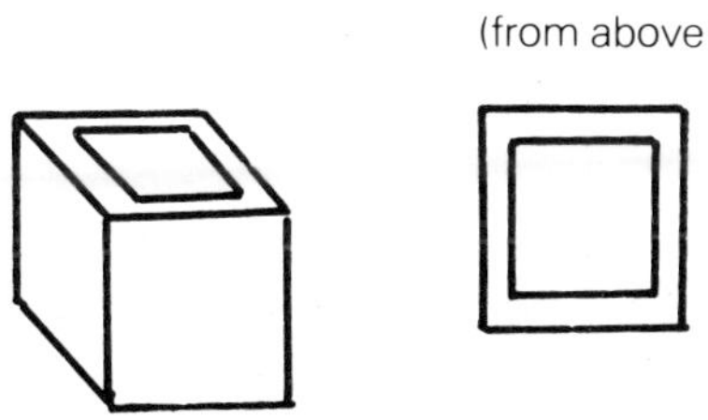

Fig. 7.21 *Pillar blocks.*

Random reconstituted stone This varies from the standard reconstituted stone in that you have three or four different units to use. To lay you can either design your own pattern or use one recommended by the manufacturer. Use their literature also to help calculate the quantities required.

3 Screen blocks

These are an attractive form of block walling which give an effect of light with pleasant patterns. They are strictly non-load-bearing and need support pillars every 2.7 m (9 ft). The mortar mix should be on the weak side for these blocks, e.g. 1 : 7, since a strong mix contracts during drying and may crack the rather fragile blocks. The blocks are 30 × 30 × 10 cm (12 × 12 × 4 in), i.e. approximately 11 per sq m (9 per sq yd). (When ordering be sure to add an extra 5% to the total since the blocks are very susceptible to breakage during transit.) The pillar blocks (Fig. 7.21) are usually 23 × 23 × 15 cm (9 × 9 × 6 in). Lay as for blocks, starting with the end pillars and building the wall between them using a builder's line and inserting a pillar every 2.7 m (9 ft). Use 'weathered' pointing.

Note 1. Firm footings are essential for screen block walls since the slightest degree of settling is likely to crack the wall. Thus we would recommend using 'solid pour' or exposed footings (see p. 80) for this work.

Note 2. There are two ways of reinforcing screen block walls: using expanded metal along the courses, and putting reinforcing rods in the pillars.

Expanded metal: this should be considered for almost any screen-block walling regardless of size, and is built in as shown in Fig. 7.22. Place mortar along the course and work the strip of metal (available in various sizes from most builders' merchants) well into it. Add more mortar if necessary to cover it and lay blocks on top. The expanded metal should be added to every other course.

Reinforcing rods: these help strengthen high walls and should be set into the footing where the

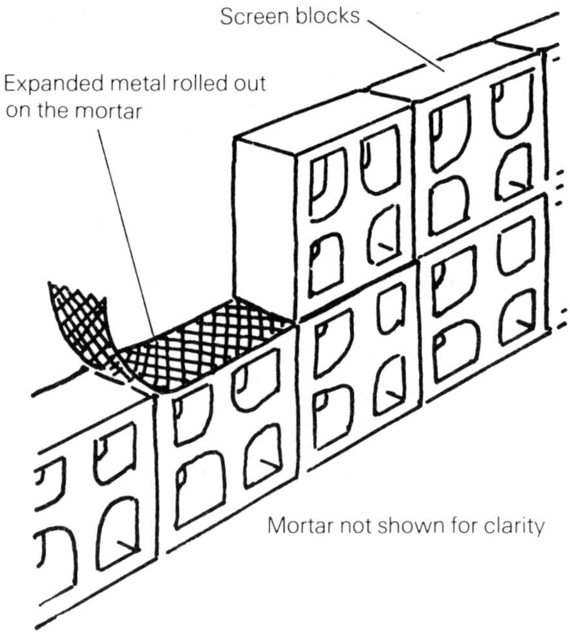

Fig. 7.22 *Using expanded metal to reinforce a screen block wall.*

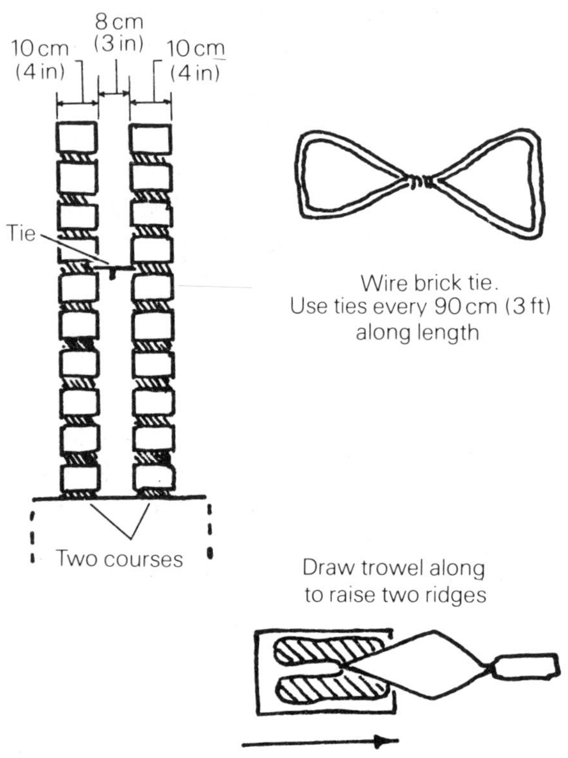

Fig. 7.23 *Double course brick wall.*

centre of each pillar is to stand. Build pillars around them and fill with concrete when the pillars have set.

It is worth noting that, if you have time, it is much cheaper and relatively simple to make your own blocks. Use manufactured moulds such as Auriol Kwik-Kast, the recommended mix being three parts coarse, washed, sharp sand to one part cement, using a little water to make a semi-dry mix. There are a number of mould types, so find out what is available and follow the manufacturer's instructions for the best results.

Note An interesting variation on screen block walls is to combine them with brickwork. This can be done either by simply using bricks instead of pillar blocks (for brick pillars see p. 149) or, for an even more decorative effect, courses of bricks can be combined with the screen blocks. This technique makes a number of designs possible, depending on the degree of 'walling' or 'screening' required.

4 Brickwork

This used to be the standard walling material but the price of bricks nowadays makes blocks a quicker and cheaper alternative. The universal appeal of brick walls needs no introduction here, and it is sufficient to say that if you can afford them, they will provide a much more pleasing effect than blocks. Concrete blocks can never compare with the muted colours and shapes of a well-weathered brick wall. Should you be able to use bricks, the commonest form of wall is the 'stretcher-bonded' 28 cm (11 in) cavity wall (Fig. 7.23). (Single brick walls can be used for low, non-load-bearing walls, but they are not stable enough for higher work or retainers.) For the cavity wall, two walls are built simultaneously 8 cm (3 in) apart, tied every six courses with brick ties laid across the cavity. Footings should be 45 cm (18 in) wide. (For footing depth see Table 7.1, p. 77.) Be sure of a good mortar mix consistency. Build as for blocks, corners first, using a builder's line along each wall. Avoid a uniform mortar bed for bricks: place a blob on a brick and draw the trowel down the middle, raising a ridge on either side. Lay the next brick on these ridges, tap down, butt and check with spirit-level. Cavity walls can either be finished off with coping stones (see below) or with brick coping as shown in Fig. 7.24. For reinforcing cavity walls see p. 81. 'Raked' or 'rough' pointing both look well with brickwork.

To calculate quantities of bricks allow approximately:

72 per sq m (60 per sq yd) for single walls
144 per sq m (120 per sq yd) for cavity walls.

Note 1. Double walls: good, strong walls can also be built by building two walls together (without the cavity) and by bonding the walls with header courses. This means that the stretcher courses alternate with courses of bricks laid across the width of the wall, presenting their short sides (or heads) to the wall face. Figs. 7.25a and b illustrate two popular patterns for header-bonded brick walls. These should be built along the same lines as described above and for calculating quantities note that two header bricks equal one stretcher. An additional point to notice about building walls using these patterns is that, because the composition of the courses alters, it is necessary to insert 'closers' (cut bricks) at the ends of courses to maintain the correct spacing and complete the course. Fig. 7.25c indicates how these should be used.

Fig. 7.24 *Brick coping on a double wall.*

Note 2. Pilasters for brick walls: these serve the same purpose as pilasters in block walls (see p. 87), and Figs. 7.26a and b show how they should be incorporated into single (10 cm (4 in) wide) walls and double (20 cm (18 in) wide) walls respectively.

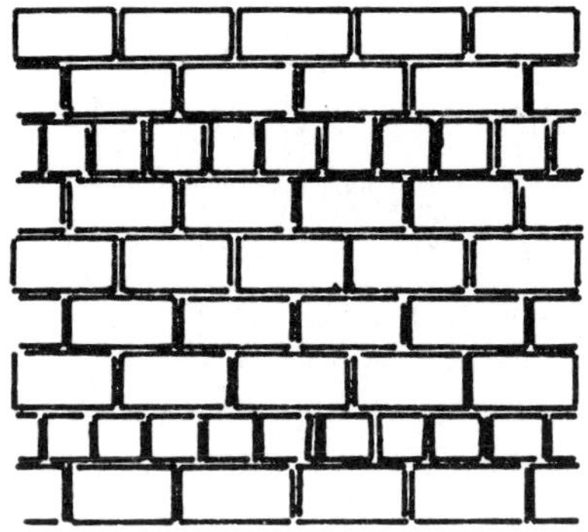

(a) Standard header bond

(b) Flemish bond

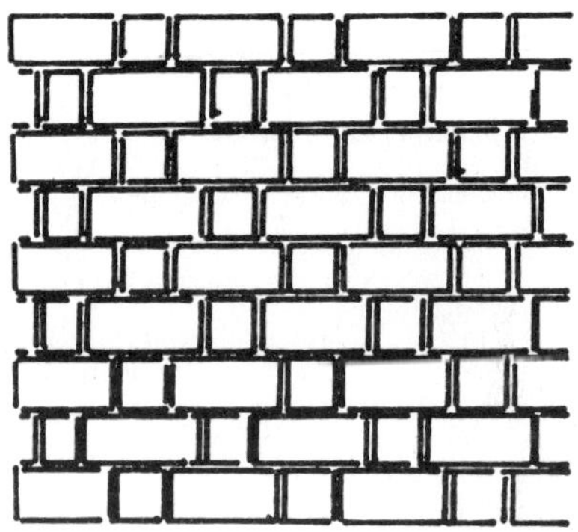

(c) Closer-brick cut lengthways

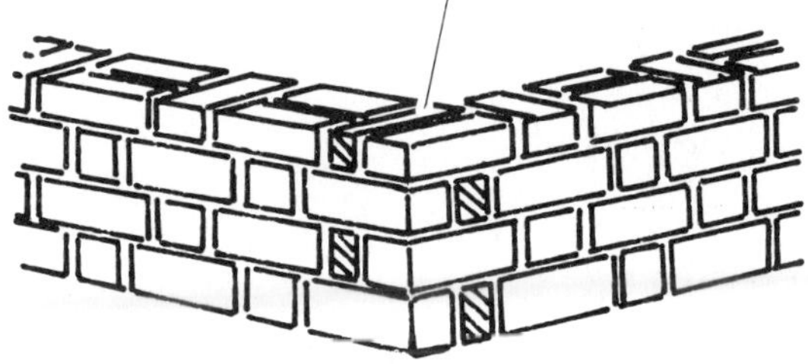

Use of closers in decorative bond brick walls (closer bricks are shaded)

Fig. 7.25 *Three examples of header bonded double walls.*

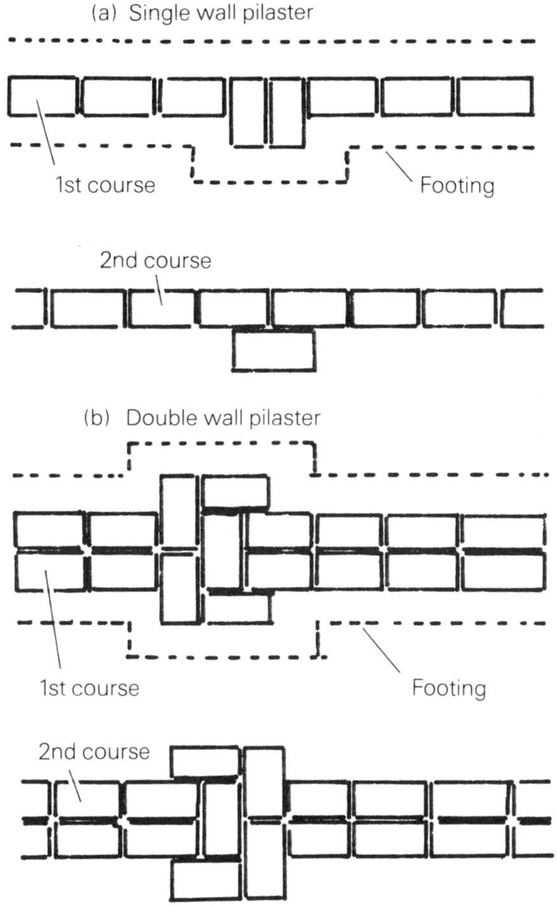

Fig. 7.26 *Pilasters for brick walls. Third and subsequent courses will alternate designs of 1st and 2nd courses.*

COPING STONES

These provide a neat finish to all kinds of wall described above, unless of course, you wish to fill block or cavity walls with earth for planting flowers. They also give the wall a much more weatherproof finish. The most popular form of coping stones are the 'saddlebacks', which are available at most builders' merchants and are easy to lay. They come in various sizes to suit the different blocks. Consult your dealer for details. Lay one on either end of the completed wall on a thin mortar bed that you have raised into two ridges by drawing the trowel down the middle. Ensure that there is an equal overhang (Fig. 7.27a) on either side of the block below. Run out the builder's line between them off the back edge, and lay the copings to the line (Fig. 7.27b). You may then point between the stones if required. To cut coping stones see Cutting blocks, p. 82.

Alternative ways to cap brick cavity or hollow block walls are either to use a mortar finish as shown in Fig. 7.28a or by a row of header bricks laid on edge, Fig. 7.28b. In the first case, expanded metal is laid along the wall under the top course and the gaps or cavity in the top course filled with mortar. For the second method you first place the bricks on edge along the course and cut the last brick to fit the exact length. Remove the bricks and re-lay on a mortar bed, placing each successive brick in position with a good

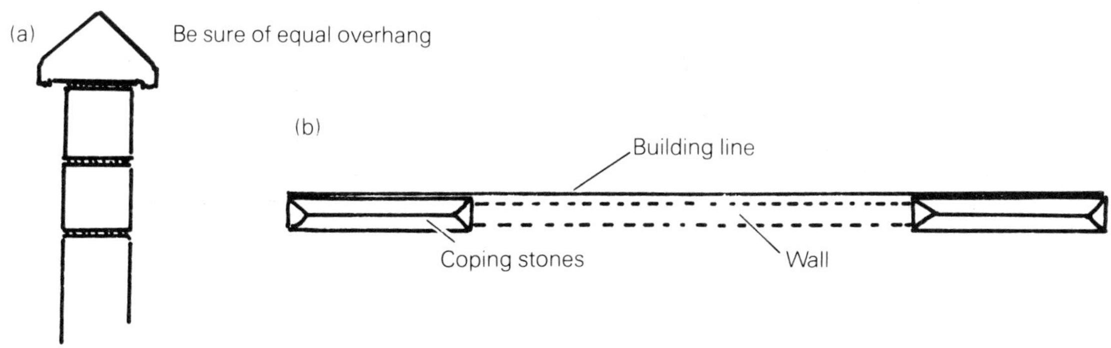

Fig. 7.27 *Laying coping stones.*

slice of mortar on its face. (Check as you go along that you are maintaining a uniform joint thickness.) Position the cut brick two or three units from the end to give a neater finish.

RENDERING

To render

When the wall, block or brick, is finished and the mortar is dry, it can now be rendered if required. Rendering is spreading a 0.7 cm ($\frac{1}{4}$ in) thick layer of mortar all over the face of the wall (or faces on a dividing wall), and giving the mortar a uniform finish, either smooth, brushed with a sponge, or marked with a trowel. A very plastic, sticky mix is required. Glues or bonding agents are available from builders' merchants which make better mixes for big jobs.

What you will need

1 : 4 mortar mix, with a generous quantity of plasticizer. 1 tonne (1 ton) of sand will cover 58 sq m (70 sq yd) of wall at 0.7 cm ($\frac{1}{4}$ in) thick. Calculate the area of the wall you wish to render, and, using the above figures, work out your sand and cement requirements.

To apply

Before mixing the mortar prepare the wall by brushing any loose material or dust off the face and by placing a long board or plastic sheeting along the bottom of the wall to catch the droppings. Mix the mortar and place it on a clean spot-board near the wall. Take a good-sized blob of mortar on a steel float and, starting along the top, spread the mortar on to the wall with a single, smooth stroke. Repeat over the entire face of the wall. Smooth the finish out to an overall uniform depth on completion. When this coat is dry (leave at least one day) repeat, giving the wall another coat for strength if required.

Note 1. Care should be taken when rendering to check that the mortar is not sliding down the wall and 'bellying out' at the bottom. Keep an eye on the areas you have covered and go back smoothing out any suspect places. To be effective and long-lasting the render must be well stuck to the wall. 'Bellying-out' occurs if the mortar is too wet or if insufficient pressure is used when applying. Do not attempt to render a new wall until it is well set.

Note 2. If you wish to render the surface of an old wall or if you are rendering a new wall in dry weather conditions, it will help the render to stick and make the job easier if you give the wall a good soaking with a garden hose. Spray the wall surface until the water stops soaking in.

When the rendering has been allowed to 'go off' for an hour or so it can then be sponged or marked as required. This should not be attempted too soon after application, since it will pull the mortar off, nor should the mortar be allowed to dry completely since this will make marking it very difficult.

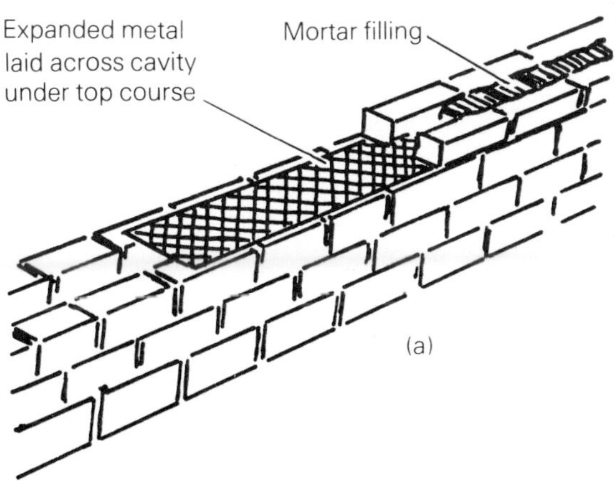

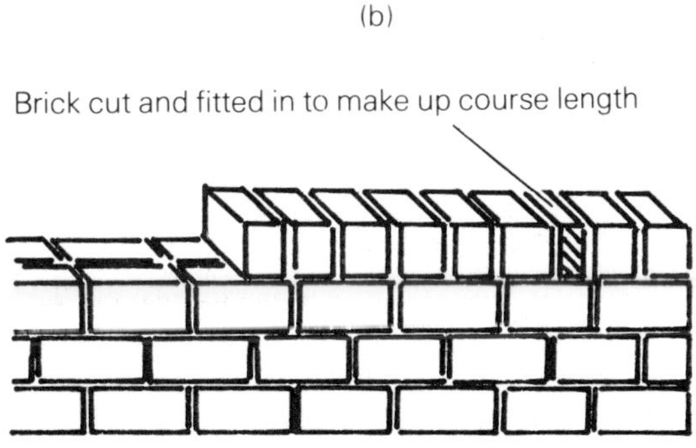

Fig. 7.28 *(a) Capping a cavity wall.*
(b) Capping a double wall with on edge headers.

5 Stone walls

Stone walls have long been one of the most prominent features of our countryside. The products of endless labour and often great skill, they represent for many people the essence of traditional building. This may go a long way to explain why they are so popular a feature in suburban gardens; a stone wall of colour and texture sympathetic to the house or buildings associated with it, blends naturally with its surroundings (Plates 5 & 6) and brings a feeling of the countryside into town gardens. Carefully planned and sympathetically blended, they can greatly enhance a garden, but overdone or built with unsuitable stone they can easily look out of place, self-consciously 'twee' and even rather absurd. Small gardens which seem to be bursting apart with huge stone features, walls or rock gardens that dominate everything around them will never look natural or uncontrived. It is a shame but it illustrates the main problem with stone walls: the actual construction, whatever the type of wall, is not in fact very difficult but finding suitable stone is.

There are two basic types of stone that can be used. First, the actual 'walling stone' which has been 'dressed' at the quarry. 'Dressing' means that the corners have been squared and the best side 'flattened' into a face (Fig. 7.29). Thus the stones are of more or less regular shapes and have at least one good 'face' which is used on the outside. Using this kind of stone the builder can produce a regular 'coursed' wall, i.e. with the stones lying in rough courses like bricks. It is with this kind of stone that most traditional walls were built. However, it is now very hard to come by dressed stone in reasonable quantities and it is usually rather expensive; very few quarries produce it on a regular basis, if at all. This means that people have to use the second type of stone available: rough quarry stone. This is commercially available at most quarries and often at garden centres etc., and is a fraction of the price of dressed stone. It is rough, undressed stone which is built together in an irregular, uncoursed wall, which will not have the same regular-faced effect as dressed stone. This is not to say that rough stone is not suitable for garden walls, just that more care is needed to blend the stones. Check before ordering on the average sizes of the stones available and avoid getting over-large ones. Large, undressed stones will be needed, however, if you are constructing rockeries or stone features, see p. 150.

Basically then, a wall built of dressed stone will tend to be coursed and more regular, and a rough stone wall will tend to be uncoursed and less patterned. There are slight differences in approach to these two types of wall so reference should be made to the building technique suitable for the type of stone you manage to acquire. When looking for stone use the telephone directory for addresses of quarries or possible suppliers. Dressed stone is sometimes available from demolition sites or from farmers who are removing a wall. It is well worth asking such people – you never know your luck.

Note 1. The batter of the wall faces is most important; dividing walls taper towards the top. To check this while building, construct a batter gauge, see p. 87. Walls over 1.2 m (4 ft) high of either sort, divider or retainer, need a batter for strength. They also look better when finished.

Note 2. Just as for concrete block or brick walls, footings of some description will be necessary; see Table 7.1, p. 77. The corners, if any, should be built up first.

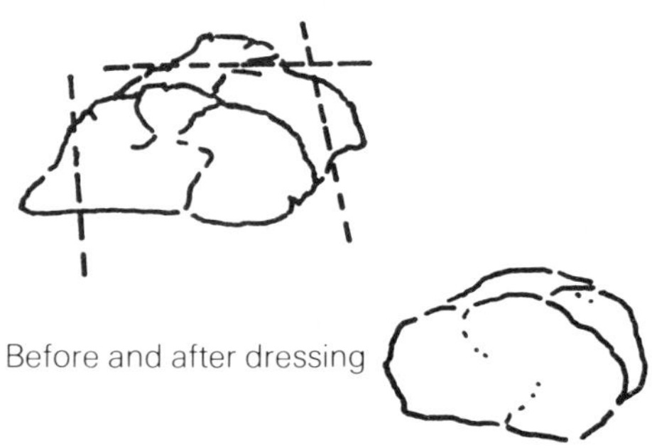

Fig. 7.29 *'Dressing' stone.*

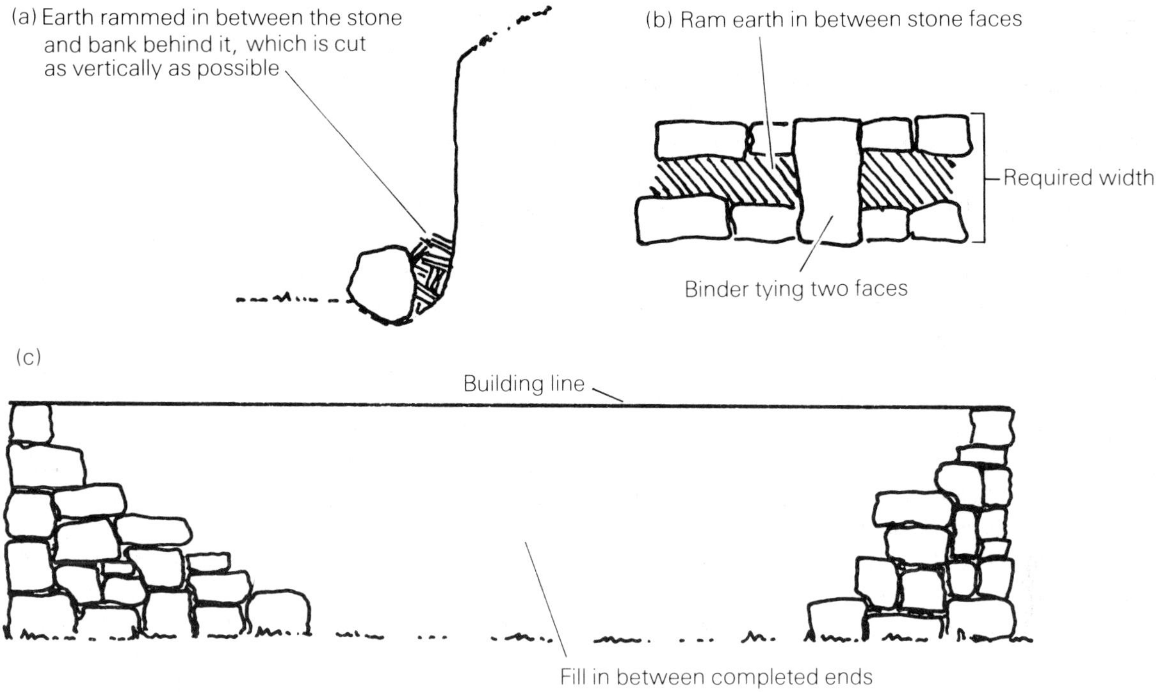

Fig. 7.30 *Coursed stone wells. (a) Commencement of retaining wall. (b) Commencement of dividing wall. (c) Use of building line.*

DRY-STONE WALLS

A dry-stone wall is one where no mortar is used. The stones are built carefully together and the spaces between them filled with rammed earth. These are very suitable for gardens, being ideal for low retainers and various types of feature; they may also be built with gaps in their faces suitable for planting wall flowers in. Where there is a lot of weight on the wall and strength is needed, i.e. retaining walls over 1 m (3 ft 6 in), semi-dry or cemented walls are more suitable.

1 COURSED DRY-STONE WALL

This technique is suitable for wall building with dressed stone. Low terraces and flower-bed borders look particularly pleasant built in this manner. Work out first what kind of wall you require, divider or retainer, and using Table 7.1, see p. 77, check the type of footing required.

What you will need

Stone. Shovel. Rammer. Builder's line. Spirit-level.

Measuring up

Work out the height, length and width (see below) required, i.e. divider or retainer, and then the total area. Stone weighs approximately 1660 kg per cu m (25 cwt per cu yd). Use this figure to work out your stone requirement, e.g. a 90 × 90 × 45 cm (3 × 3 × $1\frac{1}{2}$ ft) section of wall would use 830 kg (12 cwt) of stone. See Table 7.1 for footing requirements.

To build

Clear the grass and vegetable soil from the line of the wall, dig and lay footings if required. Build up the two ends, using larger stones if possible, to a height of about 45 cm (1 ft 6 in). If the wall is a retainer place stones as close to the bank as possible making a tight fit (Fig. 7.30a). As each stone is laid, ram loose earth down behind it until the stone is firmly held. When the stone is firm place another beside it and ram firm. Then place one on top of them and ram earth around it. Continue to fill in along the line of wall.

If the wall is a divider, work out how wide the base should be in relation to the finished wall height from Table 7.1, p. 77. Place two stones with their faces outward, at the required distance apart across the width. Ram earth in between them (on wide walls small stones can also be used as filler). Continue to build up the two faces as for retaining walls, ramming earth and small stones in between them (Fig. 7.30b). At intervals along each course lay a binding stone across to tie both faces together.

When you have two ends, stretch the builder's line between the top outside edges. (A retainer requires one line, a divider two lines.) Now, using the line as a guide, fill the gap between the two ends, up to the level of the line, placing stones and filling the gaps with earth (Fig. 7.30c).

When this is complete repeat the process, building up the corners 45 cm (1 ft 6 in), stretching the line between them, and filling in the gap until the required wall height is reached.

Note 1. If a batter is required check it every two or three courses.

Note 2. Every so often a small stone may be left out and the gap filled with earth. This will enable you to insert wall flowers or creepers later on. If you have the plants at the time of building it is an idea to insert them as you go along, as this will minimize any disturbance.

2 UNCOURSED STONE WALLS (UNDRESSED STONE)

The actual building technique, placing stones and ramming earth, is the same as above but the preparation for this kind of wall is slightly different to suit the type of stone. Unlike dressed stone, rough stones come in all shapes and sizes, some better than others. To avoid the common error of running out of good stones halfway through a wall, it is a good idea to sort out the stones before starting.

When you have the footing ready, with all vegetable soil and grasses removed, sort the stone into a number of heaps along the line of the wall. Each heap should have a fair share of the largest, smallest, good and bad stones. When building, use each heap for the section of wall it faces. This will ensure a good spread of stone types (Fig. 7.31).

Quantities should be estimated in the same way as for dressed stone, and the footing requirements worked out from Table 7.1 as above. For tools and measuring up see above.

To build

Place the largest stone of each heap along the line of the wall and do a quick visual check for straightness (Fig. 7.32a). Repeat on the other side if you are building a divider. When positioning these and subsequent stones, try them in a number of positions until you find the side they sit best on or the side that presents the best face.

Now, using a variety of sizes, fill in between them, placing stones and ramming

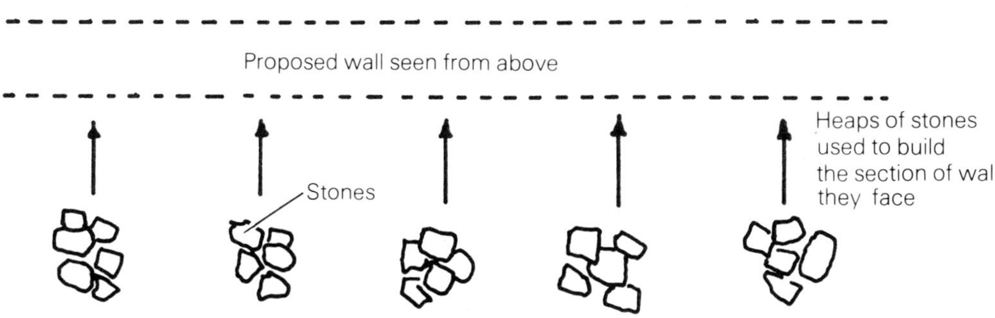

Fig. 7.31 *Uncoursed stone wall : preparation.*

the earth, up and along in pyramid shapes (Fig. 7.32b). Check every so often that the face of the wall is relatively straight and that there is the required batter.

When this first phase is complete, place the largest remaining stones in the heaps at the lowest point opposite them, and build up with smaller stones into pyramids again, checking the line of the face and batter (Fig. 7.32c). Carry on in this way until the tops of the pyramids reach the required height. When this happens fill in the gaps between them to complete the wall (Fig. 7.32d).

Using this system there will be a good, even spread of stone quality and the majority of the largest stones will be in the bottom half of the wall; this not only adds strength to the wall, but also tends to look neater when completed. As with coursed walls, small stones may be left out at various points to create gaps for planting later.

SEMI-DRY STONE WALLS

Where added strength is required, either on high walls over 1.2 m (4 ft), or on steep sites, without losing the 'dry-stone' effect 'semi-dry' stone walls can be used. These are built in exactly the same way as dry-stone walls, whether coursed or uncoursed, divider or retainer, with the difference that a mortar mix is used to replace the rammed earth in the middle of the wall. The idea is to construct a cemented wall where no cement shows on the outside. With careful use of the mortar it is possible to build a wall to look completely 'dry', with only the back edges of the face stones in contact with the cement. It is, however, a much stronger wall. A cement mixer will help if the wall is to be a large one.

What you will need

Stone. Building sand. Cement. Shovel. Builder's line. Trowel.

Measuring up

Estimate stone quantities as for dry-stone walls (see p. 95). Sand for mortar mix: use about 30% (weight) of the total weight of stone used. Mortar mix should be 1 : 4. Use this ratio to estimate the cement requirement.

To build

Build as for dry-stone walls (sort out the stone and build in pyramids), but place blobs

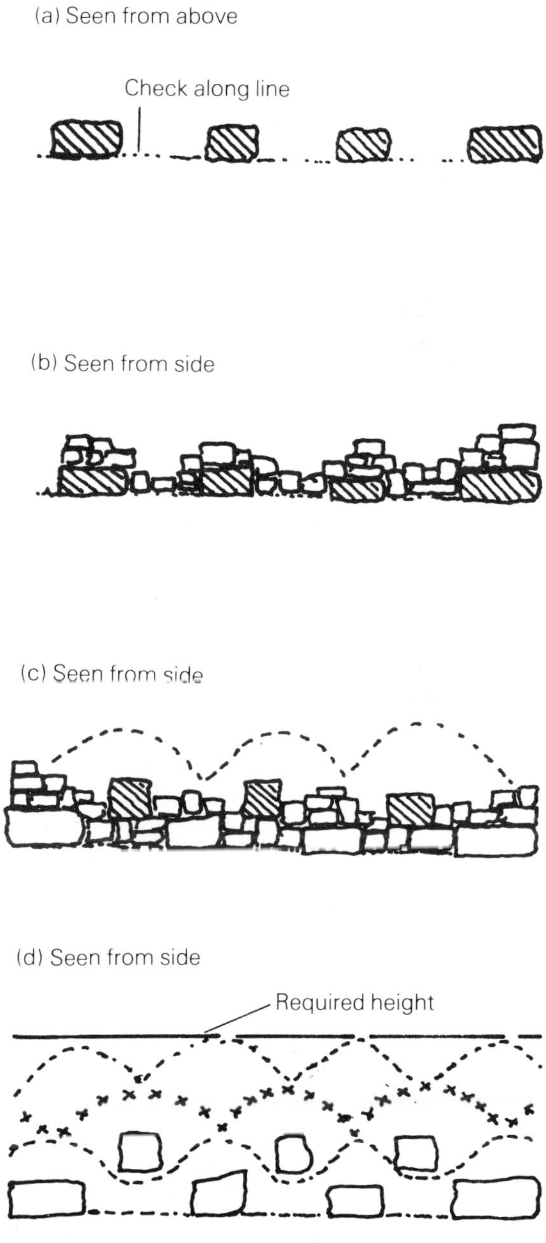

Fig. 7.32 *Uncoursed stone wall: stages in building.*

of mortar behind the stones, or between faces of a divider. Ensure that each stone is well gripped by the mortar and that none of the mix oozes out on to the face of the wall. On wide walls small stones can be used as additional filler (Fig. 7.33). This will save mortar.

Note If the walls, dry or semi-dry, run along beside paths, they can be given extra stability by ensuring that the base of the wall comes below the finished level of the path (Fig. 7.34). In this way the bulk of the path helps anchor the wall. This is particularly useful for retainers.

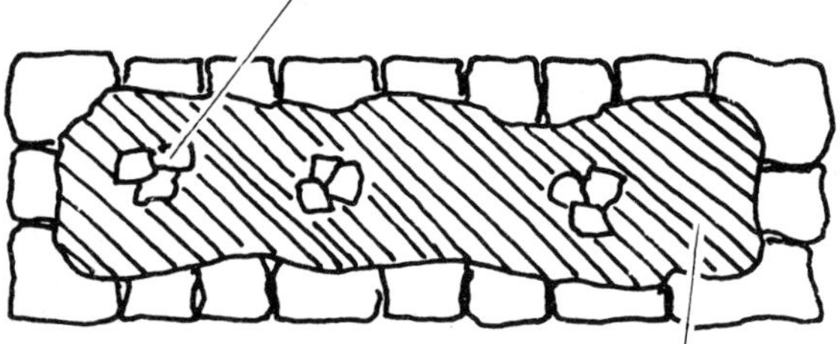

Fig. 7.33 *Semi-dry dividing stone wall showing mortar mix in middle in contact with back edges of face stones.*

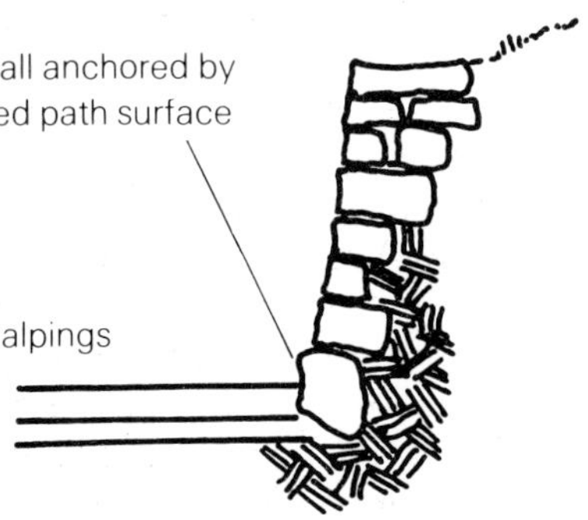

Fig. 7.34 *Additional support for a retaining wall.*

CEMENTED STONE WALLS

Where very large walls are required, for weight-bearing etc., the wall can be built as for 'semi-dry' walls using a mortar mix, and then pointed on completion along the face or faces. This is the strongest form of stone wall. The building is the same as for above, but mortar should also be put around the face stones, not just behind them. The excess mix that has oozed out on to the face of the wall as stones are placed on top of each other can be removed when the pointing is done. 'Rough' pointing is most suitable for stone walls (p. 88).

Note Reinforcing bars can be used with either dry or cemented walls; for the former they are driven into the earth footings and for the latter they are set into the concrete footings. For details see p. 81.

WOODEN RETAINERS

If suitable materials (see below) are available, wooden retainers do have a place in the garden, although the cost of timber and their relatively short life compared to stone or masonry walls points against them. Generally the posts should be set in trenches and held with concrete filled up around them.

Materials: Railway sleepers. Telephone or electricity poles. Treated softwood or split hardwood stakes.

8 Hedges

Their unique combination of visual appeal and important screening qualities have assured hedges of a permanent place in garden layouts, and while they might seem to fall outside the scope of this book, we have included them here because, whether used on their own or in combination with fences and walls, they must be allowed for when a garden layout is being planned.

A second reason for including them is that in well-established gardens there may be a length of hedge that has been neglected, growing too large or straggly for your present needs, or an alteration in the garden layout that requires a hedge to be brought back under control. Simply cutting the top off a hedge, or trimming it back, will not necessarily cause what is left to fill out and take on a well-formed shape; further measures may well be necessary. Thus we also cover in this chapter techniques for restoring old hedges to good order, work that is just as important for creating the kind of garden you want as laying paths or building walls.

1 New hedges

Using a hedge around part or all of the garden instead of a fence or wall has a number of distinct advantages. In the first place, the hedging plants (in addition to the seasonal delights of colour changes, flowers and berries) bring a harmony to the garden, blending with the general shapes and colours to form a natural backdrop for the other garden plants that neither fences nor walls can match. They will also attract wildlife, particularly birds, to the garden by providing roosts, food and nesting places. Secondly, it has been shown that a good, bushy hedge (and here the bulk below 1.8 m (6 ft) is important) can play a significant part in cutting down outside noise, while at the same time acting as an efficient screen and windbreak, creating sheltered, private areas in the garden.

On the other hand, it is important to be aware while planning the garden that some hedging plants (quickthorn, for example) are best planted in double rows, and that all hedges need plenty of room for their roots, and should be accessible for regular management once grown. The latter points are particularly important if the hedge is to be planted along the back of a flowerbed, since the root systems will compete for nourishment with the flowers, while weeds and brambles will flourish beneath it. Careful planning, providing space for everything, and regular maintenance should, however, overcome these problems.

Apart from using hedges on their own, one very effective arrangement which combines the advantages of both is to plant them along the inside of a wall or fence. This gives you a solid barrier on the outside, while inside the hedge provides height, which will save on fence or walling materials, depth, which will increase the screening effect, and more inter-

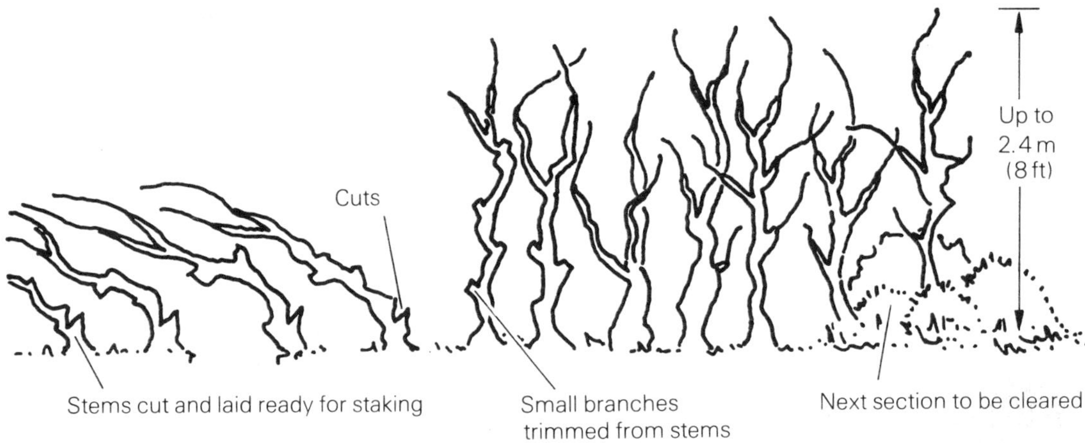

Fig. 8.1 *Preparing and laying a hedge.*

esting perspectives from the house and garden. A further development of this, if you are building a wall or erecting panels with gravel boards, is to build earth up along the inside and plant a low hedge on top. This way you maintain the height of the barrier, while at the same time providing sites for rockeries, small waterfalls and backdrops for water features.

For further ideas on combining fences with hedges and climbing plants see pp. 70 and 150.

When choosing your hedging plants, be sure first to have a clear idea of what you want and exactly how much space is available, and second, to spend some time looking at nursery catalogues, and visiting gardens and garden centres. The range of plants that can be used for hedging is surprisingly wide and it could be that you will find something more suited to your particular needs than the obvious and traditional choices.

2 Restoring hedges

The problem with hedges that have been neglected and allowed to run wild is that, while the top branches grow up and out, the base dies away, starved of light and smothered by weeds and brambles. Thus gaps begin to appear, and the hedge loses its main purpose – good bush growth below 1.8 m (6 ft).

The exact extent of the treatment required to encourage new, healthy growth and restore the bulk of the hedge will depend on: (1) how badly it has become overgrown; (2) the amount of gaps that have formed and the health of the individual plants and (3) the extent to which the hedging plants have grown out of shape. To find out these things and to rectify them, work should proceed in the steps outlined below.

Note The work outlined below should be carried out between March–May or September–October. It should not be attempted at times of growth or when there is a likelihood of heavy frosts.

(1) Trimming and clearing Trimming and clearing the hedge represents the first stage of the work, and where the hedge is in fairly good condition, this alone may be sufficient. The work should aim to clear the base and body of the hedge of all weed and bramble growth, to cut out all dead or sickly hedge plants and branches and cut the outgrowth of the hedge, down and back, until it takes on the required proportions. Trimming should be done where possible with single, upward strokes.

(2) Re-planting If, when trimmed, the hedge has a few distinct gaps where dead

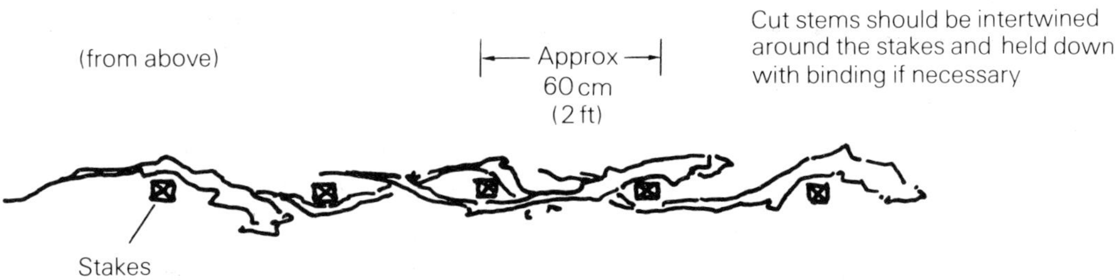

Fig. 8.2 *Staking the hedge.*

plants have been removed, these should now be filled with replacement plants. It is important before planting new specimens to clear the hedge bottom of debris and decayed wood, and if the soil is particularly poor to replace it with fresh, well-composted earth.

(3) **Laying** Some, hedges, however, will have grown so straggly and out of proportion that neither trimming nor re-planting will solve the problem. If, when cleared, the hedge is full of gaps at the base while the upper growth has reached about 2.4 or 3.6 m (8–12 ft), an alternative to removing the whole hedge and starting again is to 'lay' it. This is a process whereby the tall stems are cut (enough to be bent over without breaking off) and laid down along the line of the hedge, interwoven between stakes, thereby forming new bulk for the hedge, re-shaping it and filling in the gaps. Any stems between 2.4 and 3.6 m (8 and 12 ft) and 5–10 cm (2–4 in) thick are suitable for laying provided they are strong and healthy. The laying procedure which should be done during the winter months and never at times of growth is described below.

LAYING PROCEDURE

What you will need

1.5 m × 5 × 4 cm (5 ft × 2 × $1\frac{1}{2}$ in) hedging stakes. (These are available from builders' merchants and some garden centres, and the exact dimensions will alter from area to area.) Estimate stakes at one every 60 cm (2 ft). Bill-hook or small axe. Rubber Maul. Heavy leather gloves.

To lay

1 Clear hedge as for above.

2 Fig. 8.1: Cut stems (between 15–30 cm (6 in–1 ft) from the ground) about three-quarters of the way through with a firm, downward stroke. Bend stem over to an angle of about 30°. Do not twist them, and on slopes always lay them uphill.

3 Fig. 8.2: After you have cut and laid several stems, go back along the hedge driving a stake in every 60 cm (2 ft) along the middle of the hedge. Work the stakes down in between the laid stems and knock them into the ground (approx. 30 cm (1 ft)) with the maul. The stems are thus held in place, interwoven round the stakes.

4 When the laying is complete and the stakes are in position, check that all the stems are lying properly, binding any that spring loose to the stakes, and cut off any excess stake length.

The hedge should now be left alone until new growth starts and the plants begins to fill out again. Once fresh growth is well established, trim the hedge regularly.

9 Gates

Hanging gates requires precision and concentration but is not otherwise difficult. There are a lot of different factors and measurements to be taken into consideration whilst working, and a loss of concentration can result in uneven gates, gates that will not shut properly, gates that stick at one point and so on. This should not, however, put you off attempting to hang gates; a steady, step-by-step approach and a thorough reading of this chapter should remove all difficulties.

There are two basic types of gate: wooden and metal, but there are, of course, many different designs and sizes. First, you should deliberate not on what design to have, but on how many (double or single gates) you want, where exactly to put them and which way the gates will open. If the site is flat you should have no problems, choose double or single gates as preferred. If, however, there is a slope through the gateway of more than 5 cm (2 in) in the proposed length of gate when in the open position, you will need double gates (i.e. shorter individual lengths), or you should re-locate the gate to open the other way. Bear in mind also that gates on a road or footpath should, if possible, open inwards and so avoid being a potential hazard. Spend some time on these questions, since a correct decision now will make things much easier when you come to install the gates.

Having established how many gates you require and exactly where they, or it, will go, you can then decide which type to install. It is really a matter of taste and of blending the gate in with existing fences or walls. Metal gates tend to look better with block walls, while wooden ones look better with brick, stone or rails. In terms of durability there is not much between them, but for factory-made gates, metal ones are probably cheaper. To help you choose a design, and particularly if you want to make your own gates, we have included a number of alternatives at the end of this chapter.

It is considerably quicker to hang metal gates, since when you buy them they come complete with hinges, fasteners and bolts already in place (Fig. 9.1a). Wooden gates, on the other hand, need all these accessories fitting to them as you go along; not difficult but time consuming (Fig. 9.1b). The technique described below for hanging wooden gates is also applicable to ready-made morticed gates. Follow the same procedure for home-made gates, making allowances for different dimensions.

Note 1. If the driveway etc. is at an angle to the gate, then metal gates may make life easier since they allow for a swing of over 90° either way round the post (Fig. 9.1c). Wooden gates will have to be hung on the opening side of the post to give sufficient swing.

Note 2. It is advisable with all types of gate to hang them slightly high in the middle to allow for natural sag in the materials and the effects of time (Fig. 9.1d).

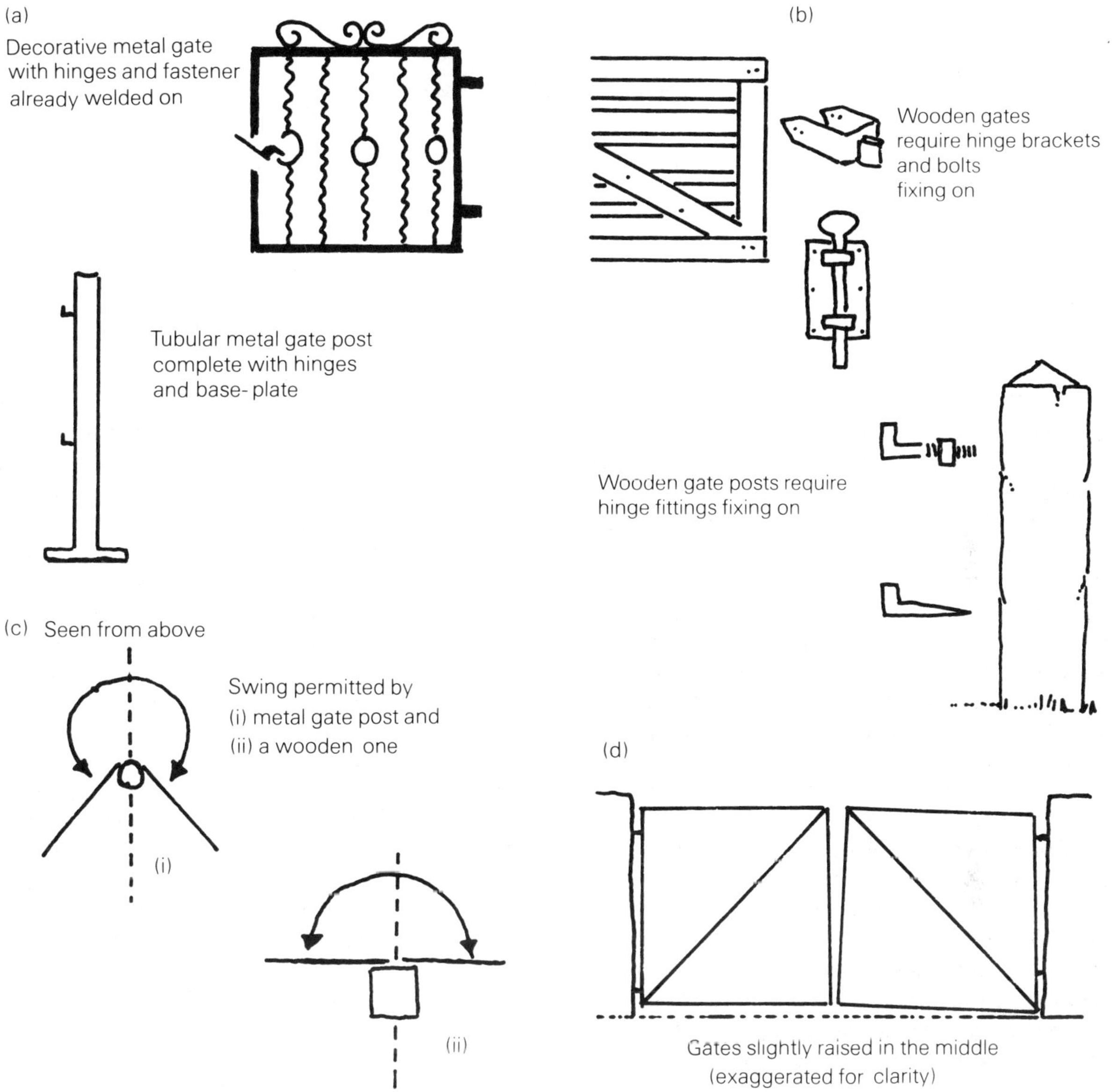

Fig. 9.1 *Metal and wooden gates : comparison of fittings and 'swings'.*

1 Metal gates

Decide first whether to have double or single gates: a matter of taste unless the ground is sloping (see p. 102).

What you will need

Gate(s). Posts (gates and posts should be supplied together). 76 kg (1½ cwt) of concrete mix (see p. 14) per post hole. Pickaxe. Shovel. Spirit-level. Tape-measure. Small 8 cm (3 in) wood block. Rammer.

Measuring up

When measuring width of gate allow for (a) two post widths, (b) 4 cm (1½ in) gap between

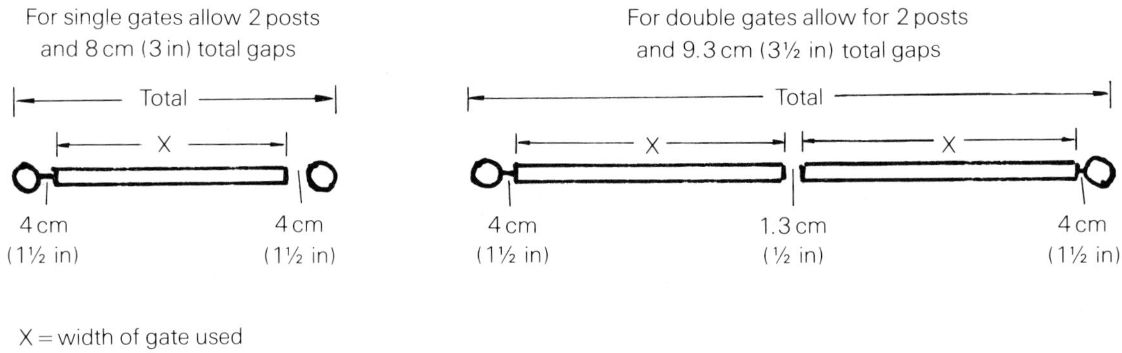

Fig. 9.2 *Single and double gates : measuring the horizontal gaps.*

gate and posts (either end for single gates) and (c) an additional 1.3 cm ($\frac{1}{2}$ in) gap in the middle for double gates (Fig. 9.2).

Always try to measure from a fixed point, i.e. the end of a wall, or, if there is none, decide where one post will be and measure from there. This avoids unnecessary inaccuracies.

Note Gates must clear the ground along their whole lengths. Therefore always, on any gate, allow at least a 8 cm (3 in) clearance underneath gate when closed.

To hang

Having determined and allowed for any slope in the ground, calculate the height of the hinges above ground level. To do this measure the distance between the bottom hinge on the gate to the bottom of the gate, X, and add 8 cm (3 in) for ground clearance. The total, Y, will now be used to fix the gate post at the required height (Fig. 9.3).

Step 1 Excavate hole (Table 9.1, see p. 104) for first post. Holes should be at least 45 × 45 cm ($1\frac{1}{2} \times 1\frac{1}{2}$ ft). Place post in hole and work concrete mix under the post until the bottom hinge fitting is at the required height, Y, above ground level (Fig. 9.4). Always use concrete.

Step 2 Hang gate on post and prop post in upright position. Place 8 cm (3 in) wooden block under the free end of the gate. Fill about half the hole with concrete to give additional support while leaving room for adjustments (Fig. 9.5).

Step 3 For double gates repeat the operation for the other gate, measuring position of second post from that already fixed. See 'Measuring up' for distances to be taken into account when measuring the width of a gateway.

Step 4 When the gate(s) are hung and temporarily blocked, adjust the posts until the gates are square and level with each other, check that there is a 1.25 cm ($\frac{1}{2}$ in) gap in the middle between double gates, top and bottom. When satisfied, level up the posts, fill up the holes with concrete, ram the concrete tight, re-check posts and gates, make any necessary adjustments and leave with the blocks and props in position.

Note Do not, if possible, use or remove the gate(s) until the concrete has set, i.e. at least two days. Then, after the posts have firmly set, fit any additional features such as locks, or stop-plate for double gates.

Table 9.1 Calculating the depth of post holes

Height of post above ground level, up to :		*Depth of post below ground level*	
m	ft	m	ft
0.90	3	0.75	$2\frac{1}{2}$
1.2	4	0.83	$2\frac{3}{4}$
1.5	5	0.90	3

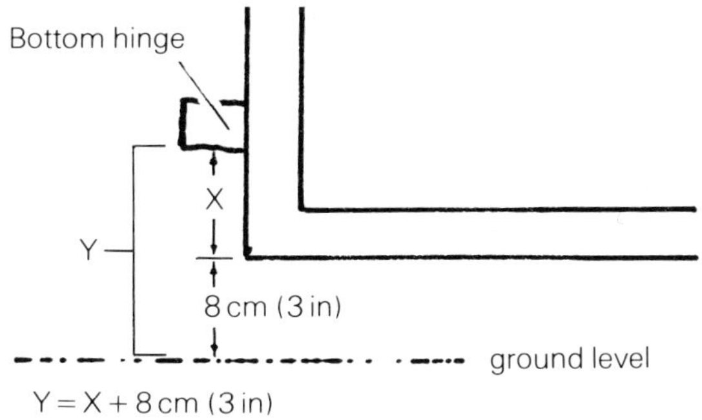

Fig. 9.3 *Calculating height of hinges above ground level.*

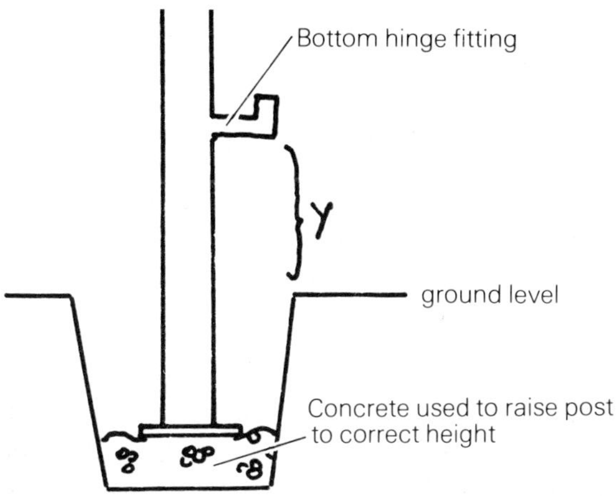

Fig. 9.4 *Erecting metal post.*

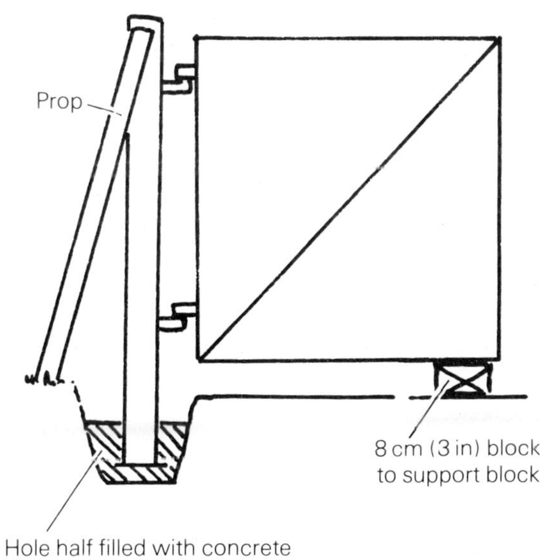

Fig. 9.5 *Hanging the gate on the post.*

2 Wooden gates

Three general points first:

1 Wooden gates will inevitably swell or sink a bit over the years. To compensate for this happening allow a slightly larger gap between double gates, i.e. 2 cm ($\frac{3}{4}$ in).

2 Square wooden gate posts allow a swing of 90°. If this is insufficient for your purposes it is advisable to position the hinges on the side of the post you want the gate(s) to open on.

3 Wooden gates, especially good, solid oak ones, are rather heavy and awkward and we therefore advise using an assistant to hang the gates and to help support them while you make any adjustments.

What you will need

Gates. Posts. Post hinge fittings. Gate hinge brackets and closing mechanisms. 75 kg ($1\frac{1}{2}$ cwt) of concrete per post hole. Shovel. Pickaxe. Spirit-level. Tape-measure. Wood auger or electric drill (the bits should be of slightly smaller diameter than the holes in the post hinge fittings). Spanners (to suit bolt sizes). Heavy carpenter's or lump hammer.

Measuring up

Allow gaps across width as for metal gates (see p. 104). Always try to measure from a fixed point. (When you order the gates the dealer should supply the correct posts and all necessary fittings and bolts. Check that he will do so before ordering.) If using home-made gates work out post lengths from Table 9.1 (p. 104) and order hinges and fittings from a hardware store or builders' merchant.

To hang

Step 1 To fix gate brackets on to gate: position brackets on upright, evenly spaced top and bottom and mark bolt holes. Remove brackets and drill out the holes. Re-position brackets and fix with bolts. Screw up tight (Fig. 9.6).

Step 2 Work out depth of bottom of gate

post below ground level (see Table 9.1) and mark ground level on the post (Fig. 9.6b). (A rough check to see that the mark is in the right place: height of post *above* ground will be height of gate plus 15 cm (6 in).)

Step 3 Work out position of bottom hinge fitting on post above the ground-level mark, i.e. position of bottom hinge fitting above ground-level mark will be X (see p. 104) plus 8 cm (3 in), (Fig. 9.7a). The bottom hinge fitting is pointed at one end to be driven into the post. Work out and mark the position of this hinge in the middle of the post (either on the front face or on one side, depending on your opening requirements) and drill a hole of slightly smaller diameter than the fitting a couple of centimetres deep. Place fitting in the hole and hammer it home until it is tight and firm. Check it every few centimetres to ensure that it is going in upright and not turning to either side.

Step 4 The top hinge fitting is a modified bolt (Fig. 9.7b) which is fitted through the gate post and screwed tight. To fit: measure distance between the hinge brackets on the gate and reading off the bottom hinge on the post, mark position of the top one using this measurement. Before drilling this hole out, use a spirit-level to position the mark directly over the bottom hinge. Drill out the hole (of

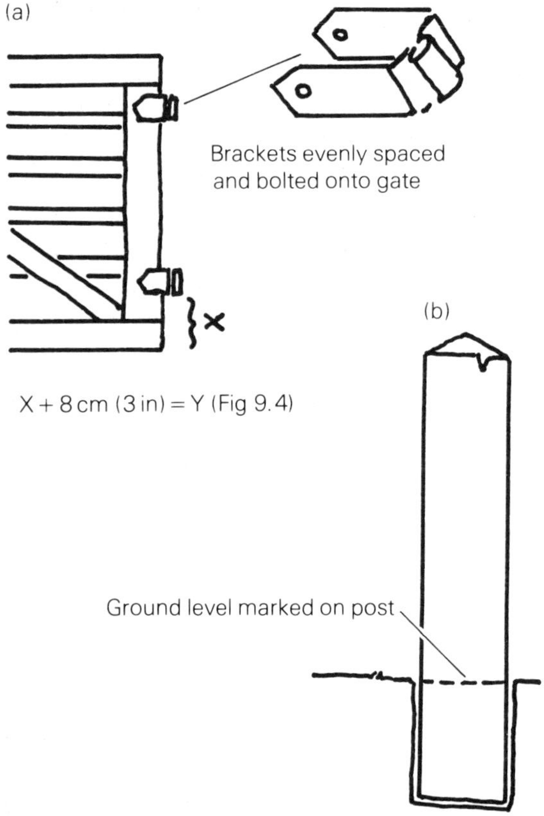

Fig. 9.6 *Wooden gates:*
(a) Fixing gate brackets.
(b) Fixing position of post.

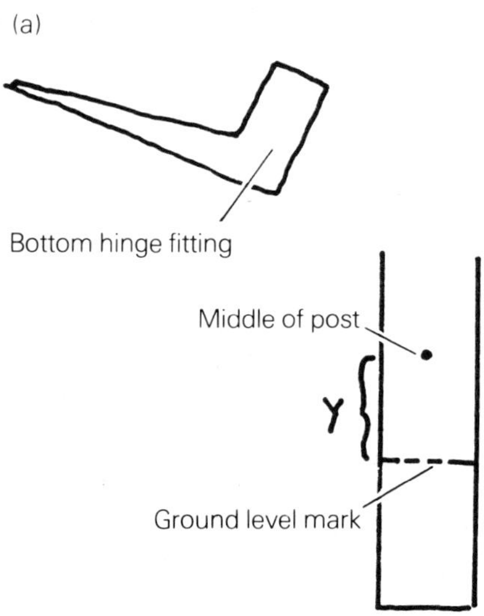

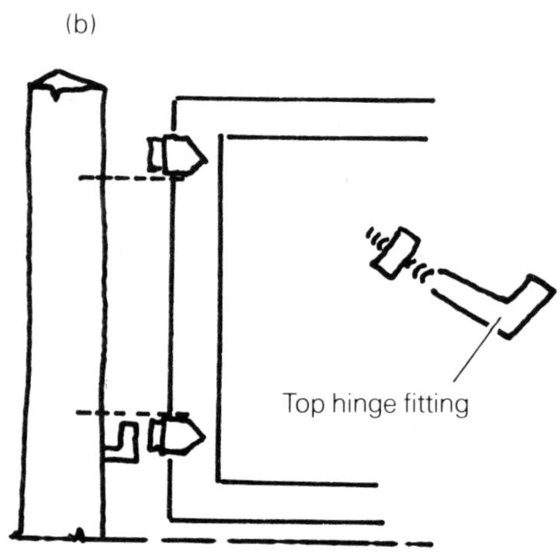

Fig. 9.7 *Wooden gates: positioning top and bottom hinges.*

slightly smaller diameter than the bolt) and hammer the fitting through. Bolt up tight.

Step 5 Once all the hinges and brackets are in position you can erect the posts and hang the gates. This procedure is the same as for hanging metal gates (see p. 105). Fit all locks and catches once the concrete is dry.

Note 1. If you are using braced wooden gates be sure to hang them the right way up (see below).

Note 2. If you are hanging wooden or metal gates over 1.2 m (4 ft) long on free-standing brick or block posts, be sure the posts are sufficiently reinforced. If they are not, the weight of the gates, particularly if anyone swings on them, may well snap the post off just below the bottom hinge bracket. The best way to prevent this is to set a reinforcing bar into the concrete footing, build the post around it and then fill up the middle with concrete when the masonry has set. If, however, the post comes at the end of a length of wall make sure it is well tied into the courses of the wall. In either case you should build the hinge brackets in as work progresses. (For positioning hinge brackets see p. 106.)

Making your own gates (wooden)

Two points before starting:

1 When making your own gates it is worth the extra cost to buy good-quality timber. It should be well seasoned and preferably treated with some kind of preservative. If it is not you should creosote or paint it. If your timber is selected carefully the gate will be less prone to warping or generally going out of shape and should have a very reasonable lifetime.

2 The second point is that, as mentioned in the introduction to this chapter, accuracy in measuring is essential if the gate is to fit properly and look good when hung. To ensure this be careful not only to measure and mark the timber properly, but also, for the braces in the frame to work efficiently (see below), to be as accurate as possible when cutting the timber.

The biggest problem with gates, particularly those over 1.2 m (4 ft) is that, as time passes the head of the gate (see Fig. 9.8) starts to drop, pulling the gate out of shape. Thus, the most important part of the gate's design is the brace (Fig. 9.8) which is fitted diagonally across the frame to help keep the head of the gate up. To do this the brace should always be fitted to the bottom of the frame at the heel end and to the top at the head end (Fig. 9.8). (This is also true of braced doors which should be hung from the side at the bottom ends of the braces.) Once the braced frame (or 'z' frame) has been constructed a variety of materials can be used for

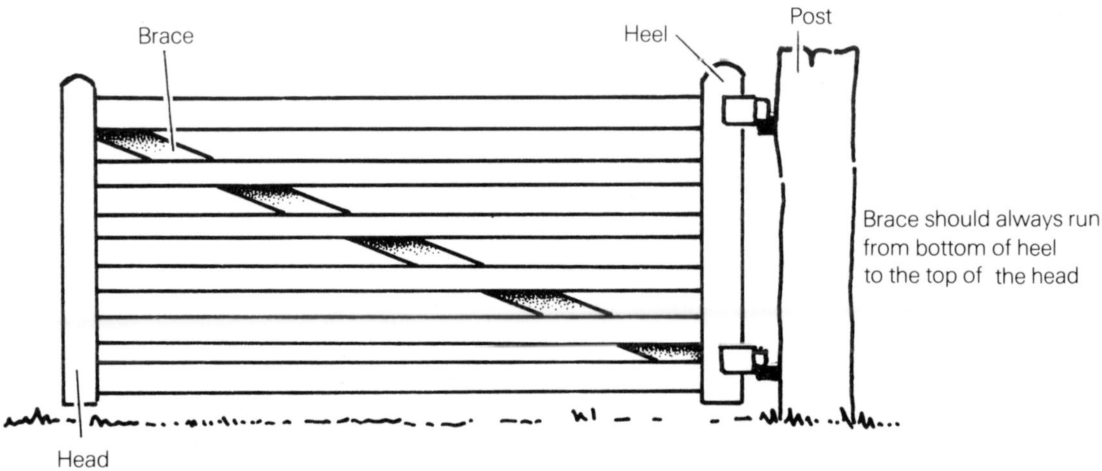

Fig. 9.8 *Components of a braced gate.*

the face of the gate, either matching a fence if there is one, or creating a contrast with a fence or wall.

To make the 'z' frame

The size of timber used for the frame should be determined in relation to the length of the gate and the weight of the face material. Your dealer should be able to advise you on suitable sizes but as a general rule, for gates under 1.2 m (4 ft) long the head and heel should be at least 10 × 5 cm (4 × 2 in) and the top and bottom rails 10 × 5 cm (4 × 2 in) or 8 × 5 cm (3 × 2 in). For longer gates (field gates etc.) the head and heel should be 15 × 5 cm (6 × 2 in) and the top and bottom rails 13 × 5 cm (5 × 1 in) or 10 × 5 cm (4 × 2 in). The bolts should be ordinary coach bolts with washers at least 10 cm (4 in) long and up to 1 cm ($\frac{3}{8}$ in) in diameter.

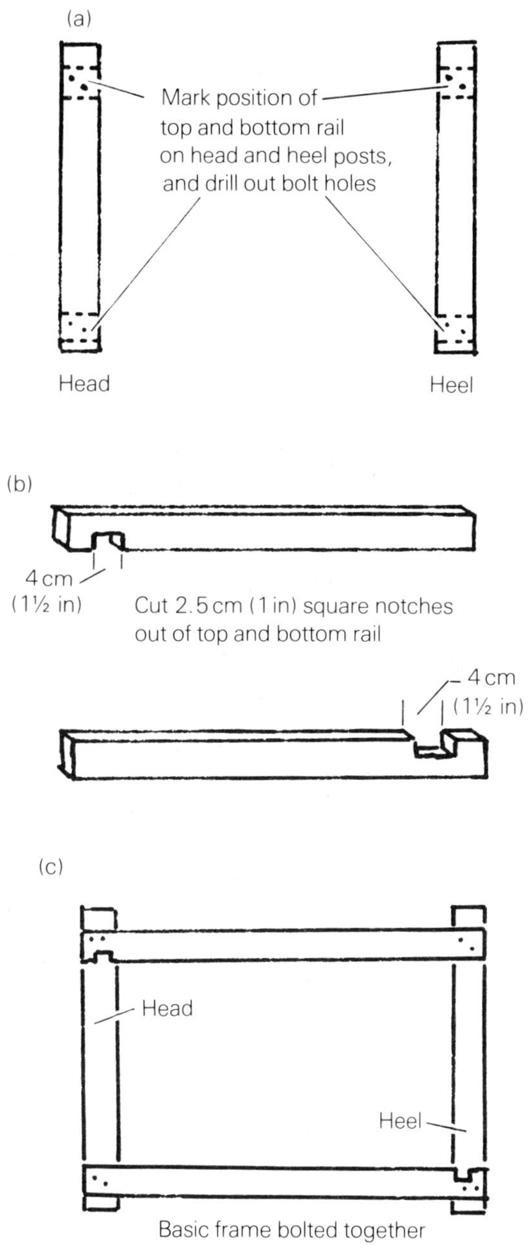

Fig. 9.9 *Forming the basic gate frame.*

Step 1 Cut head and heel posts to length. Next, using an adjustable square or protractor, mark on them the exact positions of the top and bottom rails and bolt holes (Fig. 9.9a). Drill out the holes.

Step 2 Cut top and bottom rails to length and cut out a 2.5 cm (1 in) square notch 4 cm ($1\frac{1}{2}$ in) from one end of each (Fig. 9.9b). Lay the rails in position under the head and heel and, using a pencil inserted into the holes in the head and heel, mark the position of the bolt holes on top and bottom rails. Drill out holes.

Step 3 Lay out rails on top of head and heel, and checking that all the corners are square, bolt the four together (Fig. 9.9c).

Step 4 Lay the brace in position across the frame. (Do not cut to exact length before doing this.) On the inside edge of the brace mark it as shown in Fig. 9.10a. When cutting out, remember to allow for the tabs.

Step 5 Mark and cut out tabs, to correspond exactly with the positions of the notches on top and bottom rails. Tap brace into place and drill bolt holes in brace, head and heel. Bolt brace firmly in position (Fig. 9.10b).

You now have the basic 'z' frame to which the face material, hinges and fittings can be attached.

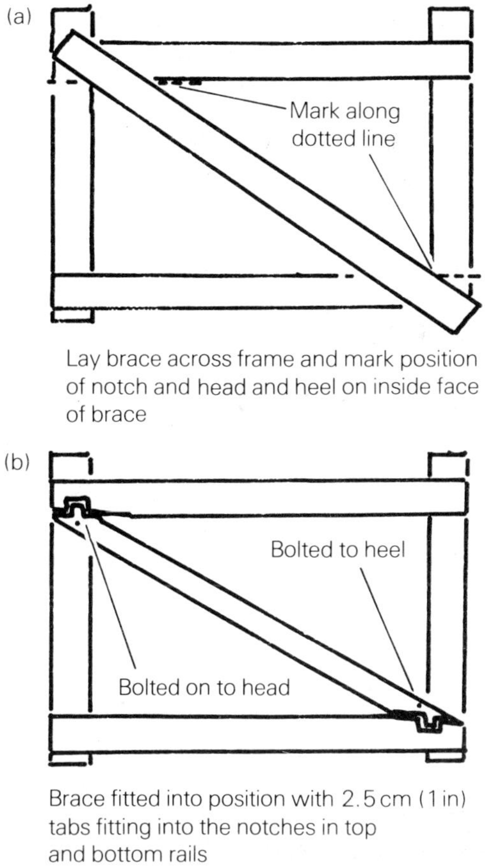

Fig. 9.10 *Cutting and fitting the brace for 'z' frame.*

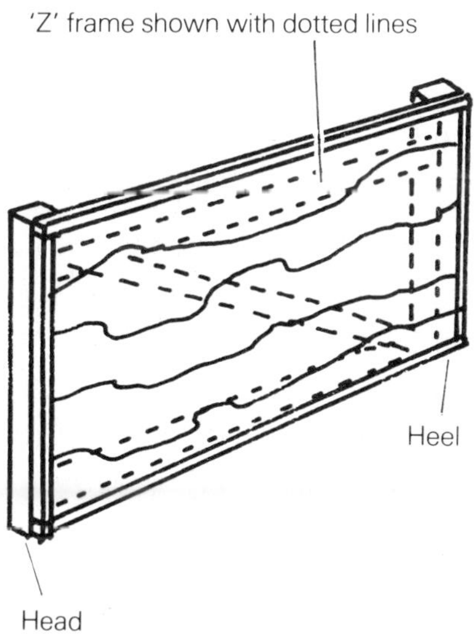

Fig. 9.11 *Lapped panel fitted onto a standard 'z' frame.*

Note In this example the top and bottom rails have been bolted on to the sides of the head and heel posts. This method is the quickest and easiest way to construct a frame suitable for most purposes. If, however, the tools and time are available the frame could be assembled using mortice and tenon joints. This method produces a neater looking and stronger frame suitable for heavy gates over 1.2 m (4 ft) long.

Suitable face materials

Lapped panels These make attractive, lightweight gates and the panels can be built at home to the required size (p. 52). Alternatively, if the gates are combined with a fence of commercially bought panels, the frames can be built to suit the standard panel size used. In either case, the struts on the back of the panel should be removed or left off, and the panel boards and front struts nailed directly on to the 'z' frame (Fig. 9.11).

Paling/close boarding Paling has long been popular for small gates and should be attached to the 'z' frame in the same way as for paling fences (p. 61). For larger gates and increased privacy, close-boarding can be used (p. 62), but since these will be large, heavy gates be sure to use a good size of timber for the frame. Give your dealer the required dimensions of the gate and ask him which size of frame would be suitable.

Note Close-boarded and 'solid' paling gates can be made to look 'invisible' by using strap hinges and continuing the face material across the front of the gate posts (Fig. 9.12). This gives a very pleasing effect, but the strap hinges will not open outwards or inwards more than 90°. Check before starting that these limitations suit your requirements.

Field-style gate These are the traditional four- or five-barred gates and can be used in long or short versions. The spacing and number of bars is a matter of taste and should be designed to complement whatever is immediately adjacent to the gate. Use 10 × 2.5 cm (4 × 1 in) timber for the bars and toenail (p. 62) them to the head and heel on the inside of the 'z' frame (Fig. 9.13). When secure, nail them to the brace. This style of gate can be made considerably stronger by rebating diagonal slots (2.5 cm (1 in) deep for 10 × 2.5 cm (4 × 1 in) bars) into the bars at the point where each one meets the brace. When fitting, tap the brace into the slots and bolt or nail firmly together. This method 'locks' the structure of the gate together making it almost impossible for it to sag along its length.

Stock gate This is a cheap and easy type of gate to make and, although it does not look particularly attractive, it may be useful as a temporary gate. Consisting of no more than a few strands of fencing wire, 8 cm (3 in) diameter poles and 5 × 5 cm (2 × 2 in) spacers, it will cost very little and can probably be made up of off-cuts from other fencing jobs.

Lay out posts and spacers and staple the wire strands to them using standard galvanized fencing staples. Fix two wire loops round the fence post at the heel end and attach gate (Fig. 9.14a). At the head end, fix a wire loop at the bottom of the fence post and a strand of wire stapled to a short length of wood at the top (Fig. 9.14b). Use these to close and secure the gate.

Others For alternative ideas on face materials see Screens, p. 150. Some of the materials suggested for screens would make very attractive gates and should be built on to a 'z' frame in the same way as those described above.

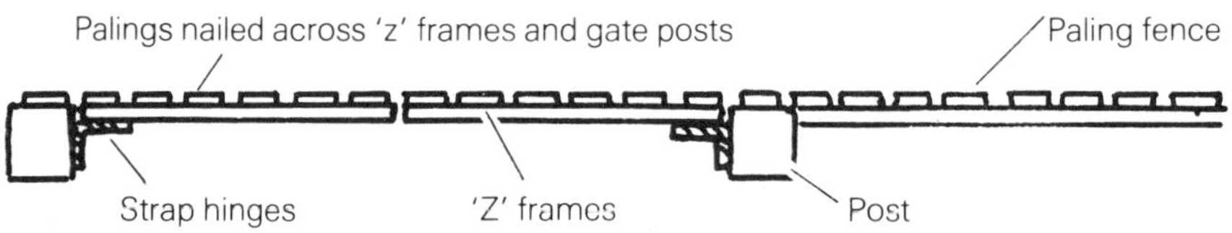

Fig. 9.12 *'Invisible' gate in a paling fence.*

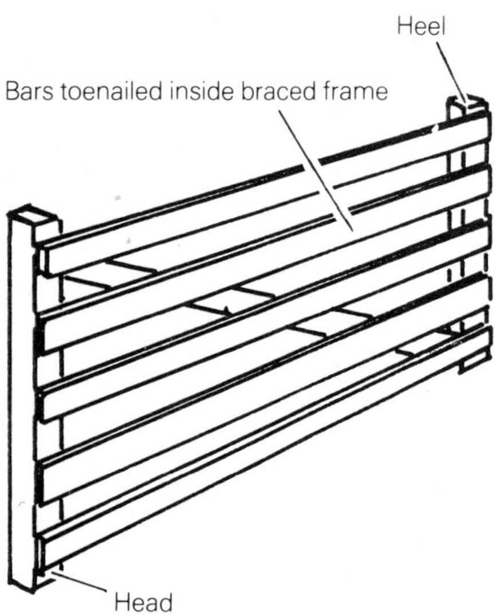

Fig. 9.13 *Fitting bars into a braced gate frame.*

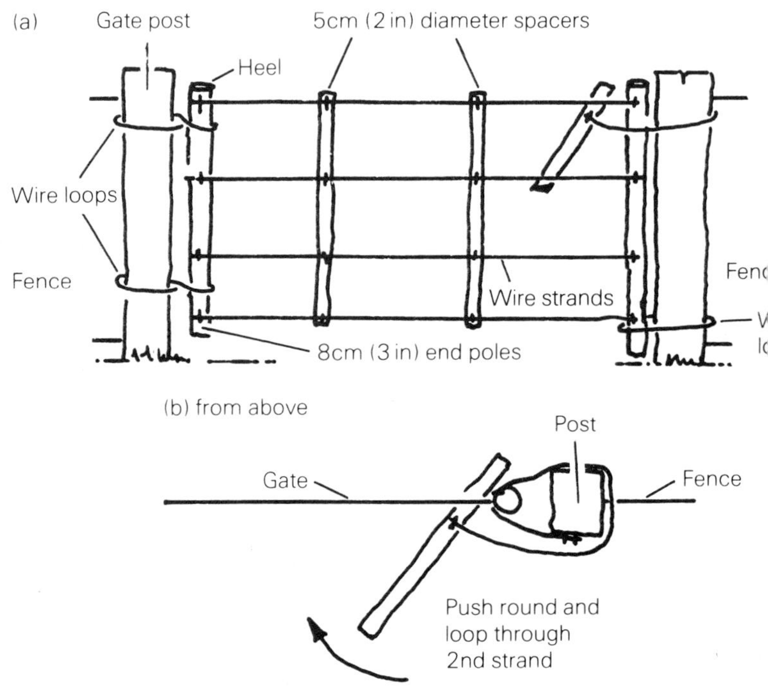

Fig. 9.14 *American style stock gate.*

10 Terraces, drives, paths and steps

Before starting work on constructing hard or flat surfaces reference should be made to Chapter 3 where we outline some of the things that should be taken into consideration while planning the work. The most important point to bear in mind at the moment, however, is that terraces and paths, etc. can be both practical and decorative at the same time. With a little imagination most of the surface materials covered here, including concrete, can be used in such a way that they serve a practical purpose and at the same time enhance the overall layout of the garden. The basic rule, covered in more detail in Chapter 3, is not to use too much of one type of material over too large an area.

The most common practical use for solid surfaces is immediately around the house to keep mud and dirt away from doors and French windows and to provide somewhere that can easily be kept clean on which dustbins and coal bunkers can stand. Most builders, as part of the building specifications, will lay a narrow strip of concrete around new houses for this purpose and this can be used as a good starting point for laying out larger areas near the house. Using the levels provided by the concrete as a guide, the surface can be extended in certain places, in front of French windows for example, into a terrace for recreational purposes or as a work area. The finished effect can be made more interesting by using different surface materials and by using layout shapes that break up the straight lines around the house. Leading off from these areas, paths can then provide access to washing lines, rotary driers, sheds and vegetable plots, and a route for wheelbarrows to incinerators and compost heaps.

The other large, solid surface usually required is a drive or parking area for vehicles. Whether or not you actually own a car, some provision must be made for parking or turning cars and, on the whole, the more solid the surface the better it will be. The size and shape of a parking area or drive will, of course, be governed by the amount of space available, the position of the house, the siting of access from the road and the amount of parking or turning space needed. The finished surface is a matter of taste and the most common 'finishes' are outlined in this chapter to help you decide on what is most suitable for your garden.

Apart from the practical uses just mentioned, in their decorative capacity terraces and paths can be used to open up, shape and complement the lawns, flowerbeds, shrubberies and views in the garden. How much solid surface is included and how it is used depends on how formal the garden is intended to look and the cost and availability of materials. As a general rule though you should consider constructing a terrace or path if there are awkward level changes to manage, unwanted objects, such as manholes, to disguise or features, such as ponds, sundials or ornaments, to highlight. Terraces can also be designed and laid in conjunction with paths to help harmonize the house and garden, linking various areas and providing access to individual points of interest. Materials should, as far as possible, be chosen to complement existing materials and the overall feel of the garden.

As with most aspects of garden construction, time spent on considering various plans and alternative finishes will not be wasted, since it is expensive and difficult to alter these things at a later date, and, most important of all, when deciding on the size of a terrace, drive or path and choosing the surface material, always keep in mind the use to which it will be put. This is particularly true if you are laying an area for turning cars or a terrace as a site for specific garden furniture. It is surprising how easy it is to underestimate the amount of room you need to turn a car or to use, for example, a table and four chairs. In the latter case as often as not one or two people will end up with the back legs of their chairs sinking gracefully into the lawn. Most of these problems can be overcome if the job is properly measured up and planned.

In the rest of this chapter we will be looking at how to lay the different types of materials, how to finish them off and how to construct steps. Before you start the jobs, however, you should ensure that the site has been properly prepared in terms of foundations (for load-bearing surfaces) and drainage. These topics are covered in detail in Chapter 5, which should be looked at before you finalize your plans.

1 Concrete

Concrete is a mixture of sand and gravel (aggregate) and cement that produces an extremely durable and tough finished surface. While it is commonly used as a finish itself it can also play an important role as the base or foundation on which other, less strong, materials can be laid. The main advantage of concrete is its strength and, while it is not a very pleasant material to work with, it is simple to lay and a variety of interesting finishes can be given to it just before it sets. It can also be dyed various colours, either during mixing or after it has been laid. The different dyes can be obtained from builders' merchants along with instructions for their use.

Concrete, on the other hand, is not the cheapest finishing material (slabs are less costly), and you will also require a cement mixer if you have large areas to lay or if time is a factor. Ready-mixed concrete is available by the cubic metre (cubic yard) (see p. 27), but it has a built-in disadvantage in that you have to lay large quantities all at once which requires assistants and a lot of shuttering. It is worth getting a quote from your local dealer, however, to see if the expense and extra work of setting up is made up for by the time saved.

What you will need

Calculated quantities of sand and gravel and cement. Cement mixer. Shovel. Shuttering boards (see Measuring up). Tamping board (this should be a 10 × 5 cm (4 × 2 in) straight-edged length of wood, long enough to span the gap between the shutters with about 30 cm (12 in) extra on either end, see Fig. 10.3). Pegs. Spirit-level. Hammer. Tape-measure. Wood or steel float. Builder's line. 8 or 10 cm (3 or 4 in) nails.

Measuring up

Concrete depths and volume:

Non load-bearing: (i.e. pedestrians only). A uniform 8 cm (3 in) depth is sufficient for finished surfaces or foundations. If there is no hardcore, the concrete should be laid on a 5 cm (2 in) layer of scalpings.

Load-bearing: Up to 0.5 tonne (½ ton): 10 cm (4 in) uniform depth. Over 0.5 tonne (½ ton): 15 cm (6 in) uniform depth.

Use Table 10.1 to calculate the volume of concrete required for your particular job once you have decided on the depth. For example, 24 sq m (28.7 sq yd) at 8 cm (3 in) uniform depth will require 1.92 cu m

Table 10.1 Concrete: examples of depths/areas/volumes

Volume of concrete	*Depth*	*Area that would be covered*	*Volume of concrete*	*Depth*	*Area that would be covered*
1 cu yd	3 in	12 sq yd (10 sq m)	1 cu m	8 cm	12.5 sq m (14.95 sq yd)
1 cu yd	4 in	9 sq yd (7.5 sq m)	1 cu m	10 cm	10 sq m (11.96 sq yd)
1 cu yd	6 in	6 sq yd (5 sq m)	1 cu m	15 cm	6.6 sq m (7.96 sq yd)

(2.5 cu yd) of concrete. Tell your dealer how much you require in cubic metres (cubic yards) and he will be able to tell you how much sand and gravel you need. Calculate cement quantities at a rate of 1 : 6 (see p. 14).

The next item to be considered is the 'shuttering'. These are lengths of wood positioned and secured with pegs to form a mould for the wet concrete. They support the concrete until it is dry and provide a guide for levelling off the surface and keeping a uniform depth; they also make work easier by dividing up large areas into more workable units. The concrete is placed between the shutters and levelled off with the tamping board.

The shutters should be lengths of stout wood at least 5 cm (2 in) thick, with clean, straight edges, and, if possible, the same depth as that required for the job (i.e. 8 cm (3 in) deep for a non-load-bearing, 8 cm (3 in) deep path), and of convenient length up to about 3.6 m (12 ft). You will only require enough shuttering for a day's work since it can be removed and re-used once the concrete is dry. The pegs should be the same as those used for concrete wall foundations (p. 78) and will be needed every 1.8 m (6 ft) along the length of the shutters and at all joints (Fig. 10.1).

To lay

Once the site has been excavated where necessary and the hardcore (if required) has been laid, the shuttering can be erected. (See Chapter 5 for site-drainage requirements and excavation and hardcore details.) If the concrete is for a path (the technique is the same for terraces etc. but on a larger scale, see p. 115), the builder's line should be stretched tight between the pegs, driven in every 1.8 m (6 ft) along the proposed edges of the path, at the height above the hardcore, or scalpings, of the required thickness of concrete. The shutters should now be laid so that the top, inside edge of the wood (make sure that this is a clean, straight edge if using second-hand timber) touches the line. Nail shutters to pegs (using extra pegs at any joints) and fix end shutters across the open ends (Figs. 10.2a and 10.3).

If the path is to be laid on level ground a slight fall to one side will be required to ensure that rain-water drains off. This fall should be approximately 1.3 cm ($\frac{1}{2}$ in) for

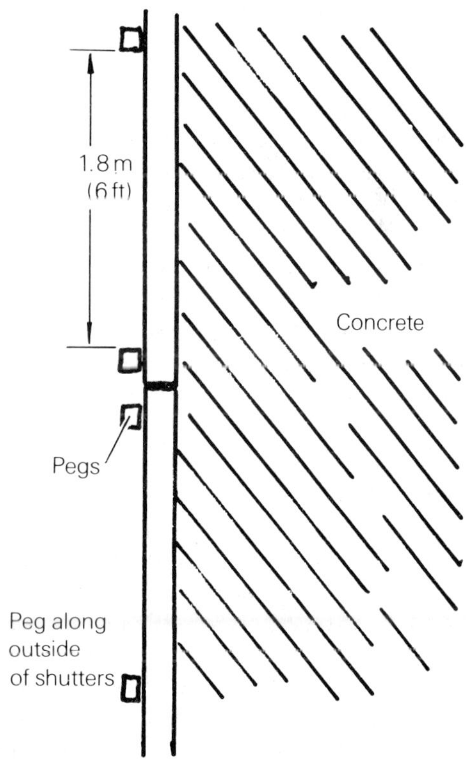

Fig. 10.1 *Concreting: use of shuttering and pegs (from above).*

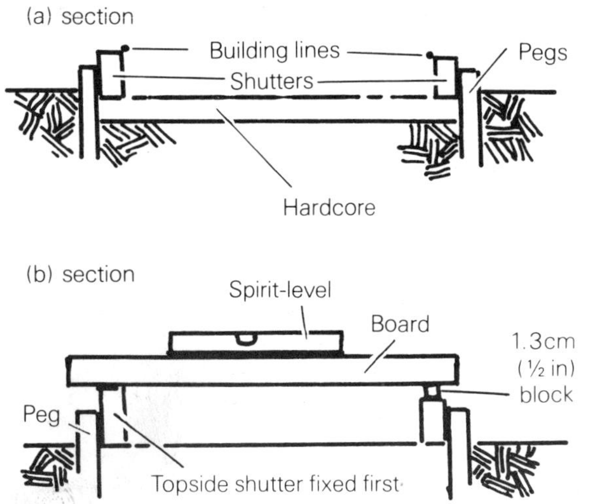

Fig. 10.2 *Concreting. (a) View of shutters. (b) Method of ensuring rain-water run-off.*

every 60 cm (2 ft) of width. This can be done using a block and spirit-level. Fix top side shutters first and then, using the spirit-level and block, fix lower side shutters (Fig. 10.2b). For run-off fall on larger areas and arranging drainage for enclosed areas see p. 41.

When sufficient shuttering has been fixed (depending on length of work session), the builder's lines should be removed and the concrete mix (for mixing see p. 14) shovelled into the shuttering, filling to about 2.5 cm (1 in) above the shutters and in 1 m (yd) stretches (i.e. do not fill too much at a time before starting to level with a tamping board). Then, starting at the top end, the tamping board is banged down across the shutters until it touches them on both sides. This action consolidates the concrete and fills any holes. The tamping board (Fig. 10.3) is then moved across the surface (starting at the end shutter and moving in the direction of laying), with a back and forth 'sawing' motion which leaves the concrete level and smooth, and at the same time drags the excess off into the next piece to be filled. If the concrete runs over the edge of the shutters when being shovelled in, or slops back under the tamping board as it is moved along, the mix is too wet and less water should be used for subsequent mixes. Alternatively, if water does not rise to the surface during the first stage of tamping, or if cutting off the excess is very difficult, the mix is too dry and more water should be added. (For ideal mix, see p. 14.)

Continue as described, shovelling in concrete and levelling off with the board until the end of the work session or the end of the path is reached. At this point the concrete should be finished off against an end stop shutter, which will be removed when work is re-commenced or with the rest of the shuttering if it marks the end of the path. Shutters should be left in place until the concrete has set.

Curing: if the finished surface of the concrete is allowed to set too fast it will be brittle and prone to flaking or crumbling. To avoid

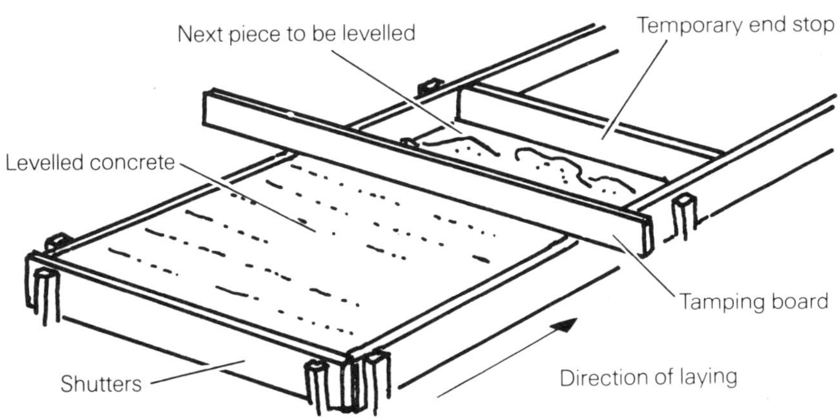

Fig. 10.3 *Concreting : levelling concrete using a tamping board.*

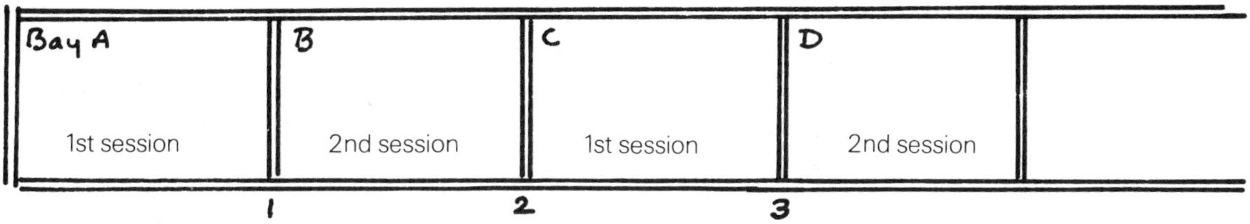

Fig. 10.4 *Concreting : alternate laying in bays.*

this, when the surface has been finished off (see below), it should either be covered in plastic sheeting which will retain the surface moisture and allow the concrete plenty of time to cure, or in some porous material (such as sacking) which can be periodically sprayed with water while the concrete sets. The longer the concrete is left to cure the stronger the surface will be, but for most purposes a curing period of two to three days will be sufficient.

Note 1. If you are laying concrete in particularly hot and dry conditions it is advisable to add a retarding agent to the mix to allow the concrete time to set properly. Such agents are available from builders' merchants with advice on their use.

Note 2. Expansion boards: since concrete has a considerable expansion co-efficient, measures should be taken on large areas or long lengths of path, to prevent the concrete cracking or splitting after it has set. Fibre boards (available at builders' merchants) are sold for this purpose and can be cut to any size for permanent insertion into the concrete to absorb any subsequent expansion. Not all concrete will crack without these boards, but it is a wise precaution to take for large parking areas etc. and the boards are not expensive.

To lay the boards the procedure is the same as above, with the difference that, at the end of the session, an expansion board is inserted along the inside of the end stop shutter, with the concrete finished off against it. The board is then left in place when the end stop is removed and work resumed.

If, however, more than one bay is to be laid in a day, they should be laid alternately as shown in Fig. 10.4. That is, bays A and C are laid in the first session with expansion boards inserted behind cross shutters 1 and 3. When bay B (and any others) are laid the expansion boards are inserted at cross shutter 2 etc. as the shutters are removed.

Where large areas of concrete are being laid the area should be divided into bays (1.5 m (5 ft) should be the maximum width of the bays if working single-handed) for convenience, and to allow the expansion boards to be inserted. Fig. 10.5 illustrates a typical division into bays and the correct order of laying.

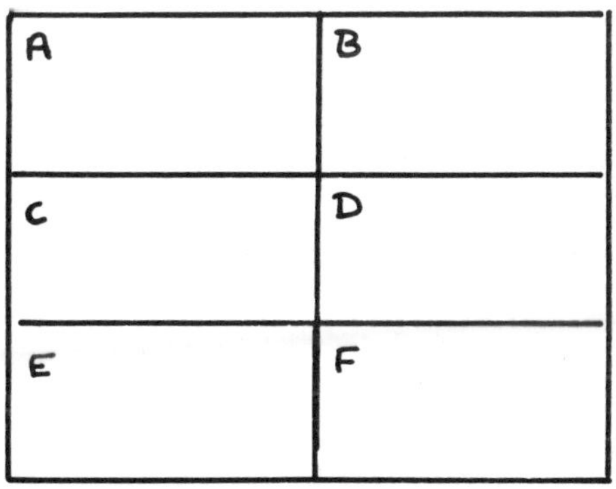

For laying one bay per session
the order should be: A, E, C, B, F, D

For two bays per session
the order should be: A + F, E + D, C + B

For three bays per session
the order should be: A + D + E, B + C + F

Fig. 10.5 *Laying large areas of concrete.*

(A session means that the concrete is laid and left to harden before any more bays are laid. How many bays you lay per session will depend on how much time you have, how many assistants to help mix and level off you can organize and so on. Plan all sessions carefully so as not to waste time or materials.)

The expansion boards will be laid against sides where the shutters are being removed from hardened bays.

Concrete mix: The ideal mix for these jobs should be sufficiently wet to mould into a ball if squeezed in the hand, but not so wet that water starts to run out. Any concrete mix that has 'gone off' before being used should not be re-vitalized, since the extra addition of water serves only to weaken the mix and bring the cement to the surface. This being so, plan carefully: work out how many bays you will lay and mix for each bay as you come to it. If you are having ready-mix concrete delivered, be sure to have enough people to help you lay it, since all your concrete will arrive at once; tell the driver what it is for so that he can add the correct amount of water.

Surface finishes

For concrete laid as a foundation, or where a lot of grip on the finished surface is required (steep drives etc.), the finish given by the tamping board is acceptable. If, however, a neater or more decorative surface is required, the concrete can be worked in a number of ways before it cures to make the finished textures more interesting.

As mentioned above, the action of tamping the concrete brings the water to the surface, and, while this helps cure the concrete properly, it also makes it difficult to see exactly what the surface looks like, how smooth it is etc., particularly if the concrete has been mixed slightly too wet. Before attempting to work on the surface finish, therefore, wait until the water has evaporated away. Once this has happened you can then treat the concrete in one or other of the ways suggested below.

(a) **Floating** When the surface is ready you can go over the concrete with either a wooden float, smoothing out any lines or ridges left by the tamping board, or if you want a really smooth, almost shiny finish, you can use a rectangular steel trowel. Whichever tool you use you should skim the surface of the concrete in wide, loose sweeps, keeping the leading edge of the tool slightly raised to avoid digging into the surface, and using as little pressure as possible. Repeat the operation if required, using slightly more pressure as the surface dries out, until you are satisfied with the finish. Use boards laid across the concrete to reach the middle of large areas. When the surface is finished, cure as usual (p. 114).

(b) **Brushing** For many concrete surfaces round the garden (whether on terraces, paths or steps) it is often useful to have a slightly rough-textured finish which helps stop them becoming slippery in wet or frosty weather. The easiest way to get this kind of surface is to use a wide-headed brush. As above, wait until the surface water has dried off and then *lightly* brush the concrete, pulling the brush gently towards you. Repeat over the whole area, avoiding as far as possible any overlap of the brush-strokes. Cure the concrete.

(c) **Exposed aggregate** This is a very pleasant way to finish off a concrete surface that leaves the stones in the concrete exposed, producing a colourful, irregular finish. To do this the surface should be floated lightly using a wooden float (see above), and then left until it is almost set hard but the surface is still slightly tacky. When this point is reached wet the concrete with a very fine spray and brush gently until the tops of the stones show clearly. (Be careful not to dislodge the stones by brushing too hard.) When you are satisfied with the finish leave the concrete to set for at least two days before using.

(d) **Imitation crazy-paving** An alternative way to finish off concrete is to mark it with crazy-paving-type patterns. This can be done using a small piece of tubing immediately after levelling is finished and before all the water has dried off the surface. Draw patterns on to the concrete and then, after the surface water has dried out, tidy up the grooves and flat areas with a trowel and soft brush, flattening or removing any loose stones or excess lumps. Cure the concrete. This technique can be used to mark the concrete with a number of different patterns, but it is a good idea to plan the patterns quite carefully since it is very difficult to erase mistakes and still keep the concrete looking smooth.

2 Basic laying techniques for slabs, bricks, crazy-paving, etc.

(a) Solid bed

A lean mix of concrete (i.e. 1 : 8) is set in shuttering (p. 113), and the finishing material, slabs, bricks, etc. is set on top while the mix is still wet (for depths of solid beds, see Table 5.1, p. 33). Where concrete or brick edgings (pp. 124–5) are being used for paths or terraces, if put in first these edgings will serve as shutters.

(b) Screed bed

A thin 2.5 cm (1 in) layer of lean mortar mix (i.e. 1 : 6) is laid on a previously laid concrete bed (for depth of concrete beds see Table 5.1). The finishing material is then set on the mortar mix while it is still wet. A uniform depth of mortar can be maintained by using 2.5 cm (1 in) laths as guides (Fig. 10.6).

(c) Mortar spots

Mortar mix (1 : 6) is applied in spots or blobs, on to the prepared hardcore or scalping base, with a spot for each corner and one for the middle (for spot depths, see Table 5.1).

Note For (a) and (b) the slab or brick, etc. is laid on the levelled bed and tapped down to level to give a good bind with the bed. For (c) the mortar spots are of generous size enabling them to spread firmly to approximately 2.5 cm (1 in) depth, as the slab, etc. is tapped down on top. All finishes should be checked regularly as work progresses with a spirit-level.

(d) Sand bed

This is the traditional method of laying brick and slate paths and terraces, and relies for its strength on the surface material being locked in place by mortared edgings and sand swept down into all the joints. When the edging material has been fixed in place (see p. 125), spread sand over the area to be covered and level it off as shown in Fig. 10.7. Place finishing materials on the sand, tapping it firmly down and butting each piece firmly up to its neighbours. Finally, sweep loose sand back and forth across the finished surface until all the joints are well filled. Periodic re-sanding of the joints will keep the brick, etc. firmly locked in place.

Note The sand-bed technique is most suitable for non-load-bearing surfaces and for use with finishing materials that come in small units such as bricks or paving-stones.

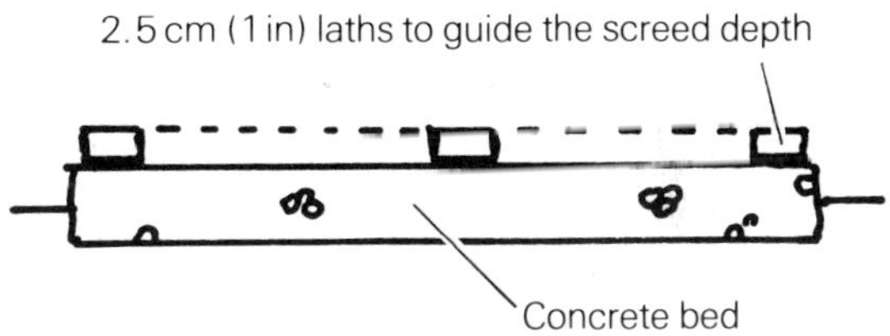

Fig. 10.6 *Screed bed : maintaining uniform depth of mortar.*

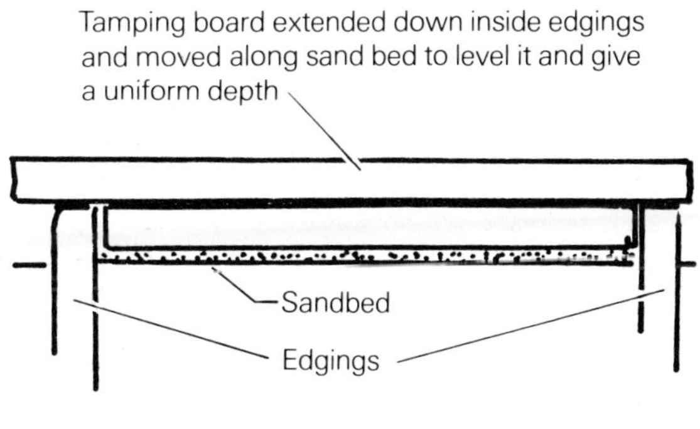

Fig. 10.7 *Levelling a sand bed*

3 Standard concrete slabs

Concrete slabs come in two standard finishes: vibrated or pressed. The vibrated slabs are the popular, smooth-finished ones which are nearly white in colour, while the pressed slabs are grey, and have a pitted, textured finish. Both are available at most builders' merchants and are cheaper than concrete. They are not difficult to lay and provide a solid, durable surface which will serve almost any purpose.

The vibrated slabs, however, have the disadvantage of quickly becoming slimy and slippery in wet or frosty weather, and both types can make a garden look somewhat bare and square if laid unsympathetically or in too large a quantity in a small area. Their other main drawback is that the standard 60 × 60 cm (2 × 2 ft) size makes them rather heavy and awkward to handle.

Note Ground preparation for the various jobs will differ slightly. Before commencing a job reference should be made to Table 5.1 (p. 33) to see what will be required in addition to the tools needed and measuring up instructions.

What you will need

Slabs. Mortar. Shovel. Trowel. Spirit-level. Builder's line.

Measuring up

The handiest size slabs are 60 × 60 × 5 cm (2 ft × 2 ft × 2 in). Two people should be used to lay them. Using these size slabs, of which there are 2.70 per sq m ($2\frac{1}{4}$ per sq yd) the quantity needed will be: the area to be slabbed in square metres × 2.70 (in sq yards × $2\frac{1}{4}$). Mortar quantities: 25 kg ($\frac{1}{2}$ cwt) per slab for mortar-spot technique – 50 kg (1 cwt) per slab for solid bed. (For strength of mortar mixes see p. 14.) It is advisable to use a 60 cm (2 ft) long spirit-level when laying the slabs, since each slab area and then the slab can be accurately checked as work goes on.

To lay

Determine the uses of path to be laid and decide on the suitable method of laying (Table 5.1, p. 33). The ground should then be prepared as indicated in the table, dug out or levelled and either hardcored or sealed with scalpings.

The builder's line should now be stretched along one side of the path and fastened to pegs at the height of the required finished level for the slabs.

Shovel in the required amount of mix for one slab and level. The first slab should now be laid on the mortar, with one edge flush with and touching the line (Fig. 10.8a). The slab is then levelled by gentle tapping on its upper surface and checked with the spirit-level. If there is to be any fall use the spirit-level with a small block (p. 113). Continue laying (Fig. 10.8b) until you have the length of path required. If the path is to be two or more slabs wide, repeat the operation line by line, using the previously laid line as a guide instead of the builder's line, until you have the required width.

To lay a slabbed area: decide on the use to which the area will be put and determine the laying technique. Prepare ground. Lay the two sides and one end using the builder's line, as for paths, and then, using a straight-

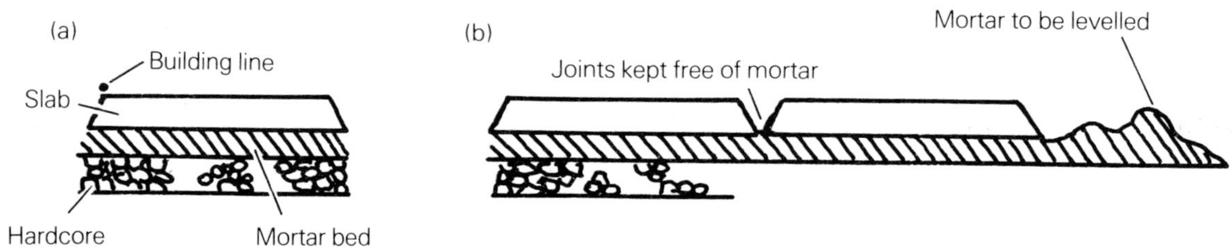

Fig. 10.8 *Laying concrete slabs. (a) Using building line to ensure the correct height. (b) Sectional view of successive slabs.*

Fig. 10.9 *Laying a slabbed area using a straight-edged board and building line.*

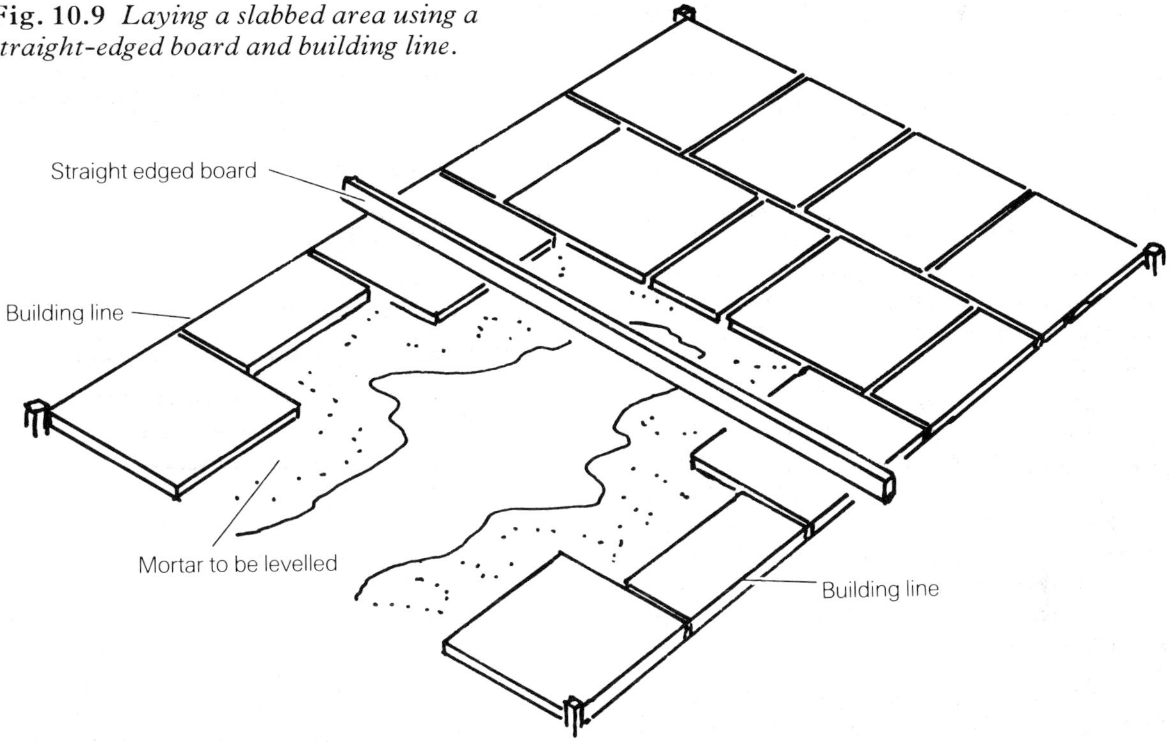

edged piece of wood to check the levels, fill in the middle sections (Fig. 10.9). For the popular, staggered pattern, every other row will have to start with a half-slab (for cutting, see p. 82).

Drainage: If the terrace is to be laid against the house, its final level above ground and the fall of the slabbed surface will be very important. Ideally, for a terrace laid flush against the house, the finished level should be at least 20 cm (8 in) below the damp-proof course of the house (i.e. two brick courses), and the fall should be away from the house walls. If the terrace is laid between two walls, then the fall should be towards one corner (see Fig. 10.10a). For arrangement of piped

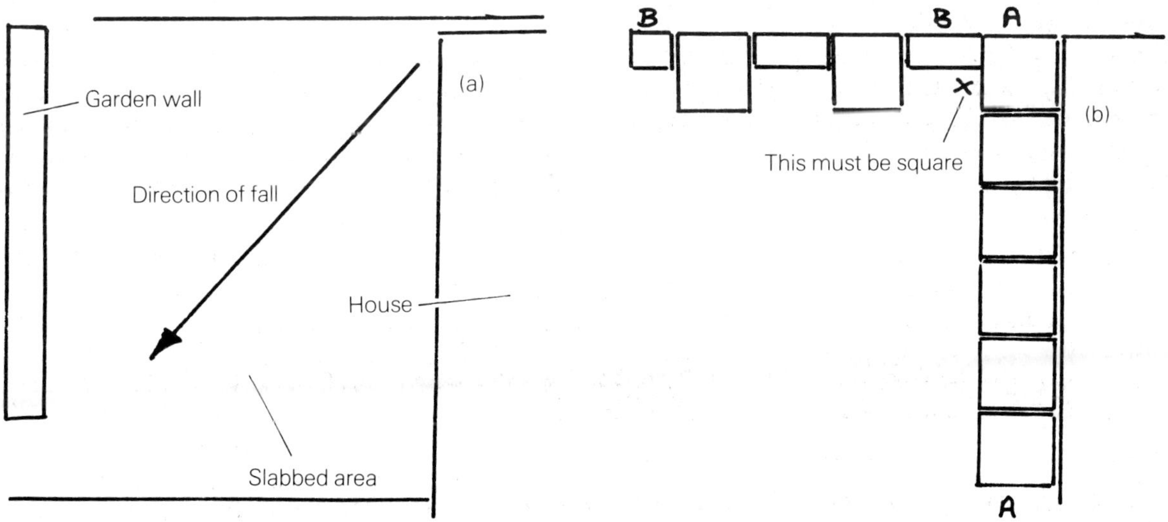

Fig. 10.10 *Ensuring correct fall away from house when laying slabs.*

drains and for terraces laid in enclosed areas, see Chapter 5.

To ensure a good fall away from the house, stretch builder's line at finished level along the house wall (20 cm (8 in) below damp-proof course), and along line AB (Fig. 10.10b). Lay first row (method chosen according to use) along line A, followed by a row down line AB. Lay middle rows moving down line AB, checking the fall at intervals with spirit-level and block. (To ensure a square corner at X, see p. 10.)

Note For decorative or coloured slabs which are to be laid in certain patterns refer to the manufacturers' literature. These types of slabs can make very attractive terraces (Fig. 10.11), but can be very time-consuming to lay. It is a good idea, however, to take a look at what is available since they may combine well with, for example, a terrace of standard concrete slabs. A coloured slab here and there will make any terrace more interesting. Most shaped and decorative slabs can be laid using the techniques outlined above unless specific instructions are given in the manufacturers' literature.

For making your own slabs, using your own designs and shapes, see p. 177.

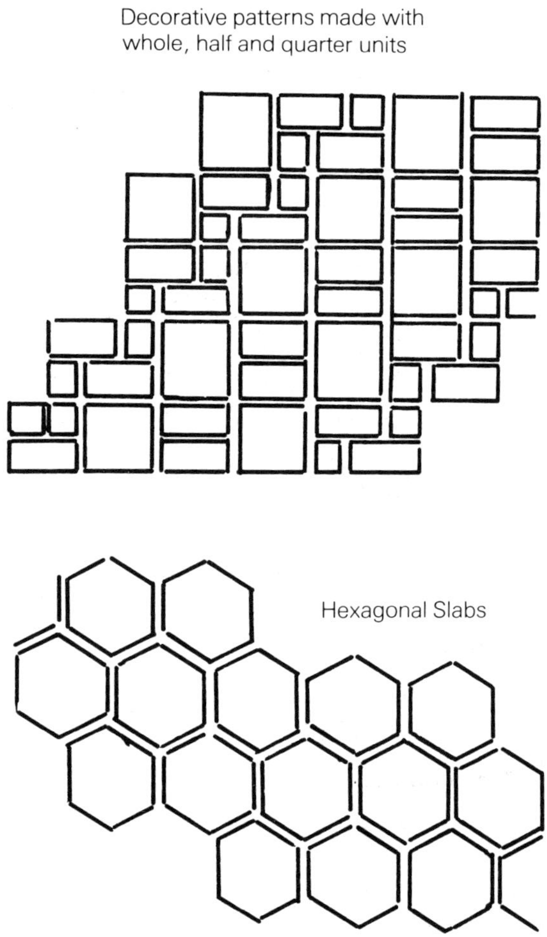

Fig. 10.11 *Two types of decorative slabs.*

4 Bricks

Brick terraces and paths, like brick walls, were once a standard feature in gardens of all shapes and sizes. Whether one thinks of the broad, sweeping terraces and walks of the stately home, the shady, moss-covered paths of the cottage garden, or the bricked yards of terrace housing, brick, in a wide range of shapes and colours, was the standard material, providing a unique warmth and variety. While it is true that new technology now produces much tougher, denser bricks that take longer to soften and mellow, the versatility of the medium and the detail of design that can be achieved, still make them one of the best materials to use around the garden.

Inevitably the modern price of brick and the introduction of so many new types of materials has led to a steep decline in the use of brickwork, but it should be remembered that with the house demolition and renovation that is continually going on, there is usually a good supply of second-hand bricks available in most areas. These will not necessarily be cheap (compared to slabs, etc.) but they will certainly be cheaper, and probably have more shades of colour, than new bricks; it is always worth finding out what is available locally. The design possibilities for terracing and paths are very wide (some of the more popular ones are shown in Fig. 10.12), and while the actual laying may be more time-consuming than when using materials with larger units, the techniques are exactly the same.

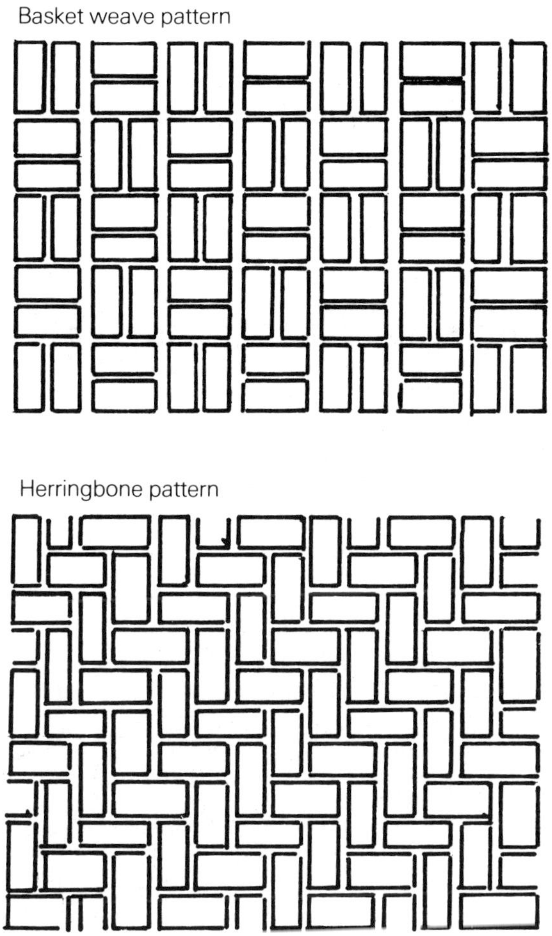

Fig. 10.12 *Two patterns for bricklaying (from above).*

Of the new bricks commonly available at builders' merchants the cheapest are the small grey or pink types, and prices range up through the red house bricks and the dark red engineering bricks to the blue/grey paving bricks with chamfered edges at the top end, but even the cheaper ones cannot compete with most other materials in price. (The only exception are the coloured slabs or reconstituted stone units.) If, however, second-hand bricks are available or you have the extra money to buy new ones, the colour effects and range of designs that bricks make possible will undoubtedly add something special to the garden. One thing to be aware of, though, is that frost will damage any irregular or soft surface causing it to flake and disintegrate. So if bricks are to be used in exposed positions across large areas, you should use the harder paving or engineering bricks.

To lay

The most convenient and readily available size of brick is the standard 23 × 11.5 × 7 cm (9 × $4\frac{1}{2}$ × $2\frac{3}{4}$ in) house brick which works out at 50 per sq m (40 per sq yd) when laid flat. Paving bricks, not always available, come in a range of sizes from 20 × 10 × 4 cm (8 × 4 × $1\frac{1}{2}$ in) to 20 × 10 × 10 cm (8 × 4 × 4 in) and laid flat will cover at the same rate as house bricks. Solid bed, screed bed, or sand bed should be used, depending on load requirement (see Table 5.1 p. 33).

Decide on your pattern and lay as for slabs, using a builder's line and laying in rows. Lay a section of the bed, in shutters as for solid bed (p. 117) to keep a uniform depth and lay the bricks on it, tapping them down for a firm bond with mortar beds, and butting them tight up to each other. Continue over the whole area, using a straight-edged board and spirit-level to keep them level. (For laying with a fall, see p. 113.) Jointing, particularly for the sand-bed technique, is most important to prevent any subsequent movement, and should be done as soon as the mortar beds have set, or immediately after laying is complete on sand beds.

5 Crazy-paving and natural slate

Crazy-paving has two main advantages, the first related to cost and the second to design. In the first case, by its very nature, crazy-paving relies on random sizes, shapes, textures and colours for its effect and therefore can only really be made up of second-hand or re-used material. Any broken stone material, old slabs, pieces of old concrete, broken up slates and so on can be used, and if they are laid on a wet solid bed it will not matter if the

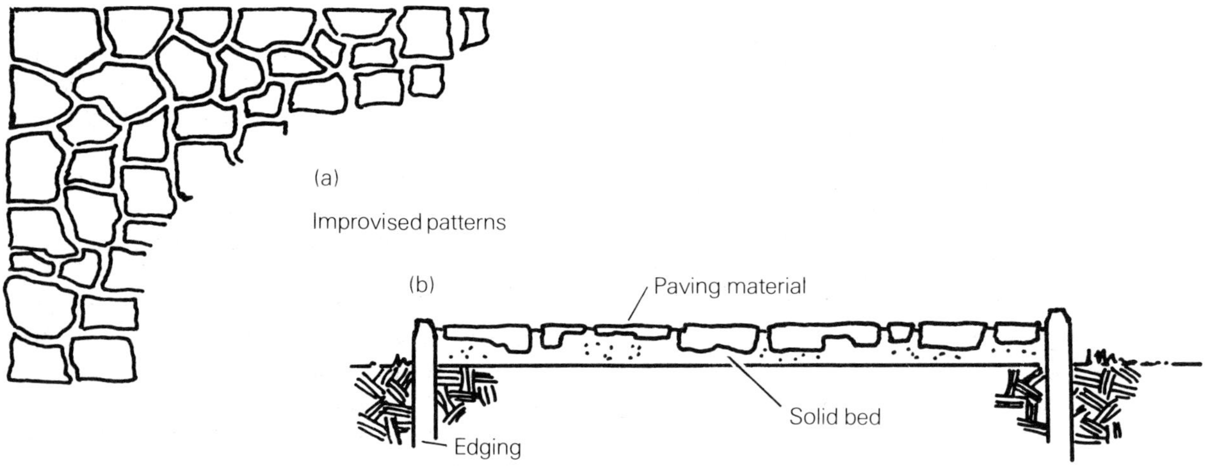

Fig. 10.13 *Crazy-paving. (a) Typical pattern from above. (b) Sectional view showing mortar bed absorbing unequal thicknesses.*

pieces used are of different thicknesses, since they can be tapped down level and absorbed by the bed (Fig. 10.13b). Plate 13 shows how pieces of old concrete path of widely varying dimensions can be used to create the levelled treads of new steps. This being so, a crazy-paving terrace, path or steps can be laid for the price of the sand and cement used; a considerable advantage when materials are so expensive.

The second point is that, again, because crazy-paving is based on random sizes and patterns, it can be used with ease in combination with all the other finishing materials covered here (Plate 11 shows it laid in combination with brick edges), since the pieces can be fitted into whatever sized spaces are left by materials with more regular shapes. Clearly this versatility opens up numerous possibilities for original designs and, in addition, wherever there is an awkward space to be filled, in corners or at the edges of more formal designs, crazy-paving gives a pleasantly informal look to terraces and paths (Fig. 10.13a).

A *rough* guide for quantities is 1 tonne of broken material per 7.5 sq m (1 ton per 9 sq yd); it should be laid using the solid-bed technique.

Decide on load requirements (see Table 5.1, p. 33). Clean off the ground and apply scalpings or hardcore if required. Lay as for bricks, erecting edgings first and using a board to maintain levels, improvising patterns as you go along using groups of large and small pieces.

Natural slate has, like bricks, been very popular in the past but is now extremely expensive and very hard to come by in large quantities. It is, however, a most attractive finish, both in texture and colour, and this alone may justify the expenditure.

Slate covers at roughly 1 tonne per 11.7 sq m (1 ton per 14 sq yd). If you obtain large pieces, for a non-load-bearing surface, then lay it on mortar spots as for concrete slabs. If you have small pieces or require a load-bearing surface (see Table 5.1), lay it on a solid bed as for crazy-paving. Improvise the pattern as you go along.

For draining large areas of crazy-paving or slate, see Chapter 5.

Note Both crazy-paving and slate will look well if jointed after laying. When laying the various materials the size of the gap left between the pieces is a matter of personal taste. If any material, slabs, bricks, crazy-paving or slate are to have a regular gap between pieces, then a spacing block of appropriate size should be used.

6 Gravel and tarmacadam

Gravel is a popular, cheap and easy-to-lay material for drives and paths. It can look untidy when first laid, but after a few months' consolidation period and regular raking and weeding, it provides an excellent, smart surface. Concrete or brick edgings are the simplest and most practical way of containing the gravel round the edges.

Prepare the ground by removing all grass and topsoil. Hardcore will be required if the earth underneath is particularly soft, otherwise a well compacted 5 cm (2 in) layer of scalpings will suffice as a base for the gravel.

Erect the edgings around the perimeter (see p. 124). Rake out the scalpings working from one side to the other, checking the depth and roll flat (a small vibrating roller should be used for drives to ensure sufficient compaction). Spread and rake the gravel over the scalpings, levelling it off by eye and making the surface as smooth as possible. (As for preparing the ground for lawns, the best kind of rake to use is the wide 90 cm (3 ft) small toothed sort. The width of the head makes it much easier to get a smooth finish.)

'Pea' gravel at 8 cm (3 in) depth will cover at an approximate rate of 1 tonne per 7.5 sq m (1 ton per 9 sq yd), (Fig. 10.14).

Tarmacadam is one of the commonest finishes of all for drives and parking areas, but it is also one that we would not recommend the amateur to attempt to lay. It is difficult to obtain and transport, tricky to lay and requires some experience and a number of specialized tools to produce an acceptable result. It is impossible to disguise badly laid 'tarmac', and invariably it will have to be taken up and re-done.

Should tarmac be required we would advise contacting a specialized contractor to do the job, who will probably save you time and money in the long run. Reputable contractors can be found through the telephone directory or local newspapers and they will usually estimate the job free of charge. The expense of the job can be cut to a minimum, however, by preparing the ground for them in advance: clearing away the topsoil or existing surface, levelling if required and hardcoring if it is to be a load-bearing surface.

Note For load-bearing surfaces, such as drives and parking or turning areas, two grades of tarmac should be used. The strength is provided by the 'base' grade (which is made up of 2.5–5 cm (1–2 in) stone in tar mix) and the surface finish is provided by 'topping' (a much finer grade which is spread thinly over the base to provide the neat, flat finish). For paths or strictly pedestrian areas 'topping' alone is sufficient, but for load-bearing areas make sure that the contractor is going to lay a good base first before finishing off with topping. Most reputable contractors will do this anyway, but skimping on the base, or omitting it altogether, is a widespread practice among less reputable contractors, and is worth warning against here. Without the base a tarmac surface used by cars will rapidly collapse and break up.

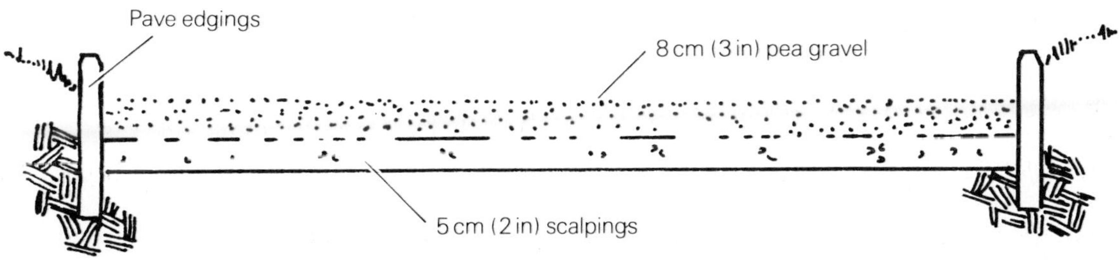

Fig. 10.14 *Sectional view of a gravel path.*

7 Concrete and brick edgings; beds in terraces; alternative designs for terraces and paths; jointing/pointing

(7a) CONCRETE AND BRICK EDGINGS

Some kind of specially laid edgings are more or less essential if a path or terrace is bordered by a flowerbed or any area of similarly loose soil. Not only do they help to finish off the area they enclose, complementing or contrasting with the surface material, but they also help retain the loose earth and prevent plant or root growth over or under the solid surface. This can be a continual problem, particularly if the surface materials have been laid on sand and it is relatively easy for root growth to find its way under the bricks, etc. If this happens it will not be long before the surface starts being disturbed by plant growth. The other main advantage of laying edgings of some sort is that, if put in position first, they will serve as shuttering for solid- or screed-bed laying, or as a level guide for spreading scalpings or sand, (see Fig. 10.7, for example). Any suitable material can be used for edgings, either continuing the colours and textures of the terrace or path finish, or contrasting with them, but in this section we will look at two of the most common types: concrete pave-edgings and bricks.

Note In the examples that follow the edgings are shown standing a few centimetres (an inch or so) proud of the flat surfaces. They could, of course, be laid so as to lie flush with the terrace or path, and which effect is used is a matter of personal taste.

CONCRETE PAVE-EDGINGS

These popular and easy-to-lay edgings are stocked by builders' merchants and garden centres and come in standard sizes: 15 or 18 cm (6 or 7 in) (height) by 90 × 5 cm (3 ft × 2 in). The concrete mix should be 1 : 9 and fairly dry.

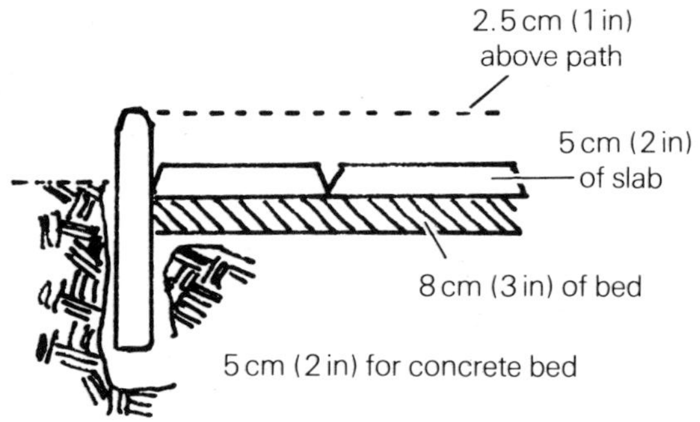

Fig. 10.15 *Concrete pave-edgings: diagram showing how to calculate depth of edging trench below ground level.*

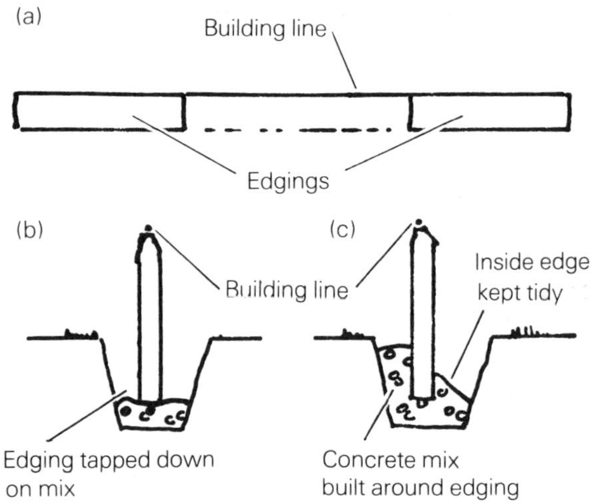

Fig. 10.16 *Laying concrete edgings. (a) Side view. (b) and (c) Sectional views.*

To lay

Dig a trench along the proposed line(s) of the edgings. The depth will depend on how high you wish them to stand above the finished level of the terrace or path; the standard height above level is 2.5 cm (1 in), since this allows for a good depth of edging below ground. In this case the depth of the trench will be: 2.5 cm (1 in) *plus* the thickness of the surface material, *plus* the thickness of the bed used, subtracted from the height of the edging used. To this should be added 5 cm

(2 in) for concrete edging bed. In the example shown in Fig. 10.15, for a slab path using 18 cm (7 in) edgings, the depth of the trench below the prepared ground will be: 18 cm minus (2.5 + 5 + 8 cm) = 2.5 cm + 5 cm = 7.5 cm (7 in minus (1 + 2 + 3 in) = 1 + 2 in = 3 in). Alter the sum to suit your requirements.

Dig out excess earth along the line of the path edge. Fix an edging (see below) at either end at the required height and run out the builder's line between the two, off the top edges (Fig. 10.16a).

Work along between them using the line as a guide for placing the other edgings.

To fix the edgings put a small amount of concrete mix, 8 cm (3 in), along the bottom of the trench in 90 cm (3 ft) runs. Place the edging on this and tap it down until the top edge lies flush with the builder's line (Fig. 10.16b). Then shovel in concrete along both sides of the edging, consolidating and firming up with a trowel (Fig. 10.16c). Make sure that the mix placed along the inside edge is tidy or it may interfere with the surface material laid against it. Cut edgings as for concrete blocks, see p. 82.

BRICK EDGINGS

If bricks are available for edging work you may well prefer to use them since their size and shape make a number of different designs possible. The basic designs are no more difficult to lay, though slightly more time-consuming than concrete edgings, and a number of variations of each can be created making it possible to develop an area of interest from what is otherwise a somewhat neglected part of construction work.

Designs

As shown in Fig. 10.17 the simplest design is to lay the bricks on their sides along the line of the edging, either flush with or slightly higher than the finished surface. A variation of this would be to lay the bricks in the same direction but flat on their faces, giving a broader, more definitive edge.

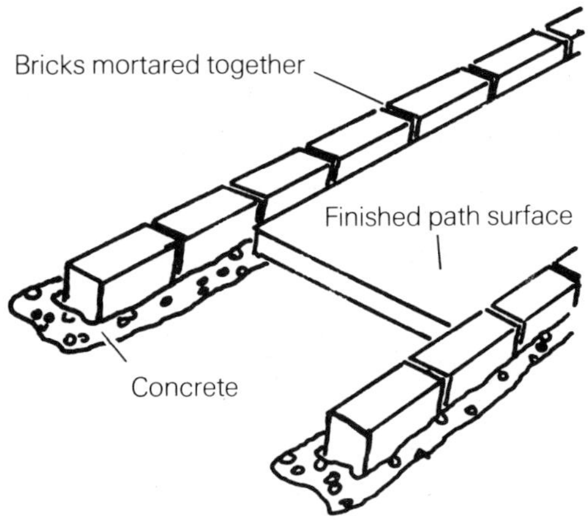

Fig. 10.17 *Bricks stood on edge and used as path edgings.*

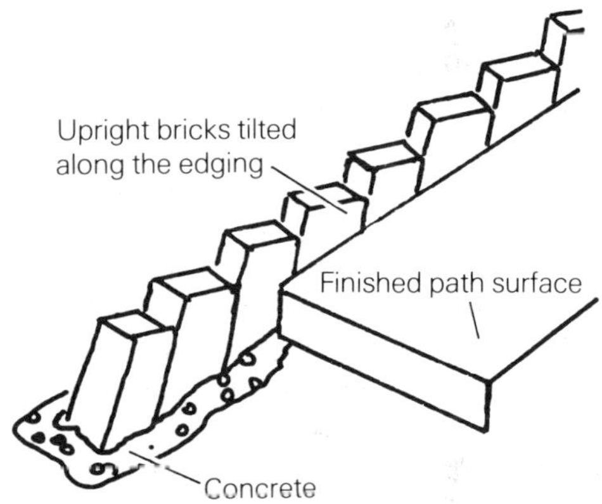

Fig. 10.18 *Sawtooth effect for edgings using tilted upright bricks.*

Alternatively, another series of designs are made possible by standing the bricks upright and varying their heights or the direction in which they point. A popular variation of this style is to tilt the upright bricks to one side, giving a saw-tooth effect to the line of the edgings, (Fig. 10.18). Whichever designs are used, or whether new ones are devised, the finished effect of carefully laid brick edgings will certainly make up for the extra time and work needed to lay them.

To lay

Bricks should be laid in the same way as concrete edgings, using a builder's line and concrete, and the initial trench depth should be

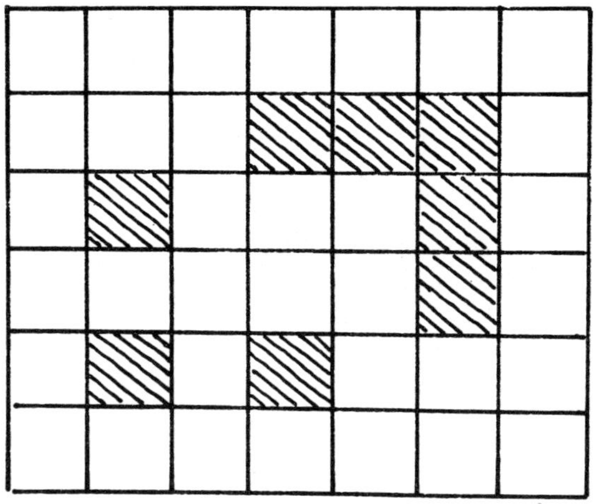

Fig. 10.19 *Leaving slabs out of a paved area creates distinctive patterns.*

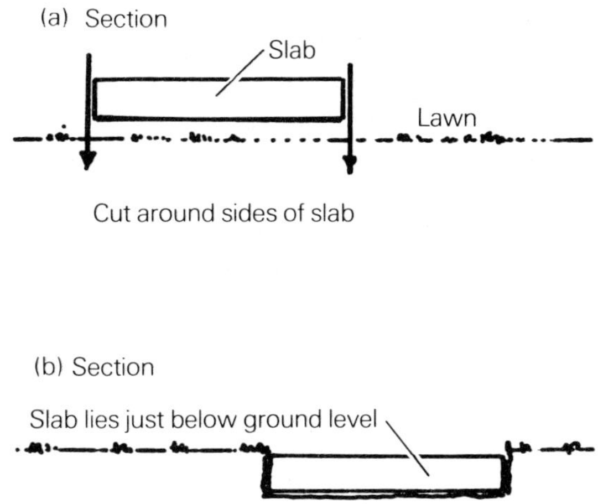

Fig. 10.20 *Setting slabs as 'stepping-stones' in a lawn.*

worked out by altering the sum shown to suit the size of brick and design being used.

(7b) BEDS IN TERRACES

Large areas of terrace can be made to look very attractive if sections of the surface material are left out. These gaps can then be filled with earth and planted with flowers and shrubs, and can be made to look even neater if they are lined with brick or concrete edgings. It should be noted, however, that the patterns for the beds should be worked out on paper (Fig. 10.19) before work commences and the surface laid or missed out according to the plan. Trying to lift out sections of the surface, and this is particularly true of slabs, once they have been laid can be extremely difficult, and the operation will most likely disturb the surrounding surface that you want to leave in.

(7c) ALTERNATIVE DESIGNS FOR TERRACES AND PATHS

While a definitive look at all the design possibilities for terraces and paths must lie outside the scope of this book, we would like to list here some of the commoner variations of style (using materials covered in this chapter) that may help to give an indication of what can be achieved with a little imagination.

Note The illustrations here show the designs used as path surfaces. Where suitable these designs can be used for terraces by repetition across the larger area.

CONCRETE SLABS

(1) A very attractive variation on the slabbed path is to space individual slabs so that they form 'stepping-stones' across the lawn. This method is one of the easiest and most effective ways of laying a path across the lawn without appearing to break it up too much.

To lay
Start by laying the slabs out on the lawn and re-arrange them until the direction and spacing of the 'steps' are to your liking. Test the spacing by walking along them and adjusting the slabs until you can walk across them comfortably.

When they are in the right positions cut the turf around each one with a spade (Fig. 10.20a). Lift the slabs aside and dig out the turf inside the cuts to a depth that will allow the slab to lie just below the lawn level (Fig. 10.20b). This will enable you to mow over the top of them.

Clean out any loose soil to allow the slab to lie firmly, drop slab into position and tap it down. Any gaps left around the slab can be filled with small pieces of the cut turf.

A variation of this style is to lay the slabs across the lawn 'diamond' fashion (Fig. 10.21). The amount of overlap can be altered to suit personal taste and the slabs laid as for above.

Note To make your own 'stepping-stones' *in situ*, see p. 180.

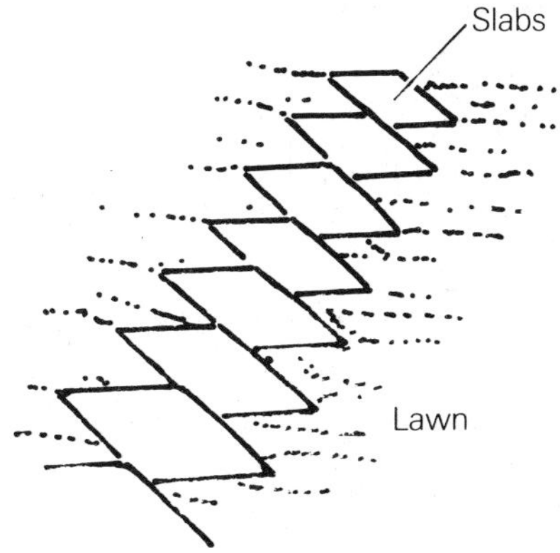

Fig. 10.21 *Slabs laid across a lawn in a diamond pattern.*

(2) Using slabs in combination with small pebbles is one of a number of attractive and unusual variations that can be used for conventional path surfaces. Fig. 10.22 and Plates 7–10) illustrate one way in which the two can be combined.

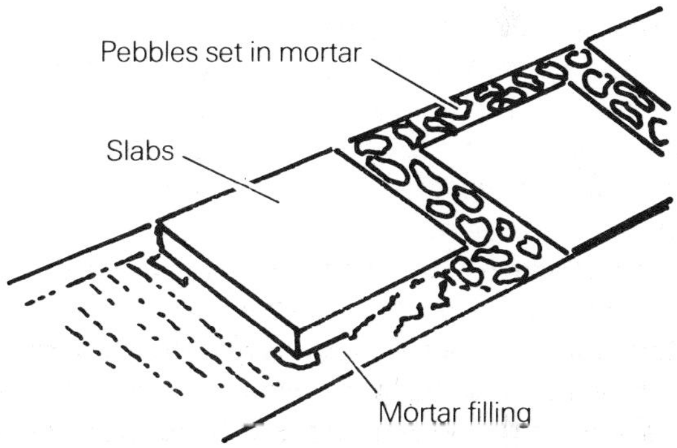

Fig. 10.22 *Combination of slabs and pebbles used as a path surface.*

To lay

For this design the slabs are laid in the normal manner using mortar spots, with the previously laid brick edgings being used as a guide for levels. The spacing and positioning of the slabs will depend on individual designs, those in the illustration being spaced at regular 15 cm (6 in) intervals down alternate sides of the path. The pebbles are then set in a mortar bed following the spaces left by the slabs. Although paths such as this one involve more work and materials than a conventional slab path, they also add variety and help lessen the formality of the concrete finish.

BRICKS

(1) Bricks can also be used in combination with slabs to bring colour and definition to terrace areas. The design shown in Fig. 10.23, for example, uses single lines of bricks to break the terrace up into smaller units. A number of variations on this theme are possible, including brick lines of varying width and areas of brick surrounded by slabs. Laying techniques will vary according to the use to which the terrace will be put and should be worked out from Table 5.1 (p. 33).

(2) Another use for bricks is to lay them

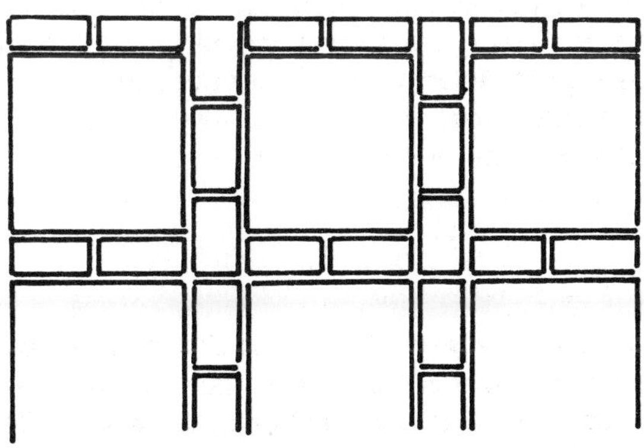

Fig. 10.23 *Combination of brick and slabs for a terrace or path.*

Fig. 10.24 *Informal brick path laid across a lawn.*

across lawns in the same way as the 'stepping-stones' of the slab paths mentioned above. They can either be spaced in groups across the lawn like the slabs, or laid in an informal pattern, such as that shown in Fig. 10.24, which, while producing a 'continuous' path, does not appear to break up the lawn too much. The same procedure as for laying stepping-stone slab paths should be used, altering the designs before cutting the turf to make sure that the spacing etc. is correct, and finally laying them just below the lawn level.

These are just a few of the many variations that can be achieved using slabs and bricks. There are, of course, almost endless possibilities using different designs and combining different kinds of materials (crazy-paving, for example). We strongly recommend that you spend some time looking at a few alternatives before committing yourself to one or the other. This is particularly true if you are using concrete, since this material is very expensive and difficult to remove or alter if you are not satisfied with the result.

(7d) JOINTING/POINTING

Whichever material is used for jointing (i.e. filling in the gaps between slabs or pieces of paving, etc.), either earth, sand or mortar, it will strengthen the terrace or path and make the finished surface more pleasant to look at. Earth or sand brushed into the joints is a suitable finish for some materials, such as bricks or slate laid on a sand bed but, of course, this can lead to a weed problem later on. Perhaps the most satisfactory all-purpose jointing material for finishes laid on screed or solid beds is a lean mortar mix (1 : 6), pushed down the joints and smoothed off (pointing) with a trowel. If a neat job is required be sure to keep the joints clear of excess screed or mix while laying the slabs etc., since cleaning them out afterwards can be a long job.

8 Steps

Although it may appear to be one of the more complicated jobs, building steps is not, in fact, too hard to organize once you have decided exactly what you want. Problems only really arise if you either change your mind halfway through a job or start work without having a clear idea of how the job will proceed, i.e. how many steps there will be etc. Once this has been worked out and you have decided on what materials to use, the building procedure is very simple, if repetitive.

The materials used will depend on what is available, what the steps are joining up with, and the overall effect required, and in fact any of the materials we have discussed above can be used, alone or in combination. Slabs, slate or crazy-paving, for example, all make good 'treads' (Fig. 10.25a), while bricks, blocks or stone can be used for the 'risers'. Alternatively, the steps can be cast in concrete or you can use large pieces of wood (i.e. old railway sleepers or split oak) in combination with one or other of the materials mentioned already. In this section we will look at three basic techniques for making steps, each one suitable for different combinations of materials.

Before going on to look at the actual construction, however, a quick word about how to work out the number of steps you need. Whatever the situation, the number of steps used will depend on the height of the risers and the depth (horizontally) of the treads, and these proportions depend in turn on how formal and regular you want the steps to be.

As a general rule though, to decide on the size and quantity of steps, first work out the total length and the total height of the step site. These figures should then be divided up as equally as possible (Fig. 10.25b), i.e. a 3.6 m (12 ft) length would divide up into four treads 90 cm (3 ft) deep each, and if the height was 1.2 m (4 ft) there would be four risers of 30 cm (1 ft) each. There is no set rule; it is a matter of juggling with the figures until you arrive at the most acceptable arrangement for your purposes. It should be noted, however, that risers of 30 cm (1 ft) are uncomfortable and difficult to negotiate and that the ideal riser height is generally considered to be 18 cm (7 in).

For situations where it is difficult to assess the overall length and height of the step site (i.e. long, low irregular slopes, etc.) or where regular steps would look out of place, the best policy is to start at the bottom, building an 18 cm (7 in) riser, and position the next step at the most convenient point (much as one does when digging out stepped footings for walls, see p. 80).

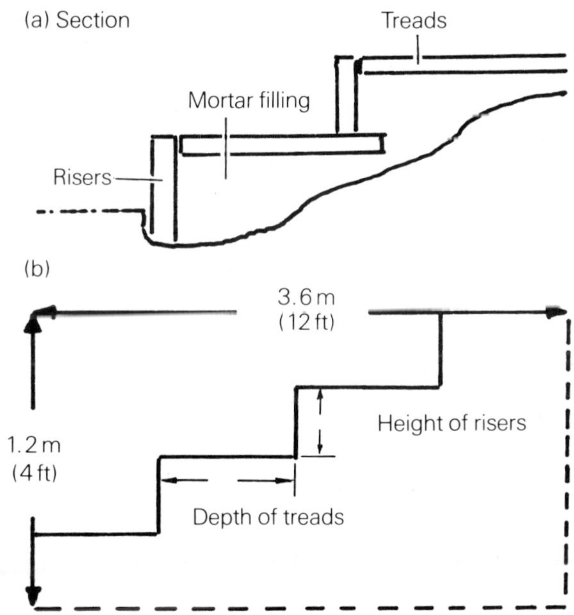

Fig. 10.25 *Making steps. (a) General construction showing arrangement of treads and risers. (b) Calculating horizontal depth and vertical height of steps.*

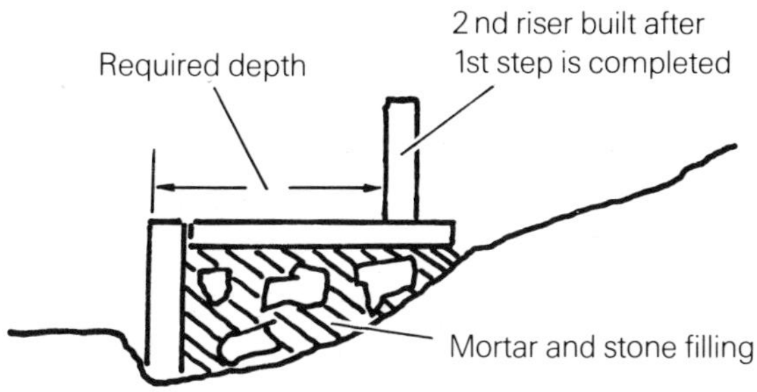

Fig. 10.26 *Constructing first and subsequent steps.*

TO BUILD

(1) Brick and crazy-paving

In this example we have used a combination of brick risers framing treads of crazy-paving (Plate 24), and, as with all types of step, each riser is built on the tread of the step below to give a solid foundation (Fig. 10.26). When starting the first riser should be built on a small footing (p. 76) if it cannot be built off a terrace or path.

Note To prevent puddles forming on the steps the treads should be given a slight fall, either to one side or from back to front. This is a matter of choice, unless the steps are cut into a steep bank where the treads will be enclosed by side walls. In these cases the fall should be from back to front.

Procedure

1 Dig out rough profile for the first few steps.

2 Mock up the first riser and check, using a board and spirit-level that you have enough clearance behind it for the tread material and mortar bed (Plate 11). Decide also at this point on the direction of tread fall and allow for it in your calculations. Dig out any excess earth now.

3 Build the riser. When it has set, fill in the tread area with rubble and sand to form a good base for the mortar bed. Mix mortar and shovel into position (Plate 12).

4 Place crazy-paving on the mortar and tap down into position, using spirit-level or a

board to check that the pieces are lying at the correct level (Plate 13). Repeat the process until the tread area is covered, fitting the pieces into an informal pattern (Plate 14).

5 Go back over the tread, checking the levels and filling the joints with mortar. Point up the mortar with a trowel and leave tread to set (Plate 15).

6 Repeat process for required number of steps.

Note Alternative materials for this technique include:
For risers : blocks or stone.
For treads : bricks, slabs, slate or concrete.

(2) **Concrete and half-stone risers** (Plate 16)

For these steps the concrete has been laid 8 cm (3 in) deep. Thus for 18 cm (7 in) risers the stone will need to be built up 10 cm (4 in).

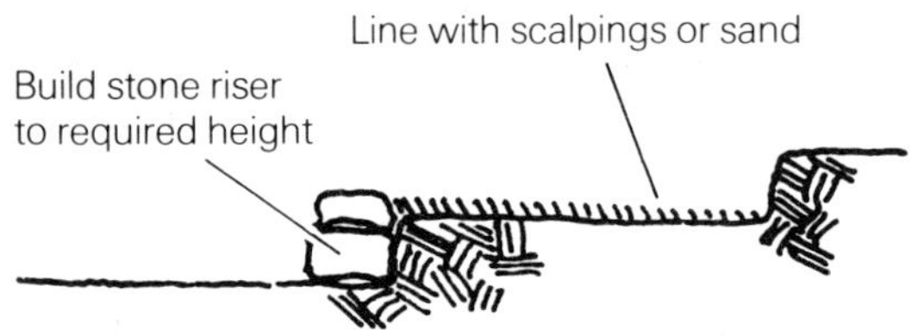

Fig. 10.27 *Sectional view of stone riser.*

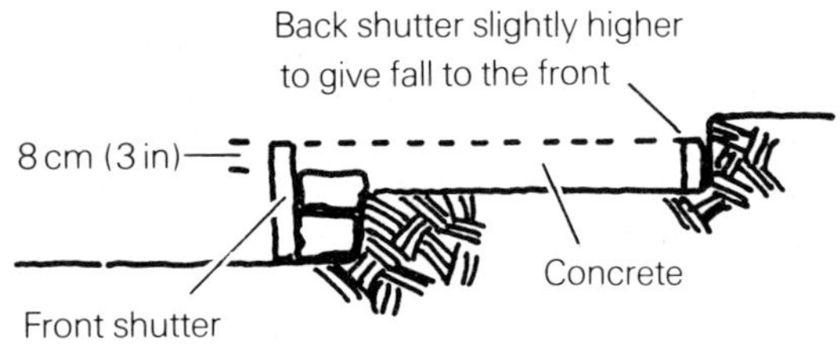

Fig. 10.28 *Setting up the shuttering for concreting.*

Procedure
1 and 2 as for above.

3 Build stone riser to required height and cover tread area behind it with sand or scalpings (Fig. 10.27).

4 Fix shuttering across the front of the step, and across the back of the tread, checking that the back shutter is high enough to give required fall (Fig. 10.28).

5 Using a fairly dry mix (if the mix is too wet it may run down over the stones), fill with concrete and level off with a tamping board (p. 114). Do not give the concrete too smooth a finish since this will become very slippery in wet weather; either leave the ridged finish given by the tamping board or brush lightly after it has set for a while. (For Finishing and Curing concrete see p. 114.)

6 Repeat for next steps when the concrete is well set.

Note Alternative materials for half-risers: bricks or blocks (laid flat).

(3) **Wooden steps**

If suitable wood can be found, very attractive steps can be made using risers in wood combined with stone, brick, etc. treads. Railway sleepers are ideal for the purpose, but oak or similar hardwoods may also be used.

Procedure
The risers should be anchored in position, using bolts or steel rods, either straight into the earth or, for greater strength, into concrete footings. Fill in tread material as for above.

As mentioned above, building steps is not difficult, but to save both time and materials avoid digging out too much earth when cutting the step profiles, since this will mean that you will need excessive amounts of filler.

11 Features

Most garden layouts rely for their full effect on various focal points; features in the garden towards which attention is directed by the surrounding layout designs. Whether these points of interest are ornaments, such as sundials, small statues or planted bowls, or something larger such as a pond, with either a waterfall or a fountain, or whether it is some planted area, such as a rockery or a pergola, where careful planting makes it stand out, they all serve the same purpose: to provide something that focuses attention and gives the layout, or a part of it, a central cohesion. As such, the various features situated around the garden play a very important role in the overall design and need to be planned and built with as much care as the walls, terraces and paths which help build up the rest of the layout.

In Chapter 3 we have discussed some of the considerations that should be kept in mind when planning gardens and features, in turn, should be fitted into wider plans for the garden as a whole. It is sufficient to point out here that almost any garden design, irrespective of its size, will be more cohesive and interesting if various features are included to catch the viewer's attention. If this can be achieved the surroundings, such as buildings or high walls, become less dominant, and the garden becomes an entity on its own.

What features are included in a garden layout depends very much on the type of layout being worked on, the practicalities of, for example, using water etc. and personal taste, but we hope in this chapter to provide some ideas on a range of suitable features, which can either be used as they stand or adapted or combined to suit particular circumstances.

Clearly, in all the sections that follow, there are a wide number of variations in design and materials used, possible for each type of feature and it is not feasible for us to pursue all these in equal detail. Thus in each section we have concentrated on giving full technical details for one or two examples of each, followed by some possible variations that can be built using the same techniques.

1 Waterfalls

Waterfalls are often thought of only in connection with large landscaped gardens or as part of a pond design. While this is not without justification, since it is in such situations that they have traditionally been found, it is a shame because they are in fact ideal material for an interesting feature in any sized garden, bringing the movement and, perhaps even more important, the sound of water into situations where it might otherwise be absent. The advantages and pleasure to be gained from this, particularly in urban surroundings, need no introduction here, and if it is impossible to create a pond or large-scale water feature in your garden, a small waterfall and catchment basin might be a suitable alternative.

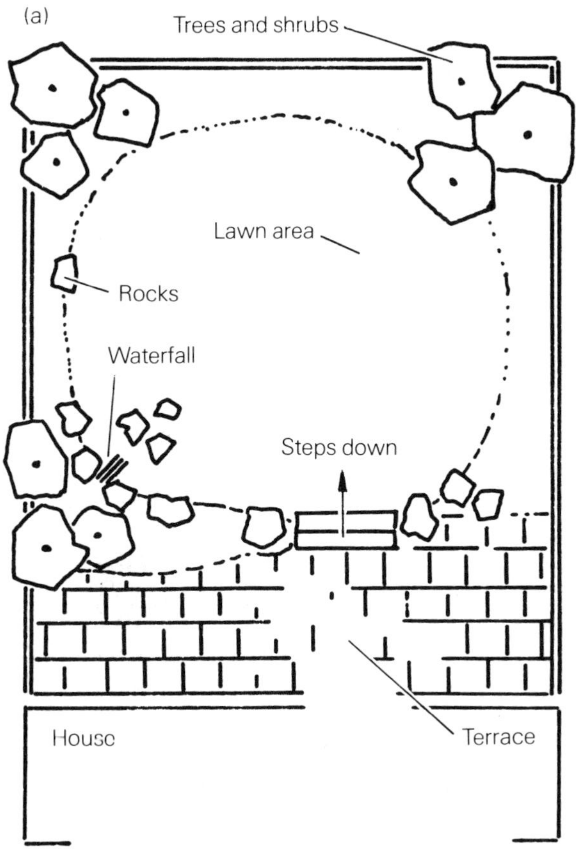

Fig. 11.1
(a) Plan showing a waterfall combined in the layout for a small garden.
(b) Arrangement of rocks for the waterfall.

Since we are going on to look at ponds suitable for the larger garden in the next section, we will concentrate here on the use of waterfalls in the small town garden, where the addition of water, even if not in large quantities, can make such a difference.

In the example shown in Fig. 11.1a a small waterfall has been used as the centre of interest in the garden of a small terraced house. Although it may not occupy a central position in the garden, it nevertheless creates an area of sound and movement which captures the attention, while the rest of the garden provides a suitable background for it. Situated as it is it also serves to draw the viewer out into the garden because, although it is not immediately visible from the house, it will be audible from the terrace behind it. The actual arrangement of the rocks can be seen in Fig. 11.1b, and using this picture we can start to analyse what is required for the construction of such a feature.

Clearly, by its very nature, the waterfall must appear to fall from higher to lower ground. Thus the illusion must be created that the waterfall is situated on the edge of higher ground, and this means raising a mound, of suitable proportions for the size of the site, against which the waterfall stones can be set. In our example, then, the level of the lawn area has been dropped and the earth from there built up around the edges, leading up to the mound in the corner. Thus, with

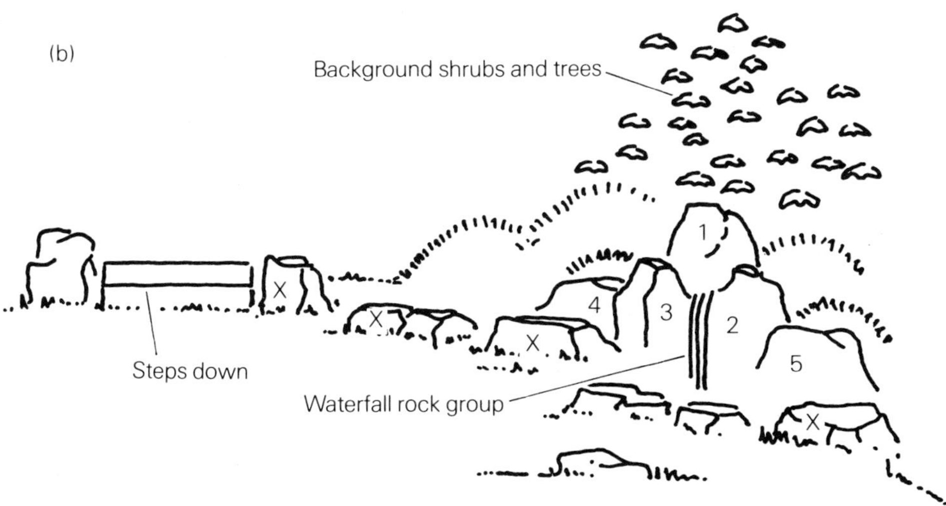

the minimum amount of earth moving, the different levels have been created which make possible the siting of a small fall.

The illusion of higher land is added to later by the bulk of the stones and dense back-planting behind the fall. This planting also serves to isolate the arrangement from the walls and building behind, framing it and concentrating attention on the path of the water itself.

Once the site for the fall has been established, the next consideration is the construction of the rock arrangement. The exact way in which water falls, the shapes and sounds it makes, depends on two main factors: first, the stones over which it falls and second, the volume and speed at which it does so. In Fig. 11.1b, the water forms a single, thin stream, emerging from between the two large stones and falling out of sight behind the stones grouped at the bottom. This pattern could be altered in a number of ways, such as those shown in Fig. 11.2a and b, where changing the position of various stones creates entirely different looking falls. In all three examples, however, the amount of sound and movement will depend on how fast the water is allowed to flow over the stones and this is regulated by stop taps or the size of pump used.

These considerations bring us on to the mechanics of the fall. Build into the arrangement in Fig. 11.1b are three crucial components: the water source, the header pool and the drain or collecting pool. In most situations the water can either be fed to the fall straight from a tap and allowed to drain away at the base, or it can be collected in a small pool and fed back up to the top by a pump. (The exception to this is, of course, where a natural source of water is available, in which case the fall is inserted at a suitable point along the water course.) At the point where the water enters the fall it is necessary to build up the volume of the water slightly to ensure a good flow down the stones. To do this a header pool is situated just behind the first stones of the fall, which allows the water to collect in sufficient volume to create, for

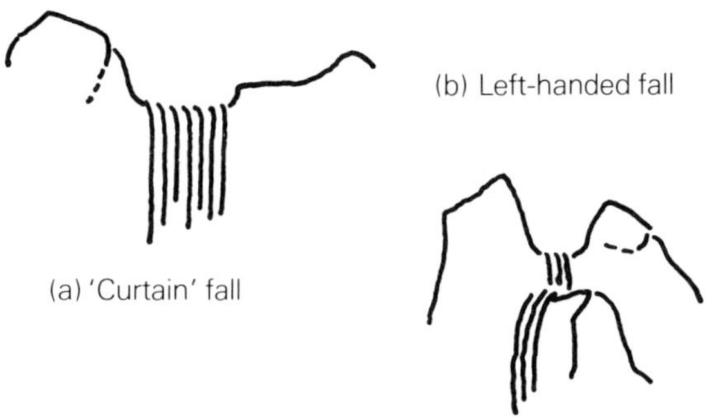

Fig. 11.2 *Two variations for waterfall design.*

example, the wide 'curtain' fall shown in Fig. 11.2a. Finally, there is the drain or collecting pool at the bottom. Whichever technique is used, collecting or draining, this area should be designed as part of the whole group and in such a way that it blends in with, in our example, the lawn which leads away from it. Here the stones are grouped together, suggesting that the water falls into a small gully, with one or two set lower into the grass stretching away from the bottom of the fall. In this way the eye is lead naturally down from the top of the fall and out across the garden, the stones forming a visual link, while at the same time controlling the water. The fall is then further blended into the setting by the use of large stones on the far side of the steps and down the edge of the lawn, continuing the theme round the garden.

These then, are the most important aspects of creating a waterfall: the mound and backup planting which form the immediate setting, the stones which form the actual watercourse, the source, header pool, and drain which control the water, and the supportive use of other stones to blend the feature in with the rest of the garden. With these things in mind, let us look at the construction details.

TO CONSTRUCT A WATERFALL

What you will need

Stone. Mortar mix: 1 : 4, sand and cement. Shovel. Trowel.

For piped source and drain 1.3 cm ($\frac{1}{2}$ in) diameter polythene water pipe for the feed. Many types of piped drains or soakaways can be used; reference should be made here to the relevant sections of Chapter 5 and the most suitable form chosen from there.

For collecting pool and pump Small pump and polythene water pipes to fit. Consult your local dealer who can advise on which type is most suitable for your particular requirements.

Measuring up

Plan your fall carefully, working out how much piping is needed to take the water from source to header pool. The source will either be a tap in or near the house, or the collecting pool if a pump is being used. Order accordingly. The stone required is almost impossible to estimate precisely, but if you work out the type of fall you want, you should be able to guess roughly how many large and small stones you will need. For example, the fall in Fig. 11.1a and b, requires six large stones for the fall group, four large stones for supportive use round the garden, and a selection of some eight smaller stones for the base of the fall and incidental filling out of the design.

To build

1 Create the mound, forming the earth to give the overall contours required (Fig. 11.3)

2 Position major stones in two stages: First, (Fig. 11.4) dig in the large stones that will help contain and shape the mound (marked X in Figs. 11.1b and 11.4). Drop stones into position and pack earth firmly around them. Fill up behind with additional soil. Second, concentrate on the fall. Stone 1 (Fig. 11.4) forms the highest point and the backdrop, while stones 2 and 3 frame the fall itself. Be sure to leave enough room at H for the header pool.

3 Decide at this point what kind of pump you are going to use. Two basic kinds are available: submersible ones that sit on the bottom of the collecting pool (or pond) and those that must be situated out of water and connected to it by pipes. Your local dealer will be able to advise on which kind is most suitable for your needs. When this is decided, work out the best position for the drain or collecting pool and dig the hole. This should now be lined with either bricks and render or concrete to make it waterproof, with pipe connections for

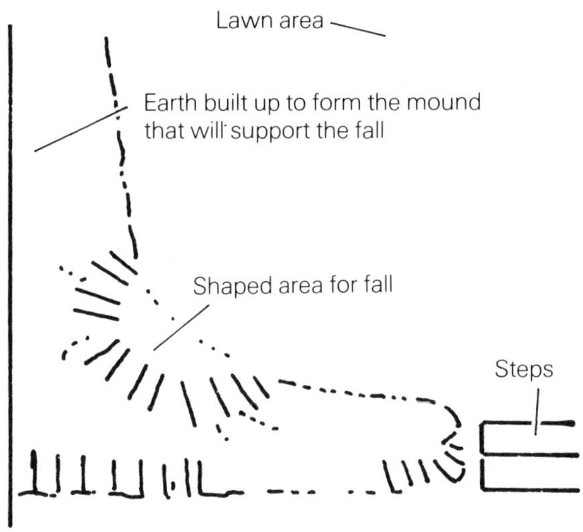

Fig. 11.3 *Creating the setting for a fall.*

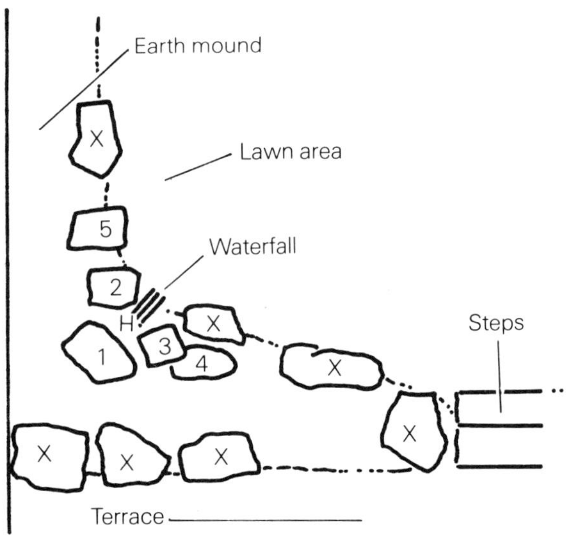

Fig. 11.4 *Diagram illustrating use of major stones: 1–5 for waterfall; X for containing the earth mound. (For elevation see Fig. 11.1b).*

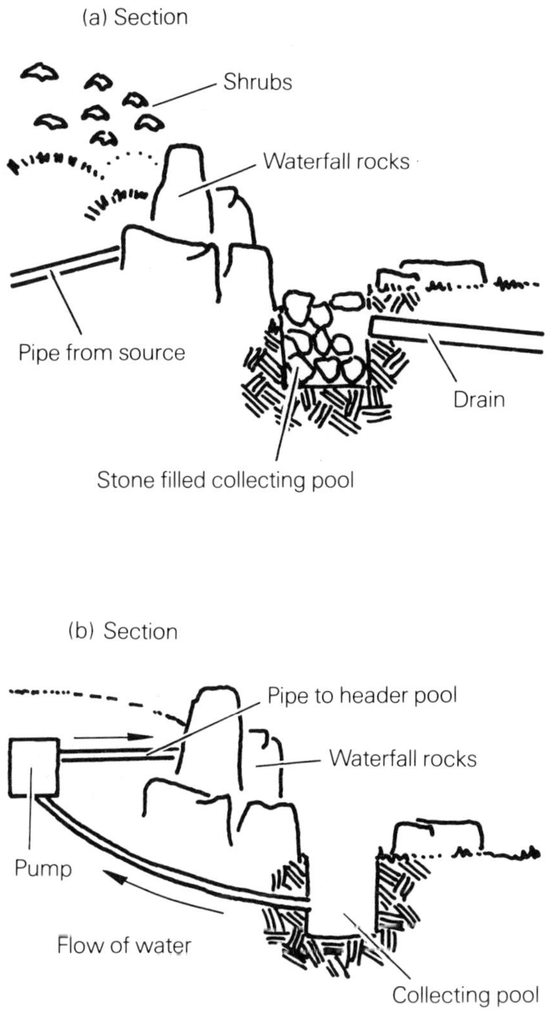

Fig. 11.5 *(a) Drain and (b) Pump arrangements for a waterfall.*

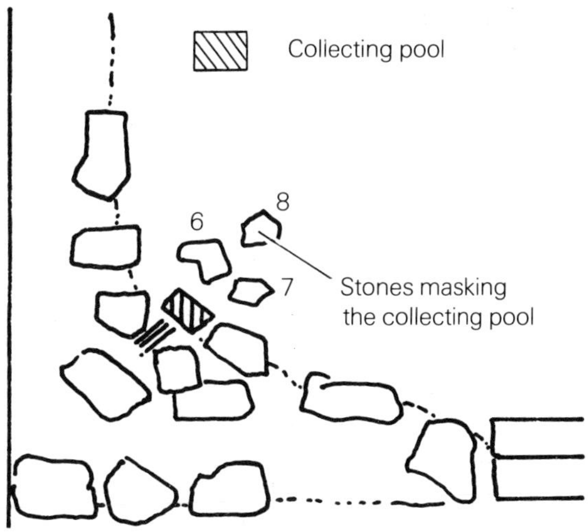

Fig. 11.6 *Filling out waterfall group with subsidiary stones (6, 7, 8).*

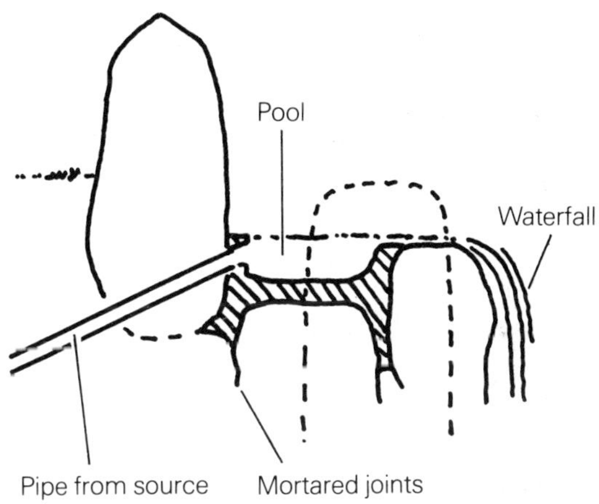

Fig. 11.7 *Sectional view of a header pool.*

pump or drains set into the lining. Submersible pumps should now be fitted into the collecting pool and connected to their power line. Lay drains (Fig. 11.5a) or water pipes; for submersible pumps lay pipes direct to header pool and for other pumps to the pump site. Non-submersible pumps are best situated in a small box (brick- or concrete-lined) behind stone 1 and let into the mound. It can then be covered in soil to cut down operational noise. Lay pipe from pump box to header pool (Fig. 11.5b). The collecting pool can either be filled with stone (Fig. 11.5a) or left open to form a pool (Fig. 11.5b), depending on the effect required and whether or not it contains a pump.

4 Fill in waterfall design with subsidiary stones (i.e. 4 and 5 in Fig. 11.4), packing the stones firmly together with soil, and position the masking stones (6, 7 and 8 in Fig. 11.6) around the drain.

5 Using a variety of smaller stones to fill in any gaps, create the header pool (Fig. 11.7) and the details of the water course. Render

the inside of the pool and mortar up the joints between stones, down the fall and around the drain.

6 Fill out the design with any additional stones and position the supporting stones leading away around the garden. For those spreading out into the lawn, use the same technique as for laying stepping-stone paths (p. 126), setting them progressively lower.

7 Plant up the backing mound. If you want to have ferns etc. growing near the actual fall, create small pockets as you build the water course which will hold sufficient soil to facilitate planting. A scattering of small gravel stones in the header pool, on ledges down the fall and around the drain will also add to the general effect.

A small waterfall of this type can be seen in Plate 17, and, although in this example it falls into a pond, it could fall into a collecting pool in thc area defined by the lowest stone on the right, across to the white 'island' stone and back up to the base of the fall, making it an interesting little feature of the kind we have been looking at here.

2 Ponds

Ponds, like waterfalls, will add entirely new dimensions to a garden, and can be created in two ways. Either, if there is an existing stream, by careful damming in the right place, or, if there is no water already present in the garden, by creating a watertight receptacle which can subsequently be filled.

An excellent example of the first kind can be seen in Plate 18, where the course of the stream has been dammed to create a small, informal pool that appears completely natural in the rustic setting. In this example the water is held back by a large piece of slate set into the earth at a point where the slightly higher ground that surrounds the pool area slopes away to lower parts of the garden. This means that the water has plenty of space to back-up and find its own level, while still being retained in one area. Situating the dam further back or further forward would have involved extensive earth moving to create new sides for the pool. The exact depth and size of the pool is regulated by the height of the dam; this could be raised slightly to increase the area of the pool or lowered to reduce it. This is very much a case of trial and error and, having dammed the stream, you should be prepared to alter it later if the resulting pool is too large or too small. One factor to bear in mind is the increased flow of water in winter, and this should be taken into consideration when siting the dam.

If you are fortunate enough to have a stream running through your property and wish to create a pool somewhere along its course, start by carefully observing the whole site (preferably over the full cycle of a year). Choose your damming point and construct dam. If there is a large, constant flow of water, you may have to dig a trench round your dam site to divert the water during construction. Make sure that any dam constructed of mortared masonry (stone, brick, etc.) is sitting on a firm concrete footing (p. 76).

Most people, however, will not have the advantage of a stream running through their garden, and so a pond must be made. Whether this is to be large or small, concrete- or plastic-lined, and with or without additional features (such as bridges or waterfalls), the basic design principles remain the same. The pond should have carefully levelled edges, an overflow and a low point to help with cleaning out. In addition to these requirements, to make ponds as attractive as possible, whether they are formal or informal, the actual materials of which they are constructed should not be visible round the edges. To meet these requirements the design should be based on that shown in section in Fig. 11.8a where the slabs surrounding a small formal pool are seen sitting on a shelf that is just below water level. (For more informal designs the slabs would be replaced by stones as shown in Plates 19 & 20.) This technique means that the plastic

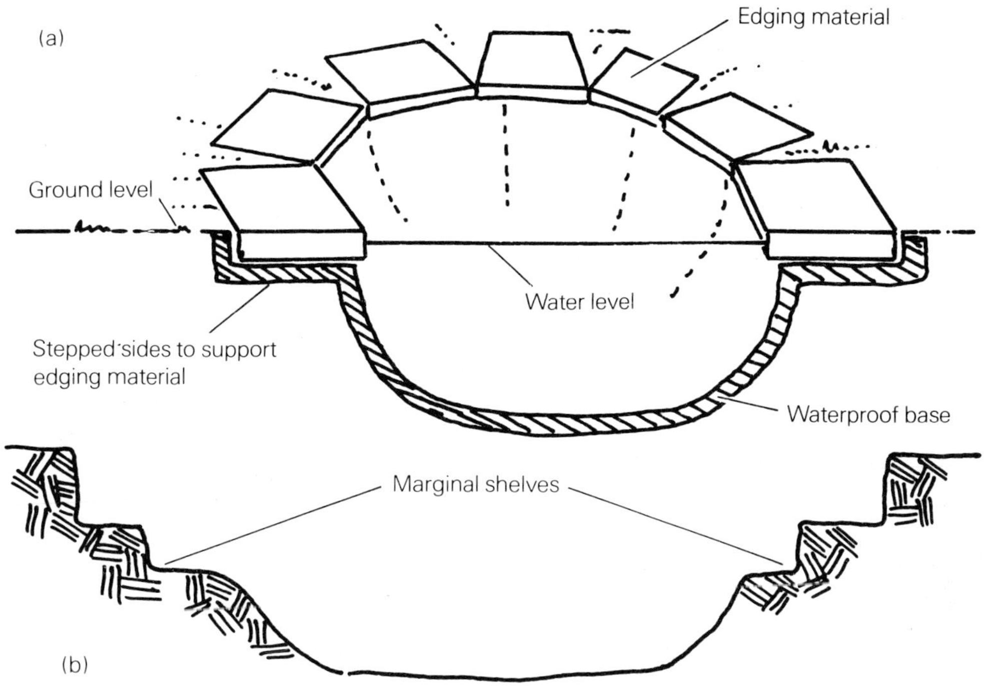

Fig. 11.8 *(a) Basic requirements for pond construction.*
(b) Section of pond showing use of marginal shelves.

lining can be brought up behind the slabs to just above water level, but will not be visible above or just below it. (Similarly if a concrete lining were used, this would also not show round the edges.)

Siting: the position of a pond will clearly depend mainly on the demands of the wider layout of which it is part, but you should bear in mind that ponds are best suited to sunny, open positions where they will not be subject to excessive leaf fall. In addition, if your garden includes a sloping area, you may consider using part of the slope to contain the pond. This technique (used to create the pond shown in Plates 19 and 20) minimizes the amount of digging required and helps blend the pond naturally into the garden around it.

The shape: The shape of a pond will depend, like its positioning, on the overall design in which it is being included, but some points about depth and the contours of the pond should be noted. To avoid excessive digging, while providing sufficient depth for fish to survive and to prevent the water freezing solid in winter, you should aim to make the pond 38–75 cm (15 in–2 ft 6 in) deep. Some aquatic plants, however, cannot thrive in deep water and so, to accommodate them at the right depth and to give their pots something to stand on, marginal shelves should be included round the sides. This means that the pond will have a double-stepped sectional view as shown in Fig. 11.8b. Again, the exact contouring is a matter of personal taste, but the pond should be designed with the above points in mind.

The construction technique outlined below covers all aspects of making ponds, using earth and concrete steps, constructing the overflow and contouring the bottom, and should be adapted to suit your particular needs and choice of edging material.

TO BUILD

What you will need

Pegs: long enough for required depth of water *plus* 15 cm (6 in). Spirit-level: at least

60 cm (2 ft) long. Straight-edged board: at least 1.8 m (6 ft) long. Pick axe. Shovel. Trowel. Tape-measure. Edging material: i.e. stone, slabs, etc. Concrete: (1 : 6) and shuttering (see p. 113). Mortar: 1 : 4).

(**Plastic Lining** rolls of special pond-lining fabric can be bought which are flexible enough to suit any pond shape. The plastic is very tough but also pliable and moulds itself to the contours of the pond base; its quality of elasticity allows it to 'give' as the weight of the water pushes it down round the sides and across the bottom. Various types are available and the best way to choose one is to visit a pond or garden centre to look at the alternatives and ask the advice of the staff. A wide range of sizes are available (although they are all square or rectangular in shape) and the following formula (provided by Lotus Pool Catalogue) indicates how to calculate the size of liner you need once the pond is dug:

Length of liner = overall length of pool *plus* twice the maximum depth.
Width of liner = overall width of pool *plus* twice the maximum depth.

Note Prefabricated moulded pools are available and if you wish to use one, buy it before preparing the hole. You should then excavate the hole and set the pool in it following the manufacturer's instructions.

Concrete lining Concrete should be laid at a uniform 10 cm (4 in) depth over the bottom. At this depth, 1 cu m (1.25 cu yd) would cover 9 sq m (11 sq yd). Use this figure to work out total requirements. Over large areas it may be a good idea to insert some reinforcing bars into the wet concrete, laying them in a criss-cross pattern. Waterproofing additive should also be used if mixing your own concrete.

Procedure

Soil base and plastic lining

1 Work out the position of your overflow. This will govern the final water level and should sit just below the finished level of the surrounding edges.

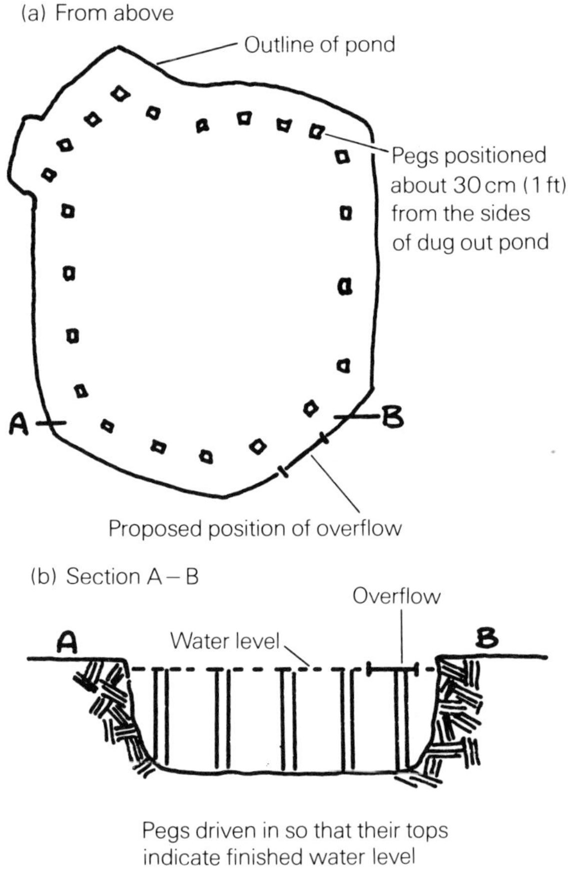

Fig. 11.9 *Pegging the edge of the pond.*

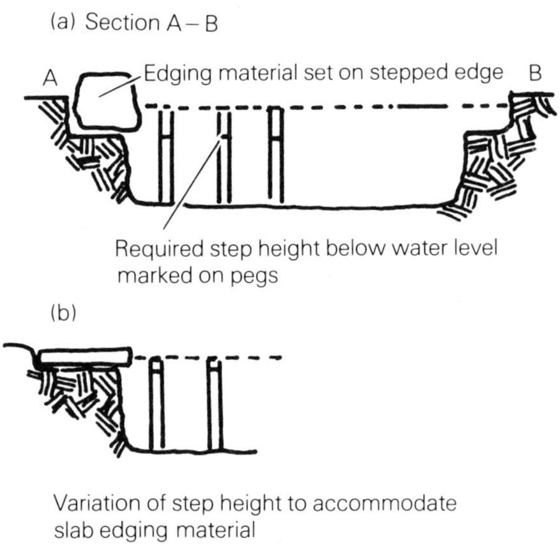

Fig. 11.10 *Using the pegs to guide construction of stepped edges.*

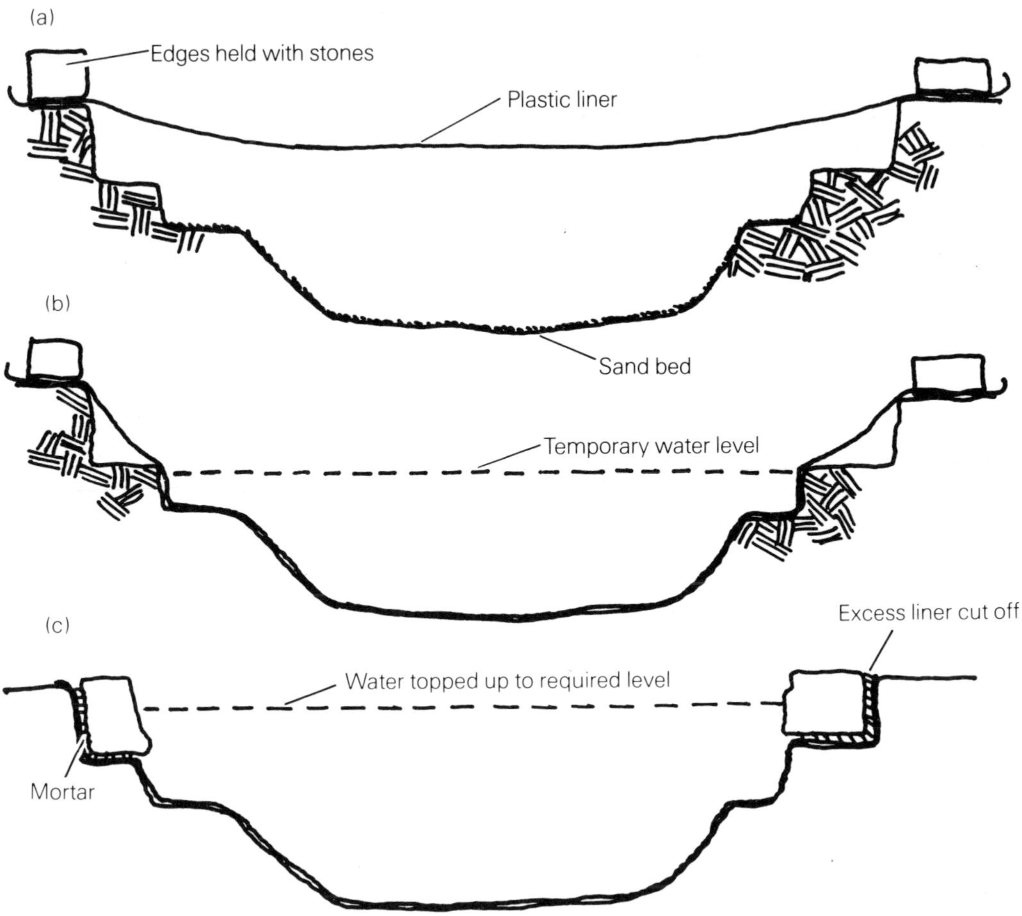

Fig. 11.11 *(a) First stage in installing plastic pond liner. (b) Filling the liner with water up to the level of the edging step. (c) Edging material set in position, and the water level topped up.*

2 Dig out pond shape, using the position of the overflow to work out the depth and to keep the edges level. Make the sides as vertical as possible. Check depth and sides by holding the board with one end on the overflow out over the pond, keeping it level with the spirit-level and reading off below it with the tape-measure. Try to give the bottom at least two levels. This will create a natural collecting area for dead leaves etc. and fish if the pond is drained and make it more interesting to look at once filled.

3 Starting at the overflow, work round the pond bottom banging in pegs (every 60–90 cm (2–3 ft), about 30 cm (1 ft) from the sides using the spirit-level (Fig. 11.9).

4 Using the peg tops as a guide, cut a step round the sides of the pool, deep enough (horizontally) for your edging material to sit on and low enough for it to sit correctly in relation to the required water level, i.e. in Figs. 11.10a and b, the steps are cut in different proportions, for stone edgings (a) and slab edgings (b). Alter to suit your needs.

5 Go round the step smoothing out the surface, removing any sharp stones etc. If the step is cut in clay subsoil, with the addition of water, it can be moulded to give a very firm, smooth surface. When you are satisfied, remove the pegs and cover the pond bottom and sides with a 2.5 cm (1 in) layer of clean sand.

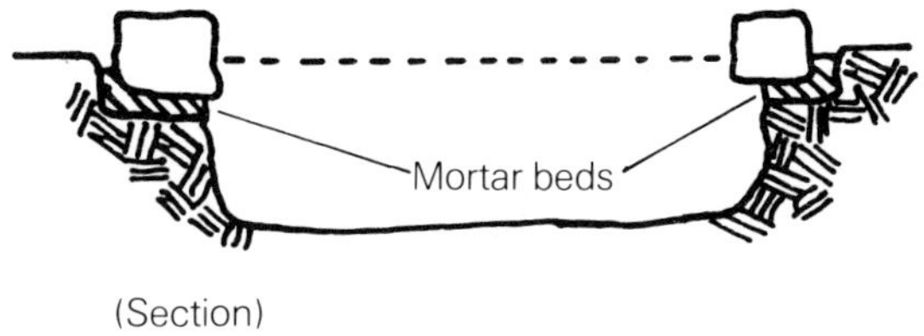

Fig. 11.12 *Pond edging material set on mortar and slightly overhanging the step.*

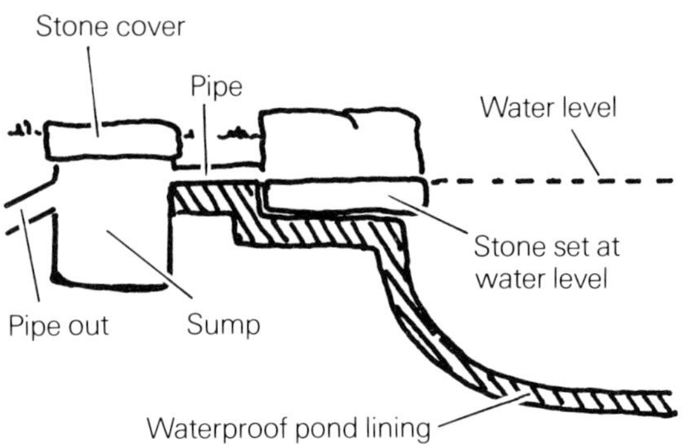

Fig. 11.13 *Arrangement for a pond overflow.*

6 Lay pond lining, bringing it well up, over the sides and out on to ground level. If you are using pond lining plastic you will find that as you stretch it out over the sand it will settle on the surface, tightly hugging the contours. For other, thicker plastic sheets you will have to smooth out wrinkles and fold overlaps into neat creases, holding them down with sand; be sure to allow generous tucks around the points indicated in Fig. 11.11. (This will allow the plastic some spare capacity as the water pins it down and stretches it tight down the sides.)

Note Avoid pond sizes that will require more than one sheet, unless the pool is to be continually topped up by a stream, for example. In these cases overlap the sheets by at least 1.2 m (4 ft) and the weight of the water plus subsequent silting should seal them pretty tight. Any initial seepage will be made up for by the stream.

7 The edging material (stone, slabs, etc.) should now be mortared into position on the step (Fig. 11.12). Place a good bed of mortar on the lining and position stone, etc. with the front edge positioned out over the step edge. (This creates a shadow under it giving the illusion of depth and hiding the pond lining. It also provides somewhere protected for fish to go.) Settle the stone firmly and fill in with mortar between the pond lining and the back of the stone. Alternatively, where you have sufficient depth, you can fill this space behind the stone with soil which will provide a suitably waterlogged site for planting rushes and other water-loving plants. Repeat the process round the pond, mortaring the stones firmly together. Cut off any excess lining that remains visible above ground level.

8 Overflow: Fig. 11.13 illustrates an arrangement for the overflow. A low stone, whose top comes level with required water level, is positioned on the step and the sump (brick-lined and rendered) situated just behind it and underground. Connect sump to drain outlet. (For suitable drains see p. 36.) Regular edging material continues round either side.

Concrete lining and sides

Prepare as for above up to and including (5). If the pond is being built in soft ground, include an 8 cm (3 in) layer of hardcore under the sand. When the base is ready, place a number of bricks (10 cm (4 in)) around the bottom of the pool and shovel in the concrete filling around and up to the tops of the bricks. Smooth off the concrete with the back of the shovel as each section is laid. Lay a uniform 10 cm (4 in) layer over the bottom and up over the step (Fig. 11.14a). Remove bricks and insert any reinforcing bars as you go along.

When the concrete is dry, erect shuttering round the sides to give a 10 cm (4 in) wall up the back of the step to just below ground level (Fig. 11.14b). Fill with concrete and leave to set.

Remove shuttering and seal the joint along

Plate 16 Steps constructed of half-stone risers with a concrete slab completing the riser and forming the tread (p. 130).

Plate 17 A small pond side waterfall with a collecting pool at its base (p. 136).

Plate 18 A carefully placed dam (in this case a piece of slate) across the path of a small stream, creates a lovely informal pool in this gently sloping garden (p. 136).

Plate 19 A pond built against a slope, with the open side built up with stone to contain the water. Stone is then used round the other edges to complete the effect (pp. 136-7).

Plate 20 Another view of the stone wall used to contain the pond. Note that the concrete path is laid up to and around the base of the wall to give the wall greater strength (pp. 136-7).

Plates 21 – 24: Rockery construction (p. 150)

Plate 21 This small sloping area between the new steps and the terrace provides an ideal site for a small rockery.

Plate 22 Three structural stones form the framework for the rockery retaining soil along the bottom and at the level change caused by the step.

Plate 23 A large, interestingly shaped stone is placed as the focal point for the rockery and others are then placed in association with it.

Plate 24 The rockery is completed by the addition of smaller stones and by levelling out the soil between the stones.

Plate 25 The completed climbing frame (p. 152) under test. The small ladder, the slide, the table, the rope ladder and the swinging rope are all moveable accessories.

the bottom with a bitumen paste (Aquaseal 88 etc.).

Continue with steps (7) and (8).

Note The pond shown in Plates 19 & 20 has three sides of earth step and one of concrete (along the path). To build this, dig out the pond bottom and position pegs as above for earth sides. Build wall along remaining side and create a concrete step as shown in Fig. 11.15. Join concrete step up with earth ones and lay lining (plastic or concrete).

Plastic lining

To lay the plastic lining, stretch the fabric over the pond and secure it round the edge with stones (Fig. 11.11a). Fill the lining with water until the water level reaches the bottom of the edging step (Fig. 11.11b). Mortar edging material into the required position and cut off excess lining. Finally when the mortar has set (two to three days) top the pond up until the required water level is reached (Fig. 11.11c).

Additional features

Additional features, such as waterfalls, bridges or islands, can be added to the pond at various stages of construction.

Waterfalls, designed and put together as indicated on pp. 131–6, can be added once

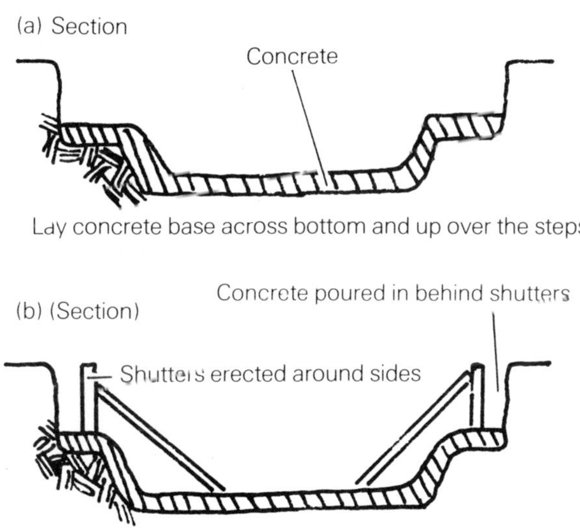

Fig. 11.14 *Procedure for laying (a) Concrete pond base. (b) Side walls.*

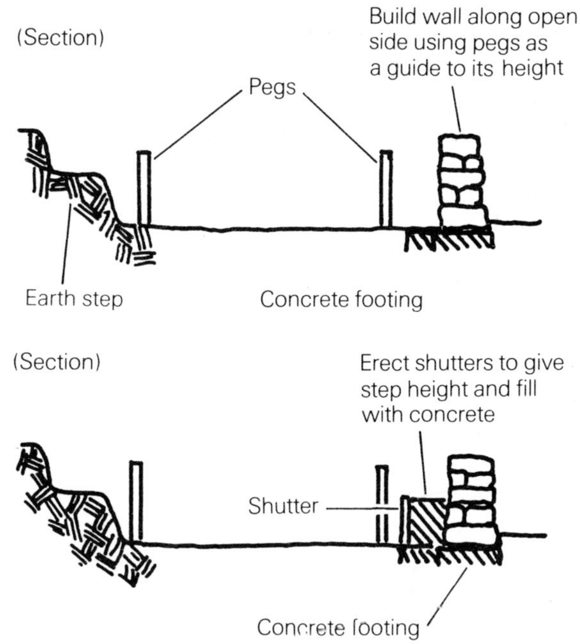

Fig. 11.15 *Enclosing the open side of a pond with a low wall and creating a concrete step inside it to match the earth step round the rest of the pond.*

the step round the pond edge is ready, building up and back off this level.

Bridges should be allowed for in the initial planning stage, and the pond shaped to give natural bridging positions (Fig. 11.16a). If you want to include a double-span bridge or stepping stones, the stepped edge of the pond should be continued across the bottom of the pond in a raised ridge and the supporting stone (for bridges) or stepping-stones mortared on to this (Fig. 11.16b).

Island stones are best positioned after the pond has been filled when you can get a better idea of how large they need to be and where the island would look best. In ponds with concrete linings these can simply be laid on the pond bottom or built up in combinations of two or three stones where the pond is deeper. For plastic linings these stones should be positioned within reach of the edge (to avoid walking on the lining) and, if well rounded or smooth, laid carefully on the lining or, if you think there is a risk of the stone puncturing the lining, on a bed of thick, clayey mud.

Any pond lining will look a bit new and stark for a while but the growth of algae and weed will cover it after a year or two. It is not a good idea to cover the bottom in building sand etc., particularly if you are going to keep fish, since these materials sometimes contain toxic traces that could be harmful to pond life. Seek advice from a specialist dealer or let the pond silt over naturally.

3 Pergolas

Pergolas are a useful and decorative way of providing some shelter for terraces and patios and for displaying climbing plants in their full glory. In this way they can either be used as extended arches stretching down a length of path, or they can be used to 'roof over' wider terraces used for outdoor entertaining and recreation. Whatever type is required we have included here some of the commoner materials used to build them and three basic designs. These may either be taken as they stand or modified to suit particular requirements.

(3a) The extended arch

The usual design for these involves a series of arches, linked at the top by crosspieces along the length of each side (Fig. 11.17). Apart from the actual construction details, an important point to bear in mind is that these structures can become top heavy and vulnerable to high winds once the climbing plants have spread over them. For this reason we would recommend using a generous amount

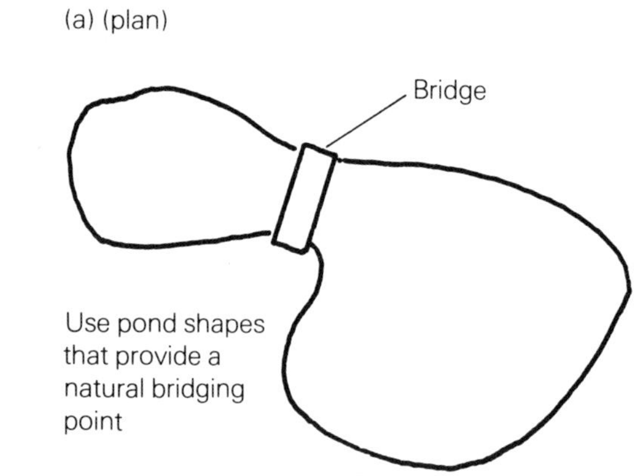

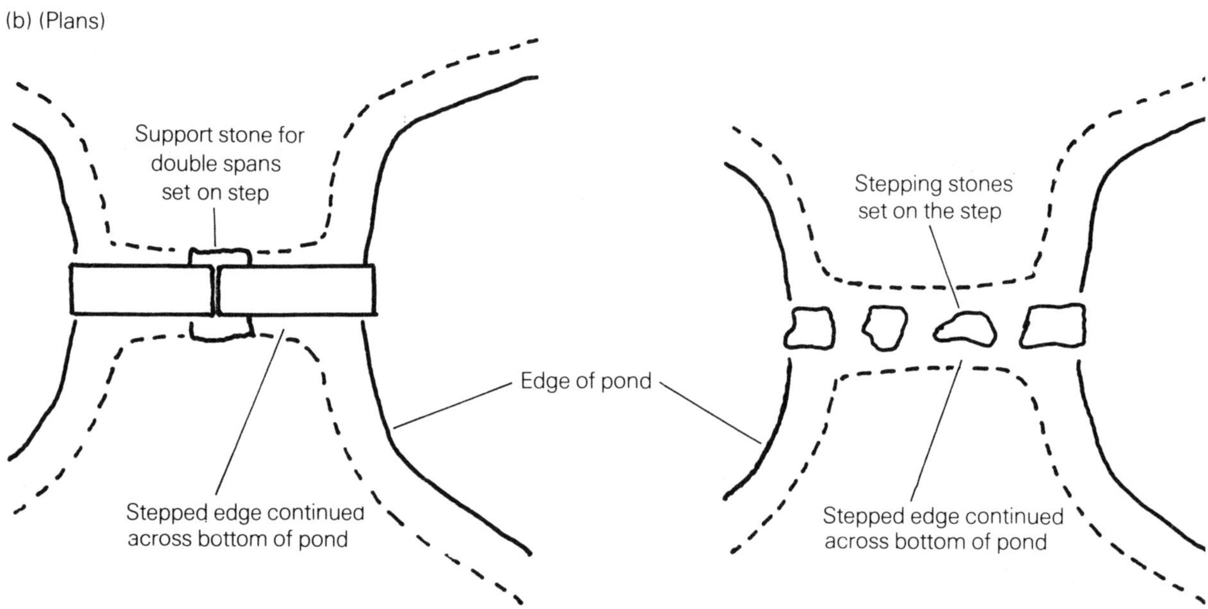

Fig. 11.16 *Bridging a pond and arrangement for double-span bridges or stepping stones.*

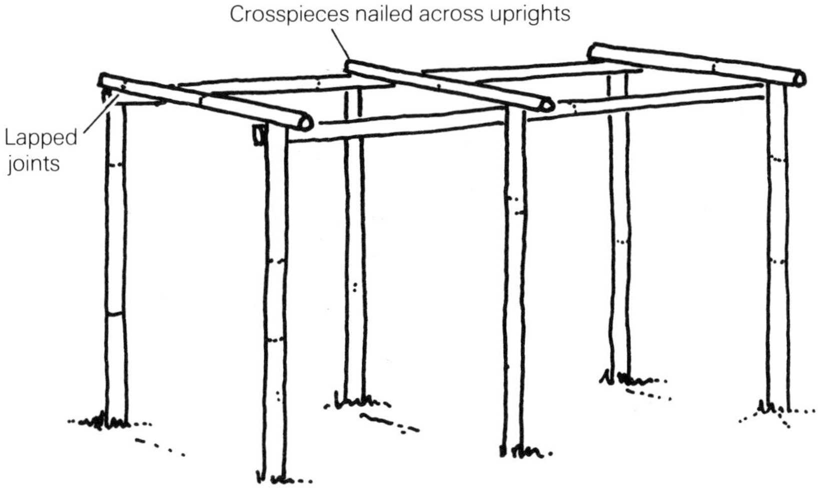

Fig. 11.17 *Design for larch pole pergola.*

of concrete to anchor the uprights. In the example shown here we have used the simplest and cheapest material, larch poles, which also have the advantage of a rustic appearance, easily blended with a variety of plants and colours.

What you will need

Larch poles. 8 cm (3 in) and 10 cm (4 in) nails. 50 kg (1 cwt) of concrete per post hole. Shovel. Spirit-level. Hammer. Hand saw.

Measuring up

When measuring up for the uprights allow for: height of pergola *plus* 60 cm (2 ft) in the ground. Other lengths will depend on the exact dimensions of individual designs, but we recommend that the pergola should be about 2.4 m (8 ft) high, with 1.2–1.5 m (4–5 ft) spans between uprights down the length. The width will be governed by the site, but should be kept in proportion with the above measurements as far as possible. Measure up larch pole requirements as for Larch pole trelliswork (p. 64).

Note Nailing is probably the most convenient way of fixing the pergola together. Bolting would be stronger but more expensive (if using bolts, keep them well greased to avoid rusting), while the cheapest and quickest way is to lash the poles together with p.v.c.-covered garden wire. On the whole, however, nails are probably the most suitable. Always try to use galvanized bolts and nails.

To construct

1 Cut uprights, crosspieces and sidepieces to length.

2 Cut notches in the top end of the uprights and both ends of the sidepieces, as shown in Fig. 11.18a.

3 Dig post holes, erect uprights and secure with concrete, checking as you fill the hole that the posts are standing straight and in line. On long runs the builder's-line method for erecting fence posts may be useful here, see p. 48.

4 Fix crosspieces in position, re-check the uprights, ram the concrete firmly down and leave to set.

5 Position crosspieces across the width, sitting them on the uprights and nail them down firmly (Fig. 11.18b).

6 You now have the basic structure. This can either be left as it is or some of the gaps can be filled in. Use either more poles (Fig. 11.19a) or p.v.c.-covered garden wire (Fig. 11.19b) for this, depending on how substantial the pergola is to look.

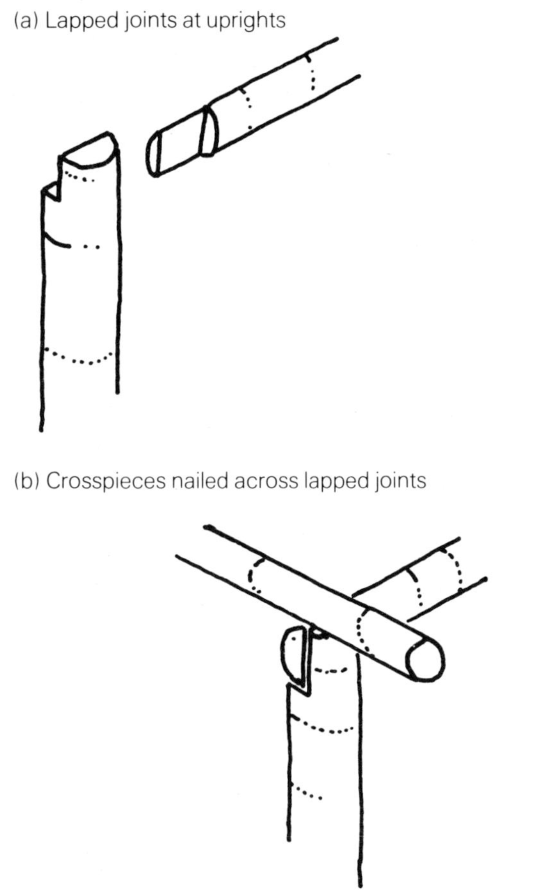

Fig. 11.18 *Details for constructing larch pole pergola.*

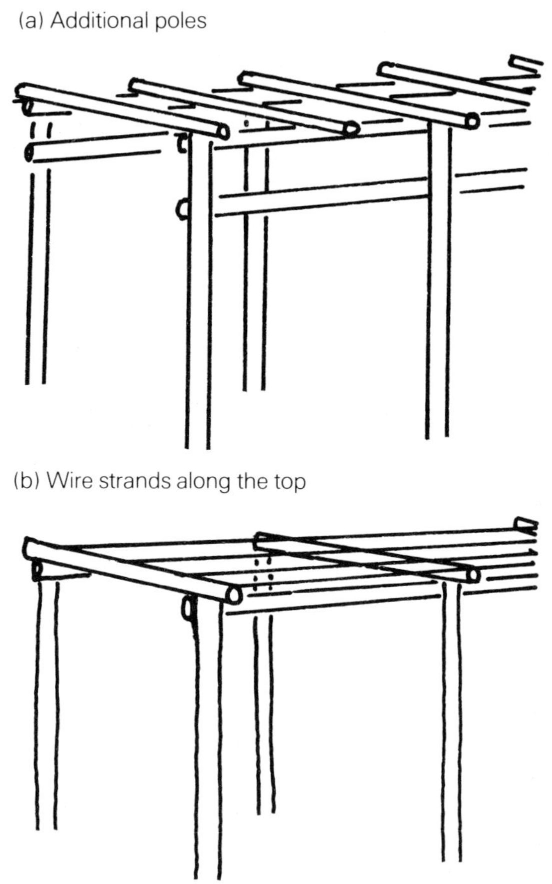

Fig. 11.19 *Variations on the basic frame using (a) additional poles and (b) wire strands.*

(3b) LEAN-TO PERGOLAS

These are commonly used when some covering for a terrace by the house is needed and thus where one half of the structure can be supported by the house wall (Fig. 11.20). Since the house wall will make the pergola much stronger than a free-standing one, concrete will not be needed. Otherwise the main details are as for the above. To attach the structure to the house, lengths of 10 × 5 cm (4 × 2 in) treated softwood should be screwed to the house wall using masonry plugs (Rawlplugs etc.) and 10 cm (4 in) screws, and the crosspieces nailed to this. Additional materials can be added in the same way as in (6) above.

(3c) CANTILEVERED PERGOLAS

An interesting variation on any pergola shape is to cantilever the crosspieces out over the side of the structure. Fig. 11.21 shows how this might be done with an extended arch pergola that runs down the side of a wide terrace. The arrangement thus arches out over the body of the terrace providing wider support for plants, and some shade on hot days without appearing to close the terrace in. This is ideal if the area enjoys a good view, either out over the garden or over more distant vistas. Construction would be the same as for (a) with the crosspieces lengthened to give the desired effect.

The above three designs are easily erected

and relatively cheap, but there are, of course, numerous possible variations. These are more substantial and would therefore be more expensive, but their longer life might make the investment worthwhile. For a more formal effect the poles could be replaced with 10 × 5 cm (4 × 2 in) sawn wood, or, to produce the strongest type of all, masonry pillars (bricks or pillar blocks) can be used instead of wooden posts and combined with 15 × 5 cm (6 × 2 in) sawn boards (Fig. 11.22). For using pillar blocks, see p. 89. Brick pillars should be built as shown in Fig. 11.23. A reinforcing bar set in concrete down the middle of either type of pillar would add considerable strength.

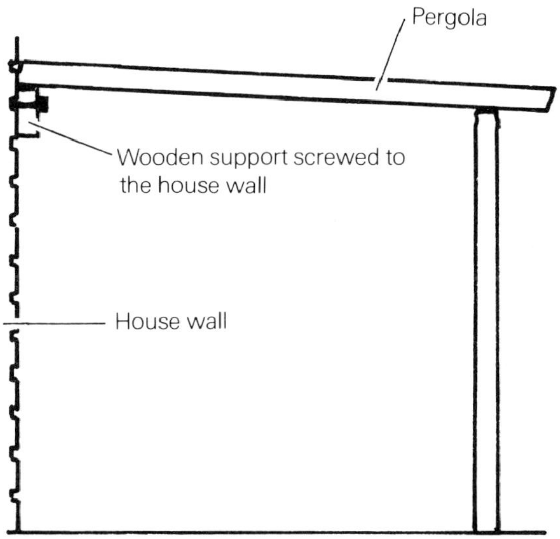

Fig. 11.20 *Sectional view of a pergola with one side supported by a wall.*

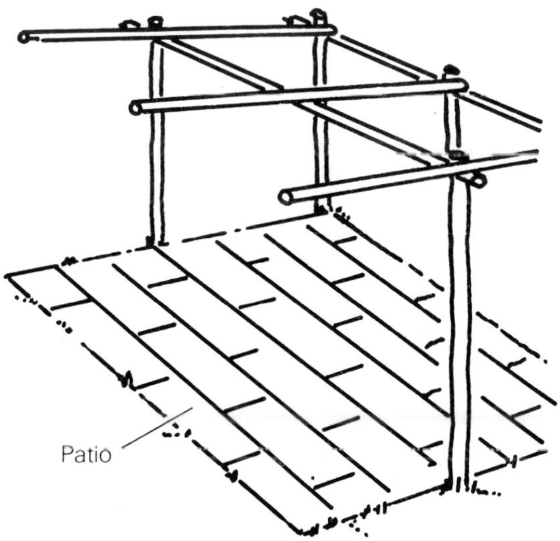

Fig. 11.21 *Pergola using cantilevered poles to provide shade for a patio.*

Fig. 11.22 *Pergola using sawn timber gives a more formal effect.*

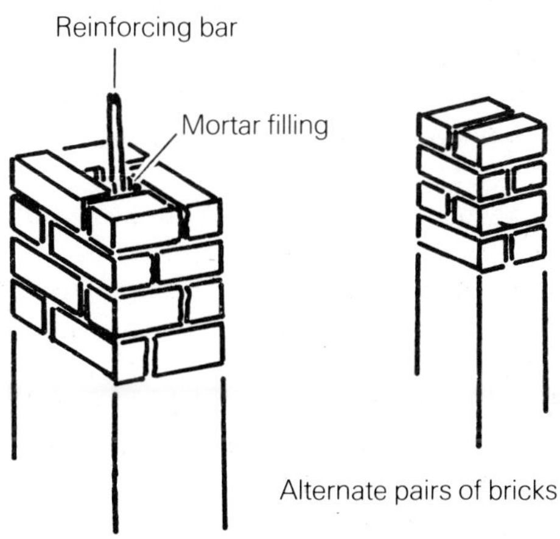

Fig. 11.23 *Two types of brick pillar for supporting a wooden framework.*

4 Rockeries

Whether a rockery is used to fill an awkward space in the garden (see Plates 21–24) or whether it is designed as a full feature in its own right, the visual success of it will depend on two factors. First, the rocks should appear as natural as possible, as though they could always have been there, and following on from the first point, they should not be too cluttered. Although a new rockery may look rather bare, it will not be long before the plants fill out the spaces and blend the whole composition together.

When selecting your stone (whether from a stream bed, a quarry or a garden centre) aim to get two or three of outstanding shape, colour or interest (stratification lines, etc.), and then a number of smaller ones that can be used in association with these.

The secret of successful rock work in this type of informal setting is to achieve an asymmetrical balance within the group, i.e. the height of one stone should be set off and balanced by the bulk of another. Thus in Plate 24, the thrusting, sharp-edged shape of the large central stone is balanced and complemented by the softer, low-lying shapes of the two stones below it to the right. In this way the group is built up around particular feature stones creating, by a series of balanced groups, an overall effect that looks natural and within which each stone relates to another. Setting the stones in this way avoids the cluttered and untidy appearance of some rockeries where the stones appear to have been piled together, more in an attempt to cover the ground than to give any hint of a natural environment. It is because of this that they look artificial and contrived.

To avoid this kind of haphazard jumble of stones the construction of a rockery should be approached systematically and the stones carefully set in the earth, rather than simply laid on it. The sequence of photographs (Plates 21–24) illustrate this approach to construction.

In the first stage (Plate 22) three 'structural' stones are positioned, i.e. they are essential for the structure of the rockery, in this case retaining earth along the bottom edge and at the change of level caused by the step. The main body of earth is still open, but already it is being defined into separate spaces. In the second stage (Plate 23), the large stone placed in association with the one beside the step, creates a focal point or fulcrum, around which the rockery revolves. In front and below this stone the foreground has been given definition by a group of three relatively flat stones. These three give some horizontal depth to the feature and in turn focus attention on the central one, whose colour and sharper profile make it stand out. Two other structural stones have been added to complete the bottom edge.

The third stage (Plate 24) is one of filling out and completing the overall design. A smooth, compact stone has been added below and to the right of the focal point, complementing its arching shape and, at the same time, providing a link between the foreground group and the higher group at the back. To the left and above the focal point, smaller stones are added to give definition to the top of the layout, which is kept relatively open so that it does not appear to dominate the slope below. Large or closely grouped stones along the top edge would make the rockery look top heavy and spoil the balance.

Once all the stones are in position it remains only to spread the soil more evenly around the stones and put in the plants. When the plants have grown and the spaces are filled, the stones will play an unobtrusive yet essential role in the feature, striking a balance between man-made and natural shapes.

5 Screens

One component of landscape design that is not frequently used in the West is the internal screen. An essential part of the Japanese and Chinese landscaping tradition, these lightweight, 'see-through' fences can be very useful to divide up the spaces of a garden

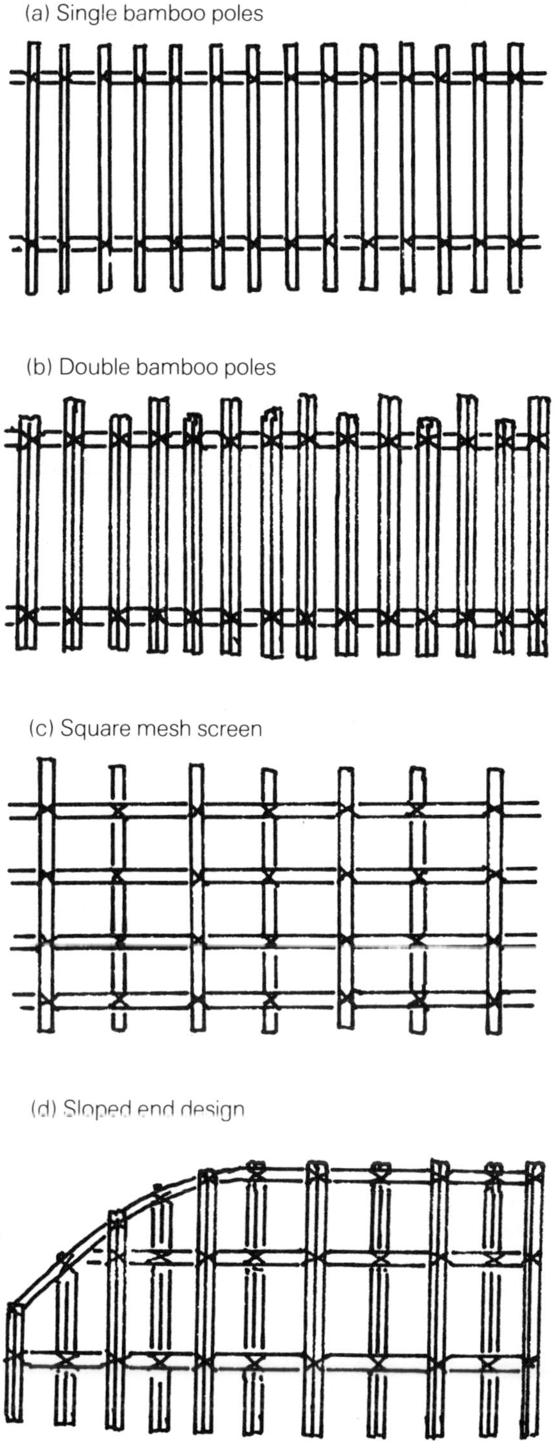

Fig. 11.24 *Various designs for bamboo screens. (All are fixed together with p.v.c.-covered wire).*

subtly, without intruding on the overall layout or blocking any views. They can also be used to form an unobtrusive backdrop for plants or ornaments, concentrating attention on the featured items while not actually cutting them off from the surrounding garden.

Designs for this type of screen can vary enormously and those shown here represent only the basic ideas of what can be achieved using one or two widely available materials with a little imagination.

BAMBOO

Perhaps the most exotic material to use is bamboo. In most places this can be bought in 90 cm (3 ft) or 1.2 m (4 ft) long canes, most commonly used to support tomato plants etc. Fig. 11.24 illustrates four common designs for bamboo screens, but the exact shapes and dimensions will depend to a large extent on what type of bamboo canes are locally available and on how large the screen is to be. For anything much over 1.5 m (5 ft) we would advise using trelliswork (p. 171), rather than screens.

The screens shown in Fig. 11.24 can either be constructed by securing the canes in a double frame (see Making your own lapped panels, p. 52), or by binding them together with p.v.c.-covered garden wire. Support posts for larger units should be 5 × 5 cm (2 × 2 in) or 10 × 5 cm (4 × 2 in) treated softwood.

BRUSHWOOD

A cheap and handy alternative is to use the bamboo canes in combination with lengths of twiggy branches (Fig. 11.25). The brushwood is held between a double frame of canes, or other suitably sized wood, and can be loosely or tightly packed depending on the required effect. These make very attractive screens that introduce an informal, rural air into the garden. Again, the screen can be bound together with wire, or more substantial units produced using heavier wood and nails.

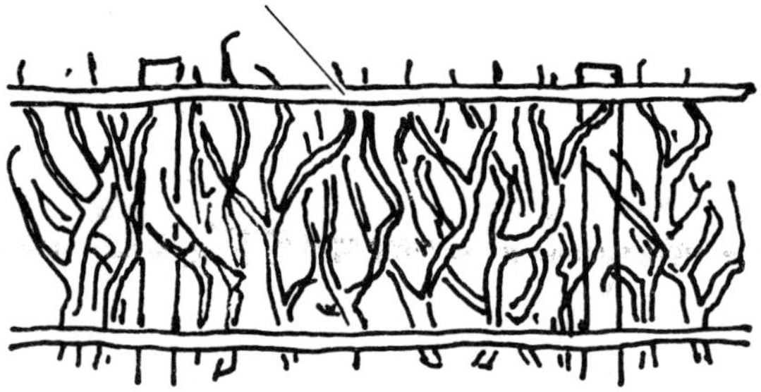

Fig. 11.25 *Brushwood screen.*

Whichever material is used, or whether interwoven trelliswork (p. 171) is used in short lengths, these screens have a variety of uses round the garden and provide a useful, cheap alternative to internal hedges or walls.

6 Children's area

In most average-sized family gardens a problem arises about where the children can play without interfering with the adults' use of the garden and vice versa. Apart from the lawn, shared by everyone, the answer to the problem may be to create a specific area in the garden where the children can dig, build, play and even plant without affecting anyone else, and so render the rest of the garden safe from possible destruction. If such an area is to be created it should be versatile enough to cope with the wide range of demands that children's play will put on it and, by so doing, retain their interest. This means that it will have to be definitive, in that it provides a focal point for a variety of activities, and yet flexible enough to stimulate the imagination and encourage the children to develop its potential themselves. Following on from this idea the facility should not be an end in itself, serving one purpose, but rather an invitation to children to centre their activities around it. It is often not enough, as many people will have discovered to their cost, simply to buy children's garden furniture, such as a swing or a slide, because although these provide continued enjoyment, each item is of such a limited nature that children will also seek other things to do. The suggested solution that we put forward here will not be cheap (good sawn wood is inevitably expensive) but the cost will be a fraction of that of any manufactured, brand-name, multi-purpose unit of comparable size and indeed of a lot of the commercially available single-purpose units (slides, swings, sandpit boxes, etc.).

The children's area suggested here concentrates a wide range of possible activities in one place and does not need the supplementary standard items of garden furniture mentioned above. The activity area centres around a climbing frame structure that can be built from standard-sized wood, available from most builders' merchants or timber yards, and does not require any specialized woodworking knowledge. The finished unit can be seen in Plate 25 and the completed activity area would include a sandpit around and under the laddered end.

The basic frame, combined with the sandpit, provides facilities for general play, extensive climbing and a play house, easing any ground space restrictions by making activities possible on at least two levels. When the accessories are added – the slide, wooden ladder, rope ladder, swinging rope (or swing) and movable table – a wide range of play activities can be accommodated. The movable accessories are designed to be sufficiently heavy and stable for safe use by very young children, and yet lightweight and compact enough to be moved around and re-positioned by children from the age of six upwards. Thus the frame can 'grow' with the children, being used in different ways as the pattern of play alters over the years. Used on its own or combined with a sandpit and even a paddling pool, the frame will concentrate activities in one area and provide for a wide range of play requirements.

TO CONSTRUCT THE FRAME

What you will need

Materials: All timber should be good-quality, planed softwood.

(a) Basic frame Wood: 8 × 8 cm (3 × 3 in): four lengths at 2.1 m (7 ft); 8 × 5 cm (3 × 2 in): two lengths at 2.4 m (8 ft); three lengths at 2.1 m (7 ft); one length at 2.4 m (8 ft) i.e. 2 at 1.2 m (4 ft); three lengths at 1.3 m (4 ft 4 in). 5 × 2.5 cm (2 × 1 in) roofing lath: 4 m (14 ft) i.e. four at 1 m (3 ft 6 in). Blockboard: two sheets of 2.4 × 1.2 m (8 × 4 ft), 1.3 cm ($\frac{1}{2}$ in) *external* blockboard. Dowel: 2.5 cm (1 in) diameter: seven lengths at 1.8 m (6 ft). Bolts: two at 10 × 1 cm (4 × $\frac{3}{8}$ in), plus washers. Screws: 28 at 10 cm (4 in); four at 4 cm ($1\frac{1}{2}$ in). Nails: 12 at 5 cm (2 in); 15 at 4 cm ($1\frac{1}{2}$ in).

(b) Table Wood: 8 × 8 cm (3 × 3 in): one length at 2.4 m (8 ft); i.e. four at 60 cm (2 ft). 8 × 5 cm (3 × 2 in): one length at 2.4 m (8 ft); i.e. two at 1.2 m (4 ft). one length at 1.2 m (4 ft); i.e. two at 60 cm (2 ft). 5 × 2.5 cm (2 × 1 in) roofing lath: 2.7 m (9 ft); i.e. two at 1 m (3 ft 6 in) and two at 45 cm (1 ft 6 in). Screws: 16 at 10 cm (4 in). Nails: 10 at 5 cm (2 in).

(c) Slide Wood: 8 × 5 cm (3 × 2 in): one length at 3.6 m (12 ft); i.e. two at 1.8 m (6 ft). 5 × 5 cm (2 × 2 in): one length at 3.6 m (12 ft); i.e. two at 1.8 m (6 ft). Screws: two at 4 cm ($1\frac{1}{2}$ in). Nails: six at 8 cm (3 in); six at 5 cm (2 in).

(d) Wooden ladder Wood: 8 × 5 cm (3 × 2 in): one length at 2.7 m (9 ft); i.e. two at 1.3 m (4 ft 6 in). 5 × 2.5 cm (2 × 1 in) roofing lath: one length at 38 cm (15 in). Screws: two at 4 cm ($1\frac{1}{2}$ in). Nails: six at 4 cm ($1\frac{1}{2}$ in).

(e) Ropes Swinging rope: approx. 1.8 m (6 ft) at 2.5 cm (1 in) diameter. Rope ladder: approx. 1.8 m (6 ft) at 1.3 cm ($\frac{1}{2}$ in) diameter.

Tools: Saw. Carpenter's hammer. Rasp (for removing sharp edges, etc.). Screwdriver. Spanner (to fit bolts). Tape-measure. Pencil. Electric drill (or brace and bit). Jigsaw.

Note 1. If constructing the frame and accessories all at once, work out total wood, screw and nail

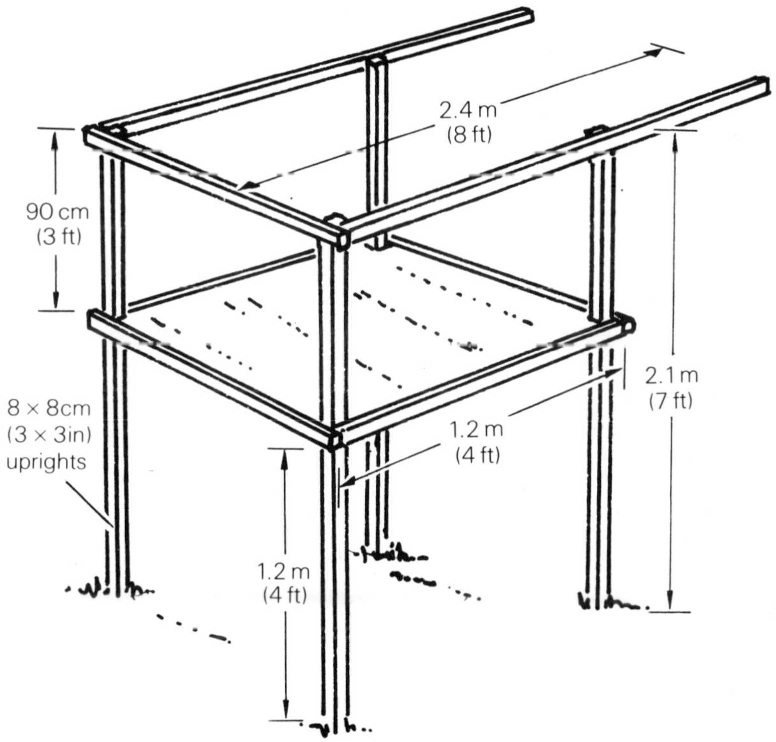

Fig. 11.26 *Main structure for the climbing frame.*

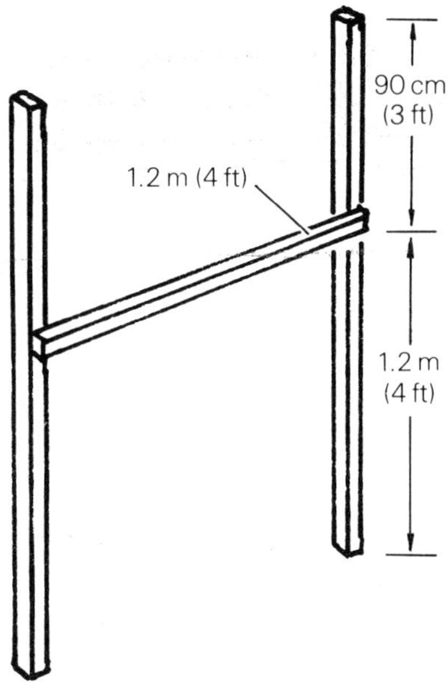

Fig. 11.27 *Forming the sides for the frame.*

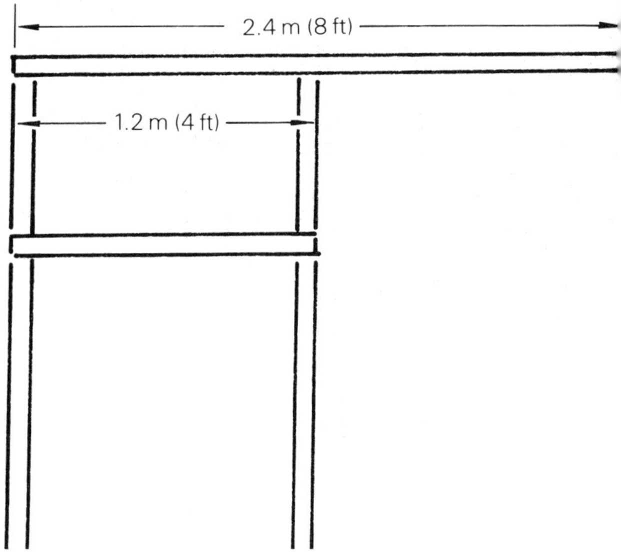

Fig. 11.28 *Adding the top cross-pieces to the sides.*

requirements and order as one lot; this way you should get a bulk discount. Specific requirements for each unit have been itemized separately so that they can be built individually and others added later.

Note 2. A number of design variations and additional accessories can easily be added, some of which can be made up from offcuts (such as the rope ladder). Construct basic frame etc. and assess what is left over before buying extra materials.

Note 3. As mentioned before, the frame is stable enough for most requirements. If, however, older or large numbers of children are going to use it, additional stability can be gained by setting the four main uprights in concrete. For this allow an extra 30 cm (12 in) on length of the 8 × 8 cm (3 × 3 in) posts for the basic frame and 25 kg ($\frac{1}{2}$ cwt) of concrete for each hole.

TO CONSTRUCT

Basic frame (Fig. 11.26)

1 Cut timber and smooth off sharp edges and any rough patches.

2 Fig. 11.27: Attach 1.2 m (4 ft) lengths to the 2.1 m (7 ft) uprights. Two screws either end, making two H-shaped units.

3 Fig. 11.28: Attach 2.4 m (8 ft) lengths of 8 × 5 cm (3 × 2 in), flush with the top of the uprights (two screws either end).

4 Fig. 11.29: Fix on the 1.3 m (4 ft 4 in) lengths of 8 × 5 cm (3 × 2 in), so that they cover the ends of the crosspieces. (Two screws either end into the uprights.)

5 Fig. 11.30: Nail 5 × 2.5 cm (2 × 1 in) laths (three nails each) along the inside of the platform crosspieces, 1.3 cm ($\frac{1}{2}$ in) below top edge.

6 Fig. 11.31: Cut a 1.2 × 1.2 m (4 × 4 ft) piece off one sheet of blockboard and cut out 8 × 8 cm (3 × 3 in) squares at the corners. Slide the platform into position and tap down until it rests on the 5 × 2.5 cm (2 × 1 in) laths, sitting flush with the crosspieces.

7 Fig. 11.32a: Take remaining 1.2 × 1.2 m (4 × 4 ft) piece of blockboard and mark out as shown. Cut shapes out with jigsaw. Keep the outcuts since these will be used as rungs for the rope ladder.

8 Fig. 11.32b: Fix on to side of frame (whichever face suits your requirements) using a 4 cm ($1\frac{1}{2}$ in) screw at each corner.

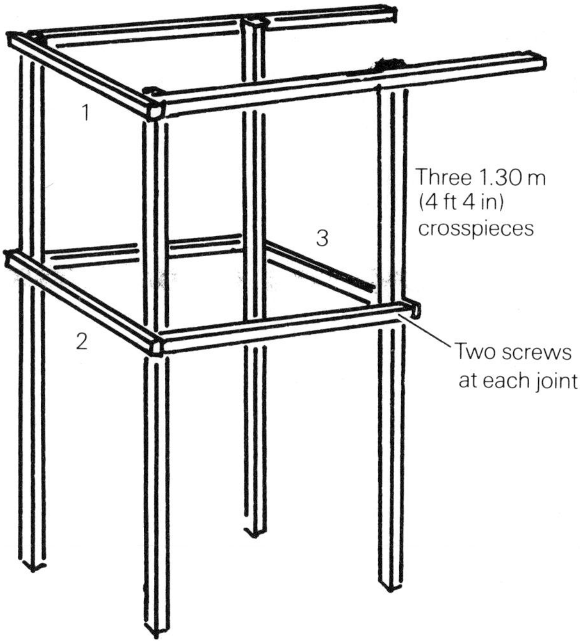

Fig. 11.29 *Joining the sides with three crosspieces.*

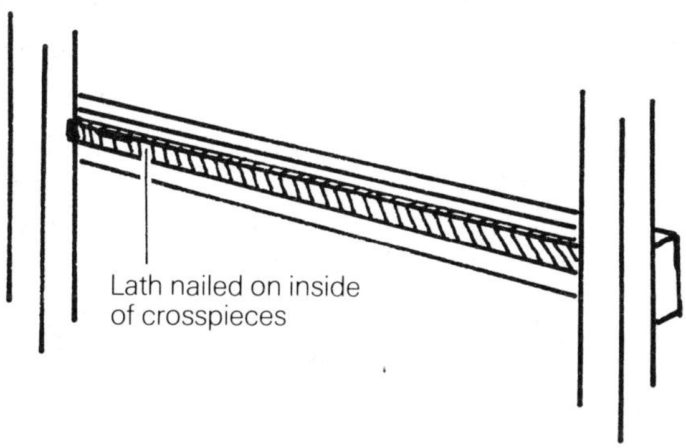

Fig. 11.30 *Nail 2.5 cm (1 in) laths around the inside of the platform crosspieces, 1.3 cm ($\frac{1}{2}$ in) below top edge.*

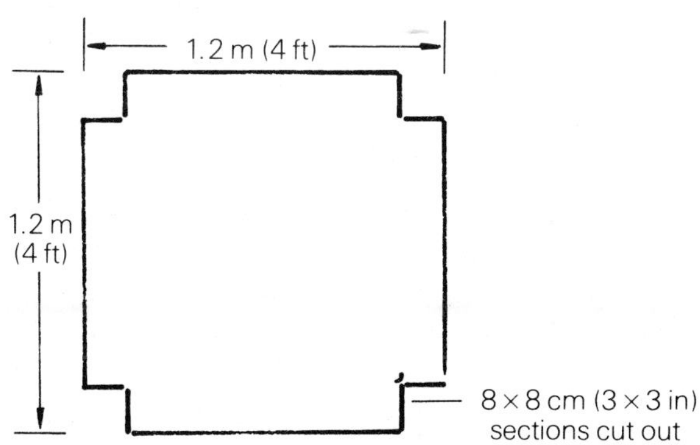

Fig. 11.31 *Cutting out blockboard to form the platform for the frame.*

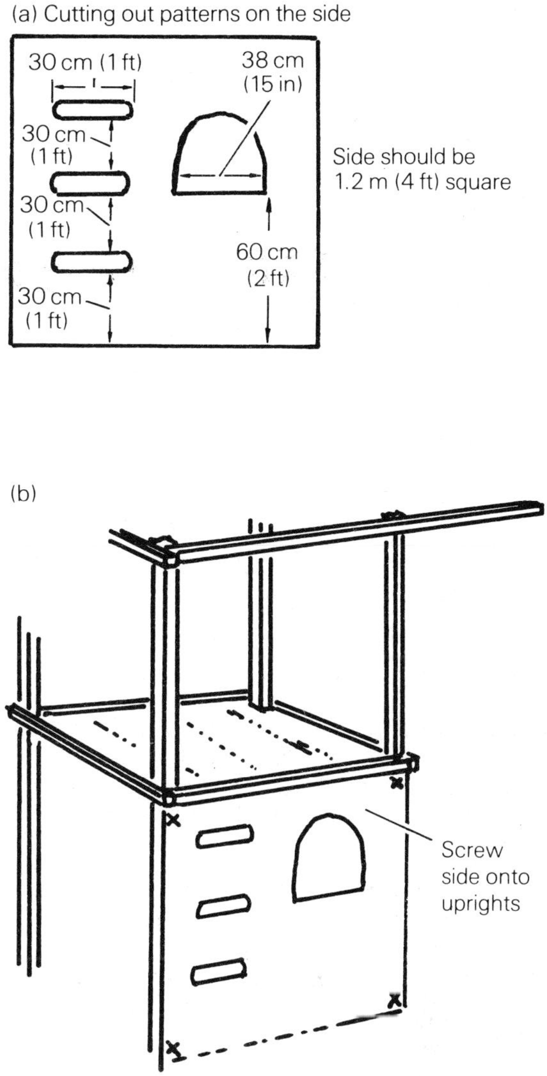

Fig. 11.32 *Cutting out and fixing on the side.*

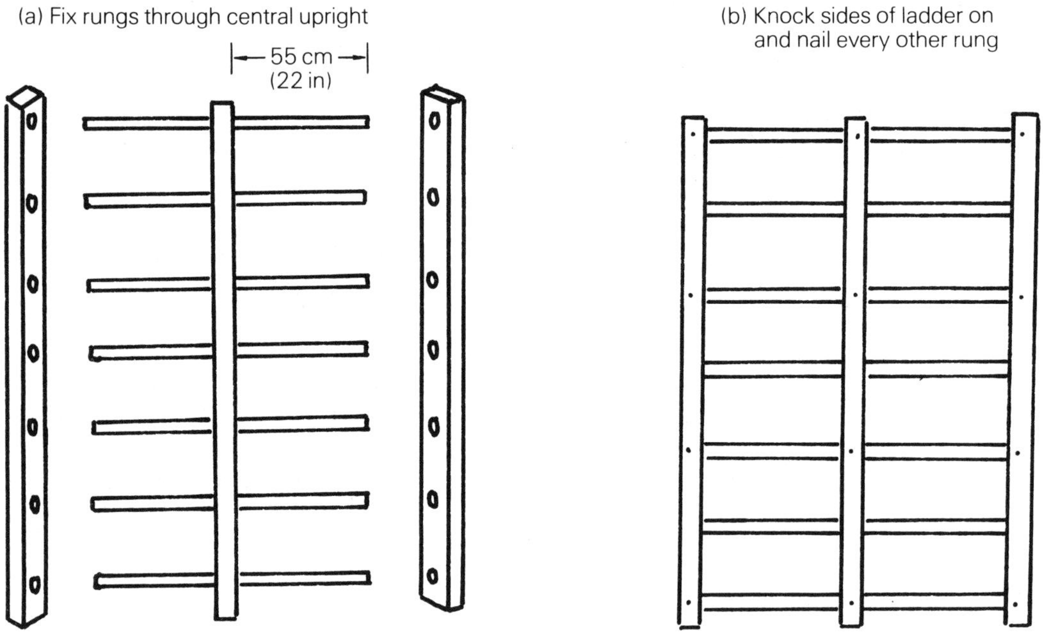

Fig. 11.33 *Constructing the ladder end.*

9a Fig. 11.33a: Cut the dowels down to 1.2 m (48 in) lengths (keep offcuts for wooden ladder rungs). Drill out seven holes with 30 cm (12 in) centres, using 30 cm (1 in) wood bit in one length of 2.1 m (7 ft) 8 × 5 cm (3 × 2 in) wood. Knock dowels through until 55 cm (22 in) sticks out either side.

9b Fig. 11.33b: Drill holes (same centres) 2.5 cm (1 in) into the other two 2.1 m (7 ft) lengths of 8 × 5 cm (3 × 2 in). Knock these side uprights on to the dowels and nail every other one on each upright using 4 cm ($1\frac{1}{2}$ in) nails.

10 Fig. 11.34: Position the ladder unit inside and flush with the tops and ends of the extended 2.4 m (8 ft) 8 × 5 cm (3 × 2 in) crosspieces. Drill out and bolt up tight.

Table

11 Fig. 11.35: Mark second sheet of blockboard as shown. Cut off 1.2 m × 60 cm (4 × 2 ft) piece (marked 'Table'). Assemble and cut wood for table (shave off sharp edges). Construct as for above, using 8 × 8 cm (3 × 3 in) lengths as legs, screwing on the 60 cm (2 ft) lengths of 8 × 5 cm (3 × 2 in), flush with the tops and outside edges of the legs (see Fig. 11.27), and then fixing on the 1.2 m (4 ft) crosspieces, overlapping the ends (see Fig. 11.29). Fix on the 5 × 2.5 cm (2 × 1 in) laths on the inside edge of sides (see Fig. 11.30). Cut notches in blockboard (see Fig. 11.31) and drop into place.

Slide

12a Fig. 11.36: Cut timber for slide, take off sharp edges and chamfer the ends of the 5 × 5 cm (2 × 2 in) lengths. Cut the 1.8 m × 53 cm (6 ft × 21 in) piece off the blockboard (marked 'slide'). Nail on to the 8 × 5 cm (3 × 2 in) lengths.

12b Fig. 11.37: When this is secure, nail the 5 × 5 cm (2 × 2 in) lengths on top, chamfered ends up, and screw the 5 × 2.5 cm (2 × 1 in) lath into position across one end of the 8 × 5 cm (3 × 2 in) supports.

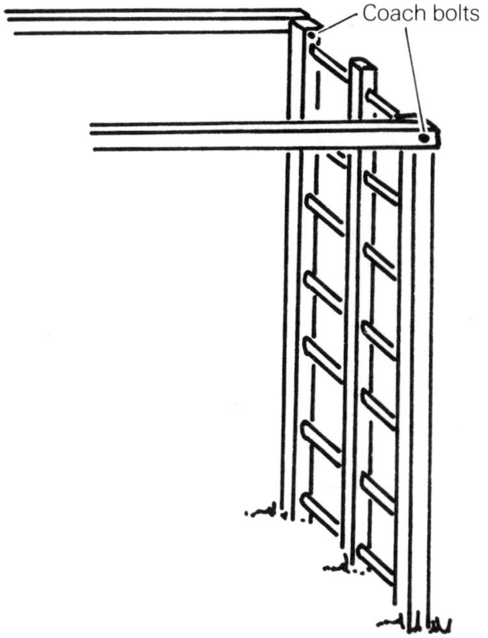

Fig. 11.34 *Fitting the ladder on to the main frame.*

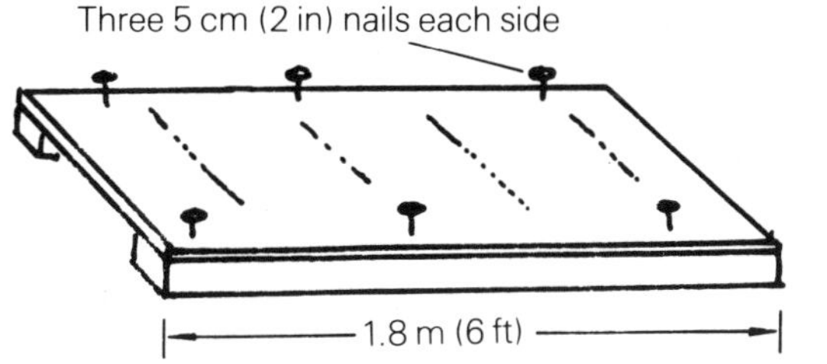

Fig. 11.36 *Slide top nailed on to two 8 × 5 cm (3 × 2 in) supports.*

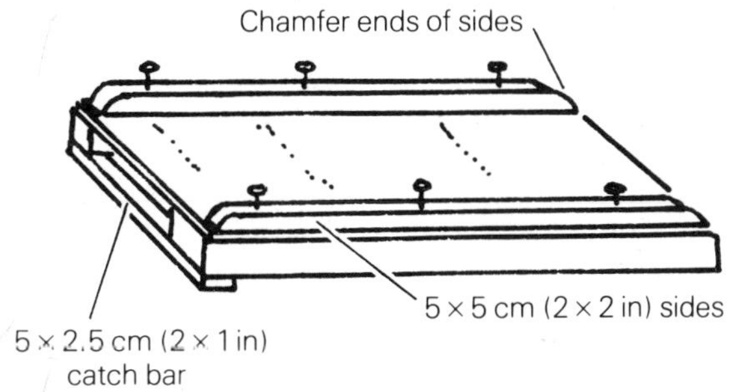

Fig. 11.37 *Adding sides and catch bar to the slide.*

Fig. 11.35 *(Right) Marking the blockboard for cutting out table top, slide etc. Dotted lines show cuts that can be made to create arch effect.*

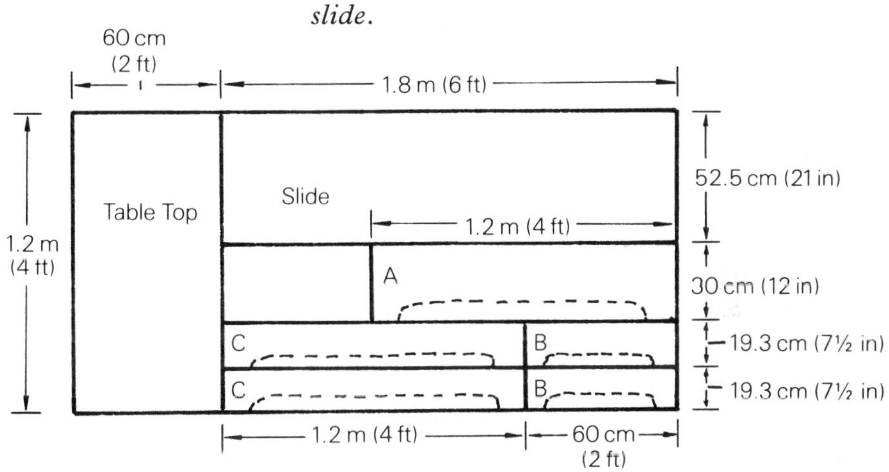

Wooden ladder

13 Fig. 11.38: Cut timber for ladder and take off sharp edges. Mark holes for rungs (approx. 26.3 cm ($10\frac{1}{2}$ in) centres. Drill holes 2.5 cm (1 in) deep, knock rungs in and nail every other one up both sides. Screw 5 × 2.5 cm (2 × 1 in) lath across one end.

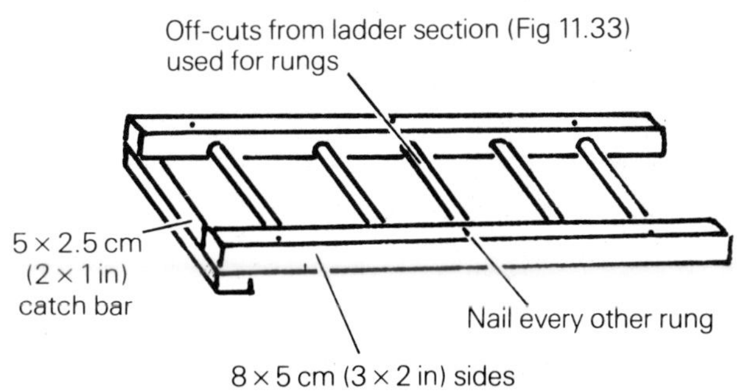

Fig. 11.38 *Assembling the small wooden ladder.*

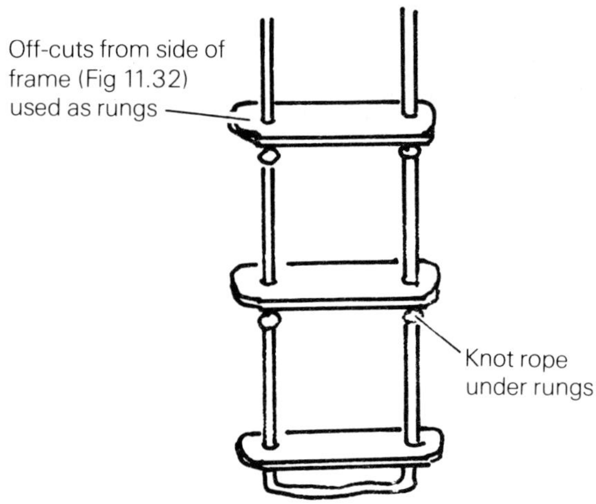

Fig. 11.39 *Assembling the rope ladder.*

Rope ladder

14 Fig. 11.39: Drill out holes for rope in the rungs, feed rope through, knotting below the top two rungs. Drill holes in main frame (several sets of holes can be drilled so that the ladder can be hung in various positions). Pass rope ends through and knot. (Plate 25 shows one position for rope ladder.) Position swinging rope where required.

15 When the main structures are complete, cut out pieces A, B (× 2), and C (× 2) from the blockboard (Fig. 11.35). These are fixed on to the main frame (A) and the table (B and C) to provide extra stability. The exact shape of the 'arch' is a matter of taste. Cut shapes and screw into position.

16 The whole structure plus accessories will now need protecting against the weather. The frame in Plates 42 and 44 has been treated with golden-brown creosote, but varnish or dark creosote could be used or the frame could be painted.

The frame can now be used either as it stands or combined with a sandpit (etc.). For the sandpit, dig a shallow depression, lay edgings (bricks etc., see p. 124) and fill with clean sand. For a concrete-lined sandpit or paddling pool adapt the techniques used for lining a pond with concrete (p. 138).

12 Lawns and flowerbeds

As we mentioned in the introduction to Chapter 5, it is important both in a new garden and one where the design is being altered, to clear the whole site first. Clearing means removing all bushes, grass, building debris and general junk that prevent you from getting a clear view of the whole site. This is important since these things obscure the levels and general shapes which might need altering. If a lawn and flowerbeds are being created at the same time ensure that all the preliminary work (clearing and forking) is also done at this stage; this way all areas will be equally advanced and can be shaped and designed at the same time, minimizing any disturbance.

Clearing and preparing an area for a lawn is not technically difficult but it does require a certain amount of hard, concentrated work. There is no quick, easy way that will produce a smooth, weed-free lawn. The method described here will suit the average garden and will not take too long.

If, of course, there is a large area to do you might consider a small cultivator (see p. 12) to help with the final turning over of the soil. However, if you do it yourself, there is no substitute for the fork and proper attention to the removing of all roots and weeds. Cultivators will break up the soil but they will not clean it (indeed they sometimes make matters worse by chopping the roots into smaller pieces); we recommend using them only after the soil has been thoroughly cleaned, to chop the earth into a fine tilth for seeding.

1 To lay a lawn

PREPARATION

What you will need
Sprayer. Weedkiller. Fork. Wheelbarrow. Rake. Shovel. Pegs. Builder's line. Seed. Garden roller.

Method
(a) **Spraying** The task of clearing soil which has either become overgrown with weeds, grasses or brambles, or which has never been cultivated, should be divided into two parts. First, the matted vegetation above ground should be dealt with and then the roots and stones. To deal with both surface matter and roots at the same time requires very strong weedkillers, which not only destroy the green cells above ground but also penetrate the soil and kill the roots. Such poisons are available but they leave the soil 'dead' for several months and seeding would have to wait while the effects wore off. It is, therefore, quicker in the long run to spray the vegetation on the surface with one of the weedkillers which is neutralized on contact with the soil, and then to dig the roots out during the first forking (see below).

There are a number of such weedkillers available; consult your dealer as to which would be most suitable for your purposes. Most can be applied with either a watering-can with a rose attachment, or a backpack sprayer (these can be hired by the day and have the advantage of a long spraying nozzle which can be used to penetrate dense vegetation). Quantities will be indicated on the bottle or in the manufacturer's literature. One application of these poisons should leave the grasses etc. shrivelled and easy to scrape off with a fork or grass rake. The more efficiently you scrape the dead matter off, the easier the first forking will be.

Once the surface is clear you will be able to see better how the area is shaped and you will now be able to plan the lawn and bed areas, pinpointing any area you want to re-shape.

Note All garden weedkillers are *extremely dangerous* if not handled with care. The types recommended here are no exception and some have no antidote if swallowed. The safest way to carry out the job is to establish a procedure and follow it every time you handle poisons. Fill the sprayer and put the poison away (even if you may need more later). Spray. Wash the sprayer carefully and then wash your hands. Repeat procedure if required. Keep children and pets off the sprayed area for at least 24 hours. Lock up poisons and *never* store them in soft-drink bottles.

(b) First forking This is the hardest part of preparing a lawn, but is is also the key to success. The aims of this first forking are as follows: to clear away any remaining dead matter; to remove all roots, underground suckers and stones; to break up the soil to a depth of at least 20–30 cm (8–12 in).

If this is done conscientiously the subsequent stages of preparation will be much easier and the lawn is much more likely to be healthy and trouble-free. The only way to achieve this is to work systematically in rows, using a wheelbarrow to carry away the rubbish as you lift it. The fork should be driven in to its maximum prong depth, the sod lifted, turned over and then broken up by dividing it with the fork. The roots and other vegetable matter should then be lifted out by hand. Stones or any other rubbish should also be removed at this point. The first forking should leave the whole area weed-, root- and rubbish-free, with the earth broken into small lumps.

Note If a cultivator is available it can now be used to break up the soil even more, but it should not be used before the first forking.

(c) First raking The whole forked area now needs raking off, after the earth has had time to dry out. This raking process will remove the lumps and stones still remaining and smooth off the surface. Again, a wheelbarrow should be used to remove any rubbish. For suitable rakes see tools, p. 12.

Once the whole area has been roughly smoothed out by the raking, you can now shape or re-shape any slopes, banks or level areas using a shovel and wheelbarrow to relocate the earth.

When you are satisfied with the overall shape turn your attention to the soil itself. If it is too sandy or clayey, acidic or alkaline, wet or dry, or just exhausted from years of supporting weeds etc. you may need to alter its composition slightly by adding peat or fertilizers. If you are not sure seek advice from your local seedsman or garden centre and carry out any necessary operations now – it might be too late once you have seeded.

The other major consideration at this point is whether or not the lawn, or any other part of the garden, is going to need an underground drainage system. If you decide that some kind of drainage is necessary, now is the time to put it in. The different types and patterns of drains for this purpose are covered in detail in Chapter 5. Besides drains, any other services or pipes to be laid underground should also be installed before the second forking.

(d) Second forking Spread and fork in any recommended soil dressings, for the lawn area, breaking up any remaining lumps of earth.

If you have been working the bed and lawn areas at the same time you should now mark off the bed areas with the pegs and line. Also, if you have any paths or terraces to lay, edgings or retaining walls to put in, you should do these jobs now to avoid disturbance later on.

The soil for the flowerbeds and lawn now require different treatment and should be considered separately.

Flowerbeds: For new gardens on land that has recently been a building site, or for land that is being reclaimed from the 'wild', the soil in the flowerbed areas will benefit from some additional preparation. Equally, if you are re-designing existing flowerbeds now it provides a good opportunity to put some life back into the soil. Basically, while soil for the lawn requires further work on the surface (see below), the flowerbeds need 'double-digging' to help create a good environment for the deeper roots of shrubs and trees.

Double-digging means opening up the soil two spits deep. The first layer is dug out and placed on one side, exposing the second layer which is broken up with a fork but left in position. This helps aerate hard-packed soils and ensures good drainage for the topsoil. Farmyard manure, compost or peat should now be mixed in with the broken soil, with any fertilizers that may be deemed useful, such as potash etc. (Consult your dealer as to which fertilizers would be suitable.) Working in rows, open up the trench, break up the second spit, add manure etc., fork first spit back into position and move to next row. This treatment will leave the flowerbeds revived and ready for planting. Later, where a particular plant needs additional compost, peat or fertilizer, this can be applied locally and does not affect the whole bed.

Make sure that all construction work, such as putting in edgings, filling in behind retaining walls or positioning stones for a rockery, is complete before planting.

Lawns: The soil for the lawn area now needs further work on the surface, starting with the second raking.

(e) **Second raking** The lawn will now require a final raking over to remove any unwanted matter which might have been brought to the surface by the second forking. This second raking should also aim to fill any little dips or level any ridges to give the area a smooth surface. The texture of the surface should now be a fine tilth; that is, it should have broken down to a fine, dry composition, free of any lumps or stones.

(f) **Rolling** When the tilth is right roll the whole area with a light garden roller, up and down in lines. Should any further dips or ridges come to light after rolling, rake over the surface lightly and roll again. Continue until you are satisfied with the surface.

SEEDING

Types

Two basic types of seed are available: 'pure' lawn seed and rye-grass mixtures (mixtures of lawn seed and rye). Lawn seed produces a very green, rather delicate type of grass, prone to moss encroachment and not suitable for heavy use. When grown, however, it looks extremely attractive and is most suitable for ornamental lawns. Rye-grass is much more robust and hard-wearing, and is strongly recommended for lawns which will be used by children or the family generally. Although it is a coarser type of grass, rye-grass, if carefully maintained, can look very smart and should be cut regularly, with care being taken to remove any 'bents' (tough stems which, if allowed to grow, are very difficult to cut with the mower). Consider carefully the use to which the lawn will be put and choose accordingly.

Note Within these two basic types are a number of varieties and mixture variations. Consult your dealer about which type or mixture will best suit your purposes.

Quantities

Grass seed of most sorts should cover at an approximate rate of 7 sq m per 0.5 kg (8 sq yd per lb). For small areas this means a rate of 68 g per sq m (2 oz per sq yd).

Method

The simplest method of seeding lawns is to 'broadcast' the seed on to the rolled earth, i.e. taking a handful from a bucket and scattering the seed with a relaxed, horizontal swing of the arm. To ensure an even coverage of the whole lawn, put a measured quantity of seed into the bucket, mark off the area it should cover with footprints and broadcast the seed evenly over the area marked. Repeat the process area by area until the whole lawn is covered. Keep any excess seed since you might need to sow one or two patches again.

Finally, to avoid the seed being picked up by the wind and to ensure good contact with the soil, the whole seeded area should be lightly raked over; this will result in the seed being tucked securely under a thin layer of tilth.

You can then only wait patiently until the seed germinates and the grass begins to grow (this will take two or three weeks). In dry weather the seed may need some watering – your supplier will be able to advise on this.

Early maintenance

Before the grass has securely taken (when it is less than 2.5 cm (1 in) high) the lawn should not be tampered with, except to remove any large, fast-growing weeds. Once the grass is growing strongly (about 2.5–5 cm (1–2 in) high) it should be mowed as soon as possible. The first few cuts should be done with a sharp cylinder mower set relatively high, since this will not disturb the roots and will also roll the lawn. Rotary mowers tend to knock and pull the grass in its infant state, and will blow away any ungerminated seed. Grass thrives on being cut, which helps it to spread and thicken, whereas weeds tend to die off. Thus once the first cut has been made, the lawn should be cut as often as possible, to control weeds and encourage strong grass growth.

After a couple of weeks it will become clear whether there are any patches where the grass has not taken, and these areas should be re-seeded. If the lawn as a whole does not seem to be growing readily then an application of lawn fertilizer (available with advice and instructions from most garden centres and seedsmen) can be made in conjunction with more regular watering.

Note 1. It is very difficult to pinpoint an ideal time for seeding a lawn because so much depends on the weather; clearly it is not a good idea to seed during periods of cold, wet weather or during very hot, dry spells. Generally speaking, however, any time between March and early September is suitable, providing extreme weather conditions are not forecast.

Note 2. After much experience of laying lawns, we have found that garden birds are not any great threat to the seed. Should the lawn seem, however, to be regularly covered in finches, sparrows or pigeons, then a number of sticks with strips of silver paper tied to them placed about the lawn should scare them off. Seed treated with bird repellent is available, however, should you prefer to use it.

2 Turfing

For those who prefer an 'instant' lawn rather than waiting for a lawn to grow from seed (approximately two months is needed before a seeded lawn is really ready for use), turf is available and is simple to lay. A turf lawn is expensive compared to a seeded one, but on the other hand, once the ground has been prepared and the turf laid, it is ready for use almost immediately and can be almost guaranteed to succeed. Turf dealers can be found in the telephone directory or in local newspapers; it should be noted, however, that turf is best laid in the spring or autumn months and that it is not always available. This is because most turf comes on the market when a farmer wishes to plough a field. He will then sell the turf to a specialist company which will subsequently cut it and advertise if for sale. The cost of turf can be cut if you collect the turf yourself, thereby saving the often considerable delivery charge.

Quantities

Turf comes in standard-sized pieces of 90 × 30 cm (3 × 1 ft); hence it requires three turves per sq m (sq yd). It is usually sold by the sq m (sq yd).

Note To estimate the size of an irregularly shaped piece of ground, see p. 20.

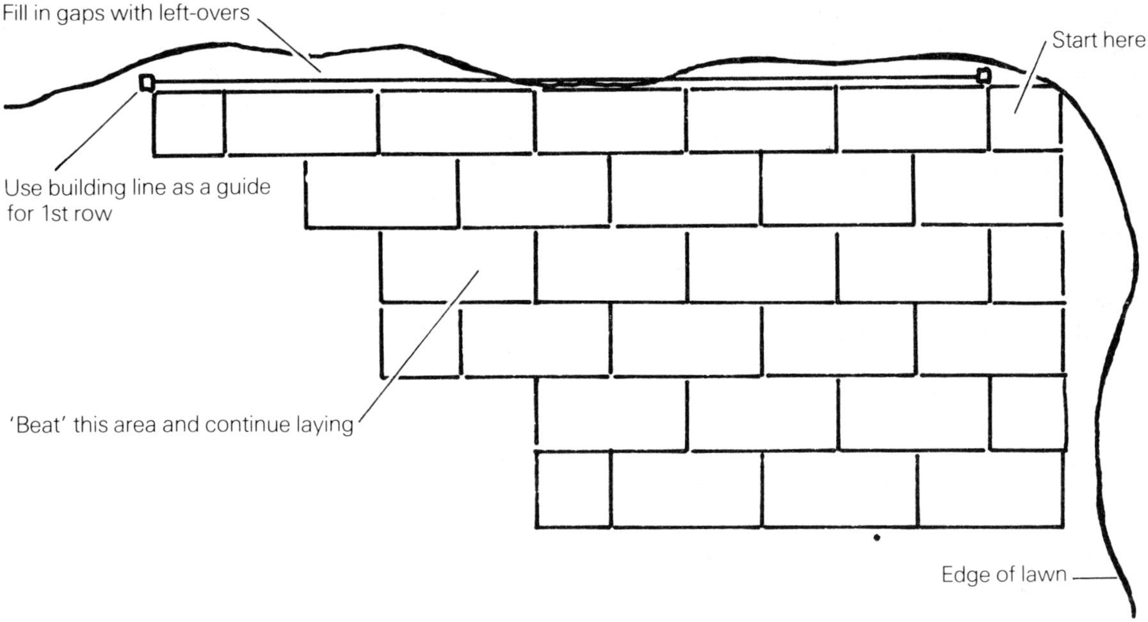

Fig. 12.1 *Laying turves; note use of half-turves to avoid cross-joints being in a straight line.*

To lay

The ground must be prepared in exactly the same way as for seeding (p. 160) up to and including the rolling. Once rolled the ground is ready for turfing. The turves will arrive either rolled up or folded over with the grass in the middle.

Take one strip and position it where the first row is to start. Unroll or open out the turf. As with slabs etc. every alternate row should start with a half-turf, to stop all the crossjoints being in straight lines. Continue to lay turves down the rows, butting them together to ensure a tight fit (Fig. 12.1).

Lay three or four rows together and, after you have an area of 10–20 turves laid, go back over the area 'beating' the turf with the back of your shovel. Good hard strokes will flatten the turf, bringing the roots into firm contact with the soil and moulding the edges neatly together. Carry on in this way, laying 10–20 turves, butting them together and then beating the area laid, until the bulk of the whole area is covered. You will now have a collection of halves and left-overs which will fill in any gaps and tidy up the edges.

Avoid having very small pieces at the end

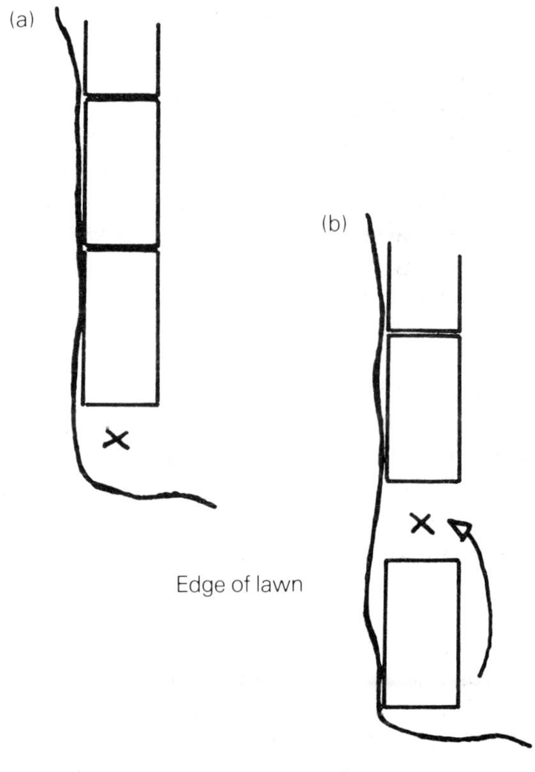

Fig. 12.2 *Diagram showing avoidance of having a small piece of turf at the end of a row.*

of a row (as in Fig. 12.2a), as they are likely to be knocked off or disturbed before the roots have taken. Instead, pull the last whole turf down to the end of the row and put in the small piece above it (Fig. 12.2b).

The turfed lawn should now be watered and left alone until the grass starts growing again. This will mean that the roots have taken, making the turf firm and secure. Any use of the lawn before this may disturb the turf and break the new roots. Once the grass begins to grow (approximately five to seven days), it should be rolled and cut. The lawn is now ready for use.

Note If, after the first few weeks, some of the turves shrink a bit, a mixture of sand and fine soil should be brushed into the cracks and then seeded with a rye-grass mix. Careful laying, butting the turves together and firm beating, should, however, eliminate this problem.

Remember, seeding or turfing the lawn should be one of the last jobs you tackle if you are constructing and laying out a new garden. Before laying the lawn work out access routes to any future construction work or, if this is not possible, leave the lawn unfinished until all the other work is completed.

13 Additional projects

1 Greenhouse staging

Staging in greenhouses serves a number of purposes, but should be designed so that it does not prevent the greenhouse from functioning properly. The point of staging is that it provides a work surface for all the jobs necessary for greenhouse propagation, somewhere to keep the pots and trays while the plants are growing, and storage space on lower levels for spare pots, containers and tools. The problem is of course, that too much 'solid' furniture in the greenhouse may prevent light getting to plants growing on ground level, and perhaps more important, it may stop the warm air circulating properly, causing cool, shaded areas which defeat the purpose of the greenhouse.

Although the actual layout of the greenhouse will depend on individual needs and

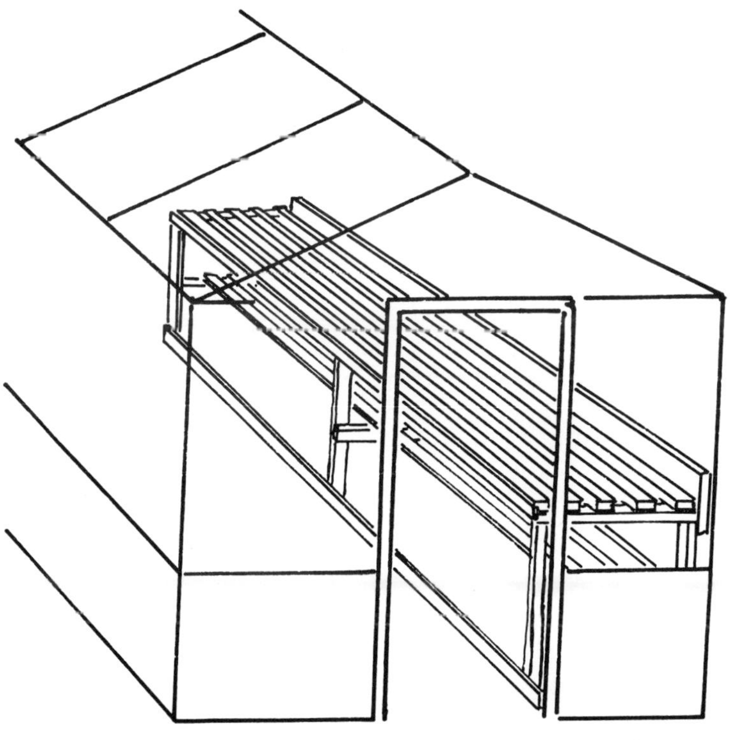

Fig. 13.1 *Complete section of staging installed down one side of a greenhouse.*

preferences, these points should be borne in mind when planning the extent and positioning of your staging.

The basic unit (Fig. 13.1) can either be used against the wall or in the centre of the greenhouse, depending on the existing layout and space available, but if used against the wall, be sure to allow for a 5–10 cm (2–4 in) gap between it and the wall for efficient air circulation. The other point to notice is that once the staging is loaded with plants and pots, it will be supporting a considerable weight, so do not skimp on timber sizes when buying the materials. Finally, in heated greenhouses, the warm air rising between the slats may hinder healthy growth by drying out the soil in the pots too quickly (this is particularly true where shallow trays are being used). To avoid this, all or part of the staging should be covered in asbestos sheeting, cut to size and laid on the slats after the unit has been built.

Dimensions for staging should be worked out to suit individual needs and greenhouse size, but generally speaking, for easy access and maintenance of plants, the unit should not be too high or too wide, since when the plants have grown it may be very difficult to reach those at the back.

TO BUILD THE BASIC UNITS

What you will need

5 × 5 cm (2 × 2 in) sawn timber: 5.5 m (18 ft) i.e. six at 90 cm (3 ft). 5 × 2.6 cm (2 × 1 in) sawn timber: 21 lengths at 1.8 m (6 ft); eight lengths at 75 cm (2 ft 6 in). 20 × 2.5 cm (8 × 1 in) sawn board: one length at 1.8 m (6 ft); Screws: 4 cm ($1\frac{1}{2}$ in) or 5 cm (2 in). Saw. Screwdriver. Brace and bit or electric drill with bits of suitable size for drilling pilot holes for the screws.

Measuring up

The quantity of wood indicated above will be sufficient for the type of unit shown in Fig. 13.1. Adjust these quantities and dimensions to suit your particular needs.

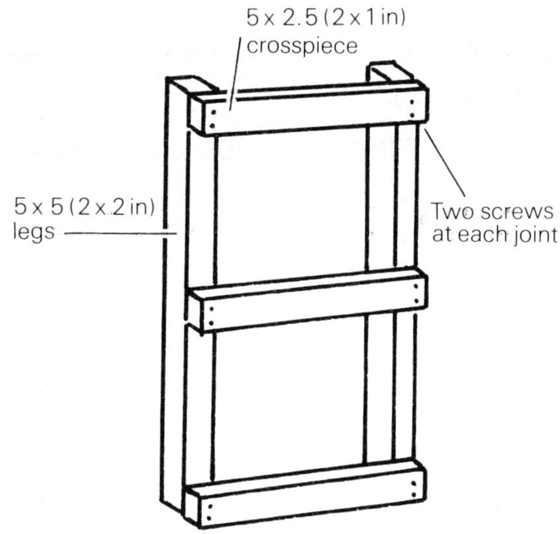

Fig. 13.2 *Constructing the support sections.*

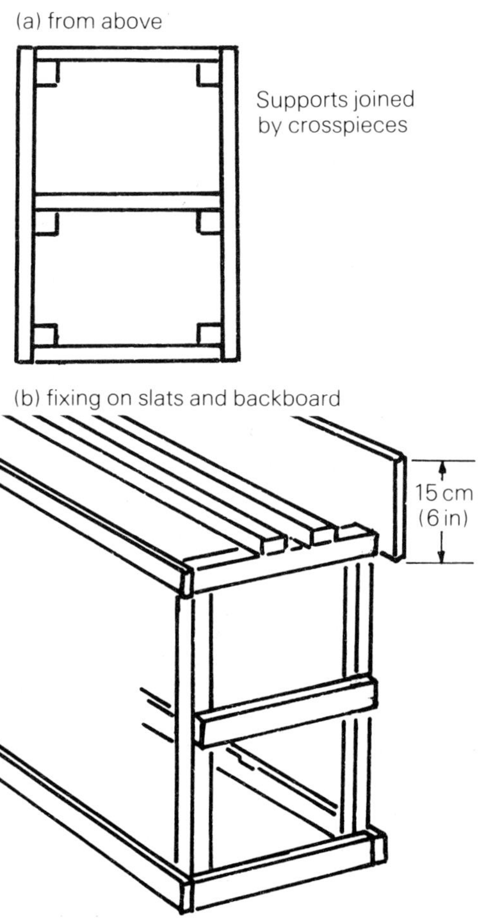

Fig. 13.3 *Assembling the staging.*

To build

1 Assemble end pieces and central support as shown in Fig. 13.2. Drill pilot holes through the crosspieces and fix on to legs, using two screws at each joint. Be sure to position crosspieces flush with the edges of the legs.

2 Put the unit together by fixing on the 1.8 m (6 ft) lengths of 5 × 2.5 cm (2 × 1 in) (Fig. 13.3a) and the 20 × 2.5 cm (8 × 1 in) board, positioning this so that it forms a 15 cm (6 in) guard rail along the back of the staging (Fig. 13.3b). Drill holes and screw together as for above.

3 Fix slats across top (12 lengths) and lower shelf (six lengths), spacing them 2.5 cm (1 in) apart and using one screw at each joint.

A variation of this kind of staging is to build brick pillars and lay a frame of slats over the top (Fig. 13.4). This makes an altogether stronger construction but of course it cannot be moved around subsequently.

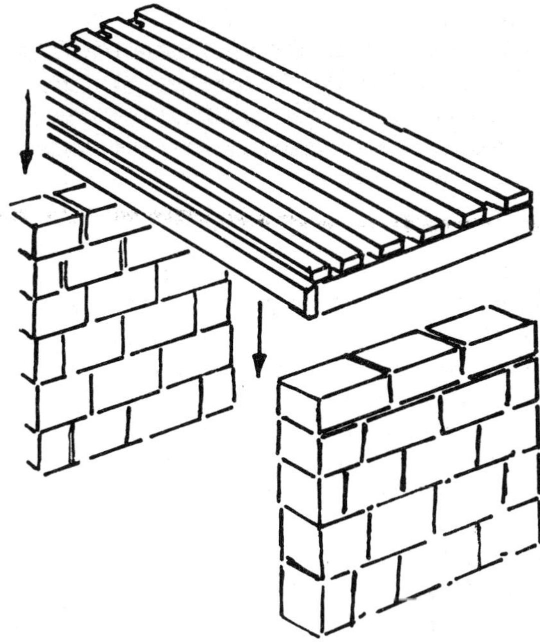

Fig. 13.4 *Slatted wooden frame fitted over brick pillars.*

2 Cold frames

In most vegetable gardens, particularly where there is limited greenhouse space, some kind of covered propagation unit is going to be useful. The designs for these 'cold frames' vary enormously, and can be anything from an old window frame propped at an angle against a wall to some very elaborate types with brick frames and sliding covers. Choice of design will depend on a number of factors, such as whether the frame is to be static (brick sides) or portable (wooden sides), lightweight (polythene-covered), or heavier (glazed), and of course, the type and size of plants to be raised in it. Governing all these points are two considerations: first, the frame should be built with a sloping top to maximize access for sunlight and second, the frame should be situated in a sheltered spot where it is protected as far as possible from the wind. A further point to note is that a plastic/polythene covering provides little protection from frost and is therefore not suitable for propagating sensitive plants early in the year.

Basic proportions for frames, whatever the design and materials used, are shown in Fig. 13.5. A frame built roughly to these proportions provides plenty of space while not being too cumbersome to handle. Larger covers etc. become heavy and awkward to use. To provide a cross-section of ideas, we have included here one design for a static frame and one for a portable frame; these should be adapted to suit your needs. Both would be glazed, but could of course, have plastic covers, in which case the polythene sheeting would be nailed on to the cover frames. Polythene is generally considered to be good for about two seasons, after which discolouration (which cuts out light) and general wear and tear will make replacement necessary.

FRAME 1: STATIC, TWO OR MORE COVERS

What you will need

Bricks or blocks: 45 × 23 × 10 cm (18 × 9 × 4 in). Mortar: 1:4. 8 × 5 cm

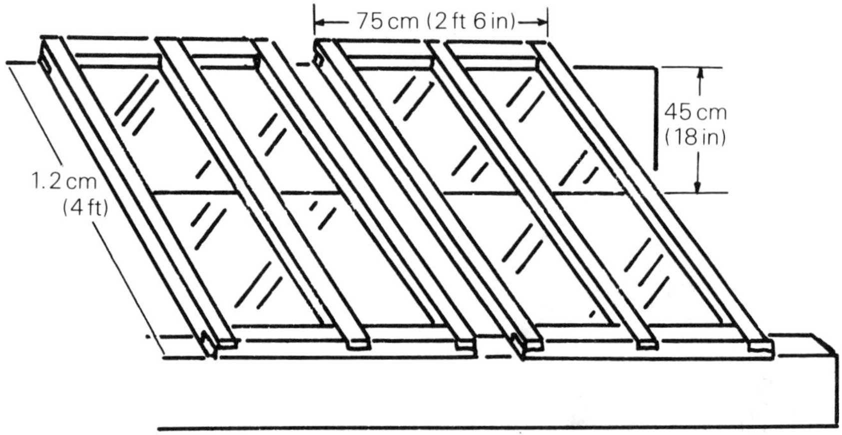

Fig. 13.5 *Standard dimensions for a cold frame.*

(3 × 2 in) and 5 × 5 cm (2 × 2 in) treated softwood. 1.3 × 1.3 cm ($\frac{1}{2}$ × $\frac{1}{2}$ in) glazing bars. Glass. Suitable nails or screws. Glazing pins. Trowel. Spirit-level. Saw. Set square. Hammer. Screwdriver.

Measuring up

Decide on exact dimensions (length and height) for walls and work out your brick or block requirements accordingly.

One cover requires: 8 × 5 cm (3 × 2 in): one length at 75 cm (2 ft 6 in). 5 × 5 cm (2 × 2 in): one length at 75 cm (2 ft 6 in); three lengths at 1.3 m (4 ft 4 in). 1.3 × 1.3 cm ($\frac{1}{2}$ × $\frac{1}{2}$ in): four lengths at 1.2 m (4 ft). Glass: four panes at 61.3 × 30 cm (24$\frac{1}{2}$ × 12 in).

Decide how many covers you require and work out total amount of materials from above.

To build

1 Fig. 13.6: Construct walls on a firm foundation of subsoil covered in scalpings. The sides should be stepped and the slope made up with mortar.

2 Fig. 13.7: Cut timber frame as shown and assemble.

3 Fig. 13.8: Nail on glazing bars. Drop glass into position, with the top panes overlapping the lower ones. Pin securely.

Lay cover on the walls so that the 8 × 5 cm (3 × 2 in) catches on the top wall and prevents the cover sliding down.

FRAME 2: PORTABLE, ONE COVER.

What you will need

Based on the dimensions shown in Fig. 13.5: 5 × 2.5 cm (2 × 1 in) treated softwood: two lengths at 45 cm (18 in); two lengths at 30 cm (12 in). 2.5 × 2.5 cm (1 × 1 in) treated softwood: two lengths at 45 cm (18 in); two lengths at 30 cm (12 in). 15 × 2.5 cm (5 × 1 in) sawn board: 9.8 m (32 ft 6 in); i.e. five at 75 cm (2 ft 6 in); five at 1.2 m (4 ft). Suitable screws or nails. Cover as for Frame 1.

To build

1 Fig. 13.9: Cut wood to lengths and assemble as shown. One length of 1.2 m (4 ft) board should be cut diagonally across its length to give the slope down the sides. Use one half on either side.

2 Assemble cover as for above (Fig. 13.7 and 13.8).

Note The frames will look better and last longer if they are painted or treated on a regular basis.

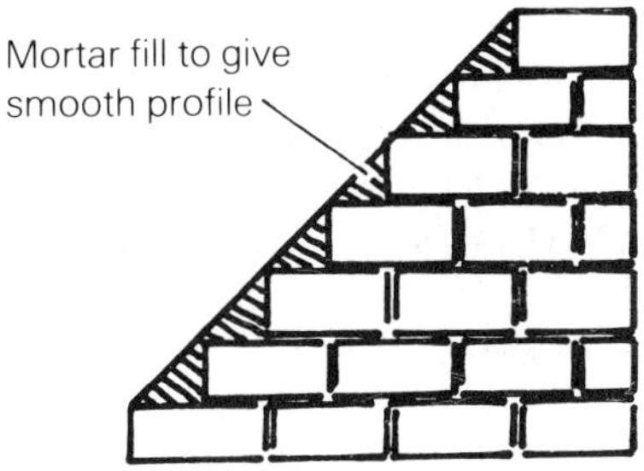

Fig. 13.6 (*Above*) *Side of brick cold frame built up with mortar.*

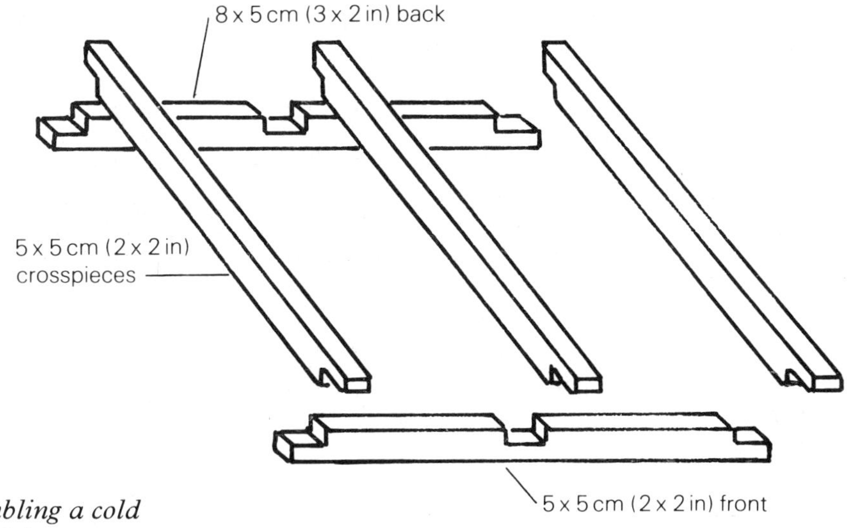

Fig. 13.7 (*Right, upper*) *Assembling a cold frame cover, cut all ends for lap joints.*

Fig. 13.8 (*Right, lower*) *Nail on the glazing bars.*

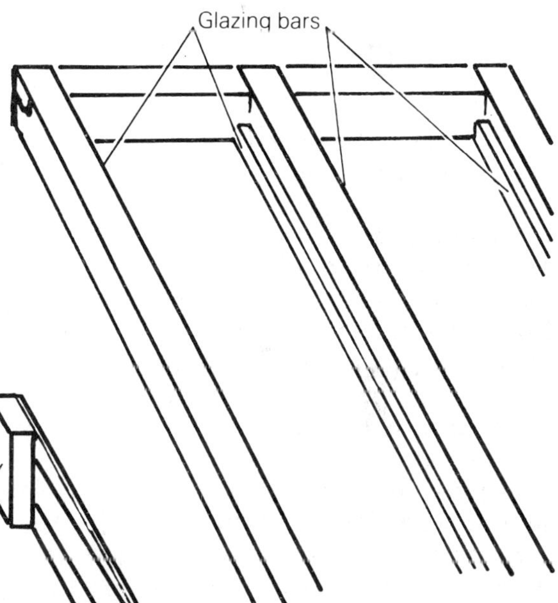

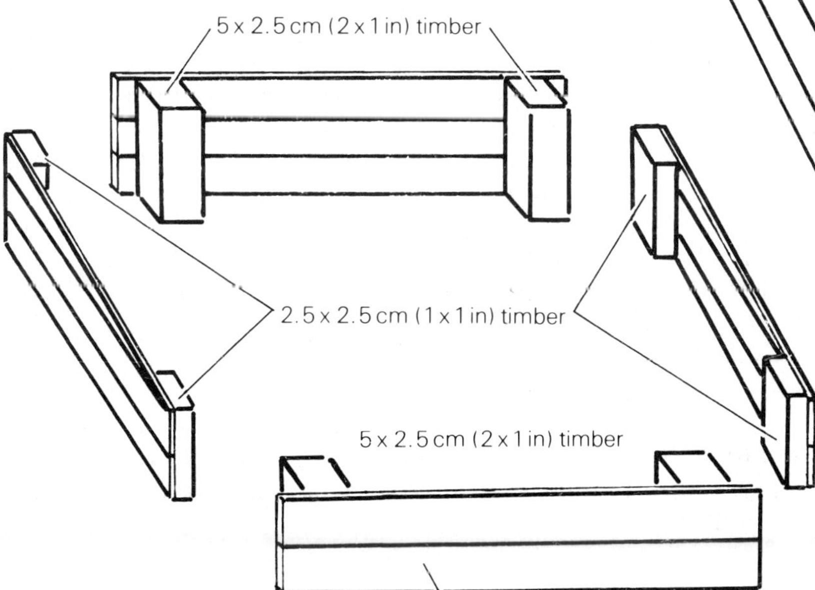

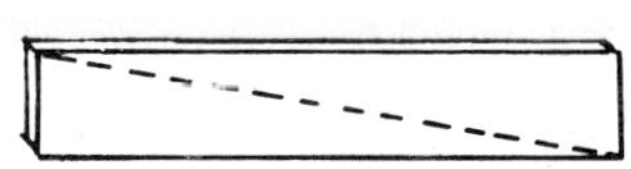

Fig. 13.9 *Assembling a wooden cold frame.*

3 Fruit cages

While fruit cages may be required to enclose large areas and be high enough to permit reasonable access for maintenance of the bushes and fruit picking, they need not be elaborate structures. The simplest design, for enclosing two or three rows of, say, four bushes each, is to erect four corner posts set in concrete and to form the frame with galvanized or p.v.c.-covered wire. Netting is then spread over this and clipped on. For larger areas and more permanent cages, it is an idea to form the sides of the frame with 5 × 2.5 cm (2 × 1 in) timber, which will make the cage more substantial and better able to support the large amount of netting required. Choice of method will depend on the quantity of fruit bushes to be caged and on how permanent the cage is to be.

Wire-framed cage

What you will need

8 × 8 cm (3 × 3 in) treated softwood posts. Galvanized or p.v.c.-covered fencing wire. Fine-mesh garden netting. Staples. Wire clips. Concrete: 50 kg (1 cwt) per post hole. Shovel. Hammer. Pliers.

Measuring up

Fig. 13.10 illustrates suitable dimensions for caging two rows (five bushes per row) of fruit. Use this to work out your wire and netting requirements. Post lengths should allow for height of cage plus 60 cm (2 ft) in the ground. Wire clips should be as for chainlink fencing (p. 72) or short lengths of thin p.v.c.-covered garden wire.

To build

1 Erect corner posts, setting them in the concrete and checking that they are upright with the spirit-level.

2 When the concrete has set, staple the three strands of wire round the posts, pulling it as tight as possible, starting with the top strand.

3 Throw netting over the cage and clip or tie it to the support strands. One corner should be left unclipped to make access easier.

WOOD-FRAMED CAGE

What you will need

8 × 8 cm (3 × 3 in) softwood posts. 5 × 2.5 cm (2 × 1 in) roofing laths. Fine-mesh garden netting. 2.5 cm (1 in) nails. Some short lengths of galvanized or p.v.c.-covered wire. Shovel. Saw. Hammer.

Measuring up

A cage to cover four rows of fruit bushes (five per row) will need to be approximately 5.5 × 5.8 m (18 × 19 ft) long and 1.8 m (6 ft) high. Fig. 13.11 shows post positions for such a cage. Post lengths should allow for height of cage plus 60 cm (2 ft) in the ground.

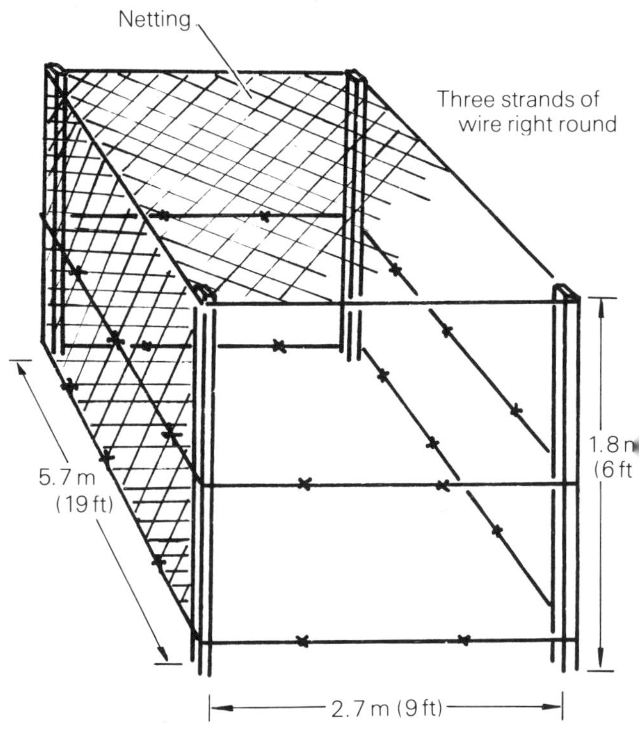

Fig. 13.10 *Wire fruit cage for two rows of fruit (5 bushes per row).*

Each side panel requires: three lengths of roofing lath at 1.85 m (6 ft 3 in); two lengths of roofing lath at 1.8 m (6 ft), (Fig. 13.12). End panels require: three lengths of roofing lath at 2.55 m (8 ft 9 in); two lengths of roofing lath at 1.8 m (6 ft) (Fig. 13.12).

To build

1 Construct side and end panels using half-lap joints as shown in Fig. 13.7 and nailing the joints together.

2 Erect posts (builder's-line method, p. 48). Stand panels in position between the posts and secure with a loop of wire (Fig. 13.12). Throw net over cage frame and nail or staple it to the bottom rail of each panel. One corner should be left unfastened for access.

Note the timber for either sort of cage should be treated regularly.

4 Small-scale trelliswork

In many situations the kind of larch pole trelliswork described on p. 64 will be unnecessarily large or impractical. Where localized support for individual plants or lightweight trelliswork along the top of a fence is required, an additional type of trellis may be useful. This is based on the basket-weave design using flexible 2.5 × 1.3 cm (1 × ½ in) slats secured in a 5 × 5 cm (2 × 2 in) frame. (Small trellises can also be made using bamboo – see p. 151.)

To construct

(Dimensions will alter according to particular requirements.) Assemble the 5 × 5 cm (2 × 2 in) frame, using half-lap joints as in Fig. 13.7. Using nails or screws fix one end of vertical slats (space according to requirements) to the frame, and slide in the

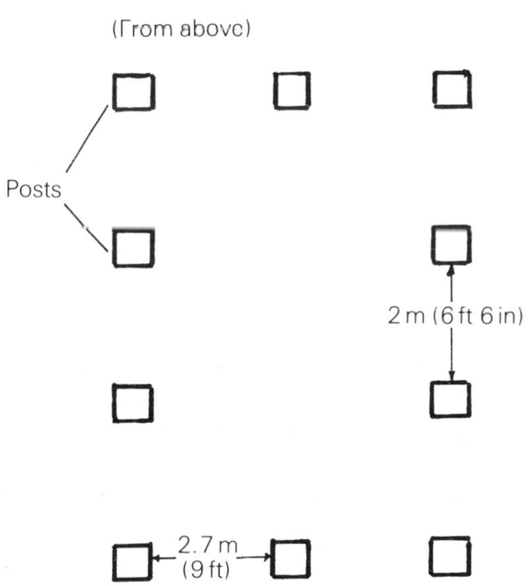

Fig. 13.11 *Spacing of posts for a wooden-framed fruit cage.*

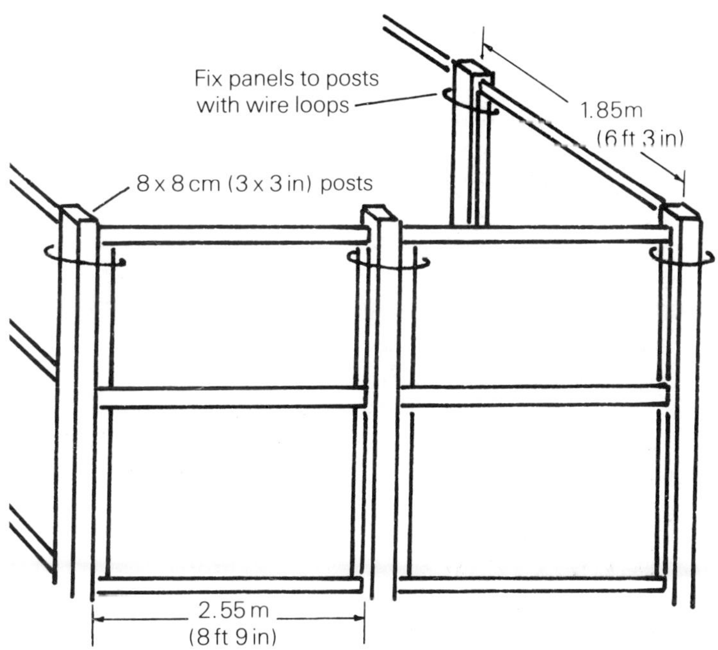

Fig. 13.12 *Wooden-framed fruit cage (netting not shown).*

horizontal ones, going over and under the vertical slats alternately (Fig. 13.13a). When the design is complete, nail or screw the ends of the slats to the frame. For free-standing trelliswork, the 5 × 5 cm (2 × 2 in) uprights should be set at least 45 cm (1 ft 6 in) into the ground. Alternatively, the trellis frame can be fixed to a wall using metal brackets.

A variation of this to to use 5 × 2.5 cm (2 × 1 in) wood for the frame and to fix the trellis along the top of a fence. (In Fig. 13.13b the trellis is fixed above a close-boarded fence.) This will provide additional screening and encourage the growth of climbing plants along the top of the fence, giving a pleasantly informal look to an otherwise rather straight and formal fence line.

5 Compost containers

Compost and the art of making it well has been the subject of long and often passionate, debate. Differing opinions on layering, additives, the time factor and what is and is not suitable for composting have been offered and refuted. One thing about which there is general agreement, however, concerns the most suitable type of bin or container in which the compost should be kept.

Wood (suitably treated with creosote, etc.) is probably the best material for making the bins since it permits better ventilation and draining than masonry, while providing more protection and insulation against heat loss than wire or corrugated iron. Further, while drainage etc. is very important, the key factor in successful composting is that the inside of the heap should reach a sufficient temperature for the rotting down process to proceed. Thus the heat must be able to build up, and to do this properly, the bin must have certain minimum dimensions, and yet not be too large, since this would lead to compaction due to the sheer weight of matter, which in turn would prevent efficient rotting down by excluding air. In addition, the compost should stand on well-drained soil, not a solid base, since this allows excess water to escape

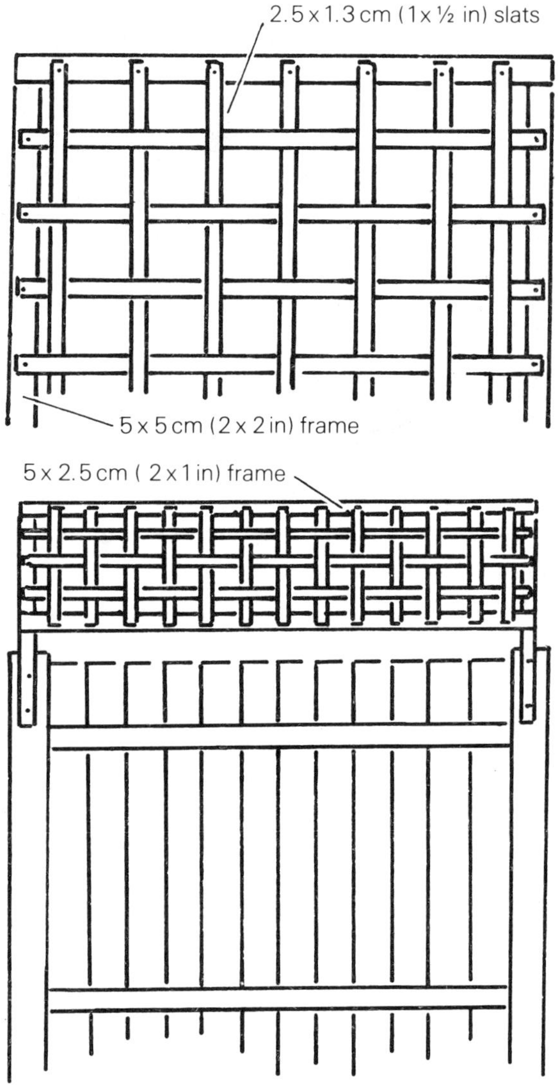

Fig. 13.13 (*a*) *Basket-weave trellis.* (*b*) *Basket-weave trellis set on top of a closeboard fence (from the back).*

while allowing micro-organisms and worms, etc. from the soil to permeate the heap and aid the rotting process. Finally, the bin should be positioned in a sheltered place, surrounded if possible by a windbreak of some description, and safely out of the way of any run-off water from roofs or trees.

A simple and practical design for a compost container is shown in Fig. 13.14. This consists of two bays (one to hold

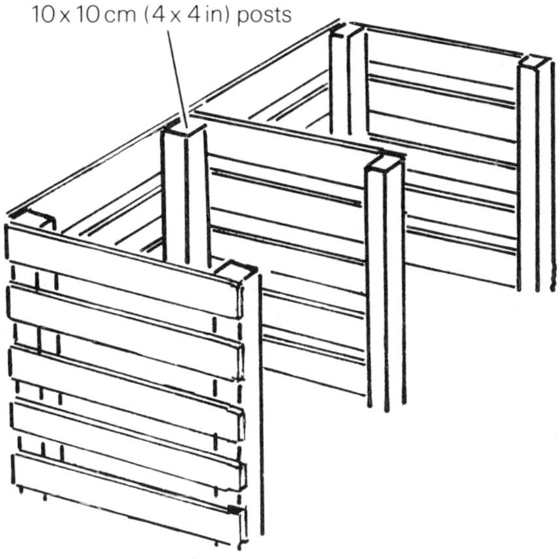

Fig. 13.14 *Two-bay, wooden compost container.*

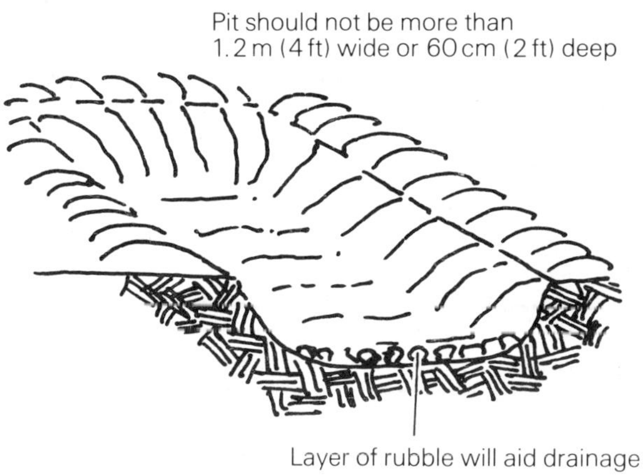

Fig. 13.15 *Sectional view of a compost pit.*

compost that is rotting down, while the other is being filled) that are left open-fronted to make filling and emptying easier, and are made of boards, spaced 2.5 cm (1 in) apart, nailed to 10 × 10 cm (4 × 4 in) posts. Material requirements should be worked out from Fig. 13.14 once the exact dimensions have been decided on. (For additional stability the posts can be extended into the ground by 30 cm (12 in) but this is not essential.)

Construct as indicated in Fig. 13.14.

Variations on this design would be to fix chestnut fencing or plastic mesh to the posts set in the ground.

An alternative to the bin method is to dig a compost pit, the advantages of this being that more heat is kept in and that the compost material is in contact with a much larger area of soil. This idea is not practical, however, in gardens where the water table lies close to the surface, since water would collect in the pit and destroy the compost. For those who would prefer to use a pit and have a suitable site, standard dimensions are indicated in Fig. 13.15. (Note sloping sides – this helps to bring the maximum amount of compost into contact with the soil. Length of pit will depend on the space available.)

6 Bird tables

No garden ever feels really complete without some form of birdlife. Whether the birds actually use the garden trees and shrubs to nest in, or whether they just visit during their daily quest for food, the life and interest they can add to a garden is unique, and one of the best ways to encourage regular visits by as many different species as possible is to erect and supply a bird table. Basically this need only be a flat surface, sheltered from the weather, where food can be placed out of reach of predatory or unwanted animals, i.e. cats, rats, etc.

Given these basic requirements, the possibilities for different designs are clearly considerable, and will depend to some extent on individual situations and usage. To provide a starting point, however, we offer here an easy-to-make design that can be used in either free-standing or hanging form as it is, or as a basis for variations tailored to suit your requirements. Since these requirements will vary, we have not specified exact dimensions for the table, roof etc., but would recommend that the tables supported by posts should be at least 1.2–1.5 m (4–5 ft) above the ground, and that the materials used should be of the sizes specified.

What you will need
8 × 8 cm (3 × 3 in) post. 5 × 2.5 cm (2 × 1 in) wood for table support. 1.3 cm ($\frac{1}{2}$ in) external blockboard for table and roof. 1.3 × 1.3 cm ($\frac{1}{2}$ × $\frac{1}{2}$ in) square-sectioned beading for table edges. 0.7 cm ($\frac{1}{4}$ in) round-sectioned beading for roof ridge. Suitable screws or nails. Wood glue. Saw. Hammer or screwdriver. Jigsaw.

To build

1 Fig. 13.16: Cut post top as shown at angle of required roof pitch. Chamfer ends of 5 × 2.5 cm (2 × 1 in) support and cut out a 2.5 cm (1 in) deep by 8 cm (3 in) wide notch in the middle of its length. Cut out a 2.5 × 2.5 cm (1 × 1 in) notch in post at required table height. Glue surfaces of both notches, slide support in (chamfered side down) and secure with nails or screws.

2 Fig. 13.17: Cut table out of blockboard and, using the jigsaw, cut out hole for post, 8 × 8 cm (3 × 3 in) and if required, a hole in which a water container can sit securely. Cut 1.3 × 1.3 cm ($\frac{1}{2}$ × $\frac{1}{2}$ in) beading to length (slightly shorter than the dimensions of the table), and glue into position round the edges of the table, leaving the corners open (this permits rain-water etc. to drain away.)

3 Fig. 13.18: Glue upper surface of the table support and underside of table (along the line where it will come into contact with the support). Fit the table over post and slide down on to the support. Clamp tight after initial impact to ensure a good bond.

Cut roof pitches out of blockboard. Glue their undersides and post top, position and secure by screwing or nailing through the blockboard into the angled sides of the post top. Cut 0.7 cm ($\frac{1}{4}$ in) round beading to length and glue into position along the ridge.

4 Erect the whole unit (using concrete if necessary) and add any required accessories, e.g. brass hooks on underside of table from which to hang fat or peanut containers. Treat the whole unit with either wood preservative or varnish.

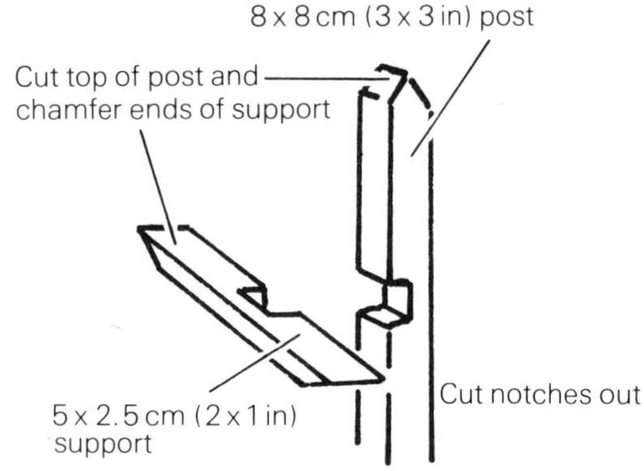

Fig. 13.16 *Preparing post and support for bird table.*

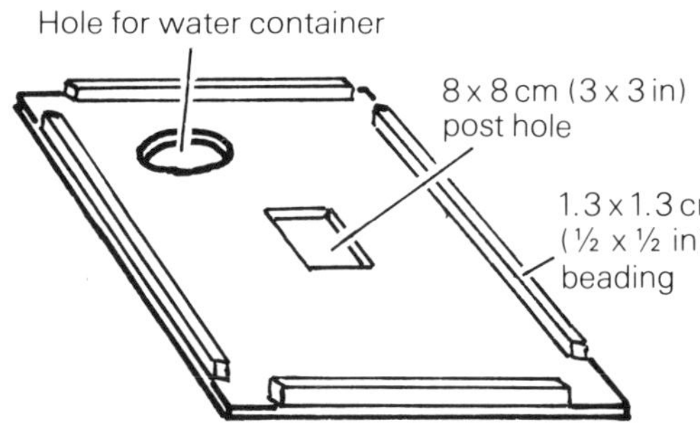

Fig. 13.17 *Putting the table together.*

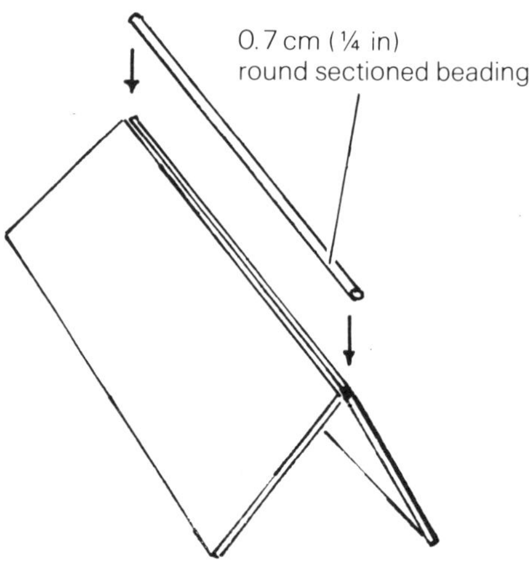

Fig. 13.18 *Assembling the roof.*

7 Water ring mains

In certain situations, either where large areas of garden need watering or where vegetables or flowers are growing at some distance from the house, it may help in saving time and effort if a ring main is laid round the garden which can be used to supply watering appliances at various points along its length. Thus instead of carrying water or running out long lengths of hose, the garden can be watered by simply attaching sprinklers or small hoses to the various take-off points. This, however, does not necessarily mean that a number of appliances can all be run at once, since effective watering, particularly by sprinklers, depends on water pressure and this is governed by the mains supply to the house.

The size of sprinklers most suited to your garden and the number that can be used at once will depend on whether you have high, medium or low pressure and you will need to establish how much pressure you have before buying appliances or planning the ring main. A simple test for water pressure is to fill a 9-litre (2-gallon) bucket from your hose and check how long it takes. If it fills in under 20 seconds you have high pressure, between 25–30 seconds is medium pressure and anything over 35 seconds is low pressure. Using this as a guide buy the appliances suited to your situation and it may be possible, if you have high water pressure, to run two low-pressure appliances at once. Your dealer should be able to advise on this.

Laying the main pipe and positioning the take-off points should be planned to allow for the type of sprinkler etc. you are using since the different models give different area coverage and water patterns. The water pattern will be either a circle, a part circle, a square or a rectangle, while coverage can range from 10.5 m (35 ft) up to about 20 m (70 ft). Thus the take-off points should be spaced so that when the appliance is moved from place to place the resulting watering areas join up to ensure total coverage of the whole area.

When the layout for the piping and the positioning of the take-off points has been finalized, the supply pipe should be laid in a narrow trench about 30 cm (1 ft) deep. (This will keep it clear of any work being done on the surface (weeding etc.) and help stop it freezing in cold weather.) The pipe should be standard polythene water pipe of suitable size to connect up with the mains, and fitted with junctions at the points where there is to be a take-off. Short lengths of pipe attached to the junctions bring the water to the surface and these can be fitted with a tap or hose connecter (with cap) and either fixed above ground to a stake or left just below ground in a covered compartment.

Remember: Once you have laid the supply main, the number and type of appliances you can run off it will depend on your water pressure. Test this before planning your layout or buying the watering appliances.

8 Re-using old artefacts and materials

As we have already mentioned at the beginning of Chapter 2, garden features built and designed for specific effects, provide cohesion and focal points for the overall layout. But in all layouts there will inevitably be small corners or lengths of path designed for practical reasons (access to sheds etc.) or the unavoidable result of carrying out necessary construction work (awkward spaces behind or beside buildings, retaining walls, etc.) that cannot play a part in the larger garden layout and remain in a kind of limbo. Such spaces or surfaces need not, however, be totally without interest and with a little imagination can be made into attractive and unexpected features in their own right.

What we have in mind here is the re-use of old artefacts and building materials as the basis for a small feature or simply to add interest to a path or set of steps by virtue of their unusual designs, patterns or colours. The former category includes anything from small pots, ceramic bowls, earthenware sinks and jugs, stone troughs, etc., through to stone counter-weights, cheese press bases, mill-stones and old cartwheels, and in addition, all the intriguing old cast-iron fittings and accessories once used by blacksmiths or around the house in kitchens and wash-houses. Items in the latter category, on the other hand, could be patterned or coloured floor tiles, carved lintels, slate hearthstones, decorative corbels or roof tiles, parts of pillars or engraved door frames (stone) or gate posts. While it is true that few of these things can be bought to order, if you keep your eyes open and search regularly in odd corners of builder's yards, visit junk shops (particularly in out of the way rural areas) sales rooms and even demolition sites of houses with old gardens and outhouses, it is surprising and often very rewarding what you can turn up and buy for a very reasonable price.

Some very attractive and unusual features have been created using the kinds of items mentioned above and they provide a very useful alternative to standard construction materials. They can also help avoid solutions such as simply concreting or ignoring awkward or out-of-the way spaces and surfaces and, as such, can add a new dimension to the garden.

14 Making your own

Buying materials from retail outlets is both convenient and useful in the sense that the items are there, ready for use, and assistants are on hand to offer advice, but there are at least two good reasons why making some of your own materials may be worth the extra effort. First, it will save you money (particularly for small quantities, for which you would not be able to get a bulk discount), and second, you can design your own units. While saving money speaks for itself, the second point has wider implications that may not be immediately obvious. One problem about buying landscaping materials from commercial outlets is that you are restricted in choice to what is available, and it is often difficult to realize the full potential of a layout due to the limited nature of the standardized materials stocked at most builders' merchants and garden centres. When making your own, you can not only vary the size and shape of the units to suit your particular layout, but you can also give them a variety of finished patterns and textures, creating paths, terraces, edgings, etc., with a totally unique look that eliminates the standardized effect of mass-produced materials.

In this chapter we cover in detail the techniques for casting the various units and then suggest ways in which the finished patterns and textures can be altered. It will become clear that once you understand the process, the design possibilities are enormous and provide an opportunity for truly creative garden construction.

1 Paving slabs

(a) SINGLE SLABS

This technique produces a single, smooth-finished slab similar to those used for terraces and paths earlier in the book (p. 118).

What you will need
8 or 10 × 2.5 cm (3 or 4 × 1 in) wood for mould sides (length and depth of sides will depend on size of slab required, but when casting at home avoid producing slabs less than 8 cm (3 in) thick). Two 8 or 10 cm (3 or 4 in) butt hinges (choose to suit mould size). Short length of wire for fastener. Saw. Hammer. Small nails. Trowel. Some grease or oil. Concrete: 1 : 4 or 5, fairly dry mix.

Note Coloured slabs, blocks, etc. can be produced either by adding concrete dyes to the mix, or by painting them once they have been cast. Find out what is available and concult your dealer as to which would be most appropriate.

To cast
Construct mould as shown in Fig. 14.1 and position on a piece of clean blockboard, plywood, etc. Cover the inside of the mould and base with a good coating of grease or oil. Mix concrete and place in mould. Tamp down *very* thoroughly, making sure that the mix fills the whole mould and is well consolidated. (The strength of the slab will depend on how well the mix bonds together during the tamping process.) Scrape off excess mix

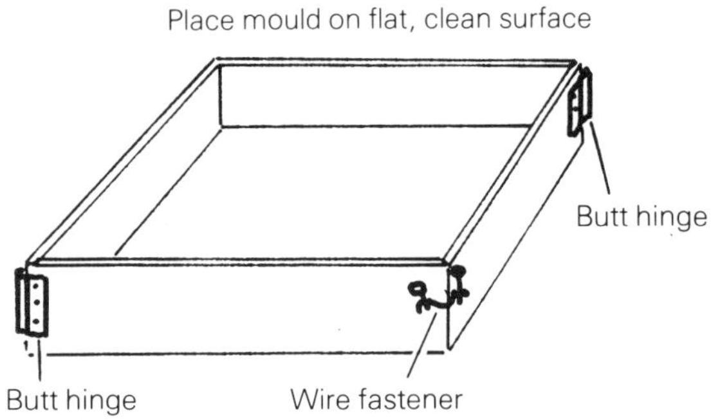

Fig. 14.1 *Mould for single slabs.*

with tamping board (p. 114) and give the slab a smooth finish with the trowel or wooden float. When the concrete has set, unclip the fastener and remove mould. Repeat for required number of slabs.

(b) GRID PATTERNS

A useful variation of this method of casting and one which will save time when laying paths etc., is to construct a mould that produces a number of different-sized units, and which, if used repeatedly down the length of the path, creates a pleasant grid pattern. Using this type of mould the 'slabs' can be cast *in situ*, thus saving time and effort.

What you will need
8 × 2.5 cm (3 × 1 in) wood. Small nails. Hammer. Saw. Spirit-level (if casting *in situ*). Some grease or oil. Concrete: 1 : 4 or 5, fairly dry.

To cast (*in situ*)
Construct mould to give required pattern of units (Fig. 14.2 illustrates one possible example). Prepare path base (p. 118) up to and including the layer of scalpings. Set mould on the prepared base, settling it firmly and checking its position with a spirit-level, making sure that there is a slight fall to one side to remove rain-water (p. 114). Oil or grease the inside of the mould generously. Fill mould with concrete, tamp and finish off as for above. Allow the concrete to set, remove the mould and re-position it on the next section of path to be laid. When the path is complete the gaps between the units can be jointed with either soil or mortar depending on the required finished look.

(c) DECORATIVE SLABS

So far we have looked at methods of casting that produce slabs with the standard smooth, unpatterned finish, but, as has already been mentioned, a variety of different decorative shapes and finishes are possible. It would, however, be impossible to cover all these in detail so we hope instead to provide a starting point by outlining three basic ways of varying the standard finish, from which further ideas can be developed. Once the moulds have been constructed, the slabs should be cast as for (a), paying particular attention to oiling the mould and tamping the concrete.

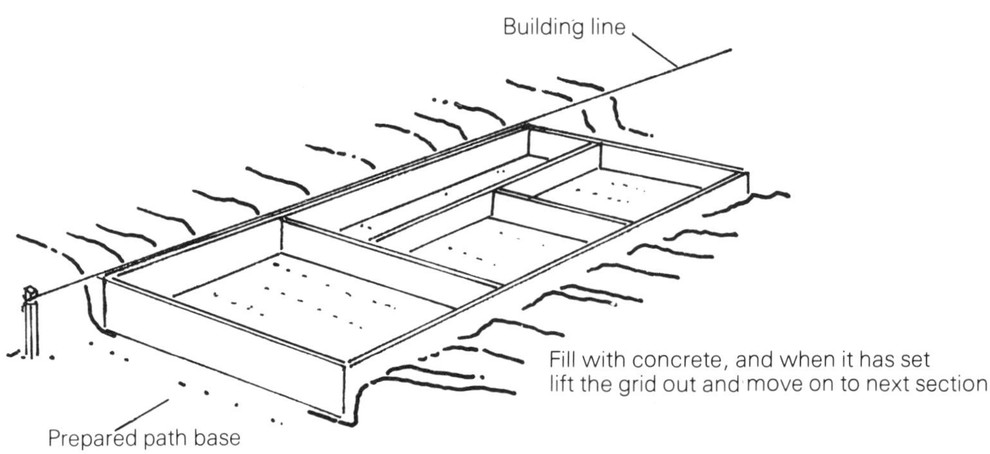

Fig. 14.2 *Grid mould for casting lengths of path in situ.*

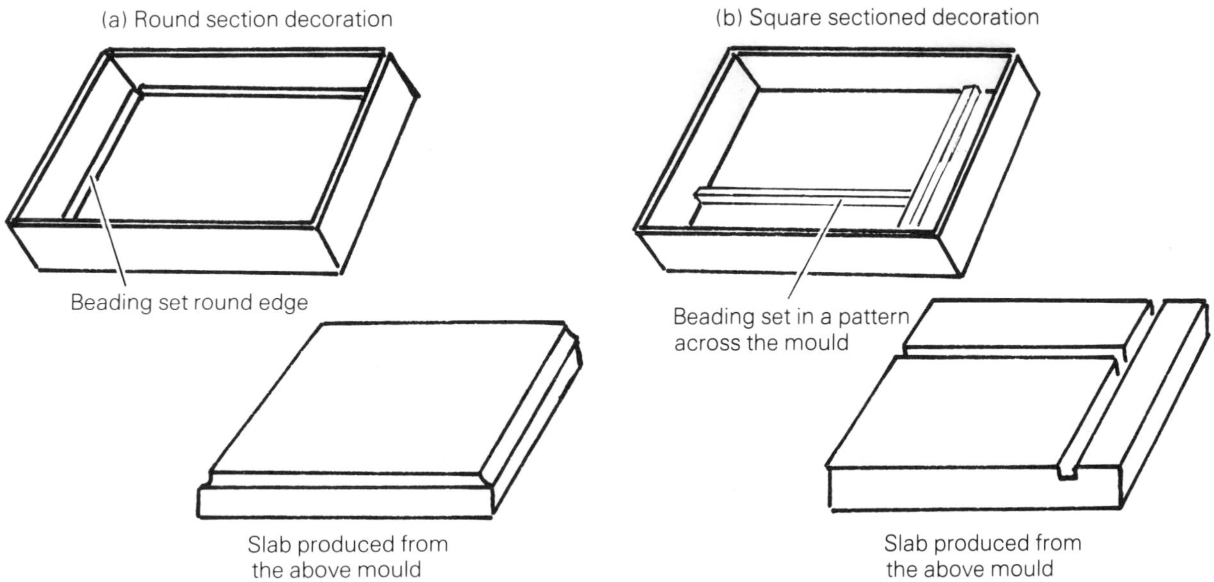

Fig. 14.3 *Producing decorative slabs : (a) decorative edges and (b) patterned surface.*

Patterned finishes

Once the standard mould has been constructed (Fig. 14.1) and positioned on a firm, clean base, lengths of beading (triangular, round or square in section) or thin piping can be arranged in the mould to create a pattern. Two examples of how this might be done are shown in Figs. 14.3a and b. In the first example the slab produced would have bevelled edges, and in the second a square-sectioned pattern across its surface. A further extension of this would be to combine the two, using piping for example, to give bevelled edges and a round sectioned pattern across the surface. Before casting, wedge the pattern material as firmly as possible into the mould, or fix with nails where appropriate, and when filling pack the first layer of concrete gently round the piping etc. before adding the bulk of the mix. Tamp thoroughly.

Textured finishes

As an alternative to giving the slabs a distinct pattern, you can alter the texture of the finish. To do this, position the mould on a firm base and cover the inside with a layer of sand, gravel, leaves or straw, indeed anything that will break up the smooth surface of the base and leave an imprint on the concrete. Cast and remove mould as for (a).

Shape variations

Up to now we have used moulds that produce straight-sided square or rectangular slabs. There is no reason, however, why the moulds should not be altered to create a variety of different shapes, either for general-purpose slabs (Fig. 14.4a) or slabs for specific jobs, such as edgings for a round pond etc. (Fig. 14.4b). Whatever shape is required, construct the mould of 8 or 10 × 2.5 cm (3 or 4 × 1 in) wood as for (a) and use flexible plywood or metal sheet to create the curves and angles.

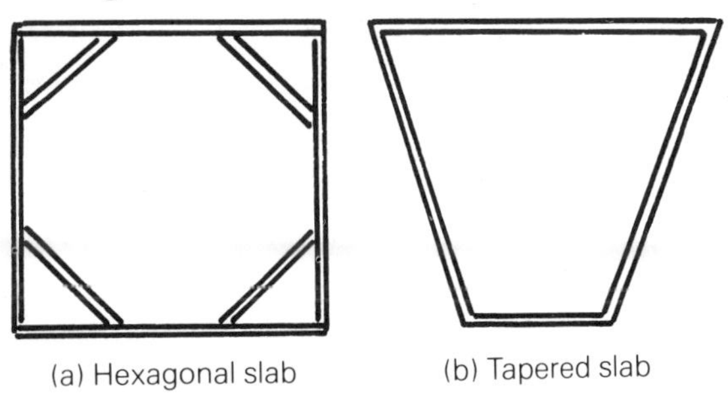

Fig. 14.4 *Two variations of the basic slab shape (from above).*

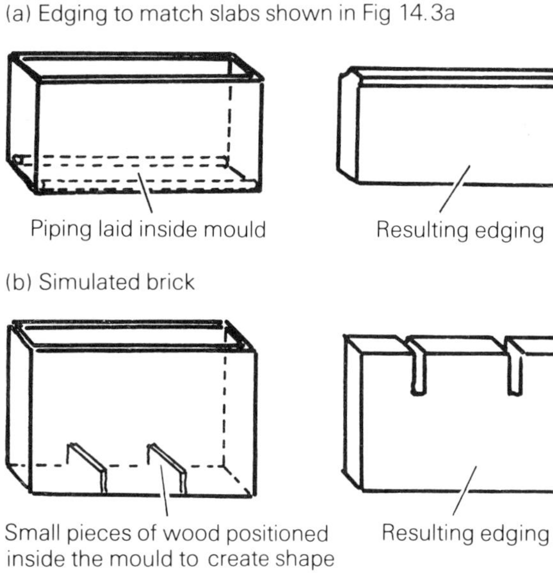

Fig. 14.5 *(a) Edging with bevelled top, and (b) Simulated brick edging.*

2 Edgings

Just as, with a little ingenuity, it is possible to make distinctive and unusual slabs for paving, so too different edgings can be cast, either to match the designs of slabs or as a feature in their own right.

To cast edgings use the same method as above: construct mould, oil or grease well, fill with concrete and finish off. Figs. 14.5a and b illustrate two possible moulds for edgings, the first (Fig. 14.5a) designed to match slabs produced from the mould shown in Fig. 14.3a, and the second (Fig. 14.5b) a kind of simulated brick edging that could have a number of uses. The concrete mix for these should be approximately 1:5 and worked well down into the mould with the aid of a short stick or trowel.

3 In situ stepping-stones

Should you wish to lay a stepping-stone-type path across a lawn, round a pond, etc. but are unable to get hold of any suitable stones, you might consider creating them yourself, using shallow holes, dug at each point where a stone would lie as *in situ* moulds. The technique is very simple and the area should be laid out in the same way as for 'stepping-stone' slab paths (p. 126); i.e., pace out along the line of the path putting down a marker at the end of each step. Alter position of markers until the direction of the path (zig-zagging, straight, curving, etc.) and the spacing between each 'step' is correct. Dig a 10 cm (4 in) deep hole at each marked point, varying the shape and size each time. Fill the holes with concrete (1 : 5, dry) – to just below ground level on lawns – tamp well and finish off. The type of finish given to the concrete will depend on how realistic you want the 'stones' to look. Generally speaking a slightly rough, contoured finish will appear more natural than a well-smoothed one, and this can be given a grainly texture by light brushing just before the surface sets (p. 116).

4 Blocks/screen blocks

As can be seen from Fig. 7.12 (p. 85) concrete blocks and screen blocks require rather elaborate moulds. For this reason, should you wish to cast your own blocks of either variety we would recommend that you buy one of the commercially available plastic moulds. These will save considerable time and effort, give a better defined result and will not add disproportionately to the cost of making your own. A number of such moulds in a range of patterns are available (e.g. Auriol Kwik-Kast) and they come complete with full instructions for use. The generally recommended mix is semi-dry, one part cement to three parts washed, sharp sand, but specific ratios for different types of blocks are given in the manufacturer's literature.

These, then, are the basic methods of casting slabs, edgings, etc. If you are going to create your own path or terrace surfaces, edgings or patterned slabs, experiment a little first and refine your technique, because this represents one of the few chances you may have to introduce new shapes and textures into the garden and to project your ideas into the finer constructional details.

Index